THE CAMBRIDGE COMPANION]
DESCARTES' *MEDIT.*

Descartes' enormously influential *Meditations* seeks to prove a number of theses: that God is a necessary existent; that our minds are equipped to track truth and avoid error; that the external world exists and provides us with information to preserve our embodiment; and that minds are immaterial substances. The work is a treasure-trove of views and arguments, but there are controversies about the details of the arguments and about how we are supposed to unpack the views themselves. This *Companion* offers a rich collection of new perspectives on the *Meditations*, showing how the work is structured literally as a meditation and how it fits into Descartes' larger philosophical system. Topics include Descartes' views on philosophical method, knowledge, skepticism, God, the nature of mind, free will, and the differences between reflective and embodied life. The volume will be valuable to those studying Descartes and early modern philosophy more generally.

DAVID CUNNING is Associate Professor of Philosophy at the University of Iowa. He is the author of *Argument and Persuasion in Descartes' Meditations* (2010) and *Cavendish* (forthcoming).

The Cambridge Companion to

DESCARTES' *MEDITATIONS*

Edited by David Cunning
University of Iowa

CAMBRIDGE UNIVERSITY PRESS

CAMBRIDGE
UNIVERSITY PRESS

University Printing House, Cambridge CB2 8BS, United Kingdom

One Liberty Plaza, 20th Floor, New York, NY 10006, USA

477 Williamstown Road, Port Melbourne, VIC 3207, Australia

314-321, 3rd Floor, Plot 3, Splendor Forum, Jasola District Centre, New Delhi-110025, India

79 Anson Road, #06-04/06, Singapore 079906

Cambridge University Press is part of the University of Cambridge.

It furthers the University's mission by disseminating knowledge in the pursuit of education, learning and research at the highest international levels of excellence.

www.cambridge.org
Information on this title: www.cambridge.org/9781107630482

© Cambridge University Press, 2014

First published 2014

A catalogue record for this publication is available from the British Library

Library of Congress Cataloging in Publication data
The Cambridge companion to Descartes' Meditations / edited by David Cunning, University of Iowa.
    pages   cm. – (Cambridge companions to philosophy)
ISBN 978-1-107-01860-0 (hardback)
1. Descartes, René, 1596–1650. Meditationes de prima philosophia.
2. Methodology.   3. First philosophy.   4. God – Proof, Ontological.   I. Cunning, David.
BI854.C35   2014
194–dc23   2013028934

ISBN 978-1-107-01860-0 Hardback
ISBN 978-1-107-63048-2 Paperback

In memory of
Annette Baier (1929–2012)
and
Paul Hoffman (1952–2010)

CONTENTS

CONTRIBUTORS

LILLI ALANEN is Professor Emerita of Philosophy at the University of Uppsala. She specializes in the history of modern philosophy with a focus on epistemology, metaphysics, philosophy of mind, and moral psychology. In addition to numerous articles, she is the author of *Descartes's Concept of Mind* (Harvard, 2003) and is the co-editor of *Feminist Reflections on the History of Philosophy* (Kluwer, 2004).

ANNETTE BAIER (1929–2012) was Professor Emerita of Philosophy at the University of Pittsburgh. She wrote seven books, including *Postures of the Mind* (University of Minnesota Press, 1985), *A Progress of Sentiments: Reflections on Hume's Treatise* (Harvard, 1991), and *Reflections on How We Live* (Oxford, 2008). Her interests were extremely wide-ranging and included moral philosophy, feminism, and philosophy of mind. She also served as President of the Eastern Division of the American Philosophical Association.

DEBORAH BROWN is Associate Professor of Philosophy at the University of Queensland. Her primary research interests are in early modern philosophy, metaphysics, and philosophy of mind. In addition to numerous articles, she is the author of *Descartes and the Passionate Mind* (Cambridge, 2006).

DAVID CUNNING is Associate Professor of Philosophy at the University of Iowa. His research focuses on early modern philosophy and in particular on metaphysics, epistemology, the history of conceptions of mind and body, and the pedagogical methods of rationalism. He is the author of *Argument and Persuasion in Descartes' Meditations* (Oxford, 2010).

xiii

OLLI KOISTINEN is Professor of Theoretical Philosophy at the University of Turku. His primary interests are in early modern philosophy, metaphysics, and philosophy of action. He is editor of *The Cambridge Companion to Spinoza's Ethics* (Cambridge, 2009), co-editor of *Spinoza: Metaphysical Themes* (Oxford, 2002), and author of *Action and Agent* (Acta Philosophica Fennica, 2001).

CHARLES LARMORE is the W. Duncan MacMillan Family Professor in the Humanities at Brown University. He has published on such topics as the foundations of political liberalism, the nature of the self, and the nature of moral judgment, and he has also written extensively on issues in seventeenth-century philosophy and on German Idealism. He is the co-author of two books and the sole author of eight, including *Patterns of Moral Complexity* (Cambridge, 1987), *Les pratiques du moi* (PUF, 2004), *The Autonomy of Morality* (Cambridge, 2008), and *Vernunft und Subjektivität* (Suhrkamp, 2012).

THOMAS M. LENNON is Professor Emeritus of Philosophy at the University of Western Ontario. His books include *The Plain Truth: Descartes, Huet, and Skepticism* (Brill, 2008), *Reading Bayle* (Toronto, 1999), and *The Battle of the Gods and Giants: The Legacies of Descartes and Gassendi, 1655–1715* (Princeton, 1993). He has published extensively on the views and arguments of the philosophers of the early modern period and on the context and climate in which those views and arguments appear.

CHRISTIA MERCER is Gustave M. Berne Professor of Philosophy at Columbia University. Her primary research area is history of modern philosophy, with a special focus on early modern Platonism, history of science, metaphysics, and philosophical method. In addition to many articles, she is the author of *Leibniz's Metaphysics: Its Origin and Development* (Cambridge, 2001) and co-editor of *Early Modern Philosophy: Mind, Matter, and Mechanism* (Cambridge, 2005). She is the North American Editor of *Archiv für Geschichte der Philosophie* and general editor of the book series, *Oxford Philosophical Concepts*.

KATHERINE J. MORRIS is Fellow in Philosophy at Mansfield College, Oxford University. She has published numerous articles on Descartes, Sartre, Merleau-Ponty, and Wittgenstein, and is the co-author of

Descartes' Dualism (Routledge, 2002) and the author of *Sartre* (Blackwell, 2008) and *Starting with Merleau-Ponty* (Continuum 2012). She is also the editor of *Sartre on the Body* (Palgrave Macmillan, 2010).

ALAN NELSON is Professor of Philosophy at the University of North Carolina, Chapel Hill. His publications focus on early modern philosophers and especially on Descartes.

LAWRENCE NOLAN is Professor of Philosophy at California State University, Long Beach. His research emphases are early modern philosophy, metaphysics, and philosophy of religion. In addition to authoring numerous articles, he is the editor of *Primary and Secondary Qualities: The Historical and Ongoing Debate* (Oxford, 2011) and *The Cambridge Descartes Lexicon* (Cambridge, forthcoming).

TAD M. SCHMALTZ is Professor of Philosophy and James B. and Grace J. Nelson Fellow at the University of Michigan, Ann Arbor. He has published on various topics in early modern philosophy. His books include *Descartes on Causation* (Oxford, 2008), *Radical Cartesianism: The French Reception of Descartes* (Cambridge, 2002), and *Malebranche's Theory of the Soul: A Cartesian Interpretation* (Oxford, 1996). He is also the editor of *Receptions of Descartes* (Routledge, 2005), and co-editor of the *Historical Dictionary of Descartes and Cartesian Philosophy* (Scarecrow, 2003) and *Integrating History and Philosophy of Science* (Springer, 2011).

AMY SCHMITTER is Associate Professor of Philosophy at the University of Alberta. Her primary research interests include history of early modern philosophy, philosophy of art, history of the emotions, and feminist approaches to the history of philosophy.

ALISON SIMMONS is Samuel H. Wolcott Professor of Philosophy at Harvard University. Her research is focused on early modern philosophy, and in particular conceptions of mind and the human being. She also has interests in medieval philosophy and philosophy of psychology. She has published numerous articles and is the editor of the forthcoming volume on consciousness as part of the series Oxford Philosophical Concepts.

CECILIA WEE is Associate Professor of Philosophy at the National University of Singapore. Her research interests are in early modern philosophy, with an emphasis on Descartes, and also classical Confucianism and environmental ethics. In addition to her many articles she is the author of *Material Falsity and Error in Descartes' Meditations* (Routledge, 2006).

ACKNOWLEDGEMENTS

I would like to express my deepest gratitude to Annette Baier, Lilli Alanen, Deborah Brown, Olli Koistinen, Charles Larmore, Tom Lennon, Christia Mercer, Katherine Morris, Alan Nelson, Lawrence Nolan, Tad Schmaltz, Amy Schmitter, Alison Simmons, and Cecilia Wee. I am grateful to each of them for all their hard work in generating papers for this volume and for coming up with such interesting interpretations and arguments.

I would like to thank Andrew Dyck, Hilary Gaskin, and Anna Lowe for their generous editorial assistance. I am also grateful to two of my graduate students, Seth Jones and Kristopher Phillips, for reading drafts of specific papers and providing very helpful feedback.

I would like to thank Naomi Greyser and Mira Grey Cunning, and also my dad, Robert Cunning. Naomi and Mira were supportive at every step of this project, and Naomi's editorial suggestions were, as always, exemplary. I have been very lucky to be able to discuss important philosophical issues with Robert in recent years. It has been an honor to share ideas with him.

And I would like to make a very personal expression of gratitude to the late Paul Hoffman for all of his help and support when I was a student in the 1990s. Paul made time. As a faculty member myself now, I have a better sense of what this involved, and to be honest I don't quite know how he did it. He made time to meet for Latin translation, to read drafts of papers, to give comments, and to talk things through, all the while being a first-rate historian and philosopher and a committed human being. He serves as an inspiration and a model.

ABBREVIATIONS AND TRANSLATIONS

Unless otherwise indicated, the chapters in this volume use the translations from volumes I and II of *The Philosophical Writings of Descartes*, edited by John Cottingham, Robert Stoothoff, and Dugald Murdoch, and *The Philosophical Writings of Descartes, Volume III: The Correspondence*, edited by Cottingham, Stoothoff, Murdoch, and Anthony Kenny. All three volumes are published by Cambridge University Press (1985, 1984, and 1991). These volumes are referred to as 'CSM 1', 'CSM 2', and 'CSMK', respectively.

References to Descartes' writings in their original language are from *Oeuvres de Descartes*, Volumes I-XI, ed. Charles Adam and Paul Tannery, Paris: Librarie Philosophique J. Vrin (1996). These are abbreviated 'AT', followed by the volume number and page.

The following abbreviations are used for titles of Descartes' works.

Meditations	*Meditations on First Philosophy*
First (or Second...) Replies	*First (or Second...) Set of Replies*
"Synopsis of the *Meditations*"	"Synopsis of the following six *Meditations*"
Principles	*Principles of Philosophy*
Passions	*The Passions of the Soul*
Discourse	*Discourse on the Method of Rightly Conducting one's Reason and Seeking the Truth in the Sciences*

Introduction

THE MEDITATIONS AND ITS RECEPTION

Meditations on First Philosophy was first published in 1641, and Descartes certainly knew that it would generate controversy. He introduces a number of radical ideas in the course of laying out his views and arguments – for example, that God might be a thoroughgoing deceiver or that He might not exist; that what we know best about bodies is not known through the senses at all and that, for example, our mathematical and non-sensory idea of the sun might be a more accurate rendition of the sun than the idea that presents it as yellow and hot; that God exists, and His will is the eternal and immutable and supremely independent cause of all reality and truth; and that the external world that surrounds us is best understood as being devoid of light and sound and sensory qualities altogether.[1] Descartes dedicates the *Meditations* to "those most learned and distinguished men, the Dean and Doctors of the sacred Faculty of Theology at Paris" (AT 7: 1). He does so in part to increase the odds that he will be heard:

Whatever the quality of my arguments may be, because they have to do with philosophy I do not expect they will enable me to achieve anything very worthwhile unless you come to my aid by granting me your patronage. The reputation of your Faculty is so firmly fixed in the minds of all, and the name of the Sorbonne has such authority that, with the exception of the Sacred Councils, no institution carries more weight than yours in matters of faith; while as regards human philosophy, you are thought of as second to none, both for insight and soundness and also for the integrity and wisdom of your pronouncements. ("Dedicatory Letter to the Sorbonne," AT 7: 5)

As we will see, Descartes spends a lot of time outside of the *Meditations* articulating the ways in which tradition and authority can keep a mind from registering the force of a rigorous argument. But tradition and authority might also be harnessed in the other direction, and Descartes is hoping that an endorsement from the Sorbonne will hold the objections of his readers at bay, at least until the arguments of the *Meditations* are able finally to get through.

Descartes had already expressed some of the controversial elements of his philosophical system earlier in *The World* and *Treatise on Man*, written from 1629 to 1633, but he decided to withhold these texts from publication when he learned that Galileo had been condemned for saying in print that the earth moves (in *Dialogue Concerning the Two Chief World Systems*, 1632). Descartes explains,

> I must admit that if the view is false, so too are the entire foundations of my philosophy, for it can be demonstrated from them quite clearly ... But for all the world I did not want to publish a discourse in which a single word could be found that the Church would have disapproved of; so I preferred to suppress it rather than to publish it in a mutilated form.[2]

The *Meditations* does not explicitly articulate the view that the earth moves, but nor does it fully articulate many other components of Descartes' philosophical system. In large part, it lays out philosophical foundations. It defends arguments that sometimes suggest or even entail a controversial position, even if the position itself goes unstated. Descartes went to great lengths to avoid the fate of Galileo, but in the end he was reprimanded as well. In 1663, thirteen years after he died, the Church put the *Meditations* and many of Descartes' other works on the *Index Librorum Prohibitorum*, or *List of Prohibited Books*.

Descartes is famous for his work as a philosopher, but he was also a renowned mathematician, geometer, and scientist. The x-y coordinate system in geometry is one of his many legacies, and indeed Descartes' achievements in mathematics and geometry are connected to his work in philosophy. One of the common fruits of math and geometry is a method that begins with results that are utterly clear and perspicuous and that leads in a step-by-step procedure to results that are clear and perspicuous themselves. Like a lot of philosophers of the early modern period, Descartes looked forward to a moment in which the claims of philosophy would achieve the level of certitude and finality that was warranted by its subject matter, so that all three disciplines would be similarly demonstrative. In his early *Rules for the Direction of the Mind*, he offers guidelines for getting as clear as possible on mathematical and geometrical concepts, and he tries to expose exactly what it is about these that allows their respective disciplines to have such certitude and stature. He says a number of things, but one is that, in both, concepts are broken down into their very simplest elements and then built back up as a function of their conceptual inter-connections.[3] This way, simple elements that go together stay together, and elements that are different are sorted in ways that appropriately reflect their differences. Descartes suggests that we take the same approach in dealing with philosophical matters,[4] and that approach will be especially prominent in the *Meditations*. As we will see, Descartes assumes that his readers are beset with numerous prejudices at the start of inquiry,[5] and these prejudices will need to be shattered if the simpler elements of our thinking are to be uncovered and viewed without obstruction. Descartes appears to hold that at bottom what it is for something to be an idea is not just for it to be a mental item, but a mental item that is intentional and that represents reality. Our most unanalyzable ideas are true and conform to the way that things are,[6] and if so, it is only composite ideas that have a chance of being fictional. True ideas inform us about the structure of reality, if only we can settle on which these are.

CHAPTERS

This volume is a companion to Descartes' philosophy, but it is a companion to the *Meditations* in particular. The distinction is very important just because the *Meditations* is a text in which Descartes has a meditator diving into inquiry from a not-yet-Cartesian (or at least not-yet-fully-Cartesian) standpoint and then gradually moving to a more considered position of reflection and clarity. The *Meditations* will present many of Descartes' views and arguments, but it will also reflect the judgments and concerns of his meditator along the way. The chapters that follow are meant to shed light on the details of Descartes' philosophical thinking, but also to highlight how the *Meditations* is literally a meditation. There will be an enormous amount of disagreement about what exactly is being argued at each point in the *Meditations*, and about when the meditator is reflecting Descartes' considered position and when the meditator is still working to get confusion out of his system, but this disagreement will be instructive.

In the first chapter, Christia Mercer discusses some of the larger historical background to the practice of philosophical meditation and how it was part of the context that informed Descartes' *Meditations* in particular. She calls attention to important philosophical meditators like Augustine, Teresa of Ávila, and Philipp Camerarius, and she notes some of the changes and developments in the practice of meditation over time – for example, a move from meditation that is seen as requiring the inspiration and assistance of God to meditation that is more individualistic. Mercer points out how Descartes incorporates a number of different influences in crafting his own meditational approach – Christian, Platonist, anti-Aristotelian, and skeptical – to best meet his specific needs and concerns.

Chapters two and three are on the First Meditation. Charles Larmore argues that the First Meditation is in effect a kind of dialogue between a commonsense empiricist meditator who subscribes to the view that all knowledge is acquired through the senses, and a skeptic who is highlighting the tensions that are internal to that view. Larmore emphasizes that no theses are positively advanced in the First Meditation, but instead the meditator is pitting aspects of his own belief system against each other. Larmore draws important connections between the skeptical project of the *Meditations* and the skeptical arguments of Descartes' predecessors, and he underscores the significance and value of the radical and ground-clearing method of the First Meditation, even if that method results in less certainty than might be desired. David Cunning focuses on discrepancies between the views and arguments that are advanced in the First Meditation and views and arguments that are defended in Descartes' larger corpus. Cunning considers in particular the way in which the deliverances of the First Meditation run counter to results that (Descartes would identify) as non-sensory and a priori – results of the sort that (he would say) are the bread and butter of philosophical investigation. It is these results that take precedence in philosophical inquiry – for example, that God is a necessary existent, that He is the eternal and immutable author of all reality, and that He would not allow us to be deceived about matters that are most evident to us. If so, there does not exist the First Meditation possibility that God does not exist, or that He created us with defective minds, or that we evolved by chance, or that our minds are constantly tricked by an evil demon. These possibilities are entertained by the First Meditation meditator, but the First Meditation meditator is not yet a Cartesian. Cunning is worried in part about explaining away the notorious problem of the Cartesian Circle – how we can effectively demonstrate that God exists and has created us with minds that are trustworthy, if all the while there exists the possibility that our minds are defective. Cunning also considers the question of whether or not the non-sensory tenets of Descartes' considered metaphysics leave room for finite minds to have libertarian independence and freedom, or if (in the First Meditation and elsewhere) he is only positing an experience of independence and freedom.

The next two chapters are on the Second Meditation. Lilli Alanen argues that in the Second Meditation Descartes is attempting to do justice to all of the cognitive faculties of a human being, but that he breaks with his predecessors and elevates many of these faculties to the level of the *I* or pure intellect. In the tradition, faculties like sensing and imagining were attributed to a lesser soul – for example the animal soul – but Descartes offers systematic reasons for discarding these and retaining the notion of the intellectual soul or mind alone. Alanen also argues that part of the Sixth Meditation argument for the view that minds are immaterial consists in the fact that the meditator in Meditations Two through Five has the first-hand experience of exercising all the cognitive faculties that are isolated in Meditation Two – especially the faculties of will and judgment – and comes to see that they are sufficiently exalted that there is no way that they could be understood to be modifications of extension or body. Katherine Morris focuses on the wax digression that appears at the end of the Second Meditation. It is clear that the discussion is meant to show that what we know best about bodies is not known through the senses, and more generally that our knowledge of non-sensory things is of the highest order, but there remain a number of important questions about the details of the wax digression. For example, there is a question about what Descartes means in saying that a feature does or does not pertain to wax, and about what it means to say that a piece of wax is capable of countless permutations, and about what it means to say that mind is known better than body. Morris offers almost a line-by-line reading of the second half of the Second Meditation, and concludes with a discussion of some of the pedagogical doctrines that might be at work behind the scenes.

The next two chapters treat issues in the Third Meditation. Descartes famously argues here that God exists, and he does so by way of some claims about the representationality of ideas. Lawrence Nolan argues that one of the reasons that Descartes' argumentation has been regarded as implausible is that he is taken too literally in his use of scholastic terminology. Descartes uses that terminology for strategic purposes, Nolan argues, and if we understand the underlying concepts that Descartes himself endorses, his argumentation is quite compelling. Nolan takes a similar approach in addressing the question of whether or not there are two separate arguments for the existence of God in the Third Meditation, and the question of what it means for Descartes to say that God is self-caused. Amy Schmitter focuses on one of the underpinnings of Descartes' Third Meditation argumentation – the notion of objective reality or representational content. Schmitter argues that in the Third Meditation discussion Descartes is making use of different elements of views of representation that were proposed by his medieval predecessors, but she argues in addition that Descartes does not assemble all of these into a final considered position in the Third Meditation. The meditator has only meditated so far, and is not yet in a position to offer a final view of objective reality. The understanding of representation that is proposed in the Third Meditation is just enough to get up and running the argument for God's existence from objective reality, and only later is Descartes able to appeal to a full-fledged theory of the content of ideas to demonstrate results about their objects. Schmitter proposes the controversial view that, in the final analysis, Descartes is a kind of externalist.

Chapters eight and nine are about the Fourth Meditation and the Cartesian tenet that minds are free to affirm truth and avoid error. Descartes subscribes to this tenet – there is no doubt – but the question is what exactly it amounts to. Thomas Lennon considers the Fourth Meditation assertion that the will consists in the ability to do or not do and argues that the assertion is simply reporting that affirming and not affirming are among the capacities of the will. The will's ability to affirm or not affirm is not a two-way contra-causal power, Lennon argues: Descartes subscribes to the view that the will is always guided by reasons that are presented to the intellect, and this is a view that was commonly assumed in the tradition. Cecilia Wee argues that for Descartes the will is free in the libertarian sense that all circumstances being identical, it has a two-way power to affirm or not to affirm. Wee considers texts that are strongly suggestive of the libertarian interpretation, and she offers a way of making sense of apparently conflicting passages as well. She concludes with a discussion of systematic Cartesian principles that might seem to run counter to the libertarian reading and argues that in fact they are fully consistent with it.

The next two chapters focus on the Fifth Meditation and Descartes' doctrine of true and immutable natures. Tad Schmaltz considers a number of different interpretations in the literature – that true and immutable natures are conceptual entities, that they are third-realm Platonic entities, and that they are identical to the things that have the natures themselves. Schmaltz points to problems for all of these interpretations and suggests that in the end there is no reading of the ontological status of true and immutable natures that squares with all of the things that Descartes says about them. But even if Schmaltz does not aim to settle the question of the ontological status of true and immutable natures, he does attempt to reconcile all of the different claims that Descartes makes about the criteria by which we identify something as a true and immutable nature. Schmaltz argues that in the end the criteria that Descartes offers are much more complementary than has been thought. Schmaltz concludes with an illuminating discussion of Kant's critique of Descartes' Fifth Meditation (ontological) argument for the existence of God. Olli Koistinen argues that the central work that is done by the notion of a true and immutable nature is to fix the externality or reference of ideas. Koistinen first offers a summary of earlier moments in the *Meditations* in which Descartes attempts to fix a notion of externality or mind-independence, but fails. In effect, Koistinen locates a continuous thread in which Descartes is seeking to make sense of how ideas can be directed at objects, and argues that it is not until the Fifth Meditation that he is finally successful. According to Koistinen, true and immutable natures are similar to formal natures in the philosophy of Spinoza, where these are part of the structure of the reality to which our ideas refer. Koistinen then argues that Descartes' Fifth Meditation ontological argument is fairly plausible if the true and immutable nature of God is not a conceptual entity but a being whose existence and externality are secured by the fact that we have true thoughts about it.

Chapters twelve and thirteen focus on the Sixth Meditation and the issue of embodiment. Thus far, the meditator of the *Meditations* has worked very hard to be a detached *I* and thereby secure the fruits of non-sensory philosophical reflection, but embodiment is integral to what we are, and the constant attempt at detachment is not sustainable. Deborah Brown separates two different questions that are being addressed in the Sixth Meditation (and in the *Meditations* more generally) – "What am I?" and "Who am I?" The questions are similar, and Descartes does not distinguish them as explicitly as he might. Sometimes Descartes fleshes out the nature of the self in terms of its thinking, willing, understanding, affirming, etc. – in short, all of those aspects of the *I* that are divorced from its embodiment. In these cases, Brown argues, Descartes is addressing the question *What am I?* In other passages he fleshes out the nature of the *I* in ways that highlight that it is not just a mind, but an embodied person and human being. Brown points to passages outside the *Meditations* in which Descartes emphasizes the intimate union of a person's mind and body, and how this union reflects our everyday default condition. For example, Descartes remarks in one of his letters that philosophical reflection is something in which it is appropriate to engage only a few hours per year,[7] and he says in the opening paragraph of the First Meditation itself that the wholesale examination of his opinions is something that he will undertake *semel in vita*, or once in life. Brown also explores the details of Descartes' view that a human being or mind–body union is more than just the sum of its mental and physical parts. Alison Simmons discusses the ways in which the second half of the Sixth Meditation works to rehabilitate the senses given that they were treated as an impediment to philosophical inquiry earlier on. In the first five Meditations, and the first half of the Sixth, the meditator goes to great lengths to detach from the senses and arrive at non-sensory clear and distinct perceptions, but in the second half of the Sixth Meditation the senses are heralded for their ability to secure truth. Their role is not to secure truth about how reality is in itself – that is the province of detached philosophical reflection – but instead they provide us with signals and prompts that are essential for navigating our environment and preserving our mind–body union. According to Simmons, the senses present us with a narcissistic picture of our surroundings that makes prominent what is relevant to us and our well-being – where we traffic in things like "empty" space, hot and cold, color, sound, tastes, joy and fear. Sensations make possible a view of the world by which we can know what to seek or avoid, and how to seek or avoid it. They are also a source of (timely) motivation. If we ended the *Meditations* thinking that only non-sensory perceptions are truth-conducive, we might over-emphasize our status as thinking things, and we might fail to appreciate all of the cues that sensations afford to assist us in our role as human beings.

In chapter fourteen, Alan Nelson enters into a comprehensive discussion of Descartes' dualism and its influence. Nelson also considers parallels with Spinoza and argues that for all the distance that Spinoza would put between his system and the system of Descartes, they are in surprising respects similar on the question of substance dualism. Descartes is not a Spinozist, and Spinoza is not a substance dualist, but he is borrowing machinery from Descartes' theory of distinction in a way that exhibits Descartes' pervasive influence. Nelson also discusses some of the ways in which Cartesian dualism had an impact on later figures, for example Locke and Berkeley. In the final chapter, Annette Baier argues that Descartes' considered conception of God is extremely unortho-dox and that Descartes is not especially shy about hiding this conception, even in the *Meditations* itself. She points to passages in which Descartes suggests that, for example, God has an imagination (which would have to involve extension), and that God is to be identified with Nature.

THE METHOD OF THE MEDITATIONS AND ITS APPLICATION

In the second set of objections to the *Meditations* Descartes is asked to put the arguments of the *Meditations* into a deductive syllogistic order.[8] There would certainly be some benefit in seeing the premises of Descartes' metaphysical system laid out explicitly, and seeing how they are supposed to entail its central tenets. At the very least there would be full disclosure: it would be clear which of the claims of the *Meditations* was a result that Descartes was advancing, and it would be clear when and where the support in their favor was lacking. Euclid was not shy about showing his hand, and left very little to the imagination. Descartes himself appreciates the payoff of the syllogistic method, but at the same time he has reservations. He thinks that it is quite suitable in the case of geometry:

The difference is that the primary notions which are presupposed for the demonstration of geometrical truths are readily accepted by anyone, since they accord with the use of our senses. Hence there is no difficulty there, except in the proper deduction of the consequences, which can be done even by the less attentive, provided they remember what has gone before ... In metaphysics by contrast there is nothing which causes so much effort as making our perceptions of the primary notions clear and distinct. Admittedly, they are by their nature as evident as, or even more evident than, the primary notions which the geometers study; but they conflict with many preconceived opinions derived from the senses which we have got into the habit of holding from our earliest years, and so only those who concentrate and meditate and withdraw their minds from corporeal things, so far as is possible, will achieve perfect knowledge of them. (*Second Replies*, AT 7: 156–57)

It is fairly easy to see the force of the argument that when two parallel lines are bisected by a third line, "corresponding angles" are equal. But Descartes thinks that metaphysical arguments are much different. They would be just as straightforward as geometrical arguments if we had a clear grasp of the primary notions of metaphysics, but there is the rub. Descartes can present the arguments of the *Meditations* in the order of premises and conclusions, but if we are not in a position to grasp the premises, and if in some cases we are inclined to reject them, the venture will be short-lived. We would be better off to concentrate and meditate and to clear away the obstacles that make metaphysical premises come off as dubious.

The ideal scenario would be one in which we could just assemble all of the metaphysical premises that are true and then draw the implications that fall out of them. So Descartes writes that in order "to philosophize seriously," we must

give our attention in an orderly way to the notions that we have within us and we must judge to be true all and only those whose truth we clearly and distinctly recognize. (*Principles* II.75, AT 8A: 38)

He adds however that, before we are able to do that, we have to "lay aside" our unexamined opinions and take steps to make sure that they are kept at bay. After we concentrate and meditate,

we contrast all this knowledge with the confused thoughts we had before, [and] we will acquire the habit of forming clear and distinct concepts of all the things that can be known. (Ibid.)

We recognize the difference between results that are extremely clear and results that only seemed to be clear – but only after a lot of work.

Descartes speaks of notions that "we have within us," and to which we are to "give our attention in an orderly way," calling them "common notions" or "primary notions." An example is the claim that something cannot come from nothing. He writes,

When we recognize that it is impossible for anything to come from nothing, the proposition *Nothing comes from nothing* is regarded not as a really existing thing, or even as a mode of a thing, but as an eternal truth which resides within our own mind. Such truths are termed common notions or axioms. The following are examples of this class: *It is impossible for the same thing to be and not to be at the same time*; *What is done cannot be undone*; *He who thinks cannot but exist while he thinks*; and countless others. It would not be easy to draw up a list of all of them; but nonetheless we cannot fail to know them when the occasion for thinking about them arises, provided that we are not blinded by preconceived opinions. (*Principles* I.49, AT 8A: 23–24)[9]

In the ideal case we could just list the primary notions and then derive the conclusions that (in conjunction) they entail. The problem, for Descartes, is that a person can be confused and not recognize the truth of claims that upon reflection are obvious. Philosophy is very hard, he might add, and so there might be truths that are in fact self-evident, but that we do not see to be obvious at first sight. An example that Descartes offers but that is very controversial is that God's existence is self-evident. In the Fifth Meditation, he writes:

If I were not overwhelmed by preconceived opinions, and if the images of things perceived by the senses did not besiege my thought on every side, I would certainly acknowledge him sooner and more easily than anything else. (AT 7: 69)

Descartes may well be wrong about whether or not it is self-evident that God exists, and he may be wrong about what should be identified as the primary notions of metaphysics. However, in making sense of the text of the *Meditations* it is important to note that later in the *Meditations* (and upon reflection) a meditator will recognize things to be true that he did not recognize to be true earlier – when he was struggling against his entrenched opinions and *was* besieged by the objects of sensation. Nor can a meditator just turn it all off. Confusion will rear its head at moments that are the least opportune, and the meditator will say what is on his mind.

Descartes is imagining (or at least hoping) that his readers will make a sincere attempt to examine their beliefs and to pay close attention as the reasoning of the *Meditations* unfolds. He writes:

I would not urge anyone to read this book except those who are able and willing to meditate seriously with me, and to withdraw their minds from the senses and from all preconceived opinions. ("Preface to the Reader," AT 7: 9)

Descartes is asking us to engage in a very rigorous intellectual exercise. He regards himself as a teacher in the *Meditations* – employing the ancient method of analysis, which he calls "the best and truest method of instruction" (*Second Replies*, AT 7: 156) – and he will not revert to lecture-mode. Part of the reason is that he does not simply want to impart information. Instead, he thinks that we should accept a result only when we see for ourselves that it is true:

One should allow oneself to be convinced only by quite evident reasoning . . . The thought of each person – i.e. the perception or knowledge which he has of something – should be for him the 'standard which determines the truth of the thing'; in other words, all the judgements he makes about this thing must conform to his perception if they are to be correct. Even with respect to the truths of faith, we should perceive some reason which convinces us that they have been revealed by God, before deciding to believe them. Although ignorant people would do well to follow the judgement of the more competent on matters which are difficult to know, it is still necessary that it be their own perception that tells them that they are ignorant; they must also perceive that those whose judgement they want to follow are not as ignorant as they are, or else they would be wrong to follow them and would be behaving more like automatons or beasts than men. (*Appendix to Fifth Objections and Replies*, AT 9A: 208)

The *Meditations* is going to have a peculiar structure. There is a meditator or *I* who is going to confront a number of views and arguments, and this meditator will be accepting views and arguments only when he sees for himself that they are true. If Descartes is right, however, the meditator is not in the best position to recognize the truth of the primary axioms of metaphysics. That is just to say that the meditator is not in the best position to see the truth for himself, and that what he does recognize to be true might well be false. To the disappointment of Mersenne (in the second set of objections), the *Meditations* does not begin with a list of arguments in which Descartes' own views are defended in premise–conclusion form. Descartes is convinced that most of his readers would never understand such arguments, and would probably even reject them. He will structure the views and arguments of the *Meditations* in such a way that a meditator can follow along and eventually be able to distinguish what is actually true from what only seemed to be so.

Descartes takes the confusion of the pre-*Meditations* thinker – or the mind that enters into the project of the *Meditations* – to be pronounced indeed. There are four causes of confusion that he identifies more generally.[10] The first is that there are opinions that we formed in childhood that we never examined and that we have held for so long that we habitually affirm them as truisms. For example, we came to believe that what is not sensible is not real: we were preoccupied with securing food and shelter and with protecting our bodies from (sensible) dangers, and so non-sensible objects were nothing to us, and we formed the belief that they are not anything at all. We also came to believe that the colors, tastes, and sounds that are a vivid and forceful component of our sensory experience are literally in the world, exactly as we sense them. In childhood we do not have the time or leisure to check to see if we are right about this, and (in the case of most of us) the opinion carries into later life. Descartes says:

Right from infancy our mind was swamped with a thousand such preconceived opinions; and in later childhood, forgetting that they were adopted without sufficient examination, it regarded them as known by the senses or implanted by nature, and accepted them as utterly true and evident. (*Principles* I.71, AT 8A: 36)

That is, we not only form habitual opinions, but we also come to have a degenerate standard of what it is for a result to be obvious or evident. A problem of course is that from the very first line of the *Meditations*, the meditator will affirm or deny results as a function of what he sees for himself to be true.

A second cause of confusion falls out of the first. We take our long-standing opinions to be unimpeachable – and to be evident – and we conclude that any claims that oppose them are to be rejected. Descartes writes:

It is not easy for the mind to erase these false judgments from its memory; and as long as they stick there, they can cause a variety of errors. For example, in our early childhood we imagined the stars as being very small; and although astronomical arguments now clearly show us that they are very large indeed, our preconceived opinion is still strong enough to make it very hard for us to imagine them differently from the way we did before. (*Principles* I.72, AT 8A: 36–37)

A person who agrees to take on Descartes' challenge of working through the *Meditations* will find it difficult to register the force of the views that Descartes is defending. The person will be inclined to reject the views if they conflict with the assumptions that they have brought to inquiry, and at the very early stages of inquiry the person is likely to reject the only premises – the primary notions of metaphysics – that can be leveraged in their defense.

The third source of confusion that Descartes identifies is that we become exhausted if we think very long about things that are abstract and insensible. Instead, we find it easier to think of things that can be pictured:

Our mind is unable to keep its attention on things without some degree of difficulty and fatigue; and it is hardest of all for it to attend to what is not present to the senses or even to the imagination. This may be due to the very nature that the mind has as a result of being joined to the body; or it may be because it was exclusively occupied with the objects of sense and imagination in its earliest years, and has thus acquired more practice and a greater aptitude for thinking about them than it has for thinking about other things. (*Principles* I.73, AT 8A: 37)

As in the case of the other two sources of confusion, here Descartes is not saying anything that is too controversial.[11] It is difficult to think thoughts that are highly abstract, and sometimes we need to catch our breath. Indeed, an important component of the pedagogical method of the *Meditations* is that it attempts to give us relief when we *do* become exhausted from philosophical reflection, or when a vivid sensible particular is the only thing that will keep our attention. But Descartes is strategic: attention to a sensible particular will always guide us in the direction of a distinct and evident perception, for example in the Second Meditation discussion of wax (AT 7:30–34), or in the First Meditation introduction of the demon (22). He also speaks vividly of an edifice (18), wind and fire (26), the sun (39) and other hot objects (41), the stamp of a craftsman (51), mountains and valleys (66–67), and winged horses (ibid.). Descartes thinks that imagistic thinking can be a threat to philosophical investigation, but it can also be instrumental.

The first three causes of confusion work in concert with each other. Philosophical reflection is difficult insofar as it deals in a very abstract subject matter, and we might be inclined to regard the results that it delivers as ephemeral. If there are long-held opinions to which we have a much greater allegiance than to claims that we are just coming to know, it is likely that we will regard the latter with suspicion. If we are self-respecting minds and not automata, it is presumably the more dignified thing to do.

The fourth cause of confusion that Descartes isolates is that we tend to get into the habit of focusing our attention on terms and words rather than the ideas for which the terms and words are used to stand in. He writes:

Because of the use of language, we tie all our concepts to the words used to express them; and when we store the concepts in our memory we always simultaneously store the corresponding words. Later on we find the words easier to recall than the things; and because of this it is very seldom that our concept of a thing is so distinct that we can separate it totally from our concept of the words involved. The thoughts of almost all people are more concerned with words than with things; and as a result people very often give their assent to words they do not understand, thinking they once understood them, or that they got them from others who did understand them correctly. (*Principles* I.74, AT 8A: 37–38.)

The fourth cause of error is of course related to the third. Descartes holds that finite minds find it very difficult to attend to things that are abstract and cannot be pictured, and he is now saying that in communication and also in our own thinking we tend to rely on imagistic words instead. If so, it is going to be easy for us to pass over and miss the contents of our ideas. Unless we engage in a very careful reflective analysis, we might have very little sense of what we are talking or even thinking about. Descartes goes to the extreme of saying that the four causes of confusion are very prevalent and that "most people have nothing but confused perceptions throughout their entire lives" (AT 8A: 37).

Descartes identifies four general sources of confusion, but he does not thereby think that the readers of the *Meditations* are all going to be confused in the same way. That is, the *I* of the *Meditations* is not necessarily one voice. For example, Descartes says about the additional proof of the existence of God that he offers in the Fifth Meditation that he is offering it "so as to appeal to a variety of different minds" (*First Replies*, AT 7: 120). He says that some minds are more prone to grasp the existence of God as self-evident (like in the Fifth Meditation) and that "others come to understand [it] only by means of a formal argument" (*Second Replies*, AT 7: 164). He speaks in similar terms about the argument for the existence of God that appears at the end of the Third Meditation. He says that he provides it for the reason that not every mind will have understood the primary notion that is at the center of the earlier argument that he had offered:

There may be some whose natural light is so meagre that they do not see that it is a primary notion that every perfection that is present objectively in an idea must really exist in the cause of the idea. For their benefit I provided an even more straightforward demonstration of God's existence based on the fact that the mind which possesses the idea of God cannot derive its existence from itself. (*Second Replies*, AT 7: 136)

In a similar vein, Descartes refers to the mind as a corporeal wind or fire (in the Second Meditation), and as having a nutritive component, and he speaks of the color and smell and sound that are known so vividly to pertain to a piece of wax.[12] Outside of the *Meditations* he notes that in those instances he was taking a point of view that is not his own – for example, a thinker along the lines of Hobbes or Gassendi who regards thought as material, or a more Aristotelian thinker who has a very different view of mind, and who takes color and smell and sound to be in objects literally.[13] Descartes says more generally that in the *Meditations*

it was not my intention to make a survey of all the views anyone else had ever held on these matters, nor was there any reason why I should have done so. I confined myself to what I had originally believed spontaneously and with nature as my guide, and to the commonly held views of others, irrespective of truth or falsity. (*Seventh Replies*, AT 7: 482)

The *Meditations* reflects a number of the different possible positions that would be entertained from the first-person point of view of a variety of minds. These positions will then be tackled head on, and they will be tackled in the light of results that the meditator will (upon reflection) recognize to be undeniable. The anticipated audience of the *Meditations* would appear to include mechanists and Aristotelians, theists who do not have a clear idea of God, skeptics, and atheists.[14] It would appear to include individuals who have never had a completely non-sensory perception, and at least some who have secured enough distance from the senses that they do have non-sensory perceptions: for example expert geometers and skeptics. The latter group of individuals might be reluctant to identify their non-sensory perceptions *as* non-sensory,[15] and they would be lacking a guarantee that maximally evident non-sensory perceptions are veridical.[16] There would also be readers who lack a fully articulated worldview but incline toward a commonsense empiricism that assumes that reality is pretty much as we sense it. Descartes announces to

those who are over-diffident about their powers that there is nothing in my writings which they are not capable of completely understanding provided they take the trouble to examine them. (*Principles*, "Preface to the French Edition," AT 9B: 13)

Descartes allows that philosophy is not easy, but he thinks that one of the central reasons is that it is extremely laborious to neutralize the four sources of confusion that stand in the way of our grasp of notions that (upon reflection) are obvious.

It is finally worth noting that, although the *Meditations* was (originally) published in 1641, Descartes had already put forward a lot of the very same views and arguments in Part four of *Discourse on Method*, published in 1637. In the *Discourse* he lays out most of the skeptical arguments (AT 6: 31–32) that appear in the First Meditation, and we encounter much of the material of Meditations Two through Six as well: the argument that if I am thinking or doubting I must necessarily exist (32); the argument that if there exists an idea of God that is infinite, it (like everything) requires a sufficient cause, and hence an omnipotent and perfect being exists (34); the argument that if God exists and created our minds, our clear and distinct (and utterly evident) perceptions must be true or else He would be a deceiver (38); the argument that the essence of God includes existence and hence that God exists (36); the argument that collections of waking perceptions are more evident and complete than dream perceptions and hence that waking perceptions contain some truth (40); and (at least a version of) the argument that minds are immaterial substances that are really distinct from bodies (32–33, also 35). The *Meditations* and the *Discourse* are still quite different, however. The *Meditations* is longer – it is just over fifty pages (in the CSM pagination), where as the *Discourse* is barely five. There is no question that some of the difference is due to additional arguments and clarifications that Descartes presents in the *Meditations*. In the preface to the *Meditations* he remarks that his

purpose there [in the *Discourse*] was not to provide a full treatment, but merely to offer a sample, and learn from the views of my readers how I should handle these topics at a later date. ("Preface to the Reader," AT 2: 7)

Another difference is that the more autobiographical *Discourse* reflects Descartes' own route to Cartesianism. The *Meditations* is written to an audience, and includes material that is meant to forge a route for a variety of minds.

Virtually every commentator will agree that there is at least some confusion in the *Meditations*, and that there is in some cases a distinction between the views and arguments that are advanced by Descartes' meditator and the views that are advanced by Descartes himself. The interpretive disagreement is about which are which and about the point (if any) at which the *Meditations* finally begins to reflect Descartes' perspective alone. Much of the discussion here has been about the issue of when Descartes is speaking in his own voice in the *Meditations*. This is largely a literary and interpretive issue, but it is crucial that we address it if we are to cull the views and arguments that Descartes is actually advancing and keep them separate from views and arguments that are more provisional. Only then can we assess Descartes' thinking and determine its applicability. An important aim of this volume then will be to present a cross-section of the interpretive possibilities so as to provide a sense of the lay of the land.

A final question to articulate is whether Descartes in the first sentences of the *Meditations* is seeking to locate a better foundation for some of the very same beliefs that he has held all along. He certainly appears to be doing this. For example, he calls into question his belief that God exists, but later he restores it on new and firmer ground. Also, in his *Principles* discussion of how to philosophize correctly, he says that "we must take the greatest care not to put our trust in any of the opinions accepted by us in the past until we have first scrutinized them afresh and confirmed their truth" (AT 8A: 38). In a number of cases, however, the updated reasons that Descartes comes to recognize as compelling lead him to similarly updated conceptions of the views that he was scrutinizing at the start.

For example, in the First Meditation he introduces the skeptical worry that we cannot make a clear distinction between waking and dreaming and that, since we cannot be certain when we are awake, we cannot be certain which of our beliefs about the sensible world is accurate or veridical. In the final analysis, however, Descartes thinks that even our waking perceptions are not wholly veridical and that qualities like color, taste, and sound are not literally in bodies in the way that we assume them to be.[17] Our pre-*Meditations* opinions about the particulars of a piece of wax, and about the rest of the bodies that surround us, and about the "empty" space that divides them,[18] are for the most part confused, and so one of the reasons that the *Meditations* is working to make us withdraw from the senses is to help us to achieve a more accurate conception of what bodies are actually like. In the Sixth Meditation, Descartes will recover the view that the external world exists, but it is a world that possesses the properties that "are comprised within the subject-matter of pure mathematics" (AT 7: 80).

The *Meditations* will also recover the view that God exists, or that there is a necessary existent that is eternal and immutable and is the creator of all substances and their modifications (Third Meditation, AT 7: 45). A pre-*Meditations* meditator might affirm this result, but if he is attending more to the linguistic terms in which it is couched, or to the image of a bearded man on a cloud, he would miss the force of the result, and also the force of its implications. In some cases the object of his thought might not even be God.[19] Or, if he is thinking of God, he might pass over and fail to notice an apparent consequence that falls out of a proper understanding of God's nature:

If a man meditates on these things and understands them properly, he is filled with extreme joy ... Joining himself willingly entirely to God, he loves him so perfectly that he desires nothing at all except that his will should be done. Henceforth, because he knows that nothing can befall him which God has not decreed, he no longer fears death, pain or disgrace. He so loves this divine decree, deems it so just and so necessary, and knows that he must be so completely subject to it that even when he expects it to bring death or some other evil, he would not will to change it even if, *per impossible*, he could do so. He does not shun evils and afflictions, because they come to him from divine providence; still less does he eschew the permissible goods or pleasures he may enjoy in this life, since they too come from God. He accepts them with joy, without any fear of evils, and his love makes him perfectly happy. ("To Chanut, 1 February 1647," AT 4: 609)

Here Descartes is sounding a bit like Spinoza, where the eternal and necessary and immutable being starts to look very different from the necessary being that is more common in the tradition. Descartes does not lay out his Stoic ethics in the *Meditations* itself, but what is important for our purposes is the extent to which he lays out views and arguments that might be a departure from the initial thinking of his meditator. Also important for our purposes is the way in which the considered views and arguments of the *Meditations* lead to consequences that are then tenets of the larger Cartesian metaphysic. Descartes advertises a small number of goals for the *Meditations* – most centrally, to establish the existence of God and the real distinction between mind and body – and much of the rest of his system will be unpacked later on.

It is certainly appropriate for Descartes to highlight that confusion often stands in the way of philosophical truth. The lingering question of course is what *is* true, and what reasons and motivations Descartes can leverage for thinking that he has gotten things right. Even if we were prepared to agree with Descartes that the primary notions of metaphysics – whatever they turn out to be – are obvious upon reflection, not everyone would agree with respect to the particular axioms that Descartes has in mind. In the chapters that follow, the authors make a number of attempts to highlight the positions that Descartes is defending, the motivations that are supposed to stand in favor of these positions, and the obstacles that are presumed to get in their way. There will be controversy in the case of a number of important philosophical and interpretive issues, in part because of disagreement about how to understand the relevant passages, and in part because of disagreement about where to draw the line between Descartes himself and the would-be Cartesian meditator. The central aim of the volume is to present some of the different approaches that can be taken in making sense of the *Meditations* – to extract its most insightful views and arguments, and to point out the critical junctures in which things are perhaps going awry – and to encourage further work.

NOTES

1. See for example the First Meditation, AT 7: 21; the Second Meditation, AT 7: 30–32; the Third Meditation, AT 7: 39; the Third Meditation, AT 7: 45; the Sixth Meditation, AT 7: 81–83.
2. "To Mersenne, End of November 1633," AT 1: 271.
3. See for example Rules Six and Seven, AT 10: 381–92.
4. For example Twelve and Thirteen, AT 10: 411–38.
5. For example *Principles* I.71–74, but see the discussion in section three below.
6. See for example "To Mersenne, 16 October 1639," AT 2: 597, and "To Clerselier, 23 April 1649," AT 5: 356.
7. "To Princess Elizabeth, 28 June 1643," AT 3: 692–93.
8. AT 7: 128. Six sets of objections were included at the end of the first edition of *Meditations on First Philosophy* in 1641, along with Descartes' responses. A seventh set of objections and replies was added to the second edition, published in 1642. The objections were solicited by Descartes himself from such philosophers as Thomas Hobbes, Antoine Arnauld, Marin Mersenne, and Pierre Gassendi, among others.
9. Descartes provides a similar list in *Second Replies*, AT 7: 145–46.
10. These are discussed in *Principles* I.71–74.
11. In our own day, we might think hard about an issue, and then identify ourselves as undergoing a brain cramp.
12. AT 7: 26, 27, and 30, respectively.
13. *Seventh Replies*, AT 7: 350–51, 477.
14. For references to the theist reader who does not have a clear idea of God, *Second Replies*, AT 7: 130–31, and *Fifth Replies*, AT 7: 365; the skeptic, *Seventh Replies*, AT 7: 476–77, and "To Hyperaspistes, August 1641," AT 3: 433; the atheist, "Dedicatory letter to the Sorbonne," AT 7: 2.
15. For example, in the First Meditation meditator's pronouncement that "whatever I have up till now accepted as most true I have acquired either from the senses or through the senses" (AT 7: 18).
16. See Descartes' famous example of the atheist geometer in *Second Replies*, AT 7: 141. Descartes also assumes that many skeptics have perceptions that are completely non-sensory, because they are sufficiently withdrawn from the senses (AT 7: 476–77).
17. For example *The World*, AT 11: 3–10, and *Principles* IV.198, AT 8A: 321–23. Note that the meditator does not come around to this view even by the end of the *Meditations*; he considers his beliefs that heat and sound and taste are literally in objects and concludes more circumspectly that "it is quite possible that these are false" (AT 7: 82). The meditator offers the

same assessment of other pre-*Meditations* beliefs as well (AT 7: 82–83). Descartes holds that the beliefs are actually false.

18. For example *Principles* II.11–18.
19. In *Appendix to Fifth Objections and Replies*, Descartes goes so far as to say that if all that we have in mind is a finite image when we believe that "God exists," then we are not believing in the existence of God at all, and so are atheists (AT 9A: 209–10).

1 The methodology of the *Meditations*: tradition and innovation

Descartes intended to revolutionize seventeenth-century philosophy and science. But first he had to persuade his contemporaries of the truth of his ideas. Of all his publications, *Meditations on First Philosophy* is methodologically the most ingenuous. Its goal is to provoke readers, even recalcitrant ones, to discover the principles of "first philosophy." The means to its goal is a reconfiguration of traditional methodological strategies. The aim of this chapter is to display the methodological stratagem of the *Meditations*. The text's method is more subtle and more philosophically significant than has generally been appreciated.

Descartes' most famous work is best understood as a response to four somewhat separate philosophical concerns extant in the seventeenth century. The first section describes these. The second section discusses how Descartes uses and transforms them. A clearer sense of the *Meditations'* methodological strategy provides a better understanding of exactly how Descartes intended to revolutionize seventeenth-century thought.[1]

EARLY MODERN METHODOLOGY: TRADITION AND INNOVATION

In order to understand the methodological brilliance of the *Meditations*, we need to recognize both its continuity and discontinuity with earlier philosophical traditions and its clear-headed response to difficulties of the period. Scholars have long noted Descartes' Augustinianism, skepticism, anti-Aristotelianism, Platonism, and interest in the tradition of religious meditation. For each of these traditions, a strong argument has been made that it was a main inspiration for his thought.[2] In fact, Descartes borrowed heavily from all of them. This should not come as a surprise. The early seventeenth century is teeming with philosophical options from which philosophers casually borrowed and whose boundaries were porous. Like so many of his contemporaries, Descartes picked and chose ideas that suited his purpose at the moment, blending them together to solve the problem at hand.

In this section, I survey the traditions that formed Descartes' intellectual milieu and from which he drew. They help us see the *Meditations* as traditional and innovative. They are as follows.

The Search for Stability

The Europe of Descartes' youth was a period of religious, political, and philosophical instability. It contained a startling array of philosophical options and eager zealots passionately arguing against one another. The Protestant reformers had splintered into warring factions, and the Counter-Reformation was in full swing. The period is packed with people bemoaning the falsities and misunderstandings around them while claiming the power of truth.[3] The English philosopher and statesman Francis Bacon exemplifies this attitude. In an essay published in 1597, entitled "Of Truth," he discusses "the Difficultie, and Labour, which Men take in finding out of *Truth*." He warns that falsities and lies corrupt the mind when they "sinketh" and "setleth in it." But he avers that despite the human capacity for "depraved Judgments, and Affections, yet *Truth* which onely doth judge it self, teacheth, that the Inquirie of *Truth*, which is the Love-making, or Wooing of it" and the understanding "of *Truth*, which is the Presence of it, ... is the Sovereign Good of human Nature." Indeed, "no pleasure is comparable, to the standing, upon the vantage ground of Truth."[4]

Platonism

Descartes was willing to use any material at hand to create, in Bacon's words, a "vantage ground" for truth. Fifteenth- and sixteenth-century humanists had often woven together quotations and ideas explicitly drawn from ancient philosophical schools and many believed that, whatever their apparent differences, these traditions could be made to cohere.[5] It is no wonder that, by the early seventeenth century, the boundaries of philosophical schools had become porous and sectarian categories unclear.

Descartes insists that he does not intend to build his system explicitly out of the ideas of Plato or Aristotle. He makes this point in *The Search for Truth*: "I hope too that the truths I set forth will not be less well received for their not being derived from Aristotle or Plato" (AT 10: 498). But this attitude toward the explicit use of ancient ideas is consistent with drawing heavily from the rich philosophical traditions available to him. Descartes suggests as much when he explains,

everything in my philosophy is old. For as far as principles are concerned, I only accept those which in the past have always been common ground among all philosophers without exception, and which are therefore the most ancient of all. Moreover, the conclusions I go on to deduce are already contained and implicit in these principles, and I show this so clearly as to make it apparent that they too are very ancient, in so far as they are naturally implanted in the human mind. (*Letter to Father Dinet*, AT 7: 580)[6]

The main point I want to make here in relation to Descartes is that Platonism was ubiquitous in the early modern period. Because Platonist doctrines were interpreted in radically different ways in the fifteenth, sixteenth, and seventeenth centuries and because early modern thinkers were happy to combine ideas from diverse sources, the task of identifying and then tracing the divergent paths of Platonism through the period is virtually impossible. The designation 'Platonism' is frustratingly vague although various strands and loosely connected doctrines can be associated with the term.[7] With this vagueness in mind, we can turn to the "Platonisms" of Descartes' intellectual milieu. They derive from three main sources.

First, when the Aristotelian Latin texts and ideas were imported to Europe from the Arab world in the thirteenth century, they were steeped in Platonism. Scholasticism resulted from the blending of Platonized Aristotelianism and medieval Christianity, which itself had Platonist roots. Thus, despite the philosophical subtlety of scholastic thinkers and despite their commitment to the Philosopher, they unknowingly promulgated a wide range of Platonist ideas, about the soul, the intellect, and the relation between the divinity and the world.[8]

A second major source of early modern Platonism is Augustinianism. The philosophy of Augustine laid the groundwork for medieval Christianity in the fifth century and set the stage for the reformations of Christianity that occurred a thousand years later.[9] Luther himself emphasized the importance and profundity of Augustine's thought, as did Counter-Reformation theologians. For example, the important French Catholic Antoine Arnaud wrote to Descartes that "the divine Augustine" is a "man of the most acute intellect, and entirely admirable not only in theology but also in philosophical matters."[10] When early modern reformers and Catholic counter-reformers turned to Augustine for inspiration, they were absorbing Platonist ideas.

Italian Renaissance thinkers who translated and interpreted Plato's works constitute the third source for early modern Platonism. At the beginning of the fifteenth century, few thinkers in the Latin west had access to more than a couple of Plato's dialogues;[11] by the end of the century, thanks to Marsilio Ficino's translations and editions, all of "the divine Plato's" works were in print.[12] Not only did Ficino produce the first Latin translation of Plato, his commentaries and interpretations form the materials for all of early modern Platonism. And the awkward truth about Ficino's Platonism is that it owes as much to the thought of Plotinus, whose works he also translated, as to Plato himself.[13]

Search for a New Philosophy

In the decades leading up to Descartes' *Meditations*, Europe was full of philosophers trying to replace Aristotelianism. Whether the ideas were based on the ancient philosophies of thinkers like Democritus, Lucretius, and Epicurus or were newly formed, the goal was to forge a new account of the world. Each of these competing philosophies had to find a way to convince readers of its truth. The rhetoric was often flamboyant. To cite one such prominent example, Galileo provokes his readers to accept his proposals as follows:

Philosophy is written in this grand book, the universe, which stands continually open to our gaze. But the book cannot be understood unless one first learns to comprehend the language and read the letters in which it is composed. It is written in the language of mathematics, and its characters are triangles, circles, and other geometric figures without which it is humanly impossible to understand a single word of it; without these, one wanders about in a dark labyrinth.[14]

This passage from *The Assayer* is so often quoted that it is easy to overlook Galileo's threat: either the reader will follow him and learn to read the language of "the book of nature" or be forever lost in a dark labyrinth.[15]

Medieval Meditations

When Descartes chose to present his first philosophy in the form of a meditation, he was doing something provocative: he was placing himself and his proposals in a tradition going back to Augustine's *Confessions* of 397–98 CE and announcing as much to his early modern readers. In order to recognize the fascinating ways in which Descartes uses and transforms the meditative discourse, we need to know more about it. In this subsection, I summarize the meditative tradition that began with Augustine and developed in important ways in the late medieval and early modern period, and that formed a crucial part of Descartes' education.[16]

In Cotgrave's French–English dictionary published in 1611, the English given for the French *meditation* is: "a deep consideration, careful examination, studious casting, or devising of things in the mind."[17] The history of Christianity contains an evolving set of spiritual exercises where the point is to acknowledge the divinity deep within oneself and devise a mental process to find it.[18] For many Christians, the underlying assumption is that we must learn how to turn our attention away from ourselves and on to God. In a striking passage, the Gospel of Mark has Jesus claim: "If any want to become my followers, let them deny themselves and take up their cross and follow me."[19] For Paul and many other early Christians, our sinful nature makes this turning to God impossible without the direct help of Jesus Christ. Paul summarizes the point succinctly: "just as sin came into the world through one man," so "through the one man, Jesus Christ," we "receive the abundance of grace" so that we might be "set free" from sin (Romans 5: 12–17; 6: 7).

Augustine of Hippo (354–430) is the single most influential meditator in the history of philosophy. Deeply moved by the epistemological pessimism of Paul, the *Confessions* contains the remarkable story of his decades-long effort to find ultimate truth and attain enlightenment. After years of struggle, Augustine realized that his corrupt nature could not find enlightenment on its own: "But from the disappointment I suffered I perceived that the darknesses of my soul would not allow me to contemplate these sublimities."[20] Rather, "wretched humanity" will remain in darkness without the direct help of Jesus Christ. As this radical epistemological claim is put in the Gospel of Matthew, "no one knows the Father except the Son and anyone to whom the Son chooses to reveal him" (Matthew, 11: 27). For hundreds of years after Augustine, the direct help of Jesus was considered a requisite for knowledge of the most significant truths about God and the human soul. Only when such divine help was conferred on the believer could there be the right "turning around" or conversion. Spiritual exercises developed to encourage self-improvement and increase the chances of attaining divine help. Their point was to teach meditators how to "take up the cross" and ready themselves for illumination. For the vast majority of medieval Christians, the final step in self-improvement required the intervention of Jesus Christ.

After generations of meditative practices based loosely on Augustinian ideas, the twelfth century witnessed a flourishing of systematic meditative treatises. Written from the first-person perspective, these spiritual exercises contain detailed steps about how to prepare to receive divine help.[21] The author of such a meditation counsels the creation of a receptive state of mind through prayer and/or attention to one's unworthy soul and then makes precise recommendations on how, when, and where to meditate. The main point is usually to learn to identify with Christ, especially with his sufferings, and to avoid temptations, demonic and otherwise. The striking thing about these "affective meditations" is that, as a recent study shows, they "ask their readers to imagine themselves present at scenes of Christ's suffering and to perform compassion for that suffering victim in a private drama of the heart." These writings "had serious, practical work to do: to teach their readers, through iterative affective performance, how to feel."[22]

This tradition of spiritual meditation developed in close proximity with the rise of scholasticism. Meditative exercises absorbed philosophical terms and nuance. Authors came to explicate meditative steps in terms of the faculties of memory, imagination, intellect, and will. The faculty of imagination became particularly important in affective meditations, where the goal was to imagine the emotional reality of Christ's sufferings as vividly as possible so as to elicit the right affect. Some meditations contain instructions for how to meditate over a short period of time; others would be used throughout a year.

Early Modern Meditations

The Reformation changed the course of meditative practices. After the reformers rejected the sanctity of saints and demanded a reconsideration of their role in spiritual life, there was a general reconsideration of meditative practices. The Catholic theologians at the Council of Trent (1545–1564), in the words of one scholar, "shaped new models of spiritual accomplishment."[23] Before the Reformation, saints were considered to be direct interveners in the lives of believers. Believers prayed to saints for help. After Trent, saints became paragons of spirituality, offering lessons on how to live a proper life. Against the Protestant reformers who took Biblical study to be a sufficient means to salvation, Catholic meditations used saints as inspirational.[24]

In this context, it is not surprising that sixteenth-century spiritual leaders offered imaginative reformulations of spiritual exercises. The Catholic church moved quickly to canonize post-Reformation spiritual advisers like Ignatius of Loyola (1491–1556) and Teresa of Ávila (also called 'Teresa of Jesus' (1515–1582)). Ignatius himself grounded the proper religious life in an education that included a rigorous pedagogy mixed with meditative exercises. The Jesuits founded schools and universities around the world including the one Descartes attended in La Flèche. During Descartes' youth, Teresa of Ávila was enormously popular for her humble and poignant reflections on the proper Christian life and the means to illumination.[25]

As this brief history of post-Augustinian meditations suggests, it has dramatic phases and moving parts. The popularity of new spiritual exercises and the Catholic commitment to the role of saints in spiritual development inspired hundreds of early modern meditative manuals. To be sure, the traditional spiritual exercise persisted, but there quickly developed variations on that tradition and many new meditative modes, including many written by Protestants. In order to discern the rhetorical subtlety in Descartes' *Meditations on First Philosophy*, it is important to see it as a clever negotiation of this diverse literary landscape.[26]

I would like to offer a few brief examples of that diversity. The meditations summarized here represent the heterogeneity of early seventeenth-century meditative options. For our purposes, the most important differences among early modern meditations are in the goal of the exercise, the faculties and other elements that contribute to that goal, the power of demons to distract from it, and the role of the author in relation to the reader and to God.

I begin with an early seventeenth-century commentary on a canonical medieval meditation on the passions of Christ. The English title of the work expresses a good deal about its goal: *Saint Bernard, his Meditations: or Sighes, Sobbes, and Teares, upon our Saviours [sic] Passion*. The text contains a translation of major parts of Bernard of Clairvaux's (1090–1153) twelfth-century meditation, but it does more than that. "To the Reader" explains: "these divine and comfortable Meditations on the Lords Passion, and Motives to Mortification . . . [are] selected out of the workes of S. Bernard, and other ancient Writers, not verbally turned into English, but augmented with such other Meditations, as it pleased God to infuse into my minde."[27] As a divinely inspired commentary on Biblical passages about the passions, relying on earlier Christian canonical writings, the work is full of direct proclamations to God and to the soul: "Learn therefore (oh my soule) to imitate the blessed Savior."[28] The book's goal is to engage the reader to meditate on the sacrifice and sufferings of Christ in order that the reader's soul might learn to imitate him.

In 1607, Antonius Dulcken published a book entitled *A Golden Book, On Meditation and Prayer*, which is an edition and translation (into Latin) of an important Spanish work by Pedro de Alcántara (1515–82). The latter had become famous in the late sixteenth century partly because he had been the spiritual adviser to Teresa of Ávila and partly because he was frequently seen to levitate in his cell. He was canonized in 1669. Pedro de Alcántara's *Meditations* nicely captures the point of many affective meditations: "Meditation is nothing other than the means to use our imagination to make ourselves present. . . in the life and passion of Christ."[29] But Pedro de Alcántara also emphasizes the role of the intellect, acknowledging that some "meditations require the intellect more."[30] The Dedicatory Letter that Dulcken wrote for his edition exemplifies the Tridentine emphasis on saintly lives and an underlying epistemological optimism based on them. He explains that all people contain "the seeds of virtue in our souls," which only need to be properly nourished. Because saints have "supernatural affections," they encourage human hearts "to grow" in the right way.[31]

Carlo Scribani, a Jesuit, published a book in 1616, entitled *Divine Love*. Although it has the structure and focus of a traditional meditation, this very long and very odd work asks the reader to focus on the passions of Christ with the goal of immortality. Scribani concedes in his nearly 600-page work that one of the main difficulties in igniting "the flame of divine love" is that humans are weak and that demons provoke that weakness.[32] He asks: "Where are you my love? ... You are not in the bread, or in the virgin milk ... or in the cross or the sword."[33] He insists that by focusing on the nature of divine love, we can overcome all difficulties. He speaks erotically of the love between Mary and Christ and between Christ and his followers. According to Scribani, this love "inebriates us," causes "a stream of tears," and "creates torrents of love."[34]

A huge two-volume *Meditations on the Mysteries of our Holy Faith*, published in 1636, marks a shift in the power of the intellect and the role of education in meditative exercise. This work, by the Spanish Jesuit, Luis de la Puente (1554–1624), is a grand and thoroughly scholastic treatment of topics common to meditations. For example, the second treats the "mysteries of the passions" and the resurrection, before moving to the trinity and then to "the most perfect attributes" of God. The text cites Aquinas and other "Scholastic Doctors" in an attempt to give "a rational account" of conflicting views about the mysteries. The hope here is to create a "fount of spiritual science [*scientia*]."[35] The frontispiece of the book summarizes its approach: the author sits in his priestly robes with a crucifix on one side and a pile of books on the other.

Early modern spiritual meditations differed significantly in terms of points of emphasis and modes of presentation. Consider, for example, Philipp Camerarius' *Historical Meditations* of 1603. The point of this huge, two-volume work in French, is to show that the history of philosophy is full of diverse ways to purify "the heart" and approach God. Camerarius' work does not fit any of the models usually offered of early modern meditations. It is not itself a meditation, in the sense that it does not ask the reader to meditate, and it appears to suppose that we do not require God's direct assistance in accessing fundamental truths. Rather, it begins with the assumption that there are different ways of coming to God and different ways of purifying one's heart;[36] it then sets about discussing those historical figures who presented "vain and useless efforts" and those who offered help in attaining a "true heart."[37] Although Camerarius is critical of many philosophers, he compliments many others, including non-Christians. From "Greek sages" to Cicero and beyond, he acknowledges that "pagan" thinkers were able to understand the right approach to virtue. Within a few pages, he quotes Homer, Augustine, and the Emperor Justinian in evaluating their views.[38] There is a chapter on the "virtues and vices of the ancient Romans."[39] For our purposes, it is important that he offers a thorough analysis of Plato's cave allegory. Camerarius is particularly concerned to note that this famous story from Book VII of the *Republic* proves how easily people remain in "false opinion and vain ignorance."[40]

The books described here represent only a small sample of the range of meditations published between 1603 and 1639.[41] My intention is to show that, although the tradition of spiritual mediation persisted well into the seventeenth century, there was a great variation among them and that post-Reformation Europe developed new meditative modes.

When Descartes entered the Jesuit school La Flèche in 1606, at the age of ten, his Jesuit teachers (and the professors who had trained those teachers) were thoroughly educated in this diverse meditative culture. As part of his education, Descartes would have studied Jesuit classics like Ignatius' *Spiritual Exercises* and very likely the works of Teresa of Ávila, which were extremely popular in the period. When Descartes was composing his *Meditations* in the final years of the 1630s, he was fully aware of this complicated context. It is noteworthy that the French translation of the *Meditations* that appeared in 1647 had the title *Les méditations métaphysiques de René Descartes*. Subsequent French editions also gave it the title *Metaphysical Meditations*.[42]

DESCARTES

Descartes' *Meditations* was written to revolutionize seventeenth-century philosophy and science. Section 1 described four methodological traditions extant in the early seventeenth century. In order to forge his revolution, Descartes needed to respond to each of these. Some he used; others he transformed. It is time to consider how.

The Search for Stability: Meditation and Reorientation

We have noted the religious, political, and philosophical instability of the early seventeenth century. Philosophers were eager to cast aside the lies that "corrupt" the mind in order to find, in Bacon's words, "the vantage ground of Truth." But as Bacon also admits such "finding out of the Truth" requires "Difficultie, and Labour." In his *Meditations*, Descartes encourages his readers to do this labor. The traditional spiritual meditation demanded that readers shift attention from themselves to a greater and greater identification with Christ. To return to the Gospel of Mark, the meditators learn to "deny themselves and take up their cross" so that they shed "the world" and gain "their soul" (Mark 8: 34, 36). This reorientation of the self requires practice and a willingness to reconsider one's world.

As we have seen, beginning with Augustine's *Confessions* and persisting through the early seventeenth century, the main goal of spiritual meditation is a reorientation of the self so that the exercitant is prepared for illumination. The means to this goal is a series of intensive meditative exercises. The assumption is that, if the meditator becomes properly reoriented, then the chances of divine illumination are greatly increased. As we have also seen, there are differences in the roles and significance assigned to the meditator's memory, intellect, will, and imagination, but the assumption remains that only by identifying with Christ and experiencing his love will illumination occur.

One of the most rhetorically stunning features of *Meditations on First Philosophy* is that it frames the search for metaphysical truths in meditative terms. For his seventeenth-century readers, Descartes' title itself would imply three things about their task: they would have to struggle to reorient their relation to themselves as experiencers of the world; they should expect such reorientation to be difficult and require rest along the way; and they could hope for illumination if they properly applied themselves. The meditative framework for the "first philosophy" prepares readers to be thoroughly changed. It is a brilliant way to prepare them for a revolution.

The Meditations *as a meditation: steps in reorientation*

Descartes' *Meditations* both uses the meditative tradition and transforms it in important ways. It is now time to explain how. In her most important work, *Interior Castle*, Teresa of Ávila describes one of the main elements in spiritual illumination in terms roughly similar to those of the *Meditations*. She explains that although we begin with "a distracted idea of our own nature," the goal is "a notably intellectual vision, in which it is revealed to the soul how all things are seen in God."[43] Descartes' Meditation One creates "a distracted idea" of one's self, which the meditator confronts in Meditation Two. In Meditations Three through Five, the meditator is lead to more and more notable instances of "intellectual vision."

It will be helpful to list the standard elements of meditative exercises and note how Descartes used, rejected, and transformed them. Here are the main steps in reorientation.

STEP 1: DESIRE TO CHANGE. The authors of spiritual meditations begin with the assumption that readers want to find the way to truth and enlightenment. There is no reason to read a spiritual meditation unless one is seeking help. Descartes can assume no such thing. Unlike his spiritual cohorts, he has to convince his readers of the need to meditate on "first principles" and to reorient themselves metaphysically. In the first paragraph of Meditation One, he famously attempts to engage his readers in the need, once in life, "to demolish everything completely and start again right from the foundations" (AT 7: 17). Given the familiarity of his readers with the meditative tradition, Descartes' rhetorical strategy here is clever. His meditator takes a step that virtually all meditations ask their readers to make, namely, to admit their past mistakes and in that sense reject the foundations of their past lives.[44] Like the authors of spiritual manuals, Descartes believes that all his readers need complete reorientation. And like them, he assumes that, although his readers might be confused in different ways and to different degrees, they all need to "start again."[45]

STEP 2: DOUBT AND DEMONS. As we have seen, many meditations discuss the dangers of demons. In his two-part *Lives of the Saints* of 1583, Alonso de Villegas writes about the ease with which demons lead people astray. For many authors, the only way to avoid the power of demons is to learn to meditate properly. It is clear that Descartes intended the skeptical arguments of Meditation One to force his readers to doubt all of their beliefs. Scholars have long debated the strategy of the arguments and debated their cogency. But the rhetorical subtlety of the Meditation has not been sufficiently noticed. Given the religious and philosophical turmoil of the period and given the common warnings about demons, his early modern readers must have found the deceiver argument particularly poignant. Whether they were Catholic or Protestant, they wanted to avoid demonic power and find a secure foundation for true beliefs. When Descartes framed the presentation of his philosophy as a meditation and then introduced a deceiving demon, he was both forcing his readers into the philosophical equivalent of sinfulness and signaling to them that he was doing so. Whatever the soundness of the demon-deceiver argument, its rhetorical force must have added to its power, especially given recent warnings of thought-controlling demons.[46] Echoing the language of Alonso de Villegas and others in the tradition, he writes: "I will suppose therefore that ... some malicious demon of the utmost power and cunning has employed all his energies in order to deceive me" (AT 7: 22). For some readers, this possibility must have sent chills up their spine. Similarly to current religious meditations, the warning is: struggle against demons or be doomed.

STEP 3: THE MEDITATING SUBJECT AND THE AUTHORIAL VOICE. In his *Confessions*, Augustine describes the step that must be taken to find God:

These books [of the Platonists] served to remind me to return to my own self. Under Your guidance I entered into the depths of my soul. . . . I entered, and with the eye of my soul, such as it was, I saw the Light that never changes casting its rays over the same eye of my soul, over my mind. . . . What I saw was something quite, quite different from any light we know on earth . . . It was above me because it was itself the Light that made me, and I was below because I was made by it.[47]

Following Augustine, meditators assumed that the "changeable" mind could only reach the "unchangeable" truths "by turning towards the Lord, as to the light which in some fashion had reached it even while it had been turned away from him." Thanks to God's intimate presence in the human mind, humans can attain knowledge, though only "through the help of God."[48] But even with divine help, as he explains in *Confessions*, "the power of my soul ... belongs to my nature" and "I cannot grasp all that I am. The mind is not large enough to contain itself."[49] Because the mind is mutable and finite, it can never grasp the whole of its contents; with the help of God, however, it can grasp some part of it.

As these passages from *Confessions* suggest, the author of spiritual exercises often speaks directly to God to praise the divinity and to ask for help. The spiritual adviser has attained illumination and so can speak with authority. In the *Confessions* Augustine speaks only to God, and so the advice he offers the reader is indirect. Instead of telling his readers what to do, he shows them his life. But it is clear that the authorial voice is that of someone who has experienced illumination.

Most late medieval and early modern spiritual meditations offer explicit advice to their readers about how to reorient themselves. In her *Interior Castle*, Teresa of Ávila constantly addresses "her sisters," offering them directions based on her own experience. She frets about the obscurity of these "interior matters," admitting to her readers that "to explain to you what I should like is very difficult unless you have had personal experience."[50] She asks God for help and beseeches those who are struggling along with her: "But you must be patient, for there is no other way in which I can explain to you some ideas I have about certain interior matters."[51] In the end, if her readers follow her advice, they may attain illumination.[52] But there is also a constant instability in the process of spiritual development. Teresa is clear about the precariousness of the journey to enlightenment because its success depends entirely on God's support. She writes: "whenever I say that the soul seems in security, I must be understood to imply for as long as His Majesty thus holds it in His care and it does not offend him." Even after years of practice, one must "avoid committing the least offence against God."[53] Teresa insists in *My Life* that the soul can never trust in itself because as soon as it is not "afraid for itself" it exposes "itself to dangers." It must always be fearful.[54] For Teresa and for many other meditators, there is never real spiritual security, and so there must be constant meditation.

Like Teresa, Descartes' meditator has to have an intellectual vision. Like Augustine and the spiritual exercises inspired by his *Confessions*, Descartes' truth-seeker must begin his journey to illumination by learning "to return to my own self." As he writes in Meditation Two: "But I do not yet have a sufficient understanding of what this 'I' is" (AT 7: 25). But the authorial voice of the *Meditations* differs significantly from that of spiritual meditators. Descartes' meditator has no idea of where the journey will lead or how the demon deceiver will be overcome. In an Augustinian mode, Descartes shows his reader a process of struggling toward illumination. But unlike the speaker of the *Confessions*, the speaker of the *Meditations* is not yet enlightened. While Descartes himself has clearly devised his first philosophy, the meditator does not let on that there is a clear path to illumination. At the beginning of Meditation Two, he writes: "It feels as if I have fallen unexpectedly into a deep whirlpool which tumbles me around so that I can neither stand on the bottom now swim to the top ... I will proceed in this way [continuing to doubt my beliefs] until I recognize something certain, or, if nothing else, until I at least recognize that there is no certainty" (AT 7: 24). To the reader, the authorial voice seems much more humble: it begins in confusion, turns to despair, and then moves only slowly to clarity.[55] And, in the end, it is much more optimistic: the meditative journey implies that any human being who takes the steps described will attain illumination. Unlike Augustine and his followers who restrict human knowledge to a mere part of the truth, and unlike Teresa and others who suggest that illumination does not effect stability, Descartes' meditator is able to grasp the entirety of "first philosophy" once and for all. Compared to the instability of religious illumination, Descartes' promise of certainty must have seemed appealing. And because his meditator moves from confusion to certainty, Descartes' readers might have felt more optimistic about their own struggle.

STEP 4: THE ARDUOUS JOURNEY. The reorientation of the self in spiritual exercises takes time and effort. It is no wonder that the meditative journey is slow and arduous. Many early modern spiritual advisers preach the development of discipline, which they often explicate in terms of the faculties of memory, intellect, and will. The acquisition of such discipline requires brief periods of intense attention and must be punctuated with periods of rest. Given the fickleness of human attention, one has to develop the capacity to concentrate and then practice what was learned.

Descartes' *Meditations* has all these features. Concerning discipline and rest, each of the first three Meditations constitutes a breakthrough that leaves the meditator discombobulated and in need of rest.[56] The end of Meditation One displays an attitude common in the discourse of spiritual exercise, namely, the fear of backsliding and inescapable darkness: "I happily slide back into my old opinions and dread being shaken out of them, for fear that my peaceful sleep may be followed by hard labour when I wake, and that I shall have to toil not in the light, but amid the inextricable darkness of the problems I have now raised" (AT 7: 23).

Like his early modern predecessors, Descartes' meditation also involves the redirection of the intellect, the proper application of memory, and the strengthening of the will. For example, Meditation Two concludes with a standard insistence: "But since the habit of holding on to old opinions cannot be set aside so quickly, I should like to stop here and meditate for some time on this new knowledge I have gained, so as to fix it more deeply in my memory" (AT 7: 34). In Meditation Four, the meditator realizes that in order "to avoid error," he must remember "to withhold judgement on any occasion when the truth of the matter is not clear" (AT 7: 62). Then, echoing a common sentiment about the weakness of will and the human propensity to error, he acknowledges:

Admittedly, I am aware of a certain weakness in me, in that I am unable to keep my attention fixed on one and the same item of knowledge at all times; but by attentive and repeated meditation I am nevertheless able to make myself remember it as often as the need arises, and thus get into the habit of avoiding error. (Ibid.)

I have noted that early modern meditations began to highlight the role of the intellect. In the next section, I argue that the "pure" intellectualism of the *Meditations* owes more to Platonism than do standard spiritual meditations. But it is worth noting here that, by the end of Meditation Five, Descartes is willing to state: "if there is anything which is evident to my intellect, then it is wholly true" (AT 7: 71).

STEP 5: ILLUMINATION. The main point of spiritual exercises is to be illumined. The authors who talk about illumination differ in their accounts, but a common assumption is that the experience involves a full recognition of the beauty and love of God. One is taken by that love and changed accordingly. As we have seen, Francis Bacon avers: "no pleasure is comparable, to the standing, upon the vantage ground of Truth." For many early modern philosophers, whether Protestant or Catholic, there is a close relation between truth, love, and pleasure. Teresa describes her experience of God as "absolutely irresistible ... It comes, in general, as a shock, quick and sharp ... and you see and feel it as a cloud, or a strong eagle rising upwards, and carrying you away on its wings."[57] We will discuss the illumination that occurs in the *Meditations* in the next section. For now, the relevant point is that although Descartes appropriates much of the language and imagery of Christian spirituality, he has dropped all talk of divine love. He mentions the beauty of God at the end of Meditation Three, but it does not function as a motivating force or even an attraction. Descartes' account of illumination differs significantly from the tradition in that it is virtually devoid of affect.

But it is also easier to attain than the tradition allowed. Although Descartes recognizes that the path to illumination will not always be easy, he is committed to the view that proper meditation will lead to insight. In *Second Replies*, he acknowledges that for those who have "opinions which are obscure and false, albeit fixed in the mind by long habit," it may be hard to become accustomed "to believing in the primary notions." But he insists:

Those who give the matter their careful attention and spend time meditating with me will clearly see that there is within us an idea of a supremely powerful and perfect being ... I cannot force this truth on my readers if they are lazy, since it depends solely on their exercising their powers of thought. (AT 7: 135–36)

In the end, however, those who are not lazy and who practice will be properly illumined.

Transforming Platonism

Section 1 listed the three main sources of Platonism in early modern thought: scholasticism, Augustinianism, and the Plotinian Platonism promulgated by Ficino. Although there is no reason to believe that Descartes ever made any thing like a thorough study of Plato's philosophy, his education would have given him a familiarity with Platonist ideas from these three sources. A Jesuit secondary school education in the seventeenth century retained a pedagogy structured around scholastic textbooks, with special attention paid to the thought of Aquinas. Scholars have long noted the Platonist ideas in the writings of Aquinas, whose popularity had increased in the Counter-Reformation. He became a pillar of the new Jesuit order after its formation in 1540 and was declared a "Doctor of the Universal Church" by Pope Pius V in 1567.[58] Descartes' Jesuit education also contained huge amounts of Augustinianism. As we have seen, the medieval tradition of spiritual meditation grew out of Augustine whose ideas inspired early modern Reformers and Catholics alike.[59] Concerning the Platonism promulgated by Ficino and other humanists, it is unlikely that Descartes' secondary education required a study of Plato's works, but his teachers were familiar with Platonism, and their textbooks would have included Platonist ideas.[60]

Given the ubiquity of Platonism in early modern Europe, it is not surprising that Descartes appropriates Platonist ideas. Some of these bear a close resemblance to Augustinian sources; others suggest non-Augustinian Platonist roots. For example, elements in the epistemological journey described in Meditations Two, Three, and Five bear a striking similarity to Plato's cave allegory. In Book VII of the *Republic*, when the truth-seeker escapes his chains and turns from the shadows, he looks with difficulty at the fire in the cave. Once he accustoms himself to the fire's illumination, he moves with difficulty to the entrance of the cave, where he is nearly blinded by the sun's brightness. He slowly becomes accustomed to that light until he is able to gaze upon the sun and see the realities it so beautifully illuminates. In Plato's words, once the truth-seeker "is able to see ... the sun itself," he can "infer and conclude that the sun ... governs everything in the visible world, and is ... the cause of all the things that he sees" (516b). In *The Republic*, the epistemological moral is that the truth-seeker is able to grasp the Good itself and see how it is "the cause" of everything else.[61]

What makes the *Meditations* so clever is that it uses all of these traditions to suit Descartes' particular needs. On the one hand, as we have seen, he explicitly models his work on Christian spiritual meditations. On the other, he replaces an essential feature of those exercises with exercises that are devoted to "the pure deliverances of the intellect."[62] As we have noted, Augustinian notions of sin make divine intervention a requisite for illumination. Descartes ignores the standard Christian need for intervention and relies instead on a purer form of Platonist intellectualism, according to which the intellect needs no such help. Similar to Augustine and the Augustinian spiritual tradition, Descartes' journey begins with a turning "inward." But unlike that tradition, his meditator is able to escape the shadow-world without the aid of any divine or human source.

The narrative arc that begins with the first paragraphs of Meditation Two and ends with the conclusion of Meditation Three roughly parallels the steps that Plato's cave-dweller takes: it begins with disorientation and confusion, moves to a first glimpse into the nature of things (the nature of mind and body), followed by the dramatic moment when the ultimate reality is apprehended. Plato's truth-seeker sees the light of the sun at the edge of the cave; Descartes' has his first glimpse of God. Neither needs divine help.

At the end of Meditation Three, Descartes neatly combines elements drawn from religious meditations with those of the Platonist tradition to create a dramatic epistemological shift. Although the argument for the existence of God occupies much of Meditation Three, its conclusion strongly suggests that one of the main points of this part of the meditative exercise is to reorient the intellect so as to recognize its cognitive range and it relation to God: "I perceive ... the idea of God, by the same faculty which enables me to perceive myself" (AT 7: 51). Although Descartes emphasizes the importance of having turned his "mind's eye" upon itself, the result is illumination. The meditator perceives God. As a conclusion to Meditation Three, he writes that, before "examining" this idea of God "more carefully and investigating other truths which may be derived from it, I would like to pause here and spend some time in contemplation of God; ... and to gaze with wonder and adoration on the beauty of this immense light, so far as the eye of my darkened intellect can bear it" (AT 7: 52).

The first paragraph of Meditation Four summarizes the lessons drawn from the meditative enterprise: "During these past few days I have accustomed myself to leading my mind away from the senses" and recognized that "very little about corporeal things ... is truly perceived, whereas much more is known about the human mind, and

still more about God" (AT 7: 52–53). As a consequence of this meditative exercise, "I now have no difficulty in turning my mind . . .
towards things which are the objects of the intellect alone."
Descartes is perfectly clear that it is "the human intellect" by itself
that knows these things. Looking forward toward the next phase of
meditation, he writes: "And now, from this contemplation of the true
God, in whom all treasures of wisdom and the sciences lie hidden,
I think I can see a way forward to the knowledge of other things" (AT
7: 52–53).

For seventeenth-century readers of the *Meditations*, this was
surely a dramatic moment. Descartes' meditator had reached the
point of reorientation: he has escaped the shadows of doubt to attain
illumination, accomplished by his own intellectual endeavors. The
lesson is clear: the human intellect is able to make the arduous trek to
illumination entirely on its own. Descartes' readers would have been
fully aware of the difference between this journey to illumination and
the Augustinian one. And many readers would be familiar with the
story of the cave, if not the details of Plato's *Republic*.[63] It seems
likely that Descartes is here cleverly engaging with these Platonist
traditions to suit his needs. By elegantly interweaving different
Platonist strands he creates something both old and revolutionary.

Reorientation and New Philosophy

The revolution that Descartes hoped to effect was primarily a scientific one. Scholars have persuasively argued that his main concern
was to furnish the world with a science that would replace
Aristotelianism and explain "the whole of corporeal nature."[64]
Descartes believes that the "establishment" of his new philosophy
would render the Aristotelian system "so absolutely and so clearly
destroyed . . . that no other refutation is needed" ("To Mersenne,
22 December 1641," AT 3: 470). As I have noted, when he claimed
his system would replace Aristotle, he joined a chorus of early modern voices announcing that a philosophical revolution was at hand.
But unlike most others, by the mid-seventeenth century, Descartes'
proposals had become one of the "new philosophies" that had to be
taken seriously.

The similarities between the "pure intellectualism" of Galileo in
The Assayer and that of Descartes are obvious. For both natural

philosophers, the mind turns itself upon its concepts, reflects on them, and discovers the truths therein contained. Also, like Galileo, Descartes believes that if the mind does not attend to its concepts in the right way, it will remain in a world of its own prejudices. But Descartes goes well beyond Galileo in offering a first philosophy that will ground his physics and doing so in a way that gradually prepares his readers for a revolution. After the illuminations of Meditation Five, Descartes concludes that meditative exercise by summarizing what he has learned and preparing his readers for the science of nature that will come:

Thus I see plainly that the certainty and truth of all knowledge depends uniquely on my awareness of the true God, to such an extent that I was incapable of perfect knowledge about anything else until I became aware of him. And now it is possible for me to achieve full and certain knowledge of countless matters, both concerning God himself and other things whose nature is intellectual, and also concerning the whole of that corporeal nature which is the subject-matter of pure mathematics. (AT 7: 71)

The success of Descartes' proposals in natural philosophy is surely due to their innovation and explanatory power. But we should not let their success hide the power of the *Meditations'* rhetorical arc. While it is impossible to gauge the exact contribution that its meditative rhetoric made to its philosophical success, the methodology of re-orientation must have cushioned the blow of its proposals. In grounding his account of nature in first principles discoverable through a reorientation of the mind, Descartes was preparing his readers to accept radical change.

CONCLUSION

The goal of this chapter is to contextualize the methodology of Descartes' *Meditations* in order to reveal the subtlety of its rhetorical strategy. Historians have long noted the work's brilliance and originality. The same has not been true of the richness and finesse of its method. I have tried to show some of the complicated ways in which Descartes uses, ignores, and transforms traditional philosophical and religious elements to create a work of astonishing subtlety. He negotiated a complex philosophical landscape to set a path that would surprise, illumine, and *change* his contemporaries. The *Meditations* is much more than a series of arguments. It is an attempt to reorient the minds of its readers and ultimately to forge a revolution.[65]

NOTES

1. On the relation between Descartes' first philosophy and concern to argue for his natural philosophy or physics, see especially Hatfield 2003 and Garber 1992.
2. For example, Menn 1998, chapters three and four; Broughton 2002; Curley 1978; Garber 1986; and Schmaltz 1991, Popkin 1979, chapters nine and ten; Hatfield 1985 and 1986.
3. For some of these, see Cunning 2010, chapter 10.
4. Bacon 2000, 7–8.
5. Mercer, 2000, 2002; Kraye and Stone 2000.
6. In this letter, Descartes describes his reaction to the Seventh Set of Objections, written by Pierre Bourdin. The letter is to Bourdin's superior, Father Dinet, who had taught Descartes at La Flèche. (See CSM 2: 64–65.) Descartes is clear that he was very concerned that this one man's views did not represent "the balanced and careful assessment that your entire Society had formed of my views" (AT 7: 564).
7. It is an awkward truth about prominent Platonists that they put forward elaborate theories that are sometimes only remotely connected to the texts of the Athenian philosopher himself. On the heterogeneity of early modern Platonism, see Kristeller 1979 and Mercer 2002. On the question of what Platonism is, see Gerson 2005.
8. As the Renaissance historians Copenhaver and Schmitt 1992 have written: "Given the quantity of Platonic material transmitted" through Arabic authorities "or generally in the air in medieval universities, it is not surprising that parts of Thomist metaphysics owe more to Augustine, Proclus, or Plotinus than to Aristotle" (133).
9. Augustine himself acknowledges his Platonist sources, noting the special importance of the thought of Plotinus. See, e.g., Augustine's *Confessions*, VII. 10 (16).
10. For the importance of Augustinianism in seventeenth-century France and for other examples of major figures proclaiming the importance of the "divine Augustine," see Menn 1998, esp. 21–25.
11. Twenty-first century scholars are often surprised to discover that, despite the importance of Platonism in medieval Europe, very few of Plato's texts were available. Only the *Timaeus* was widely available. Dialogues as important as the *Republic* and *Symposium* had been lost and had to be "rediscovered" in the Renaissance. On Descartes' relation to the *Timaeus*, see Wilson 2008.

12. For more on this history, see Copenhaver and Schmitt 1992, esp. chapters 1 and 3.
13. Much has been written about Ficino, his thought and influence. A fine place to begin an exploration of these topics is Allen 2002 and Garfagnini 1986.
14. *The Assayer*, in Drake 1957, 237–38.
15. There has been important recent work done on the "emergence" of science. For an overview and reference to other works, see Gaukroger 2006. It is noteworthy that few of these studies discuss the role of Platonism in the period.
16. The standard treatment of the relation between Descartes and Augustine is Rodis-Lewis 1954. Also see Janowski 2000, and esp. Menn 1998.
17. Cotgrave 1611.
18. For an interesting comparison between ancient and early Christian notions of self, see Barnes 2009. For an important study of religious meditations, see Stock 2011.
19. All Biblical quotations are from the New Revised Standard Version. Mark 8: 34.
20. Augustine, *Confessions*, VII.20.26–27. Also see XIV.15.21.
21. Bennett 1982, 32.
22. McNamer 2010, 1–9. Since Bynum 1987, scholars have increasingly discussed the gendered aspect of such meditations. For a summary, see McNamer 2010, 3–9.
23. Leone 2010, 1.
24. Alonso de Villegas published his *The Lives of Saints* in 1583. On Alonso de Villegas and the role of saints in the Counter-Reformation, see Leone 2010, 4 and *passim*.
25. Teresa of Ávila's fame has hardly decreased. For the importance of her writings to modern Spanish literature, see Du Pont 2012.
26. I agree with Rubidge that "Descartes's *Meditations* do not resemble Loyola's Spiritual Exercises more than other devotional manuals" (28), though I think the similarities between Descartes' work and other early meditations are more philosophically significant than Rubidge suggests. For a helpful account of those manuals, the role in them of memory, intellect, and will, and references to earlier studies, see Rubidge 1990.
27. Bernard of Clairvaux 1614, A 3r.
28. Ibid., 33.
29. Ibid, 2v.
30. Ibid, 136–37.
31. De Alcántara 1624, 2v–3r.
32. Scribani 1616, 582.
33. Ibid, 565.

34. Ibid, 2v–4r. Scribani also published a more standard meditations. See Scribani 1616.
35. De la Puente 1636, 3–5.
36. Camerarius 1603, 2–3.
37. Ibid, 334.
38. Ibid, 3–5.
39. Ibid, 183.
40. Ibid, 167.
41. Catholics wrote the majority of early modern meditations. But Protestants also took up the meditative banner. For example, a famous Lutheran theologian, Johann Gerhard (1582–1637), published a Latin work that went through several editions and was translated into English and German. For the English version, see Winterton 1627.
42. The first French translation is: *Les méditations métaphysiques de René Descartes. Traduites du Latin par M. le D.D.L.N.S.* [i.e. Louis Charles D'Albert de Luynes]. *Et les objetions faites contre ces Meditations ... avec les réponses de l'Auteur.* Traduites par Mr. C.L.R. [i.e. Claude Clerselier] (Paris: Camusat), 1647.
43. Teresa, 1921, 6th mansion, chapter 10. For a major Latin edition of her works, which were originally in Spanish, see Teresa de Jesús 1626.
44. On the similarity between some of the steps in spiritual exercises and those in the *Meditations* and on their goal of illumination, see Hatfield 1986, esp. 47–54. But the historical context is more complicated that he suggests. Also see Rorty 1983.
45. Scholars have interpreted the rhetoric and skepticism of Meditation One in different ways. See for example Wilson 2003 and Broughton 2002. Cunning is very helpful in introducing the notion of the "unemended intellect" and emphasizing the fact that Descartes' strategy here is to offer a means for any sort of reader (whether Aristotelian, mechanist, atheist, or theist) to follow the method and discover the truths. See Cunning 2010, esp. 7, 28–33, 103.
46. See Cunning 2010 and reference to other sources, 62–63, esp. 1 40.
47. *Confessions* VIII.10.
48. Ibid., XIV.15 (21).
49. Ibid., X.8 (15).
50. Teresa, 1921, Mansion 1, chapter 2.
51. Ibid., Mansion 1, chapter 1.
52. Ibid., Mansion 6, chapter 10.
53. Ibid., Mansion 7, chapter 2, section 13.
54. Teresa, 1904, chapter XIX, section 22.
55. See also Curley 1986, 153–57; Hatfield 1986, 69–72; and Cunning 2010, 37–43, 217–30.

56. In a famous letter to Elisabeth of June 28, 1643, Descartes writes that one should spend "very few hours a year on those [activities] that occupy the intellect alone" (AT 3: 692–93).
57. Teresa, 1904, chapter X, section 3.
58. For a summary of the range of Aristotelianisms in the early modern period, the place of Aquinas in the Counter-Reformation, and citations to other studies, see Stone 2002.
59. Scholars have often noted the striking similarities between Descartes' ideas and those of Augustine. The latter is also concerned with proving that the self exists in the face of skeptical arguments. His response is summed up in the statement "Si fallor, sum," which is recognized to be the distant antecedent of Descartes' defense of the same idea. For more on Descartes' relation to Augustine, see Menn 1998. But despite striking similarities between some of Augustine's views and those of Descartes, it is doubtful that Descartes knew Augustine's texts very well. He denies direct knowledge of those works and I see no reason not to take him at his word. The similarities between his ideas and Augustine's are easily explained by the ubiquity of Augustinian ideas in the period. For a recent scholar who does not take Descartes at his word, see Brachtendorf 2012.
60. Robert Black has shown that in late medieval and Renaissance secondary schools, students learned about Plato's cave allegory. Students also learned, in Black's words, the "basic doctrines of the ancient philosophical schools," including Plato, who was called "semi-divine and preferred by the gods themselves" (Black 2001, 305–07).
61. For a brief discussion of the similarities between Descartes' *Meditations* and Plato's cave allegory, see Mercer 2002, 37–39. Buckle 2007 argues for a similar point, but seems unaware of the variety of Platonisms available to Descartes.
62. This is language from Hatfield 1986, 47. I agree with Hatfield's basic point that the *Meditations* attempts to "evoke the appropriate cognitive experiences in the meditator."
63. See Black 2001, 305–07.
64. AT 7:71. See also Garber 1986, 83–91.
65. I would very much like to thank David Cunning for asking me to write up my ideas about methodological matters as they apply to the *Meditations* and then offering feedback along the way. A conversation with Gideon Manning was also very helpful. I would like to thank the Herzog August Bibliothek for offering me a Senior Fellowship so that I could use their wonderful library while researching early modern meditations.

2　The First Meditation: skeptical doubt and certainty

INTRODUCTION

Descartes' *Meditations on First Philosophy* has long been considered the founding text of modern philosophy, suggesting that philosophy begins in doubt and not in wonder as the Greeks supposed. Hegel put the idea thus: when we survey the history of ancient and medieval philosophy up to Descartes, we feel like a sailor on a storm-tossed sea who is finally able to shout "Land ahoy!," for Cartesian doubt is not doubt about this or that particular matter, but a wholesale doubt in which the human mind, rejecting the authority of nature and God, sets out to be its own guide and to make a new, "absolute" beginning.[1] Such is indeed the spirit of the First Meditation, subtitled "What can be called into doubt" and opening with Descartes recounting how the discovery of extensive error in many of the beliefs he had accepted from childhood led him to doubt "the whole edifice that I had subsequently based on them" and to undertake "to demolish everything completely and start again right from the foundations" (AT 7: 17).

As the "Synopsis of the *Meditations*" indicates, the First Meditation pursues this new beginning in a specific direction. The skeptical doubts it lays out, Descartes says, are intended only for "so long as we have no foundations for the sciences other than those which we have had up till now," since their goal is to show how "the mind may be led away from the senses" (AT 7: 12). In other words, the First Meditation has as its aim to demolish the notion that knowledge rests upon the senses and to prepare the way for the different conception of knowledge developed in subsequent Meditations. This non-empiricist conception will not only insist on the existence of innate ideas; it will also assert, as in the wax example of Meditation Two (AT 7: 30–34), that even our most

48

elementary beliefs about material things, such as that our sensations are of objects enduring over time, have their basis not in the senses themselves, but in the judging activity of the intellect.

The skepticism of the First Meditation has therefore a strictly theoretical function. It is designed to discredit an empiricist view of knowledge and does not represent, in some respects is too radical to represent, a way of life, as the ancient skeptics of the Pyrrhonist and Academic schools understood their skepticism to do. It serves to "lead the mind away from the senses" – a refrain that runs through the *Meditations* and *Replies* (AT 7: 4, 9, 14, 52, 131) – and toward a recognition of the supremacy of the intellect.

The First Meditation falls into three parts: a preliminary section (the first two paragraphs) setting down the rules for the inquiry to follow; the central part which carries out the skeptical overthrow of empiricism; and a final section (the last two paragraphs) explaining how to take this outcome seriously despite the force of habit. I shall focus on the central part and return to the preliminary section at the end.

THE OBJECT OF SKEPTICAL ATTACK

The skeptical doubts in Meditation One were not particularly novel, as Descartes acknowledged. Most had figured in the writings of the ancient skeptics and, with the publication of a Latin translation of Sextus Empiricus' *Outlines of Pyrrhonism* in 1562, had already inspired a host of neo-Pyrrhonian thinkers in France, from Montaigne (*Apologie de Raymond Sebond*, 1580) to Charron and La Mothe Le Vayer.[2] The Meditation raises worries, for example, about the general reliability of our perceptual beliefs, given the ease with which they can conflict. It also contains the argument that, some dreams being as vivid and detailed as any waking experience, we are unable to determine at any given moment whether we find ourselves in the one state or the other. All these tropes, Descartes conceded in the *Second Replies* (AT 7: 130), were like a lot of "warmed-over cabbage."

The significant exception is that even the existence of an external reality is put into question: with what reason, Descartes asks, can we claim to know that a world exists apart from our own impressions and opinions (The First Meditation, AT 7: 22–23)? This worry was absent from the ancient repertoire, and not by accident. Greek skepticism stopped short of putting into doubt the existence of the world, since it aimed to constitute a way of life. The skeptic, according to Sextus Empiricus, assents to the way things appear and only doubts or suspends judgment about "whether the object is in reality such as it appears to be."[3] The neo-Pyrrhonian thinkers of the sixteenth and seventeenth centuries followed the same line, since they too wished to live their skepticism. Montaigne, for instance, generally understood "the appearances" to which alone the skeptic assents as the apparent qualities of things. Once near the end of the *Apologie*, just before his grand conclusion that "we have no communication with being," Montaigne equated "the appearances" with the merely subjective impressions (*passions*) of our senses.[4] He did not seem to realize, however, that a skepticism so conceived must prove difficult to practice. Descartes, by contrast, intended from the start that the doubts in the First Meditation would have a purely epistemological function. As he says in the first paragraph, they are doubts he is taking up once in a lifetime and in a situation of leisure, free from all practical concerns; the interest is not in action but in knowledge alone (*non rebus agendis, sed cognoscendis tantum*, AT 7: 22). That is why he arranges the doubts systematically, in order of increasing scope, so as to arrive at their ultimate quarry, the belief in a mind-independent reality.

In the third paragraph Descartes formulates the empiricist principle at which all these doubts are aimed: "Whatever I have up till now accepted as most true I have acquired either from the senses or through the senses" (AT 7: 18). Several points about this principle call for clarification. One concerns what Descartes had in mind by distinguishing between beliefs acquired "from" and acquired "through" the senses, since the *Meditations* does not explain the distinction. An answer appears in the record of the conversations that the young Dutch philosopher Frans Burman conducted with him in 1648 about various problematic passages in his writings. There Descartes says he meant that some of our beliefs are thought to derive from what we ourselves have seen and others to come through hearing what people tell us (AT 5: 146). The conception of knowledge at issue was therefore a broadly based empiricism, though the doubts presented focus solely on first-hand experience and do not address the reliability of testimony.

There is also the matter of who, on Descartes' view, can be presumed to espouse this empiricist principle. Among philosophical schools, the

Aristotelian establishment of his time was unquestionably uppermost in his mind. The idea that all knowledge is grounded in sense experience occurs often in Aristotle's writings. The *Metaphysics* opens with the general statement that knowledge rests on experience, and experience on memory and sense perception (980a21–981a3). The *De Anima* argues more specifically that "since no one can ever learn anything without the use of perception, it is necessary even in speculative thought to have some mental image to contemplate, for images are like sense impressions, only without the matter" (432a7–10). Passages such as these led Aquinas in his *Summa Theologiae* to expound a systematic empiricism (I, q. 84, a. 6–7) according to which "the origin of our knowledge is from the senses." The formulation in his *De Veritate* – "there is nothing in the intellect that was not first in the senses" (q. 2, a. 3, arg. 19) – had become by the sixteenth and seventeenth centuries a byword of Scholastic philosophy as a whole.

Nowhere does Descartes in the *Meditations* name Aristotelianism as the principal philosophical target of its skeptical arguments. But in a letter to Mersenne of 28 January 1641, he spelled out his hidden agenda:

These six Meditations contain all the foundations of my physics. But please do not tell people, for that might make it harder for supporters of Aristotle to approve them. I hope that readers will gradually get used to my principles, and recognize their truth, before they notice that they destroy the principles of Aristotle. (AT 3: 298)

In teaching us to detach our mind from its dependence on the senses, the *Meditations*, he believed, would not only establish the metaphysical truths listed in their subtitle – the existence of God and the real distinction between mind and body – but also serve to validate thereby another anti-Aristotelian component of his thought, namely his mechanistic physics, which no longer attributed to bodies quasi-mental powers or "substantial forms." That Descartes saw leading the mind away from the senses as an attack on Aristotelian orthodoxy is explicit in the earlier version of the argument of the *Meditations* that is Part Four of the *Discourse on Method*. There he opposed this task to the standpoint of "the scholastic philosophers [who] take it as a maxim that there is nothing in the intellect which has not previously been in the senses" (AT 6: 37).

EMPIRICISM, PHILOSOPHICAL AND EVERYDAY

As the letter to Mersenne reveals, Descartes had a strategic reason to refrain from assigning a philosophical pedigree to the empiricism his array of skeptical doubts was to demolish: he did not want to give his Aristotelian-minded readers an excuse to dismiss his book straightaway. But there was also another reason. Descartes did not think that empiricism is solely or even primarily a philosophical theory. Embodied creatures that we are and impelled from infancy to view the world in terms of the body's needs, we have a natural inclination, he believed, to suppose that knowledge derives from the senses (The Sixth Meditation, AT 7: 75–76). Aristotle and his followers dressed up this common sentiment in systematic form. The skeptical arguments of the First Meditation are therefore aimed at more than just a doctrinal school. Their object is a way of thinking to which every reader must feel some attraction. As Descartes remarked to Burman in discussing the matter, anyone "who is only just beginning to philosophize" is bound to see in sense experience the source of all knowledge (AT 5: 146).

Descartes' conviction that empiricism forms a deep-seated tendency of our thinking helps to explain why he introduces the empiricist principle in the First Meditation as one that "I" have up until now accepted. He cannot mean that he himself was committed to it. The notion that knowledge rests on sense experience had long ceased to command any allegiance on his part. In his early notebooks of 1619–22, Descartes does seem to have adhered to a sense-based epistemology (AT 10: 218–19). But he had certainly abandoned it by 1628, more than a decade before the *Meditations*, when he wrote in *Rules for the Direction of the Mind*,

If someone sets himself the problem of investigating every truth for the knowledge of which human reason is adequate – and this, I think, is something everyone who earnestly strives after good sense should do once in his life – he will indeed discover ... that nothing can be known prior to the intellect, since knowledge of everything else depends on the intellect, and not *vice versa*. Once he has surveyed everything that follows immediately upon knowledge of the pure intellect, among what remains he will enumerate whatever instruments of knowledge we possess in addition to the intellect; and there are only two of these, namely imagination and sense perception. (AT 10: 395–96)

If the empiricist principle is now invoked as one that "I" have hitherto accepted, the meditating "I" must be understood, not as Descartes himself, but as a persona he has constructed and with whose reflections he expects his reader to identify. The "I" in the First Meditation represents, as Descartes noted to Burman, someone "who is only just beginning to philosophize" and who is therefore disposed to endorse the notion that all knowledge is acquired via the senses.

Not all that the meditating "I" says in the First Meditation would Descartes reject. There are in particular the two paragraphs that precede the statement of the empiricist principle and that specify the nature of the investigation to follow in this and subsequent Meditations. Descartes too believed, as does the meditating "I", that it is important, once in a lifetime, to examine the worth of all our existing beliefs, not one by one but with regard to their supposed foundations, to do so free from all practical concerns, and to endorse only those beliefs that are "completely certain and indubitable." These preliminaries are far from innocuous. Descartes wants his everyman reader to think it goes without saying that one should proceed on their basis, yet they involve some questionable assumptions, as I discuss later (§6).

Overall, however, the *Meditations* should be read as the story by which the meditating "I" gradually comes to coincide in belief and outlook with Descartes himself. In the First Meditation, we meet the sentence, "I see plainly that there are never any sure signs by means of which being awake can be distinguished from being asleep" (AT 7: 19). That is the complaint of an empiricist defeated by skeptical doubt and not anything Descartes would say, as his resolution of the dreaming doubt at the end of Meditation Six makes plain:

I now notice that there is a vast difference between the two [dreaming and being awake], in that dreams are never linked by memory with all the other actions of life as waking experiences are ... When I distinctly see where things come from and where and when they come to me, and when I can connect my perceptions of them with the whole of the rest of my life without a break, then I am quite certain that when I encounter these things I am not asleep but awake. (AT 7: 89–90)

Indeed, these lines represent the point at which the "I" has come to speak fully and unhesitatingly in Descartes' own voice. For determining whether a given perception coheres systematically with the rest

of one's experience, in order to ascertain whether it counts as veridical, is a clear instance of what he meant in holding that knowledge
cannot be based on the deliverances of the senses, but only on the
judging activity of the intellect.[5]

One apparent obstacle to regarding the First Meditation as focused
on empiricist notions of knowledge is that it puts even mathematical
beliefs into question. Unconcerned about whether their objects exist
in the physical world (AT 7: 20), such beliefs survive the doubt that,
for all we can tell, we may be dreaming; they succumb only to the
later doubt about whether an omnipotent God may be a deceiver,
giving us a mind that leads us astray even in what we consider we
know perfectly. Many have supposed that mathematics is understood
here as having a basis other than the senses, their reliability having
been discredited, and that Descartes must have in mind something
like his own view of mathematics as founded upon innate ideas. After
all, Meditation Three refers back to this passage when raising a
similar doubt about the reliability of his new criterion of knowledge,
clear and distinct perception, with particular reference to mathematical beliefs (AT 7: 35–36).

However, this interpretation is off the mark.[6] The only conception of
knowledge mentioned in the First Meditation is one which holds that
everything (*nempe quidquid*) accepted as true rests upon sense experience, and the "Synopsis of the *Meditations*" states explicitly that the
aim of the Meditation is to detach the mind from the senses. Descartes'
own non-empiricist theory of knowledge only begins to emerge in the
two subsequent Meditations. To be sure, the truths of mathematics are
described in the passage in question as containing "something certain
and indubitable" (AT 7: 20), as constituting "the most perfect knowledge" (AT 7: 21). But they are never said to be "clearly and distinctly
perceived," and this is not surprising, since that notion is not formulated
until Meditation Three. Moreover, it is easy to understand how an
empiricist could maintain the validity of pure mathematics even after
the doubt about dreaming has undermined all sense-based beliefs about
the natural world. At the ready is the theory of mathematics propounded
by Aristotle himself. Mathematics, according to him, deals with the
quantitative forms of sensible things (real or apparent) that are considered in abstraction from whether those things exist or not and that
are made the object of formal proof.[7] Though the supreme doubt involving an omnipotent God can be applied, not just to this abstractionist

account of mathematics, but also to the idea that mathematical concepts are innate and mathematical truths clearly and distinctly perceived, Descartes does not so extend it until Meditation Three. In the First Meditation, the concern lies solely with the senses as the supposed source of knowledge.

THE METHOD OF DOUBT

Though no skeptic himself, Descartes displayed a rare appreciation of the form that skeptical argument should take. In general, the philosophical skeptic aims to challenge, not this or that particular belief, but the very possibility of human knowledge. Therefore, the only coherent way for the skeptic to argue is by drawing out contradictions within the standpoint of those who profess to know various things about the world. It would be illegitimate to appeal to any opinions of one's own about, say, the unreliability of perception or of reasoning (for the skeptic supposedly makes no claim to knowledge of this or any sort), and it would be ineffectual to rely on assumptions in one's argument that are alien to the position under scrutiny. One must instead discredit assertions of knowledge by showing how they conflict with other views and principles that their advocates already accept or would have to admit; one must show that they fail on their own terms. Skeptical arguments, we could say, need to proceed by *internal demolition*. Neither in the seventeenth century nor in our own time has this requirement always been well understood, though the ancient skeptics (both Pyrrhonist and Academic) usually hewed to it closely.[8] Unlike many modern thinkers, Descartes grasped the point as well, to judge by the structure of the First Meditation.

There the empiricist principle of knowledge introduced in the third paragraph is subjected to a series of skeptical doubts whose common feature is that they undermine from within a continually revised, but weakened version of the idea that knowledge derives from the senses. These skeptical doubts do not rely on premises derived from Descartes' own philosophy. They pit against the empiricist principle other beliefs that the empiricist would accept, as well as possibilities of error that, given that principle, he cannot rule out. The goal is to prove that the empiricist is not entitled to make the knowledge claims he does since he cannot satisfy the standards for knowledge he himself sets down.

This strategy of internal demolition becomes apparent if we regard the First Meditation as in effect a *dialogue* that Descartes has staged between the empiricist and the skeptic in order to clear the way for his own philosophy.[9] The two figures can be regarded as warring voices in the mind of the meditating "I," who is inclined toward empiricism, but is also familiar with skeptical worries, precisely because they arise from within the empiricist perspective. Descartes himself in *The Search for Truth* (an incomplete work, published posthumously) presented the material of the first two Meditations as a dialogue between Polyander, a novice philosopher initially attracted to empiricism, Epistemon, a doctrinaire empiricist, and Eudoxus, who raises the various skeptical doubts and then goes on to expound the basic elements of Cartesian epistemology. I will follow suit. Incidentally, the dialogical structure of the First Meditation shows how misleading is the usual image of Descartes as a solitary thinker – arriving at his essential insights "shut up alone in a stove-heated room" (AT 6: 11), fleeing Paris for the anonymity of Holland (AT 6: 31) – that he did much to create in the *Discourse on Method*. Indeed, it bears remembering that Descartes published the *Meditations* accompanied by six sets of *Objections* and *Replies*.[10]

Here, then, is a reconstruction of the main steps in the central part of the Meditation (AT 7: 18–21) as a dialogue between the two figures. The empiricist is obliged to amend his fundamental principle again and again in response to each new charge by the skeptic that he is caught in an internal contradiction, until at last, reduced to silence, he must admit complete defeat:

EMPIRICIST: Knowledge is possible on the basis of sense experience.
SKEPTIC: But perception of small and distant objects is fallible.
EMPIRICIST: Nonetheless, perception of close, medium-sized objects is veridical.
SKEPTIC: What of the possibility that you are mad?
EMPIRICIST: I would be mad even to consider that possibility.
SKEPTIC: Still, you must acknowledge that in the past you have mistaken dreams for veridical perceptions. In fact, there are no sure signs by means of which dream perceptions can be distinguished from waking ones. How can you rule out the possibility that any perception of some close, medium-sized object is actually a dream?
EMPIRICIST: Even so, the sensible elements of any perception, whether I am awake or dreaming, resemble things in reality.

SKEPTIC: For all you know, these sensible elements could be purely
                  imaginary.
EMPIRICIST: Maybe, but the simplest elements in these perceptions –
                  mathematical notions of extension, quantity, and magnitude –
                  express truths, even if they do not refer to anything in nature.
                  Pure mathematics remains certain.
SKEPTIC: Still, there is the possibility of an omnipotent God, who created
                  you and could have given you a mind such that even what you
                  think you know most perfectly is actually false. Or if you
                  believe your origin was some natural and more imperfect
                  course of events, you have all the more reason to wonder
                  whether your mind does not mislead you here.
EMPIRICIST: [silence].

Rewriting in dialogue form the skeptical attack on the empiricist
conception helps to guard against two frequent sources of misinter-
pretation, each induced by a failure to perceive Descartes' insight
into proper skeptical method. It will not be wrongly supposed that
either the empiricist's assumptions or the skeptic's doubts express
Descartes' own views, although it was certainly his view that the
empiricist cannot successfully answer the skeptic.

Consider the doubt about dreaming. As indicated earlier (§3),
Descartes did not hold that we are unable to distinguish reliably
between dreaming and waking, since later in Meditation Six he
explains how, given his own conception of knowledge, we can do
so. His point was that the empiricist has no dependable basis for
making the distinction, and this failing is what he uses the skeptic's
doubt to demonstrate. Thus, the dreaming doubt takes for granted
that if we have a waking perception of a close, medium-sized object,
then the perception is veridical, the worry being whether we can
determine that we are in fact awake. Such an assumption is scarcely
one that Descartes himself would endorse, as the mechanistic theory
of vision in the *Dioptrics* (1637) attests; there he argued that though
our sensory organs respond systematically to the world, the images
they give us under the best of circumstances need not resemble the
way things are (AT 6: 112–14).[11] That assumption reflects instead the
Aristotelian belief that perception under normal conditions is not
subject to error,[12] which is why in this context it goes unquestioned.
The skeptic's doubt concerns whether the empiricist, even with that
belief, can reliably show that he is actually perceiving and not

dreaming. It does not challenge whether waking experience is normally veridical.[13] From beginning to end, the doubt is formulated as questioning whether there are "any sure signs by means of which being awake can be distinguished from being asleep" (AT 7: 19) and as concerned with "my inability to distinguish being asleep and being awake" (AT 7: 89). Its eventual resolution consists in indicating how to determine that we are awake: we check whether the perception in question coheres with the rest of our experience. The dreaming doubt offers a perfect example of how the skepticism of the First Meditation proceeds by way of exposing internal contradictions within the empiricist conception of knowledge.

Descartes' understanding of skeptical method also explains why the doubt that we might be like deluded madmen who "maintain that they are kings when they are paupers, or say ... that they are pumpkins, or made of glass" is not taken seriously. The meditator exclaims that "such people are insane, and I would be thought equally mad if I took anything from them as a model for myself" (AT 7: 19). Some have claimed that Descartes dismissed this doubt because questioning whether we are sane would wreck the very enterprise of reasoning about the proper basis of belief and of establishing the sovereignty of reason.[14] As a recasting of the Meditation in dialogue form makes plain, however, the one who rejects the doubt about madness is not Descartes himself, but rather the meditating "I" who is still committed to the empiricist principle. Moreover, such a person is right to reject the doubt. The chance that one may be mad forms no part of the perspective of someone following the natural inclination to trust in the senses.

Yet then, of course, Descartes has the skeptic go on to raise another possibility – namely, that we may be dreaming – which the empiricist cannot similarly dismiss, since dreams are part of everyone's experience, and which does serve to undermine from within the conviction against which the doubt about madness was directed: the perception of close and medium-sized objects under normal conditions cannot count as reliable, as the empiricist supposes, if there are no "sure signs" within experience as such (as opposed to how the intellect may combine the givens of experience) by which waking perceptions may be distinguished from dreams. Why, one might ask, does Descartes let the madness doubt be raised at all, if it fails to be properly internal? In order, I surmise, to highlight how devastating is the equally powerful dreaming doubt, which does have the appropriate form. (Note the exclamation, "Oh excellently done [*praeclare sane*],[15] as if I were not a man who sleeps at night," by which the meditator moves from dismissing the first doubt to launching the second). The First Meditation does not hold back on doubts that might imperil Descartes' own position. Its concern lies entirely with the deficiencies of empiricism, and the doubts it pursues are those that reveal how this conception of knowledge fails on its own terms.

THE SKEPTIC'S UNDOING

So well did Descartes appreciate the true character of skeptical method that at the beginning of the following Meditation, when skepticism appears triumphant, he turns the tables on the skeptic by means of this very method. He shows that the skeptic is caught in self-contradiction. In general, the skeptical point of view consists in suspending judgment about what others claim to know, and the scope of the skeptic's doubt at the end of the First Meditation seems boundless: so far as the skeptic knows, "there is absolutely nothing in the world, no sky, no earth, no minds, no bodies" (AT 7: 25). Yet, Descartes argues, the existence of at least one thing, namely of oneself as a thinking being, is implied by the very claim that one is doubting, and thus the skeptic contradicts himself in claiming to withhold judgment about the reality of absolutely everything. Moreover, *cogito, ergo sum* forms the cornerstone of the *Meditations'* new, non-empiricist conception of knowledge. For as Meditation Two goes on to argue, one expression of the fact that our existence as thinking beings is indubitable even when the existence of material objects may be in doubt is that the ability to attribute (truly or not) our changing sensations to an enduring material object, such as a piece of wax, involves the synthetic activity of judgment.

How precisely the skeptic is refuted in Meditation Two has been an object of controversy. Supposedly, the skeptic, contrary to his claim of suspending judgment about all reality, is in fact committed to the truth of *sum* ("I am"), since that proposition follows from a premise, *cogito* ("I think"), that he cannot deny. Yet if *cogito, ergo sum* is understood as an argument in which Descartes himself advances the premise and then draws the conclusion,[16] no skeptic need feel discomfited. Such an argument seems hopelessly circular, since any reasons for not yet assenting to a conclusion as elementary as *sum* would entail doubts about the premise as well. Besides, ever since antiquity skeptics had pointed out a basic difficulty in regarding proof as a vehicle of knowledge: the premises themselves stand in need of justification, yet seeking to justify them must lead to either infinite regress, circular reasoning, or unargued assumptions.

The key, however, is to realize that Descartes proceeds by using against the skeptic the skeptic's own technique of internal demolition. The inference from "I think" to "I am" does not, at least initially, constitute an argument advanced by Descartes (or by the meditator as his mouthpiece). Instead, the skeptic himself is shown to provide the premise, so that his skepticism undermines itself.[17] When the meditating "I" first formulates the inference, "If I convinced myself of something then I certainly existed" (AT 7: 25), he is speaking from the skeptic's point of view, as the immediately preceding sentences show:

I have convinced myself that there is absolutely nothing in the world, no sky, no earth, no minds, no bodies. Does it now follow that I too do not exist? No, if I convinced myself . . . .

So too in the next two formulations of the indubitability of *sum*, which follow in rapid succession: the premise to the effect that he is thinking comes from the skeptic stating the doubt about an omnipotent deceiver. *Cogito, ergo sum* enters the scene, not as an argument Descartes himself puts forward, but as an inference to a truth about existence (*sum*) whose premise the skeptic cannot help but affirm in the very act of professing his skepticism. As a result, he contradicts himself when claiming to suspend judgment about all reality. Of course, if even the skeptic must acknowledge the certainty of *sum*, then so must everyone. *Cogito, ergo sum* becomes an argument we all must endorse. Accordingly, the meditating "I" promptly switches from demolishing from within the skeptic's position to announcing a truth that everyone can now take as established, no matter what else they may believe: "*I am, I exist*, is necessarily true whenever it is put forward by me or conceived in my mind."[18]

One last point about the skeptic's downfall, which brings us back to the First Meditation. In the passages cited from Meditation Two, the skeptic is portrayed as saying he is convinced that there is no world or that there is an omnipotent deceiver, such assertions embodying the fatal premise to the effect that he is thinking. Yet no real skeptic would talk in such terms, as Gassendi complained in the *Fifth Objections* (AT 7: 257–58). The business of skepticism is not to deny prevailing opinions, but to show that those who affirm them are not, by their own lights, entitled to do so. Descartes knew this very well. He has the skeptic speak in this fashion because, as he explains in the final section of the First Meditation (AT 7: 22–23), it is easier to withhold assent from the everyday sort of beliefs in question if they are imagined to be false. Having the skeptic speak as he should will not alter the outcome. Insofar as the skeptic claims that he doubts that anything can be known to exist, he falls into self-contradiction, since that claim too entails that he is thinking and thus that he exists. Such is indeed how *Principles* I.7 and *The Search for Truth* (AT 10: 514–15) demonstrate the self-refutation of the skeptic.

CARTESIAN CERTAINTY

The central part of the First Meditation consists in a dialogue between empiricist and skeptic in which the views expressed are not by and large those of Descartes himself. They represent opposing tendencies in the mind of a meditator who has an allegiance to the principle that all knowledge rests upon the senses, but who is also alert to the doubts to which this conception of knowledge must give rise. However, the preliminary section of the Meditation – the first two paragraphs preceding the formulation of the empiricist principle – is a different matter. Having realized how doubtful is the edifice of belief accepted since childhood, the meditator lays down for the reform to be pursued a number of ground rules with which Descartes certainly agreed. He too held that we must, once in our lives, set aside all existing beliefs and "start again right from the foundations," doing so free from all practical concerns (having "rid my mind of all worries and arranged for myself a clear stretch of free time"), and "hold[ing] back my assent from opinions which are not completely certain and indubitable" (AT 7: 17–18). These three rules involve some questionable assumptions, despite Descartes' insinuation that someone just beginning to philosophize would naturally endorse them.

What, for instance, of the rule that we are to look to the foundations (*fundamenta*) of knowledge? Descartes is assuming that some of our beliefs rest essentially on others, and those on still deeper justifying beliefs, and that the whole edifice is only as secure as the basic principles (*principia*) by which we designate the ultimate source of reliable belief. Has not Descartes introduced without argument, and with unfortunate consequences for later philosophy, a "foundationalist" model of knowledge?[19] I agree that one would do better to reject such a model and, instead of supposing that all our beliefs stand in need of justification, recognize that justification properly pertains to change in belief, as when we consider reasons to accept a new belief or to reject a belief we already hold.[20] However, the complaint fails to do justice to the intellectual context. Foundationalist notions were already well ensconced. The idea that all knowledge rests upon the senses pervaded the thinking of the time, most notably in the Scholastic establishment. Descartes was not injecting a foundationalist view of knowledge where none had been before, but rather seeking to replace the reigning form with another.

More problematic is the rule announced in the second paragraph of the First Meditation to govern the subsequent debate between empiricist and skeptic:

> Because reason persuades me that I should hold back my assent from opinions which are not completely certain and indubitable... it will be enough, for the purpose of rejecting all my opinions, if I find in each of them some reason or other for doubt. (AT 7: 18)[21]

Indeed, each of the different versions of the empiricist conception is rejected because of skeptical doubts that point to the slightest possibility of error, however remote, that it is unable to exclude. This rule embodies a very stringent conception of *certainty*, justified by only the bald assertion that it is a dictate of reason ("reason [*ratio*] persuades me"). It is often said that Descartes was possessed, and wrongly so, by a "quest for certainty." Yet the problematic element is not so much the idea that knowledge requires certainty (it sounds strange to say, "I know it's raining, but I'm not certain") as the particular meaning he attached to the latter, namely *indubitability*. No belief, the First Meditation declares, will count as certain if we cannot eliminate even the slightest, most improbable way in which it might turn out to be false. Exhibiting an otherwise exemplary understanding of the properly internal strategy of the skeptic, why should Descartes have decided to impose from without so significant a principle of his own?

For consider: though indubitability is presented as a dictate of reason, it is not a requirement an empiricist must be inclined to endorse. On the contrary, I have already noted that for Aristotle sense perception serves as the basis of knowledge because of its reliability, not under all possible, but under normal, conditions: ordinarily, the Aristotelian would say, we feel certain of the truth of what we see, even if the occasional dream may trip us up. Indeed, quite apart from philosophical theory, we generally consider in everyday life a belief to be certain if we have eliminated the possibilities of error that we have some positive reason to fear, that we have some evidence to think may be at work. We do not think we must dispose of every conceivable doubt, however improbable. Descartes surely knew this. Whence then the rule of indubitability?

His answer lies in the third rule laid down in this preliminary section. Right before the demand for what is "certain and indubitable," the meditator says that the examination of knowledge claims is to take place under rather extraordinary conditions: "I have freed my mind from all cares (curis) and arranged for myself a solid stretch of free time (otium)."[22] When time is short and resources limited, when practical concerns are in play and action is necessary, we cannot afford to reject every belief for which we can imagine the slightest grounds of doubt. We must go with those beliefs for which there appears sufficient evidence. However, pursuing knowledge for its own sake is a different affair, Descartes supposed. If we look only to reasons for belief that have to do with the truth and falsity of opinions (as opposed to the utility of adopting them), if our business is not action but solely knowledge, then indubitability becomes an appropriate objective. As he declared in the *Discourse on Method*, "Since I now wished to devote myself solely to the search for truth, I thought it necessary to ... reject as if absolutely false everything in which I could imagine the least doubt, in order to see if I was left believing anything that was entirely indubitable" (AT 6: 31).

The third rule sets up what Bernard Williams aptly called the standpoint of "pure enquiry."[23] In it, Descartes supposed, reason requires that we seek beliefs immune to every conceivable doubt. Yet the question remains: why must the object of pure inquiry be the indubitable? Unfortunately, he never said, proceeding as though the point were obvious. But that is not so. On his telling, suspending all practical concerns leaves us with but a single purpose, "the search for truth." In reality, we would have at least two distinct goals: acquiring truths, but also avoiding falsehoods. The two are not the same, since if we were interested only in the former, we would believe everything, not worrying about how many false beliefs we thereby obtained, whereas if we cared only about the latter, we would believe nothing, for that would mean immediate success. Each of these options is irrational, to be sure. We need to pursue the two goals in tandem. Yet plainly there are many ways to do so. Since the two goals can come into conflict (methods of acquiring truths often yield falsehoods too; avoiding sources of error can mean missing certain truths as well), we have to determine which should take precedence in various sorts of circumstances. Thus, different kinds of rankings, different cognitive policies, are possible.

The ranking that Descartes in effect adopted, the particular weighting of the two goals of pure inquiry underlying his rule of indubitability, is evident. If the slightest, unlikeliest grounds for doubt suffice to preclude assent to a proposition, then avoiding error is being considered as always coming ahead of acquiring truths. We are never to seek to satisfy the latter goal unless we have assured ourselves of having fully complied with the former. "The search for truth" is therefore a misleading expression for what Descartes had in mind, since averting error was his foremost concern.

However, other ways exist of ordering these two goals under the conditions of pure inquiry. Instead of making the avoidance of error always paramount, we might, for instance, decide to give it greater weight only when the errors in question are of the sort that occur in the normal course of events and that there is thus some reason to expect. As for the possibility that we may have made an unusual kind of mistake (because, say, we were dreaming), we would then accord it less importance than the chance of discovering some truths, and under- take to eliminate only those possible ways of going wrong that we have good grounds to fear. The sciences operate in this fashion and do not appear to be any less "pure" for doing so. Yet many today who scarcely consider themselves followers of Descartes continue to think that practical concerns alone lead us to settle for less than indubitability, claiming therefore that because Cartesian certainty is unattainable the idea of "pure theory" must also be abandoned.

One example was Bernard Williams himself. He held that if time were not short and resources not limited, we would want as many of our beliefs as possible to be true, and as he noted, the best way thus to maximize the "truth-ratio" among our beliefs would be to reject all those containing the least possibility of error. Because we would thereby end up believing almost nothing, Williams concluded that the ideal of pure inquiry has to be discarded.[24] The mistake in this reasoning should now be apparent. Truth-acquisition and error-avoidance, even when pursued for their own sake, admit of many different combinations.

Though Descartes never explained why pure inquiry requires indubitability, his reason must have been that more was involved than just the pursuit of those two goals. That was indeed so, from his perspective. Consider again the (un-Cartesian) principle that we need only dispose of the normal possibilities of error in order to accept a proposition as true. This principle is useless without a prior conception of what constitutes the ordinary course of experience. It must already be clear what sorts of error we have good grounds to worry about. A policy of this sort makes sense therefore only if from the start we can place the prospects of human knowledge within some comprehensive view of the world. Aristotle, for instance, could see in sense-experience a reliable source of knowledge whenever standard kinds of error have been eliminated, because he also thought we determine the nature of perception itself by seeing how it fits into the natural order. To understand the mind's powers, he wrote (*De Anima*, II.4), we must look at its distinctive activities, and to understand the latter, we have to ascertain the sorts of objects on which they are typically exercised.

Descartes, by contrast, rejected the notion that the nature of knowledge can be defined by reference to a general picture of the mind's place in the world. That would be to get things backwards. How can we rightly claim to know what the world is like, unless we first settle what it is to know? The proper starting point, say the *Rules for the Direction of the Mind*, is to take the mind by itself, consider the knowledge (mathematics) it can acquire independently of the world, and then draw from this case a general method of inquiry, relying on "order and measure," which will determine what we can know of "the things themselves ... in so far as they are within the reach of the intellect" (AT 10: 378, 399). This priority of epistemology over ontology, of method over subject matter, is the sort of "absolute beginning" that, in Hegel's words, Descartes sought to effect, and it is what ruled out accepting anything as true simply because there are no ordinary grounds for doubting it. Reason, he believed, requires that we dispose of every possible sort of error, since only so can reason determine by its own lights the basic structure of the world. That is the basis of the rule, announced at the outset of the First Meditation, that only indubitable beliefs will do.

The trouble is that no beliefs, or none of substantive import, can satisfy this standard. In other words, there can be no absolute beginnings.

NOTES

1. Hegel 1971, 120–27 (Hegel 1896, 217–24).
2. Larmore 1998.
3. Sextus Empiricus 1933, I.xi, 17; see Burnyeat 1982.
4. Montaigne 1999, 601 (Montaigne 1965, 454).
5. Consider what Descartes says in reply to the empiricist objection that one sense can correct another, as when we touch a stick that looks bent in water and verify that it is straight: "The sense [of touch] alone does not suffice to correct the visual error: in addition we need to have some degree of reason which tells us that in this case we should believe the judgment based on touch rather than that elicited by vision" (*Sixth Replies*, AT 7: 439).
6. Cf. also Carriero 2009, 13, 35–37.
7. Aristotle, *Metaphysics*, XI.3, XIII.1–3 and *Physics* II.2; Aquinas, *Super Boethium de Trinitate*, q. 5–6.
8. Annas and Barnes 1985, 14, 45, 53.
9. See Larmore 2000 and Larmore 2006.
10. Cf. Marion 1996.
11. Cf. Meditation Six, AT 7:82–84.
12. See the many passages assembled to illustrate this Aristotelian view in Feyerabend 1978, 53–85.
13. Contrary to many commentators. See, for example, Wilson 1978, 20–24.
14. The interpretation has been proposed by philosophers otherwise so different as Frankfurt 2008, 53 and Foucault 1972, 56–58.
15. AT 7: 19. CSM embroider their translation of this phrase – "A brilliant piece of reasoning!" – but to the same effect.
16. So, for instance, Kenny 1968, 51–55.
17. Both Frankfurt 2008, 152, and Curley 1978, 84–88 point out that it is the skeptic who supplies the premise, though they do not recognize that Descartes is thereby deploying against the skeptic the skeptic's own strategy of internal demolition.
18. The famous phrase itself – *cogito, ergo sum* – does not appear in the *Meditations*, but only in the *Second Replies* (AT 7: 140) as well as earlier

in French in the *Discourse on Method* (AT 6: 32). However, as the previously cited passages indicate, Meditation Two clearly presents *sum* as a conclusion following from a premise to the effect that one is thinking.

19. See, for instance, Williams 1986.

20. Larmore 2008, 4.

21. I have revised the translation in CSM to conform more exactly to the Latin. It should be noted that the 1647 French translation of the *Meditations* by the Duc de Luynes, approved by Descartes, rewords the last clause of the quoted sentence – "the least grounds for doubt" (*le moindre sujet de douter*) instead of "some reason or other for doubt" (*aliquam rationem dubitandi*) – in such a way as to make even more apparent the point I am emphasizing.

22. This is a slight variation of the CSM translation.

23. Williams 2005, chapter 2.

24. Williams 2005, 31–34, 195.

3 The First Meditation: divine omnipotence, necessary truths, and the possibility of radical deception

One of the views that is defended prominently in the First Meditation is that there exists the possibility that we are deceived about matters that are utterly evident to us. The possibility takes three different forms: that God created us with minds that are highly defective; that our minds evolved by chance and so are not dependable devices for tracking truth; and that an evil demon is deceiving us every time we grasp a result as obvious.[1] It is tempting to hope that the argumentation that Descartes offers in the First Meditation is problematic, and that Descartes sees it to be problematic himself. If it is true that it is possible that our minds are deceived about matters that are utterly evident to us, it is hard to see how we would ever arrive at a result that we could trust. Commentators raised the worry immediately.[2] If there exists the possibility that our minds are deceived about matters that are utterly evident to us, Descartes would not be entitled to move beyond the First Meditation and offer any arguments, and there would seem to be no way that he could establish (in the Third and Fourth Meditations) that God exists and created us with minds that are reliable.

The First Meditation is clear in positing the existence of the possibility that our minds are deceived about matters that are utterly evident to us. If we attempt to locate an argument in Descartes' corpus that attempts to confront that possibility head on, Descartes will always be subject to the objection that perhaps the argument is no good and we find it to be compelling for the sole reason that our minds are defective. I want to suggest that we approach the First Meditation possibilities by changing the subject a bit, and indeed, by pretending that we had never read the First Meditation at all. Strange as it sounds to say, that will give us the best sense of what the First Meditation is working to do.

68

If we ignore the First Meditation for a moment, and focus on other texts, the possibility that we are deceived about matters that are utterly evident to us begins to show up differently. Elsewhere in the corpus, Descartes argues on a priori grounds that God is a necessary existent and also that He is not a deceiver. In *Principles* I.14, he writes:

On the basis of its perception that necessary and eternal existence is contained in the idea of a supremely perfect being, the mind must clearly conclude that the supreme being does exist. (AT 8A: 10)

Descartes is reasoning along similar lines in the Fifth Meditation:[3] we can know on the basis of our idea of God that His existence and omniscience and omnipotence are inseparable from His eternal and immutable nature and that, since His nature exists, He exists "as well." In these two texts, Descartes is showing his rationalist hand so to speak. He is reflecting that the sorts of arguments that are most compelling, and that are most appropriate for a philosopher to offer, are arguments that are grounded in axioms that are not known through the senses. He asserts in a number of passages that if we are too immersed in the world of sensible bodies, we will have difficulty recognizing the (otherwise) self-evident truths of philosophy.[4] For example, we would grasp the necessary existence of God as self-evident "if [we] were not overwhelmed by preconceived opinions, and if the images of things perceived by the senses did not besiege [our] thought on every side" (The Fifth Meditation, AT 7: 69). A more seasoned philosopher is in the habit of gleaning results a priori, and God's necessary existence is practically a given.

We can certainly take issue with the argumentation that Descartes offers for the view that God is a necessary existent, and I am not going to defend it here. What is important for our purposes is that in the final analysis Descartes subscribes to the view that God is a necessary existent and that he arrives at that view by what he insists are non-sensory means.

Descartes holds that God is a necessary existent, and he also holds that the possibility does not exist that God is a deceiver. He writes to Voetius:

[He claims that in my philosophy] 'God is thought of as a deceiver.' This is foolish. Although in my First Meditation I did speak of a supremely powerful deceiver, the conception there was in no way of the true God, since, as he himself says, it is impossible that the true God should be a deceiver. But if he is asked how he knows this is impossible, he must answer that he knows it from the fact that it implies a conceptual contradiction – that is, it cannot be conceived. So the very point he made use of to attack me is sufficient for my defence ... ("Letter to Voetius, May 1643," AT 8B: 60)

Descartes is arguing that God is a necessary existent and that it is a conceptual truth that God is not a deceiver. In addition, He is omnipotent in such a way that He is the author of all reality (or at least of all reality other than Himself[5]):

When we reflect on the idea of God which we were born with, we see that he is eternal, omniscient, omnipotent, the source of all goodness and truth, the creator of all things. (*Principles* I.22, AT 8A: 13)[6]

This is not an especially unorthodox thing to say about a supreme being, but Descartes takes the view (that God is the author of all reality) to an extreme. He thinks that God is not only the author of what is actual, but even the author of what is *possible*. That is in part to say – when God creates, He is not confronted with pre-existing possibilities from which to choose, but He is the author of possibility itself:

The power of God cannot have any limits, and ... our mind is finite and so created as to be able to conceive as possible the things which God has wished to be in fact possible, but not be able to conceive as possible the things which God could have made possible, but which he has nevertheless wished to make impossible. ("To [Mesland], 2 May 1644," AT 4: 118)

For Descartes, God is not confronted with facts about possible ways that things could be prior to making anything actual. That would be a limitation on His power: although He would still be able to bring about anything that is possible, He would not be in charge of what is possible itself. God is similarly the author of the essences of things. Before He creates an X, He is not confronted with a fact about what it is for something to be an X. He wills the existence of minds, for example, but He also wills that what it is for something to be a mind is to be a substance that thinks. Descartes thus says to Mersenne:

You ask me by what kind of causality God established the eternal truths. I reply: by the same kind of causality as he created all things, that is to say, as their efficient and total cause. For it is certain that he is the author of the essence of created things no less than of their existence; and this essence is nothing other than the eternal truths. ("To [Mersenne], 27 May 1630," AT 1:151–52)

For Descartes, God's power and authority are so far-reaching that He is the creator of triangular objects (if they in fact exist), but He also willed (the eternal truth) that what it is for something to be a triangle is to be an enclosed figure with three sides.[7]

Descartes holds that God is a necessary existent and the author of all reality – both actual and possible. It is an a priori conceptual truth (Descartes is arguing) that God is not a deceiver, and so He does not allow that it is possible that we find a result to be utterly evident that is nonetheless false. Descartes concludes in the Fourth Meditation:

The cause of error must surely be the one I have explained; for if, whenever I have to make a judgment, I restrain my will so that it extends to what the intellect clearly and distinctly reveals, and no further, then it is quite impossible for me to go wrong. This is because every clear and distinct perception is undoubtedly something, and hence cannot come from nothing, but must necessarily have God as its author. Its author, I say, is God, who is supremely perfect, and who cannot be a deceiver on pain of contradiction; hence the perception is undoubtedly true. (AT 7: 62)

If Descartes is right, the possibility that we are deceived about matters that are utterly evident to us does not exist. The possibility does not exist automatically, as part of the fabric of the universe. God did not create it, so it is nothing at all.

Returning now to the First Meditation, Descartes takes the three versions of hyperbolic doubt (about the reliability of our minds) to be fictional. God is in fact a necessary existent, and He did not create the possibility that our minds are deceived about matters that are utterly evident to us. He is a necessary existent, and it is a conceptual truth that He created us and anything else there might be, and so there does not exist the possibility that we were created through some other means, and there does not exist the possibility that our minds developed by chance evolutionary processes. Nor did God create the possibility that our minds are deceived by an evil demon. God did not create an actual demon, and He did not create the possibility of such a demon. The three skeptical scenarios introduced in the latter half of the First Meditation are hyperbolic, in more ways than one. For Descartes, there does not exist the possibility that we are deceived about matters that are utterly evident to us. God did not create it, and so it is nowhere to be found on the ontological grid.

We might wonder why Descartes would suggest anything to the contrary in the First Meditation. One of the reasons that he himself gives is that the meditator of the First Meditation has a confused idea of God and has not yet done the work (of later Meditations) to clear it up. He writes:

> All our ideas of what belongs to the mind have up till now been very confused and mixed up with the ideas of things that can be perceived by the senses. This is the first and most important reason for our inability to understand with sufficient clarity the customary assertions about the soul and God ... Admittedly, many people had previously said that in order to understand metaphysical matters the mind must be drawn away from the senses; but no one, so far as I know, had shown how this could be done. The correct, and in my view unique, method of achieving this is contained in my Second Meditation. (Second Replies, AT 7: 130–31)

Descartes takes the Second Meditation to be doing important work to help the meditator to think in non-sensory terms and to settle upon ideas of (immaterial) things like mind and God. At such an early stage of inquiry, the meditator is used to thinking by means of sensory images,[8] and his idea of God would have already been long polluted:

> If anyone thus represents God, or the mind, to himself he is attempting to imagine something which is not imaginable, and all he will succeed in forming is a corporeal idea to which he falsely assigns the name 'God' or 'the mind'. (Fifth Replies, AT 7: 385)

> We understand God to be infinite, and there can be nothing greater than the infinite. You are confusing understanding with imagination, and are supposing that we imagine God to be like some enormous man. (Fifth Replies, AT 7: 365)[9]

The First Meditation meditator has a "long-standing" conception of God, and a conception that runs counter to an a priori result: that God is a necessary existent, a being that is the author of all reality and that does not allow the existence of the possibility that our minds are deceived about matters that are utterly evident to us. In the rationalist tradition, Descartes is thinking that that is the kind of result that has purchase.[10]

A very different picture of the possibility of radical deception would emerge if we had never read the First Meditation. If our ideas were in order (or so Descartes would say), we would recognize that God is a necessary existent and that there does not exist the possibility that we are deceived about matters that are utterly evident to us. The First Meditation arguments are still instrumental, however, as they help us to have non-sensory perceptions in the Second and Third Meditations, and make us appreciate their authority and force.

Let us return to the hyperbolic arguments from a new perspective. The first argument is that God is omnipotent and hence that, strictly speaking, He has enough power to have created us so that our minds are mistaken about things that seem obvious. Descartes writes:

And yet firmly rooted in my mind is the long-standing opinion that there is an omnipotent God who made me the kind of creature that I am. How do I know that he has not brought it about that there is no earth, no sky, no extended thing, no shape, no size, no place, while at the same time ensuring that all these things appear to me to exist just as they do now? What is more, since I sometimes believe that others go astray in cases where they think they have the most perfect knowledge, may I not similarly go wrong every time I add two and three or count the sides of a square, or in some even simpler matter, if that is imaginable? (AT 7: 21)

If God is omnipotent, the meditator is thinking, there are absolutely no limits on what He can do. He created us, and He has enough power to have made our minds such that we are mistaken about matters that are utterly evident to us. Perhaps there are things that are more important than truth – for example faith – and God would have us focus our attention on those instead.[11] Or perhaps the acquisition of truth is important, but there is a larger context to be considered, in which human minds have a different assignment and role. As Descartes puts it a few lines later,

if it were inconsistent with his goodness to have created me such that I am deceived all the time, it would seem equally foreign to his goodness to allow me to be deceived even occasionally; yet this last assertion cannot be made.

There is clearly a reason that God allows us to err sometimes – a reason that is consistent with His goodness – and perhaps there is a reason for keeping us off the mark in general.

The second argument for the view that it is possible that our minds are deceived about matters that are utterly evident to us starts with the assumption that it is possible that our cognitive mechanisms are the product of a cause that is less than omnipotent. Descartes writes:

Perhaps there may be some who would prefer to deny the existence of so powerful a God rather than believe that everything else is uncertain. Let us not argue with them, but grant them that everything said about God is a fiction. According to their supposition, then, I have arrived at my present state by fate or chance or a continuous chain of events, or by some other means; yet since deception and error seem to be imperfections, the less powerful they make my original cause, the more likely it is that I am so imperfect as to be deceived all the time. (AT 7: 21)

If there is no skillful hand guiding the development of our cognitive processes, there would be a possibility that at some point our minds would come to have imperfections and faults. If the process is sufficiently random, it is possible that we are deceived about matters that are utterly evident to us.

The third argument is that it is possible that there is an evil genius that takes steps to ensure that we have as many false beliefs as possible. Descartes anticipates that some of his readers will find it implausible that God would have a reason for creating us to be deceived all the time. These same readers, if they believe that we have been created by God, would also find implausible the suggestion that we evolved by chance:

I will suppose therefore that not God, who is supremely good and the source of truth, but rather some malicious demon of the utmost power and cunning has employed all of his energies in order to deceive me. I shall think that the sky, the air, the earth, colours, shapes, sounds, and all external things are merely the delusions of dreams which he has devised to ensnare my judgment. I shall consider myself as not having hands or eyes, or flesh, or blood or senses, but as falsely believing that I have all these things. (AT 7: 22–23)

Perhaps this being is the devil, or a spirit that was created by God but that took a bad turn. Descartes does not explicitly mention the evident truths of mathematics or logic in the discussion of the demon, but he does mean for them to be included in the domain of things that are dubitable. He is clear that there is no belief that the demon scenario leaves untouched.[12] He writes at the start of the Second Meditation:

So serious are the doubts into which I have been thrown as a result of yesterday's meditations that I can neither put them out of my mind nor see any way of resolving them. It feels as if I have fallen unexpectedly into a deep whirlpool which tumbles me around so that I can neither stand on the bottom nor swim up to the top. Nevertheless I will make an effort and once more attempt the same path which I started on yesterday. Anything which admits of the slightest doubt I will set aside just as if I had found it to be wholly false; and I will proceed in this way until I recognize something certain, or, if nothing else, until I recognize for certain that there is no certainty. (AT 7: 23–24)

Here he is reporting that as things stand, there is no certainty, and he says the same thing immediately after the introduction of the demon:

Even if it is not in my power to know any truth, I shall at least do what is in my power, that is, resolutely guard against assenting to any falsehoods, so that the deceiver, however powerful and cunning he may be, will be unable to impose on me in the slightest degree. (AT 7: 23)

Descartes is saying here that if he cannot rule out the possibility that a demon is tricking him, then it is not in his power to know any truth.

There is not a single result that survives the First Meditation. No matter how clearly we grasp a truth of logic or mathematics, or any-thing else, we can call it into question by turning our attention in another direction and entertaining the global prospect that our minds are mistaken about matters that are evident to us.[13] We cannot call this sort of result into question while we are focusing on it – for example the result that two and three add to five – and so instead we must doubt it indirectly.[14] What Descartes will begin to do in the Second Meditation is have us arrive at non-sensory results and *not* divert our attention from them. The mind can then "tell the demon to go hang himself" if and when he does make an appearance.[15] As Descartes makes very clear,

when I turn to the things themselves which I think I perceive very clearly, I am so convinced by them that I spontaneously declare: let whoever who can do so deceive me, he will never bring it about that I am nothing, so long as I continue to think that I am something; ... or bring it about that two and three added together are more or less than five, or anything of this kind in which I see a manifest contradiction. (Third Meditation, AT 7: 36)

The more that we arrive at non-sensory results – the bread and butter of philosophical analysis, Descartes would say – the more we see that they are evident and obvious, and the more we recognize that they trump the claim that it is possible that a demon is deceiving us. The latter claim is imagistic and sensory, and attention-getting and vivid, but it is false, and is to be rejected.

A silver lining to the (confused) hyperbolical arguments of the First Meditation is that they force the meditator to focus attention on non-sensory results. There is something that the meditator is not able to doubt (AT 7: 25) even in the face of the worry that his mind might be defective: "I am, I exist." He is doubting the existence of anything that can be sensed, and he is confronted with the existence of some-thing that is not sensed and that is known with a stunning level of clarity and evidence. The meditator will be presented with more and more such results as the thinking of the *Meditations* progresses. As Descartes says in *Principles* I.75,

When we contrast all this knowledge with the confused thoughts we had before, we will acquire the habit of forming clear and distinct concepts of all the things that can be known. (AT 8A: 38–39)

We assemble primary notions like that everything has a sufficient cause for its being, and hence that an idea of God must have been produced by an omnipotent being, and that God exists.[16] We secure that God cannot deceive, that He is a necessary existent, that He is the supremely independent author of *all* reality, and that He does not allow the existence of the possibility that we are deceived about matters that are utterly evident to us. We secure results that – like "I am, I exist" – are evident in the face of the prospect of the demon, and the reason they are able to override that prospect is that they, unlike it, are cognized by the intellect and not the senses or imagi-nation. In the First Meditation we considered a series of assumptions that we took to be powerful and well thought out, but these fall by the wayside as we start to think more clearly.

Descartes would appear to have a similarly deflationary view on the existence of eternal truths that God might have created but did not. For Descartes, the possibility that our minds are defective does not exist automatically; and neither does there exist automatically the possibility that (for example) two and three add up to seven. Descartes is very clear (as presumably he should be) that eternal truths (like that two and three add up to five) are necessary: he says that "the necessity of these truths does not exceed our knowledge" ("To Mersenne, 6 May 1630," AT 1: 150). If he is assuming that a truth is not necessary unless there does not exist the possibility that it be otherwise,[17] then he holds that there does not exist, for any eternal truth, the possibility that it be otherwise. That is, he is committed to the view that God did not create alternative possible eternal truths.

Descartes does indeed say that God is the author of all reality – subject to no antecedent constraints – and that He is the author of eternal truths (or essences). There might be a worry then that Descartes' considered view is that eternal truths are necessary and that nonetheless there exists the possibility that they be otherwise. But Descartes does not understand divine freedom as a libertarian two-way power to do otherwise. Instead, God is free in the sense that He is subordinated to no external constraints and is supremely indifferent:

As for the freedom of the will, the way in which it exists in God is quite different from the way in which it exists in us. It is self-contradictory to suppose that the will of God was not indifferent from eternity with respect to everything which has happened or will ever happen; for it is impossible to imagine that anything is thought of in the divine intellect as good or true . . . prior to the decision of the divine intellect to make it so. (*Sixth Replies*, AT 7: 431–32)[18]

For Descartes, divine freedom is not a two-way power. He says by way of example that God is free in His creation of the essence of a circle.[19] In the light of his own understanding of divine freedom, what it means to say that God is free to create or not create the essence of a circle is that He is supremely indifferent and that there are no criteria or conditions independent of Him that make or even incline Him to proceed in one way rather than the other.[20]

If Descartes subscribes to the view that divine freedom is a matter of indifference, he has at least one view in common with Spinoza.[21] But Descartes appears to be Spinozistic in other ways as well. We might consider the following passage (from Spinoza) as a point of departure:

Now, we maintain that, since all that happens is done by God, it must therefore necessarily be predetermined by him, otherwise he would be mutable, which would be a great imperfection in him. And as this predetermination by him must be from eternity, in which eternity there is no before and after, it follows irresistibly that God could never have predetermined things in any other way than that in which they are determined, and have been from eternity, and that God could not have been either before or without these determinations.[22]

Descartes agrees with Spinoza that God's activity is eternal and unchanging:

It will be said that if God had established these truths [the truths of mathematics] he could change them as a king changes his laws. To this the answer is: Yes he can, if his will can change. 'But I understand them to be eternal and unchangeable.' – I make the same judgement about God. 'But his will is free.' – Yes, but his power is beyond our grasp. ("To Mersenne, 15 April 1630," AT 1: 145–46.)[23]

Descartes also uses language that recalls Spinoza's claim that in eternity there is no before and after, and in a way that raises questions about the existence of the possibility that God's eternal and immutable act could have been otherwise. He writes,

There is always a single identical and perfectly simple act by means of which he simultaneously understands, wills and accomplishes everything. (*Principles* I.23, AT 8A: 14)

Nor should we conceive any precedence or priority between his intellect and his will; for the idea which we have of God teaches us that there is in him only a single activity, entirely simple and entirely pure. ("To [Mesland], 2 May 1644," AT 4: 119)

In God, willing, understanding and creating are all the same thing without one being prior to the other even conceptually. ("To [Mersenne], 27 May 1630," AT 1: 153)

Here Descartes is speaking in terms of the relationship between God's will and intellect: God is the supreme author of all reality, and so it is never the case that He understands things that are already existent or true.[24] Instead, for God to understand something is for Him to will it and vice versa. He wills and understands the entire series of creatures by a "single identical and perfectly simple act" – one that is unchanging and eternal.[25] There is no creature that exists apart from this series, and nothing that runs parallel to it. The series might *itself* have parallel strands that are somehow a part of it, but God wills and creates these, along with any other reality, by a single act that is immutable and eternal:

Whatever is in God is not in reality separate from God himself; rather it is identical with God himself. Concerning the decrees of God which have already been enacted, it is clear that God is unalterable with regard to these, and, from the metaphysical point of view, it is impossible to conceive of the matter otherwise. Concerning ethics and religion, on the other hand, the opinion has prevailed that God can be altered, because of the prayers of mankind; for no one would have prayed to God if he knew, or had convinced himself, that God was unalterable ... From the metaphysical point of view, however, it is quite unintelligible that God should be anything but completely unalterable. It is irrelevant that the decrees of God could have been separated from God; indeed, this should not really be asserted....We should not make a separation here between the necessity and indifference that apply to God's decrees; although his actions were completely indifferent, they were also completely necessary. Then again, although there we may conceive that the decrees could have been separated from God, this is merely a token procedure of our own reasoning: the distinction thus introduced between God himself and his decrees is a mental, not a real one. In reality the decrees could not have been separated from God; he is not prior to them or distinct from them, nor could he have existed without them. (*Conversation with Burman*, AT 5:166)

There is a view of God that follows from (what Descartes takes to be) the primary notions of metaphysics, and it is not the view of the First Meditation.

We know that in Descartes' ontology there does not exist the possibility that God deceives us or that we are mistaken about matters that are utterly evident to us. We know that there does not exist the possibility that God does not exist, and we know that there do not exist possible alternative eternal truths. It would also appear that there do not exist alternative possible substances or modifications. We know that Descartes holds that God is the author of all reality, and so it is not surprising that he would say that the eternal and immutable activity of God extends all the way to modifications and in particular to the modifications of minds:

The only way to prove that he [God] exists is to consider him a supremely perfect being, and he would not be supremely perfect if anything could happen in the world without coming entirely from him. It is true that faith alone tells us about the nature of the grace by which God raises us to a supernatural bliss; but philosophy by itself is able to discover that the slightest thought could not enter into a person's mind without God's willing, and having willed for all eternity, that it should so enter. The scholastic distinction between universal and particular causes is out of place here ... God is the universal cause of everything in such a way as to be also the total cause of everything. ("To Princess Elizabeth, 6 October 1645," AT 4: 314)[26]

Descartes adds later in the letter that whenever we pray, it is "simply to obtain whatever he has, from all eternity, willed to be obtained by our prayers" (AT 4:315–16). He remarks in a different letter that

the independence which we experience and feel in ourselves, and which suffices to make our actions praiseworthy or blameworthy, is not incompatible with a dependence of quite another kind, whereby all things are subject to God. ("To Princess Elizabeth, 3 November 1645," AT 4: 333)

Here Descartes is referencing our experience of independence and freedom. There is no question that we have such an experience and that it is often a component of everyday action. Like everything else, however, it is the product of God's eternal and immutable will.

Nonetheless, it might seem odd that we would have an experience of freedom and independence. In *Principles* I.41 Descartes addresses the oddness head on. First, he notes that God wills the series of creatures by a single immutable and eternal act, and hence that there is no way to understand how our free actions are left undetermined:

The power of God is infinite – the power by which he not only knew from eternity whatever is or can be, but also willed it and preordained it. We may attain sufficient knowledge of this power to perceive clearly and distinctly that God possesses it; but we cannot get a sufficient grasp of it to see how it leaves the free actions of men undetermined. (AT 8A: 20)

Descartes is stating very clearly that we do not grasp how divine preordination leaves our free actions undetermined. He does not conclude that our actions therefore are undetermined. He says that we have an experience of freedom and independence that is in tension with the tenet that God has preordained everything for eternity, and what he does conclude is that we should acknowledge that experience and also that everything is preordained:

Nonetheless, we have such close awareness of the freedom and indifference which is in us, that there is nothing we can grasp more evidently or perfectly. And it would be absurd, simply because we do not grasp one thing, which we know must by its very nature be beyond our comprehension, to doubt something else of which we have an intimate grasp and which we experience within ourselves.

Nowhere in his corpus does Descartes speak of a clear and distinct idea of a freedom by which we have a libertarian two-way power to contravene the omniscience and omnipotence of God. We would need to have such an idea[27] if we were to affirm (by means of the will) that it is true that we have a two-way libertarian power, but what we have instead is an experience of independence.[28] Descartes is right that it is difficult to understand why such an experience would be included in the series of creatures that God has willed for eternity, but we do understand that God has preordained everything for eternity.

Another text that is potentially difficult for the view that God has immutably willed a single series of substances and their modifications for eternity is *Principles* I.37, where Descartes makes a distinction between the volitional behavior of humans and the brute mechanical activity that we find in nature. Descartes speaks in a number of texts about the brute mechanical necessity of bodies, for example in the *Discourse* Part Five sketch of how "all purely material things could in the course of time have come to be just as we now see them," without the guidance of mental entities like Aristotelian forms (AT 6: 45–46).[29] He discusses the physical components of the heart and says that

the movement I have just explained follows from the mere arrangement of the parts … just as necessarily as the movement of a clock follows from the force, position and shape of its counter-weights and wheels. (AT 6: 50)

Descartes speaks of the brute necessity of nature in other places as well.[30] In the *Principles* I: 37 passage, he makes a distinction between (what he takes to be) the purely mechanistic behavior of animals and the volitional behavior of human beings. He writes:

It is a supreme perfection in man that he acts voluntarily, that is, freely; this makes him in a special way the author of his actions and deserving of praise for what he does. We do not praise automatons for accurately producing all of the movements they were designed to perform, because the production of these movements occurs necessarily … When we embrace the truth, our doing so voluntarily is much more to our credit than if we were not able to not embrace it.[31]

The CSM translation (not above) leaves the impression of a libertarian two-way power – its translation of the last few words is "than would be the case if we could not do otherwise." But the Latin is *quam si non possemus non amplecti*. The word 'otherwise' is added in the CSM translation, and the Latin is more literally – 'than if we were not able to not embrace it'. This language is similar to the language in the Fourth Meditation, where Descartes asserts that "the will consists simply in our ability to do or not do something (that is, to affirm or deny, to pursue or avoid)" (AT 7: 57). In pointing out that the capacities of the will include affirming and not affirming, Descartes is not saying in addition that the will has a two-way libertarian power to affirm or not affirm at the very same moment. He says (famously) in the Fourth Meditation that the more the will is inclined to affirm the true, "the freer is my choice," and that if our perceptions were always clear, "it would be *impossible* for [us] ever to be in a state of indifference."[32] In *Principles* I: 37 he says that human minds have the ability to affirm or not affirm the truth and that unlike animals we are to be praised for affirming truth. But he does not think when we affirm the truth we have the contra-causal power do otherwise. He had said in the November 1645 letter to Elizabeth that the independence that suffices to make our actions praiseworthy or blameworthy is compatible with the complete dependence of all things on the will of God. He says to Mesland that "we may earn merit even though, seeing very clearly what we must do, we do it infallibly, and without any indifference" (AT 4: 117). In addition, he writes that "I call free in the general sense whatever is voluntary" (AT 4:116), and he supposes that freedom is something that is possessed by volitional minds alone.

One of the reasons that we might assume that Descartes subscribes to a libertarian view of freedom is that the Fourth Meditation delivers the result that if we refrain from affirming results that we do not understand to be true (or that are not clear and distinct), we will avoid error. The thought might be that this result makes no sense unless we have a two-way power to affirm or withhold judgment. However, Descartes is clear in the Fourth Meditation itself that when the will affirms or refrains from affirming, it does so in response to reasons. He writes:

Although probable conjectures may pull me in one direction, the mere fact that they are simply conjectures, and not certain and indubitable reasons, is itself quite enough to push my assent the other way. My experience in the last few days confirms this: the mere fact that I found that all my previous beliefs were in some sense open to doubt was enough to turn my absolutely confident belief in their truth into the supposition that they were wholly false. (AT 7: 59)

He uses similar language to describe the suspension of judgment that takes place in the First Meditation. He says that "since making or not making a judgment is an act of will ... it is evident that it is something in our power" (*Appendix to Fifth Replies*, AT 9A: 204) – that is, making or not making a judgment is in our power, and our capacities include affirming and not affirming. He then repeats that this does not mean that the will has a two-way libertarian faculty: "before we can decide to doubt, we need some reason for doubting, and that is why in my First Meditation I put forward the principle reasons for doubt" (ibid.). If there now arises the worry that God is the cause of human error because all of our volitions are preordained, Descartes points us in the direction of a wider perspective. At the end of the Fourth Meditation he says that all of our acts of will depend on God and that, insofar as they do, "they are wholly true and good" (AT 7: 60). This is a striking claim that bears repeating: all of our acts of will are wholly true and good insofar as they depend on God. Descartes then explains that error is a lack of being and truth, and that strictly speaking "it is not a thing" but a negation (AT 7: 61). The resources are there to tell a more encompassing story – although Descartes does not flesh it out for reasons that are not too hard to guess – that all of our affirmations are true insofar as they depend on God and that since all of our affirmations are true insofar as they depend on God, error is a matter of affirming an incomplete representation of reality, and our affirmations tend to be partial. But of course God can see the various gaps and blanks in our representations, and how they would look if they were more filled in.

A final reason for thinking that Descartes is not supposing a libertarian conception of freedom is that he subscribes to the view that everything has a sufficient cause for its existence. As he puts the view in the Third Meditation, everything has a sufficient cause for being exactly as it is or else there would be aspects of it that do not have a cause and hence that come from nothing (AT 7: 40–41).[33] If every bit of reality has a sufficient cause for its existence, we need to ask about the sufficient cause of the existence of a particular volition in a human mind. In Descartes' substance-mode ontology, volitions are modes of a mental substance, and their cause would either be (prior) modes, or else the mental substance itself. If the cause of a given volition is a set of mental modes, then the will does not have a libertarian two-way power. If the cause of a given volition is the mental substance itself in isolation from its modes, there is no sufficient reason why the substance would generate one volition rather than another.[34] Volitions would simply appear at random, and the "free" mind would be like a loose cannon.[35] If that seems phenomenologically implausible, and volitions are always preceded by a modification that makes their appearance less surprising – perhaps the mode, "I am about to decide" – the worry is that *that* is a mental event, with some reality, and a sufficient cause. *It* had better not just pop into existence, and on Descartes' view it can't. The free mind of the Fourth Meditation is not a loose cannon. But even if it were, it would not be able to avoid error unless the right sort of volition popped into place, at exactly the moment when it was needed.

Descartes does end the First Meditation with a remark about our freedom to resist the assaults of the evil demon. He says that

even if it is not in my power to know any truth, I shall at least do what is in my power, that is, resolutely guard against assenting to any falsehoods, so that the deceiver, however powerful and cunning he may be, will be unable to impose on me in the slightest. (AT 7: 23)

In the final analysis, Descartes of courses agrees that we all have an *experience* of independence. The question is what we are to make of this experience. A not-yet-Cartesian meditator might take it to be indicative of a two-way libertarian power to pursue alternative possibilities. However, such a meditator also asserts that it is possible that God does not exist and that the arguments of the First Meditation are "based on powerful and well thought-out reasons" (AT 7: 21–22). A Cartesian would grant that we have an experience of freedom and note that there are things that we might approach with a spirit of wonder.[36]

NOTES

1. The first two possibilities are introduced at AT 7: 21, the third at AT 7: 22.
2. See for example Antoine Arnauld, *Fourth Objections*, AT 7: 214, and Pierre Bourdin, *Seventh Objections*, AT 7: 528.
3. AT 7: 65–68. See also Cunning 2008.
4. For example *Second Replies*, AT 7: 130–31, 157, and *Principles* I.71–74, AT 8A: 35–38.

5. In *Fourth Replies* Descartes says that it can be illustrative to speak of God as being the efficient cause of Himself, but that strictly speaking God is an eternal existent that has no cause (AT 7: 240–44).

6. See also the Fifth Meditation, AT 7: 70; *Sixth Replies*, AT 7: 431–32; and "For [Arnauld], 29 July 1648," AT 5: 224.

7. See also Frankfurt 1977, 39–41; Bennett 1994, 641–43, and Nelson and Cunning 1999, 144–45.

8. Also *Principles* I.71–74.

9. Descartes appears to subscribe to the view that our imagistic ideas of mind and God (and wax …) are composite ideas that have true ideas of mind and God (and body) as underlying constituents (also Nelson 1997, 166). This view makes sense of how we can analyze our confused ideas and arrive at elements that accurately represent their objects. It also makes sense of how an idea could be *of* a thing but still misrepresent it and "provide subject-matter for error" (*Fourth Replies*, AT 7: 232).

10. See also *Second Replies*: the senses and imagination are not a good source of metaphysical truth, and "if there is any certainty to be had … it occurs in the clear perceptions of the intellect and nowhere else" (AT 7: 145).

11. See for example Popkin's discussion of late sixteenth- and early seventeenth-century philosophers who hold that human minds are not equipped to know the truth about reality. Popkin (1979, chapter 7) focuses on the view (in Marin Mersenne) that all we can know are appearances, and our minds are cut off from truth. We are built instead for faith.

12. For an alternate reading, see Olson 1988, 407. Olson argues that for Descartes these truths had better not be dubitable at the end of the First Meditation, or else no reasoning will be possible from that point on.

13. See also *Seventh Replies*: "there will be nothing which we may not justly doubt so long as we do not know that whatever we clearly perceive is true" (AT 7: 460). For evidence that Descartes holds that there are atheist geometers and skeptics who would have clear and distinct perceptions in the First Meditation; see Introduction, pp. 15–17 in this volume.

14. The Fifth Meditation, AT 7: 69–70; *Second Replies*, AT 7: 146, 166; *Principles* I.43, AT 8A: 21; and also Nelson 1997, and note 32 below.

15. *Fifth Objections*, AT 7: 327. These are the words of Pierre Gassendi, expressing agreement with Descartes.

16. The Third Meditation, AT 7: 40–45. Of course, Descartes' argumentation here is not without problems.

17. See for example Frankfurt 1977, 42, and Van Cleve 1994.

18. See also Nelson and Cunning 1999, 143–45, and Bennett 1994, 641–44.

19. "To [Mersenne], 27 May 1630," AT 1: 152.

20. See Frankfurt (1977, 44–46) and Curley (1984, 582) for interpretations that assume that for Descartes divine freedom involves a libertarian

two-way power. Note that there are passages in which Descartes asserts that we ought not say that God's power is confronted with limits or that there are possibilities that He cannot actualize – for example, in "For [Arnauld], 29 July 1648," AT 5: 224. As per the Fourth Meditation rule for judging, we should not speak of incoherent possibilities such as that two and three might add to seven, or of the incoherent prospect that God's power might come up against a limit (Nelson and Cunning 1999, 144–45).

21. See *Ethics*, Part I, definition 7 and proposition 17.

22. *Short Treatise*, 50–51. All translations of Spinoza are from the Shirley and Morgan edition.

23. See also *Principles* II.36, AT 8A: 61.

24. Also Frankfurt 1977.

25. The passage from the 1644 Mesland letter is very striking. A few lines earlier Descartes had spoken of God as confronting the possibility that contradictories might be true together and deciding whether to make that possibility actual. But then he takes it all back: "If we would know the immensity of his power we should not put these thoughts before our minds," because there is no priority between his intellect and his will, and his activity is simple, singular, and immutable.

26. See also the Third Meditation, where Descartes puts forward the view that God re-creates creatures in their entirety at each and every moment (AT 7: 48–49).

27. It is uncontroversial that Descartes holds that judgment is a matter of having an idea and making an affirmation, but see for example Nelson 1997, 164–71.

28. See also the discussion of the experience of freedom (as opposed to the idea of freedom) in Descartes' contemporary (and follower) Nicolas Malebranche. This is in Elucidation One, 552–53.

29. As Descartes puts it, "in the beginning God did not place in this body any rational soul or any other thing to serve as a vegetative or sensitive soul" (AT 6: 46).

30. For example, *The World*, chapters six and seven (AT 11: 31–48), and *Treatise on Man* (AT 11: 119–202).

31. *Principles* I.37, AT 8A: 18–19. This is a slight variation (in the last few words) of the CSM translation.

32. Ibid., emphasis added. Here we might recall the passage in "To [Mesland], 2 May 1644" where Descartes says that it is "impossible" for the will to refrain from affirming a clear and distinct idea "so long as one continues in the same thought" (AT 4: 116). The will cannot refrain from affirming a clear and distinct idea so long as it is before the mind, but the will can cease affirming the idea as long as another mental item comes before the mind instead ("To [Mesland], 9 February 1645," AT 4: 173). Descartes

says similarly of the good that "if we saw it clearly, it would be impossible for us to sin, as long as we saw it in that fashion" (AT 4: 117).

33. Also *Second Replies*, AT 7: 135.
34. Also Spinoza, *Short Treatise*, 80–84.
35. See also the discussion Van Inwagen 2000, 12–18.
36. See for example *Passions* II.70–72, AT 11: 380–82.

4   The Second Meditation and the nature of the human mind

A new philosophical entity or persona enters the scene with Descartes' discovery of the first existential judgment whose truth he can be certain of in the Second Meditation. It is called "*res cogitans*," "thinking thing" and referred to in the text variously as "I," "self," "mind," or "soul" and is the topic of this chapter. What is it and why is Descartes so excited about being able to discover his being qua thinking before and independently of knowing any corporeal things, his own body included? Descartes was no skeptic by nature – he never questioned his embodiment before he set out to apply his method of doubt systematically. Nor did he ever question it again, once he was done reordering his certainties in a new manner. How come these simple self-evident truths, "I think," "I exist," "I am," got turned into such momentous discoveries?[1] And how should the term 'thinking', introduced as a defining characteristic of the being that cannot doubt its existence, be understood?

Commentators are divided both on what exactly it is that the Second Meditation establishes about the nature of the mind, and on the sense in which it is shown to be better known than the body.[2] Is "nature" here taken in the sense of "essence" – a term that does not occur in the text – so that what the Second Meditation argues belongs to the nature of the mind would thereby be necessary and sufficient for the mind to exist as such? Or is "nature" used more in the sense of "nominal essence," picking out the thing but not what it is? Or is it perhaps something in between: the nature of the human mind but not its whole nature? What, moreover, is it that is better known about the mind than the body – is it its essence, or the plain fact of its existence? Granted that the Second Meditation establishes at least that the existence of mind as a thinking thing is

known first in the order of discoveries of the *Meditations*, and that
this knowledge is more certain than that of other things, does it also
show that the nature of the mind is better known than the nature of
the body, in some more precise sense of 'nature' to be determined?
In what follows I will examine the text carefully with these questions in mind, starting with some remarks about its historical
context.

The title of the first edition of the *Meditationes de prima philosophiae*, published in Paris in 1641, and the Dedicatory Letter accompanying it, intimates that Descartes' main concern in this work is to
prove the existence of God and the immortality of the soul (*animae
immortalitas*, AT 7: 1–2). Should we conclude that the main purpose
of the Second Meditation is to help establish the immortal nature of
the human soul?

Descartes never obtained the protection and approbation of the
theologians that he sought in this letter. The mention of the immortality of the soul is replaced in the subtitle to the second edition,
published in Amsterdam in 1642, by "distinction of the human soul
(*animae humanae)* from the body." This is demonstrated not in the
Second but in the Sixth Meditation. That Descartes did not want to
flag his argument as a proof of the immortality of the soul is in line
with his conviction that dogmas of faith fall outside the jurisdiction
of philosophy. The argument that the human mind is really distinct,
i.e., can exist apart from the body, is still important for purely philosophical and psychological reasons. Committed as he was to the new
philosophy of nature, and having shown that the vital functions
including part of the lower cognitive capacities of the human body
could be explained mechanistically without invoking special principles like animal souls, Descartes took up the challenge of defending
the nature and existence of a rational soul, traditionally seen as the
seat of higher cognitive and moral capacities, none of which could be
derived from the powers of matter conceived in terms of geometrical
extension.[3]

If the proof of the real distinction is a main topic of the *Meditations*,
the enquiry undertaken by the meditator in the Second Meditation
about the nature of the mind seems crucial in establishing one of its
central premises, which is that his essence consists in being solely a
thinking thing. In summarizing, in the Sixth Meditation, the steps
leading up to the final argument Descartes writes:

(A) Thus, simply by knowing that I exist and seeing at the same time that absolutely nothing else belongs to my nature or essence except that I am thinking, I can rightly conclude that my essence consists in this alone that I am a thinking thing. (AT 7: 78)[4]

But where exactly is this point about his "essence" established? If both the existence and essential nature of the mind were proven in the Second Meditation, i.e., it had already been shown that it is a being the nature of which is such that it requires nothing other than thinking in order to exist, its distinction from the body would thereby have been demonstrated too. Would the Sixth Meditation argument then be merely a pedagogical summary of what already had been established elsewhere? Descartes's own account in his synopsis of the *Meditations* suggests otherwise:

(B) In the Second Meditation, the mind uses its own freedom and supposes the non-existence of all the things about whose existence it can have the slightest doubt; and in so doing notices that it could not be that it should not exist itself during this time. This in fact is of highest utility, because in this way it easily distinguishes that which belongs to itself, that is, to an intellectual nature, from what belongs to the body. (AT 7: 12)

Those who expect a proof for the "immortality of the soul" are warned that he has been careful not to advance anything he could not yet strictly prove. The order he follows is that of the geometers where one sets out all the premises and concludes nothing that is not derived from evident or proved propositions.[5] The first and most important prerequisite for knowing the immortality of the soul is forming "a concept of the soul which is maximally transparent (*maxime perspicuum*), and which is entirely distinct from any concept of the body" (AT 7: 13), and this, he says, is accomplished here. The other things that are required to reach the proof of a real distinction are: the truth-rule, not established till the Fourth Meditation, and the forming of a distinct concept of corporeal nature, which is done partly at the end of the Second and partly in the Fifth. The final move from distinct concepts to a real distinction between substances, Descartes says, is completed only in the Sixth Meditation (ibid.). So he would be working from a conceptual distinction to a distinction in reality, and what the reasoning in the Second Meditation does is provide clarity on the concept of soul – on what does and does not belong to it.[6]

But Descartes cannot on the most charitable of interpretations be said merely to be rendering the concept of the soul perspicuous in the Second Meditation – at least not if this is taken to mean submitting some traditional philosophical or currently used notion of mind to mere conceptual clarification. As a matter of fact he is revising it, and in so doing introduces a new and unheard of notion of mind (understood in terms of thought) that has exercised his philosophical posterity ever since. It is supposed to be general and shared by all rational beings, yet is disclosed through reflection upon one's inner subjective experience.[7] In the text itself he is sliding between the first-person pronoun and the particular thoughts and capacities he finds in himself as an individual subject, and mind or intellect in the sense of a generic rational capacity to understand and form true judgments.

Thus, when examining his nature in the Second Meditation Descartes famously finds that he is strictly speaking "only a thing that thinks" (*res cogitans*, AT 7: 27), that thought is inseparable from him, and that the nature of his self or mind (or soul) consists in thinking alone. Having first reached the conclusion "that this proposition, *I am, I exist*, is necessarily true whenever it is put forward by me or conceived by my mind" (AT 7: 25), Descartes goes on to reflect on the nature of "this 'I'" whose existence has now been ascertained. Former beliefs about himself, e.g., that he is "a man," "a rational animal," a being with a mechanically structured body ("which can be seen in a corpse") and a soul accounting for various activities he attributed to himself, like being nourished, moving about, engaging in sense perception and thinking, are considered but discarded with the exception of the last, thinking – the only activity withstanding systematic doubt. So he concludes in an oft-cited statement:

C. I am, then, precisely (*praecise*) only a thing that thinks; that is, I am a mind (*mens; esprit*), or intelligence (*animus*), or intellect (*intellectus, entendement*), or reason (*ratio; raison*) – words whose meaning I have been ignorant of until now. (AT 7: 27)

The mind, intellect, or reason, were traditionally seen as powers of the highest psychic capacity – shared by humans and purely intellectual beings, e.g., angels and God. Few however would identify their self as an individual subject with the mind or intellectual capacity alone, or conclude that none of the things that can be sensed or pictured by the imagination belong to oneself as a mind or thinking being (AT 7: 28). In the scholastic tradition that Descartes here opposes, the moving and sensing animal body individualizing a person was a precondition for the highest part of the human soul – the intellect or mind – to exercise its capacities for understanding and reasoning. Human understanding works through abstracting intelligible forms from sensory species actualized in the sense organs, and according to the common Aristotelian slogan, there can be nothing in the intellect that was not prior in the senses. Although he rejects this natural presumption, Descartes soon finds that sensory perceptions and imaginations, as well as volitions, do show up among the thoughts he can be certain about, so must be part of his nature:

D. What then am I? A thing that doubts, understands, affirms, denies, is willing, is unwilling, and also imagines and has sensory perceptions. (AT 7: 28)

What was initially described as a mind or intellect or reason, now includes "willing and unwilling," and even "imagining and sensing."[8] Later, emotions and passions, e.g., love and hate, are added to the list.[9] This is surprising, because any functions depending on the body are still under the screen of systematic doubt, so none of the things he can imagine or sense, including his own body, can belong to his self in the strict sense with which he is here concerned, yet the very acts of imagining and sensing are now, for Descartes, part of him, taken strictly as a thing that thinks.

It is not quite clear what the dependence here is. There can be no actual sensory perceptions so no exercise of sensory capacities without bodily organs and nerves being stimulated and processing the information received. Descartes does not deny this. At this point of his reasoning, while finding himself sensing and imagining as he did before, but having not yet been able to determine what the body is, or even whether or not he is or has a body and bodily organs, he cannot take this for granted. So the conclusion he accepts for now is that these phenomena, i.e., his present sensations and imaginings (his thinking of extended corporeal things by forming mental pictures of them), are ongoing activities or states which since they are immediately noticed must be part of the thinking self whose existence alone he is certain of.

How does he arrive at this counterintuitive conclusion? Having determined that nothing, except this fact that he, qua thinking being exists, is certain, Descartes, as we already saw, lists and sets aside various spontaneous beliefs about himself that do not stand up to his present scrutiny. The first things occurring to him were that he had a face, hands, and arms and a machine composed of limbs like those of a corpse (!), and that he called a body (AT 7: 26). He appears to be stepping back from any immediate phenomenological proprioceptive experience to consider his embodied person as if from the outside, as an external observer. He sees his own body as a mechanical statue or device of the kind imagined in his early *Treatise On Man* (AT 11: 119–20). The next thing that occurred to him was that he was nourished, walked about, had sense perceptions, and was thinking. The machinery that he believed was his own body (that he "had" or possessed) performed all these various activities that he used to refer to the soul as their cause. Thus, a soul-body dualism shows up already among his spontaneous beliefs about himself: he used to think of himself as being or having a spatially configured mechanical body with a soul accounting for all these functions. Now, in putting his habitual concepts of soul and body on trial, he finds that insofar as he paid any attention to the first, he imagined it as "something tenuous, like a wind or fire or ether, which permeated my more solid parts." As to the body, by contrast, he thought he had a very distinct conception of its nature, described in terms supposedly familiar to his contemporaries as anything "determinable by shape and location and extended in space in such a way that it excluded any other body," which could "be perceived by touch, sight, hearing, taste and smell, and also be moved in various ways, not by itself, but by whatever came in contact with it." That it would belong to the nature of the body so conceived to have "the force (*vim*) to move itself, to sense, or to think," did not seem credible, and indeed he marveled that there were bodies in which such "faculties" could actually be found (AT 7: 26).

It is not quite clear exactly what conception of body Descartes' description quoted above presupposes, or why it would puzzle him that it moved or sensed. Would not the soul conceived as some tenuous ether be an explanation of sorts of these phenomena? Apparently not one he could accept, because it is materialistic. Alternatively, if Descartes were to rely on what he had learned in school, two other candidates for explaining the phenomena listed above would suggest themselves, the animal soul and the rational soul – both in themselves immaterial forms or principles. But qua forms they require matter with corresponding potencies to actualize. Descartes, moreover, had already rejected the lower kinds of form or soul in his earlier work, showing how at least some of the functions referred to the animal soul could be given a mechanistic explanation.[10] His new notion of matter, defined in terms of extension[11] excluded the entire framework of the traditional philosophy of nature with forms actualizing potencies of material bodies, in this case a naturally structured living human body with normally working organs. Descartes of course was in no position to take any of this for granted yet. He is here working to introduce a new way of conceiving sensory and cognitive functions freed from the traditional presuppositions of Aristotelian-scholastic philosophy of nature and cognitive psychology. The account quoted above of how he used to conceive himself is a picture sufficiently general to lead the reader to question usual ways of seeing cognitive capacities as depending on powers of material bodies.

What then is it that makes thinking suitable as an alternative to these old suppositions in characterizing himself? What marks out the various phenomena it covers as doubt-proof? In seeking to clarify it he goes, once more, through earlier suppositions already rejected as doubtful. The challenge he faces is to determine, without referring to any of these, what this "I (ego) who knows its own existence" is. He remarks, "Most certainly this notion thus precisely taken (sic praecise sumpti notitiam) cannot depend on things whose existence I do not know; nor therefore on those that I make up (effingo) in my imagination" (AT 7: 27–28). Inventing or making something up in imagination is picturing it with a certain shape and size as a corporeal thing, and so is no help at this point. Nothing but what is known as evidently and immediately as the existence of the self can be used in the clarification of its nature. We are stuck with the list given in passage (D) when trying to understand the new meaning of the noun-words in passage (C), and of the items on this list, the last two, imagination and sensory perception, are problematic. What then is there to learn from considering these various activities? Here's a tentative answer:

(E) Am I then not the very same (ego ipse) who is doubting almost everything, who nonetheless understands some things, who affirms that this one thing is true, denies all others, desires to know more, is unwilling to be deceived, imagines many things even involuntarily, and notices many things as if coming through the senses? (AT 7: 28)

All these cognitive acts, whether actively exercised as in doubting or understanding, or passively registered as in noticing, sensing, or imagining something, and disregarding their contents or causes, are ongoing activities that are no more in doubt than this fact that he exists. None of these, as he stresses, can be distinguished from my thinking (*mea cogitatione*) or separated from myself (*me ipso*). Nothing could be more obvious or self-evident than that it is the same I (*ego*) "who doubts, understands and wills." Likewise, even if what is imagined may be false, the very power or faculty of imagining at least must be real and part of my thoughts (*cogitationis meae partem facit*). The same holds for sensation:

(F) ... It is the same I who senses or notices corporeal things as if through the senses, since in fact I am seeing light, hearing noise, feeling heat. These are false, for I am asleep. Yet it certainly appears to me that I see (*videor videre*), hear, am warmed. This cannot be false; and this is properly what in me is called to be sensing (*sentire*), and this, precisely so taken, is nothing else than to think. (AT 7: 29)

This controversial passage has been read as offering a new definition of sensation, turning it into a purely mental phenomenon or private, inner feeling. It has also been taken to show that the essential characteristic of thinking according to Descartes has to be consciousness – what other common trait could there be uniting sensations and intellectual activities into one category? This line of reading is fuelled by the definition of thought in *Second Replies* (AT 7: 160) and *Principles* (AT 8A: 7) through that of which we can be immediately aware (*conscii*). But there are also strong reasons against it, and great care should be used with the term *conscius* here which has not yet acquired the connotations with which we are familiar.[12] An insightful defense of the more natural reading of passage (F) is offered by John Carriero, who argues that the only point Descartes needs to be seen as making here, while remaining still noncommittal as to the causes and objects of sensory perception, is that he cannot deny the appearance, or "as if" of sensing, nor that these phenomena, qua experienced, are part of his self or me (2009, 103). Perhaps the point could be put in this way: insofar as sensation and imagination are my activities or undergoings, they are kinds or modes of this same intellectual activity whereby I discover my existence as a thinking thing, i.e., whereby I see that it is evidently true that I who think necessarily exist whenever I think. The same reasoning applies to all these immediately noticed psychological acts, hence, just as the initial, primary insight "I think," they belong to me and so are part of my nature. Are they then also all essential to my nature?[13]

Carriero sees the Second Meditation reasoning as concerned with formulating the essence of the thinking thing, not as a mere conceptual enquiry.[14] Descartes, he argues, proceeds in his carefully staged argument in a traditional Aristotelian fashion from thing (res), to activity, to faculty or power and nature. Observing its own activities as a thinking being reveals its fundamental faculties or powers and its essential nature as an intellectual being.[15] Carriero prefers to characterize it as a "cognitive agent" or "cogito-being" rather than a "mind," in order to steer clear from pre-Cartesian associations of mind with intellect or intelligence on the one hand, and from the post-Cartesian readings of mind that focus too much on consciousness on the other (2009, 94). The self or being who now knows her own existence has discovered herself through understanding that something is true, and more particularly, through seeing and judging that things are thus and so: that I who think must exist as long as I think. The broader term 'thinking', Carriero argues, suits him better than 'mind' or 'intellect' precisely because judging for Descartes involves two powers, intellect *and* will, which are both covered by it. The core activities of the thinking thing, on this reading, are to understand and to judge. These, not mere phenomenal consciousness, would be essential to Descartes' notion of mind. The cognitive agent's core abilities, correspondingly, are intellect and will, both of which – according to the doctrine spelled out in the Fourth Meditation – are employed in the exercise of its distinctive and essential activity or operation: judging that things are thus and so.[16]

Carriero's emphasis on understanding and judging is well grounded in the text and makes better sense of Descartes' notion of thinking than the usual stress on consciousness.[17] A worry one may have, though, is that this reading runs the risk of simply reducing the essence of Descartes' thinking being to what in the Scholastic tradition was the highest kind of soul. In particular, can it avoid turning sensory perception and emotions into kinds of judgment? Reason or intellect as well as judging may well be, for Descartes, as for the

Scholastics, essential to mind in general – capacities that, as will be discovered later, in the Fourth Meditation – it shares with its infinite creator. Yet, it is hard to see how mind in this strict sense could form the whole essence or nature of the *human* mind. One can ask, moreover, what in this characterization of the nature of mind could ground the individuality of this particular thinking thing, whose nature Descartes set out to determine in the Second Meditation?

So there are two connected problems to consider: one is the identity of the thinking being – for all we know, thinking is exercised, but what gives this thinking subject or ego its determinate individuality? The other is the account of sensory perceptions and emotions with their characteristic feelings and sensations, something the persona meditating attends to and analyzes with such care while performing her (thought?) experiment on a fresh piece of wax, melting it by the fire in an effort to determine what the ground or evidence for her old belief that she perceives ordinary material objects so distinctly could be (AT 7: 30–31).

One might suppose that the particular body with its history, reactions, habits and relations to other things – all factors reflected in the contents and associations of these thoughts through which its nature as a thinking being is revealed to it – is what in the end determines its individual nature. Its sensations and passions, how they affect it, would be important here. The thinking thing, according to this line of reading, inherits its individuality from the flesh and blood of the author inventing it.

This cannot be Descartes' official story though. Individuation, as he understands it, goes the other way: it is the individual substantial soul that confers its particularity and identity on the human body.[18] His meditator, in spite of having resolved to take nothing for granted, never questions the unity and continued identity of his thinking self that will become such a problem for his posterity.[19] The concept of an individual substance-nature or form ("thisness") was familiar from centuries of scholastic discussions. Whether or not he is entitled to it, Descartes can rely on it in discovering his thinking self as a unitary subject with a being of its own, one that not only persists through time, but can remember and keep track both of past doubts and mistakes as well as newly won certainties, of desires and commitments, like his resolve to accept nothing but what he understands is true. The will is at center-stage here, for it is precisely through using his will (cf. [E] above) in all these different ways – now exercising its different capacities at will, now undergoing experiences without or even against its will, and now testing the limits it runs up against, that the cognitive agent gets to know itself as a unitary thinking being. It is not far-fetched to suppose that, of what Carriero considers as its two core-capacities, intellect and will, it is the latter, not the former, that gives the thinking being its determinate individuality. The intellect or reason may be distinctive for or essential to mind in general, but what makes human minds special, in addition to having these rational capacities, is, I want to claim, the will with its free power of self-determination.[20] This is not yet to say, however, that the whole nature of the human mind is reduced to its will and intellect, or that they alone are its necessary characteristics.

The self-examination undertaken by Descartes' meditator is not any ordinary Aristotelian induction, since the object observed is the very subject conducting the enquiry. If the Aristotelian induction starts from a thing or substance to determine its faculties and nature from observation of its acts and accidents (actions and passions), in Descartes' self-discovery, existence and essence are inextricably linked. Descartes does not find that he exists before and independently of his thinking but through the latter.[21] Using later points of reference, one can see his self-examination as proceeding from a phenomenological reduction of a kind, by reflecting on a selected, doubt-proof set of activities and passive acts to exclude commonsense views about himself as the human person of flesh and blood he formerly took himself to be.[22] "Using his freedom" he finds that what he is essentially is a being endowed with powers that no corporeal thing composed of the extended matter that mechanistic physics deals with could harbor.

His reply to Hobbes – who shares his conception of matter – about the Second Meditation argument, is revealing. While agreeing with Hobbes "that we cannot conceive of an act without its subject," and so cannot "conceive of thought without a thinking thing," Descartes vehemently rejects the conclusion drawn by Hobbes that "a thinking thing is something corporeal" (*Third Objections and Replies*, AT 7: 175). He agrees that the subject of any act may be understood as falling under the concept of substance – or even, if Hobbes insists, that of matter – but then matter should not be understood as "corporeal" matter but as what Descartes calls "metaphysical" matter. He goes on to note that it is "normally" said, both by logicians and "people in general," that some substances are spiritual and some corporeal (AT 7: 175–76). Acts of thought have nothing in common with acts of corporeal substances, so the substance they belong to must be incorporeal or spiritual.

This interesting exchange deserves a fuller discussion than can be given here, and so does Descartes' conclusion, which, contrary to what he pretends, goes against most logicians and common usage. In moving from his phenomenological reduction to metaphysics, Descartes does not lay out all his presuppositions. It is worth noting, however, that the text of his metaphysics of mind is rather thin. Insofar as we do not have any direct cognitive access to a substance apart from its main attribute,[23] we know nothing of this metaphysical matter except that its nature is thinking. Descartes does not venture beyond the thesis that mind, qua thinking, is something real and existing which is not reducible to corporeal matter defined through extension. None of this, besides, is fully concluded till the Sixth Meditation, but even there it remains unclear what else we actually know about the nature of the mind considered apart from the body than this fact that it is known through acts whose exercise does not depend on any clearly and distinctly understood corporeal causes. This very fact, however, we are supposed to know better than and prior to anything else. This claim is often misconstrued in terms of incorrigibility, privacy, and transparency. Though I cannot argue at length for it here, I will suggest another way of taking it.

The claim that the mind is more known (*notior*) than the body is given additional support by the analysis at the end of the Second Meditation of what our knowledge of ordinary corporeal things amounts to. Not even the commonest sensory object – "this piece of wax" – can be clearly known inductively, by sight or touch or smell or any external sense, but is known through inspection and judgment by the mind alone, implying that the nature of mind on whose judgment all knowledge depends must be better known than that of any other singular thing (AT 7: 30–34).

Every act of cognition concerning an object of sense-perception, as explained more in detail in the Sixth Meditation, requires a mind with (i) a passive faculty of receiving or registering and recognizing the sensations or perceptions it causes (AT 7: 78–79) and (ii) an active power of reflecting and passing judgments on the things causing these perceptions (AT 7: 82–83).

Descartes concludes the analysis of the wax in the Second
Meditation by noting that he finally got back to where he wanted to
be, and where his argument had led him naturally, as of itself (*sponte*).
Readers and commentators would be helped by paying careful attention to this. Where did Descartes want to end up in the Second
Meditation? Not with a full-fledged theory of the essence of the
mind in general or of the human mind more particularly. His concern
instead was all along to show the priority of the mind and its intellectual capacities (understanding and judging), both metaphysically
and in the order of knowledge, and thus to undermine the scholastic
theory of sense-perception – the foundation of the house that had to
be turned over before something else could be put in its place.[24]

Descartes suggests, and commentators often stress, that his six
Meditations are meant as a kind of spiritual exercise, and that it
takes long practice and repetition to benefit from them properly.
This holds in particular for the first two and partly for the Third
Meditation. Thus, he recommends one spend weeks on the First
and several days at least on the Second. The point of these exercises
is to "detach" the mind from the senses, to develop new habits of
thinking without relying on the senses, and in particular, to train
one's mind not to confuse intellectual things with corporeal ones –
something to which habits from childhood strengthened by bad scholastic philosophy makes one all too prone (*Second Replies*, AT 7:
131).[25] The introductory lines of the Fourth Meditation suggest that
the work of detaching his mind from the senses has been effective and
a new habit acquired, based on the insight that "there is very little
about corporeal things that is truly perceived, whereas much more
is known about the human mind, and still more about God" (AT
7: 52–53). The superiority of the cognition attained of incorporeal
things, is not, I want to stress, a matter of the number of things or
properties known about them. As already mentioned, the text of
Descartes' rational psychology is thin, and contrary to some of his
rationalist followers, Spinoza and Leibniz, Descartes does not pretend
that the difference between the human and the divine intellect is
merely a matter of the limited nature of the former.[26] That the mind,
and the existence of God, are more known or easier to know than the
body has to do with the metaphysical nature of the objects known:
their greater perfection (or reality, which amounts to the same) on the
overall scale of being and goodness (AT 7: 40–52). The priority or

superiority of our knowledge of the nature or essence of our human mind, is not a matter of its greater adequacy or distinctness as much as of its superior being or perfection – the fact that it is a unitary and indivisible substance which in spite of its finitude shares some of the perfections of its infinite creator, i.e., the capacity to grasp truth (including eternal truths) and goodness, to order its will to the highest good, or, if it so chooses, to oppose the good. The mind in understanding and using its will is active, and activity, according to old intuitions Descartes shares, is higher on the scale of being or perfection than the kind of mechanical propulsion that keeps bodies in motion but that they cannot have caused themselves.[27]

The enquiry about the mind of the Second Meditation continues in the Third with the discussion of different kinds of thoughts or ideas and their objects,[28] culminating in the analysis of judgment and the will – our highest perfection – in the Fourth. Discoveries made on the way include that of its finitude and fallibility and its utter dependence on something infinitely greater and perfect, and thus of the existence of an infinite and perfect God. This comes with the comforting insight that the omnipotent creator on whom the thinking being depends, warrants its clear and distinct ideas. Using this truth-rule to determine first the nature or essence and then the probable existence of matter in general, Descartes spells out the argument for the real distinction in the Sixth Meditation, concluding that "I am really distinct from my body and can exist without it" (AT 7: 78).

Strikingly, the argument is carried through before the existence of the human body is ascertained. Instead of dwelling on this thrilling possibility of independent existence, Descartes turns almost right away to his actual embodied condition, proving first that corporeal things exist and then not only that he has a body but that he is so closely joined and intermingled with it "that I and the body form a unit" (AT 7: 81). Imagination and sense-perception, these "faculties for certain special modes of thinking" earlier put on hold, are now called in as reliable enough witnesses. But first their nature and status as thoughts are clarified.

Descartes now claims that he can understand himself, clearly and distinctly, "as a whole" without them, but is unable to understand these faculties without himself, "that is, without an intellectual substance [substantia intelligente] to inhere in." Their objects and causes are modes of extension, but imagining and sensing count as modes of thought because their very notion includes "some kind of understanding [*intellectionem nonnullam*]" (AT 7: 78). It is the very same power which when it understands (*intelligit*; the French translation has *conçevoir*) is said to "turn in some way towards itself to inspect [*respiciat*] some of the ideas that are within it," and which is said to imagine when it turns itself towards the body to consider (L. *intueatur*; Fr. *considère*, CSM "looks") something in the body that conforms to some idea it conceives through the intellect or perceives through the senses [*vel sensu perceptae*]" (AT 7: 73). When Descartes later in the same text insists on the indivisibility and unity of his self or mind, it is taken in this strict sense of mind or thinking thing: the mind is one and indivisible insofar as it understands.[29] The nature of the mind includes the power to understand things through the senses or imagination, a power it has whether or not it is actually united to a body with the appropriate organs, but that it cannot exercise unless in fact it uses those organs and applies itself to what is conveyed through them.

Ideas of imagination include images of shapes and figures, colors, sounds, tastes, and pains that all come from the senses or memory, where sensory ideas are stored. Examining the ideas or perceptions of sensory qualities presenting themselves to him as through the internal or external senses and noticing that they were the only things "he properly and immediately sensed [*sentiebam*]," Descartes now concludes that "he sensed things altogether different from his thought, namely, bodies from which these ideas proceeded" (The Sixth Meditation, AT 7: 75). In the narrative of the *Meditations*, sensory ideas, tested by methodic doubt in the First Meditation and characterized as obscure and confused "adventitious" ideas in the Third, turn out in the Sixth Meditation to be the "the sole source" of our cognition of actually existing particular corporeal things including our own body (AT 7: 75).[30] Their evidence consists in their liveliness and the fact that they offer themselves to thought uninvited, actualizing an irresistible natural inclination or impulse to believe in the existence of the things taken to cause them (AT 7: 79–81), affecting the embodied mind in various other ways too.[31] If the reasoning in the Second Meditation uncovered the metaphysical nature and reality of my being or self, taken in a restricted sense, this very same being or self appears in the Sixth Meditation in its full human and empirical form.

I started this essay by mentioning a puzzlement as to whether the enquiry about the nature of the human mind undertaken in the Second Meditation concerns its essence or is merely conceptual, and whether it concerns the mind in general or more particularly the human mind. The fact that it includes from the start cognitive powers requiring a body to be exercised suggests that Descartes is all along concerned with the human mind, a mind destined to be and already in fact embodied, although this fact is ignored to get its intellectual nature in clearer view. If so, then the Second Meditation cannot give us the whole essence or nature of the human mind, the kind of mind that comes to life only through being united to the body of an embryo. "My nature," in the Sixth Meditation, turns out to have many senses and employments, and my particular human, embodied self is the sum of them all.[32] Thus, in correspondence with Elizabeth – his best student and reader – Descartes writes that our knowledge of "the nature of the human soul" depends on these two things, one of which is that it thinks, the other that it is united to the body and "can act and suffer with it." The second, he adds, is a topic he has written "next to nothing on," intent as he was in his published work to make the first well understood ("To Princess Elizabeth, 21 May 1643," AT 3: 664–65). To know the full nature – metaphysical, empirical, and physical – of the human mind, self, soul, or person, one must turn also to Descartes' physics and physiology, to his correspondence and to the treatise *The Passions*, but it is not evident that they all add up to a nature that can be fully known or understood distinctly in the way its nature, precisely as thinking, is understood.[33]

NOTES

1. The formula *Cogito, ergo sum*, famous from the *Discourse on Method*, does not occur in the *Meditations*. It was used by Augustine and the propositions "I think," "I exist" were textbook examples of simple self-evident truths.
2. For discussions, see Wilson, 1978, Wilson 1999, 84–93, and Ayers, 2005, 24–45.
3. *On Man*, AT 11: 202, *Discourse*, AT 6: 45–59. In his earlier writings, reason or the rational soul, retained by Descartes as the defining characteristic of human beings is postulated as directly created by God (AT 6: 59). See also "Synopsis of the *Meditations*," AT 7: 13.

4. Translations, when departing from CSM, are my own. See also "Preface to the Reader," AT 7: 8. The term *essentia* is however not used in the Second Meditation, but *natura*, which is often translated, e.g, by Anscombe and Geach, as "essence".

5. See Kambouchner 2005, 113–36, for an instructive recent account of the question of order.

6. For discussion of this controversial proof see, e.g., Wilson 1978, 1999, Alanen 1982, Rozemond 1998, Baker and Morris 1996, Secada 2000, Almog 2002, Carriero 2009.

7. This new Cartesian notion of mind with its intimate relation to that of the self or subject discovering it, has set much of the agenda for subsequent theorizing about the human mind, its nature and capacities in the Western tradition. Different traditions emphasizing one or the other of these initially interrelated aspects of this notion – its rationality and its subjectivity – tend to color (or distort, as the case may be) any later readings of it.

8. Cf. the Third Meditation, AT 7: 34; the Sixth Meditation, AT 7: 78; *Principles* I.48, AT 8A:23.

9. For example *Passions* I.25–27 and II.51–56.

10. *Discourse*, AT 6: 40–55; *Optics*, AT 6: 109–47.

11. E.g., *Principles* II.4, AT 8A: 42; the Fifth Meditation, AT 7: 63.

12. Anscombe and Geach translate *cogitatione* here and throughout this argument by "consciousness" (Anscombe and Geach, 1954). Moreover, as Carriero points out, "to be conscious" or "aware of" is often used in English translations where Descartes uses the more active Latin verb *animadverto*, better translated by turning to, noticing, paying attention to (2009, 101–2, 440n24–25; Cf. Alanen, forthcoming).

13. For an interesting alternative reading, see Shapiro 2013, who stresses the role of memory on the one hand and the moral (including cognitive) progress accomplished by the meditator as crucial for self-identity.

14. He opposes the readings of Janet Broughton, Harry Frankfurt, and Norman Malcolm. For references see Carriero 2009, 439n16.

15. Carriero 2009, 81–96 and 100–5. But see also the discussion of Jorge Secada, who sees Descartes not only as concerned with the essence of mind, but as "an essentialist," following Suarez against Aquinas in going from essence to being and not the other way around (Secada, 2000, Part II).

16. Carriero 2009, 81–94.

17. Indeed the term does not even occur in the Second Meditation. A good overview of the literature on the topic is in Simmons 2012.

18. The human mind, differently from the human body, is not made up of changing accidents or configurations, but retains its particular identity because it is a "pure substance," which holds for body only in a general

sense. See also "Synopsis of the *Meditations*," AT 7: 13–14; "To Mesland, 9 February 1645," AT 4: 167; and also the instructive discussion in Deborah Brown's chapter in this volume.

19. Not only for Locke and his empiricist successors, but also for Spinoza, who admits only one individual infinite substance, God or Nature.

20. The will is at work from the very start of the *Meditations* (AT 7: 17–18) and is omnipresent throughout the text of the Second Meditation. I argue (Alanen, forthcoming) that the will, which is given such a prominent role in the forming of judgments, and to which he seems to accord a greater freedom and independence in relation to the intellect than any of his predecessors (Alanen 2008 and 2013), is for Descartes the source and locus of individuality.

21. Cf. Secada 2000.

22. See the point about stripping off everything that does not belong to mind, made in the reply to Hobbes (AT 7: 174).

23. *Principles* I.52, AT 8A: 25.

24. Cf. the beginning of the First Meditation: "Whatever I have up til now accepted as most true I have acquired either from the senses or through the senses" (AT 7: 18). But not even the simplest bodies are strictly speaking perceived by the senses or the imagination, they "are perceived by the intellect alone." They are not distinctly perceived from the fact that they are seen or touched (animals and other machines, after all, can see or touch in some sense of the term) but from being recognized and identified, so understood, by the mind's inspection. For any object of cognition it learns to know its own nature better (AT 7: 34).

25. Among the first to make this point in the Anglo-American literature was Hatfield 1985 and 1986. For more recent discussions, see, e.g., Secada 2000, chapter 5, and Carriero 2009.

26. I discuss this in Alanen 2008.

27. It is the will too that controls the motions of the body (The Sixth Meditation, AT 7. 84).

28. See Olli Koistinen's contribution to this volume.

29. "I am unable to distinguish any parts within myself; I understand myself to be something unitary and whole (*unam et integram*)" a complete thing even when it is as a matter of fact wholly united to the whole but divisible body (AT 7: 86). This notion of the unity of the cognitive power is first expressed at *Rules for the Direction of the Mind*, Rule 12, AT 10: 416.

30. To Arnauld, who worries that his argument for the distinction between mind and body goes too far, Descartes claims he has provided stronger arguments than he had ever seen for its union with the body (*Fourth Replies*, AT 7: 228).

31. See Simmons 2001, and her contribution to the current volume.

32. That is, when it is not identified to Nature in the pre-Spinozistic sense –
nature considered in its general aspect by which Descartes understands
"nothing other than God himself or the ordered system of created things
established by God" (AT 7: 80).

33. I am grateful to Deborah Brown for support and helpful suggestions and to
David Cunning for comments on an earlier longer version.

5 The Second Meditation: unimaginable bodies and insensible minds

This essay on the Second Meditation (M2) takes its cue, very loosely, from Descartes' recommendation for reading *Principles of Philosophy* – that is, to read it once quickly, "like a novel," and then two or three times more carefully, so that by the third or fourth reading the reader should discover "solutions" to any "difficulties" encountered earlier (AT 9B: 12). The essay consists of three readings of the second half of M2, which includes Descartes' famous consideration of the piece of wax. The first section provides an initial analysis which raises a number of questions. The second section suggests some answers to these questions and attempts to reconstruct the main arguments that Descartes is offering. The third section reflects on the larger Cartesian methodologies and strategies that appear to be in play.[1]

INITIAL ANALYSIS OF ¶¶ 10–16 OF THE SECOND MEDITATION, AT 7: 29–34

¶10

¶10 constitutes a bridge between the two halves of M2. Descartes confesses to an obsessive or highly tempting thought – "I cannot stop thinking this" – which persists even after his meditation thus far, namely that

the corporeal things of which images are formed in my thought, and which the senses investigate, are known with much more distinctness than this puzzling 'I' which cannot be pictured in the imagination.

It is the combating of this thought which dominates the second half of M2; I will refer to it as "the Thought." Descartes suggests, without quite asserting it here, that the Thought is false – it is outside "the bounds of truth" – but he also seems to think that showing that the Thought is false is not enough to extirpate it. The strategy he announces for extirpating it is to give his mind "completely free rein, so that after a while, when it is time to tighten the reins, it may more readily submit to being curbed."

Descartes here hints at a distinction between an epistemological hierarchy of mental faculties: the senses and the imagination on the one hand and the intellect on the other. In the grip of the Thought, he accords to the former the accolade of "knowing with distinctness." Upon reflection, the intellect will be seen to merit this accolade instead. The identification of this non-sensory faculty as the intellect is not made until ¶16, perhaps because such an identification is an affront to the Thought.

¶11

As in the first half of M2, the investigation here involves the exploration of a particular thing – not the insensible "I", but "this wax" (haec cera). Descartes selects for investigation a particular *corporeal* thing, a parcel of stuff which is an instance of the sort of thing "which people commonly think they understand most distinctly of all" because it has an extensive set of sensible attributes: it tastes of honey, has the scent of flowers, and so on.[2] "In short," Descartes remarks, "it has everything which appears necessary to enable a body to be known as distinctly as possible." But it is also peculiarly mutable. Setting it before the fire causes it to change or to lose many of the sensible qualities with which it began, but still "the wax remains."

What exactly is this reasoning supposed to show? That whatever it was "in the wax that I understood with such distinctness," it was "none of the features which I arrived at by means of the senses." It is noteworthy that Descartes is not challenging the assumption that something about the wax was known or understood with distinctness. The challenge is rather to the view that what is known or understood is the wax's *sensible* attributes.

¶12

We have been set up to expect that, given the failure of sense-perception to deliver whatever it is in the wax "that I understood with such distinctness," Descartes will move to the faculty of imagination. The previous paragraph (¶11) was supposed to have shown that the same wax remains through changes in its sensible features and thus that the wax is "not after all the sweetness of the honey," or any other sensible qualities.[3] Rather, it is "a body which presented itself to me in these various forms a little while ago, but which now exhibits different ones." Descartes' strategy is to show that this body is not something which the imagination can grasp. If we "take away everything which does not belong to the wax," what is left is "merely something extended, flexible and changeable." He insists that "I can grasp that the wax is capable of countless changes of this kind," and then proceeds to a conclusion:

[Since] I am unable to run through this immeasurable number of changes in my imagination ... it follows that it is not the faculty of imagination that gives me my grasp of the wax as flexible and changeable.

A parallel argument shows that it is not imagination that enables my grasp of the wax as extensible. Rather, "the nature of the wax ... is perceived by the mind alone."[4]

It now seems to be presupposed that what was understood with distinctness was the *nature* of the wax.[5] Descartes' description of his procedure for arriving at the nature of the wax – to "take away everything which does not belong to the wax" – seems to introduce further puzzling terminology. What exactly is *taking away*? What is meant by *belonging to*?

Descartes takes himself by now to have shown that the Thought must be wrong. It is noteworthy that whereas we might have expected him to concentrate on showing that that the "puzzling" and insensible "I" is known with more distinctness than corporeal things, what he in fact attempts to show is that something about corporeal things – their *nature* – is known distinctly, but not via the senses or the imagination.

¶13

Here Descartes identifies "ordinary ways of talking" as a prime source of the Thought:

We say that we see the wax itself ... not that we judge it to be there from its colour or shape ... [However,] something which I thought I was seeing with my eyes is in fact grasped solely by the faculty of judgement.

There is something very strange here. On the face of it, nothing Descartes has said so far implies that I do not see the wax, even if it does imply that I do not see the nature of the wax.

¶14

This paragraph seems intended to do battle against the obsessiveness of the Thought. Descartes remarks that seekers after truth who want to "achieve knowledge above the ordinary level should feel ashamed at having taken ordinary ways of talking as a basis for doubt." He attempts to persuade us that "my perception of the wax was more perfect and evident ... now, after a more careful investigation of the nature of the wax and of the means by which it is known," than earlier, when "I believed I knew it by means of my external senses or ... by the power of imagination."

¶15

We might have the impression from the foregoing that Descartes wants to say that the wax is known *as* distinctly as the "I". However, he writes that "Surely my awareness of my own self is not merely much truer and more certain than my awareness of this wax, but also much more distinct and evident." This sentence draws a distinction between "truer and more certain" on the one hand, and "more distinct and evident" on the other, and the remainder of the paragraph attempts to show that my awareness of my own self trumps my awareness of the wax on *both* counts.

The argument for the claim that my awareness of my self is truer and more certain than my awareness of the wax seems to be that while my judgment that this wax *exists* (drawn from the fact that I see it or touch or imagine it) could be mistaken, my making such a judgement entails that "I" certainly exist. So the claim seems to be that the *existence* of my mind is "much truer and more certain" than the *existence* of the wax. This still leaves us with the question of what "much truer and more certain" *means*.

The claim that my awareness of my self is more distinct and evident than my awareness of the wax seems to concern, not the existence, but the nature of my own self and of the wax: "if my perception of the wax seemed more distinct after it was established not just by sight or touch but by many other considerations, it must be admitted that I now know myself even more distinctly." Two reasons seem to be offered in support of this claim. First, "every consideration whatsoever which contributes to my perception of the wax ... cannot but establish even more effectively the nature of my own mind." Second, "there is so much else in the mind itself that can serve to make my knowledge of it more distinct, that it scarcely seems worth going through the contributions made by considering bodily things." Neither of these reasons seems wholly perspicuous, and we again remain in the dark about what exactly is meant by "much more distinct and evident."

¶16

The final paragraph of the Second Meditation sums up the main conclusions: "even bodies are not strictly perceived by the senses or the faculty of imagination but by the intellect alone"; and "I can achieve an easier and more evident perception of my own mind than of anything else." The paragraph also calls on us to continue our meditation to assist us in resisting the "habit of holding on to old opinions" – including, presumably, the Thought.

DEEPER INTO M2

It seems that Descartes has interwoven at least three strands of argument into the second half of M2. Setting these out will allow us to address many of the questions which emerged from our initial analysis. One strand is metapsychological and concerns the scope and roles of the cognitive faculties; a second is broadly metaphysical and has to do with the "nature" of the wax; a third is epistemological (and in part ties the other two strands together), relating to the different senses in which the "I" is "better known" than the wax. Here I attempt to reconstruct these three strands of argument as far as possible.

The cognitive faculties

Part of the Thought is evidently the thesis that the senses and the imagination are our best means of arriving at "distinct understanding."

For Descartes, this thesis involves a misunderstanding of the powers of the cognitive faculties and a related confusion between the imagination and the intellect. Descartes implicitly assumes (a) that the scope of the senses is confined to sensible qualities. He asserts (b) that we can grasp the possibility of "countless mutations" and then argues that the imagination cannot grasp all of these.[6] The claim (b) then implies (by a process of elimination) the claim (c) that the faculty by which we grasp the nature of the wax is the intellect.

The assumption (a) that *what we perceive with the senses are sensible qualities* is required to make sense of some otherwise puzzling moves in the second half of M2.[7] In particular, there is the reflective first sentence of ¶12: "the wax was not after all the sweetness of the honey..." This sentence suggests that implicit in the Thought was the supposition that the wax *is* the sweetness of the honey (along with other sensible qualities). The sentence also suggests that this supposition has been undermined by the considerations of ¶11.

It is far from obvious that the Thought implies that the wax is its sensible qualities, but the conjunction of the Thought – according to which we perceive or understand the wax through the senses – and the assumption that "what we perceive with the senses are sensible qualities" *does* entail that the wax is its sensible qualities. There may appear to be something tautologous in the assumption that what we perceive with the senses are sensible qualities, but it has profound consequences. The conjunction of this assumption with the result that "the wax is not its sensible qualities" implies that we *do not perceive the wax with our senses*. Thus we can make sense of Descartes' apparently unjustified assertion in ¶13 that "something which I thought I was seeing with my eyes is in fact grasped solely by the faculty of judgement."

Descartes just asserts (b) that we can "grasp that the wax is capable of countless mutations" (in ¶11). At this stage, it is unclear whether "countless" simply means "a very great number" or "infinite." If he means "infinite," the assertion is anything but uncontroversial. Think of Gassendi's claim that

the human intellect is not capable of conceiving of infinity ... [I]f someone calls something 'infinite' he attributes to a thing which he does not grasp a label which he does not understand. (*Fifth Objections*, AT 7: 286)

But most would be inclined to accept (b), indeed to deem it obvious, if "countless" simply means "a very great number."

Descartes' principal argument in ¶12 concerns the scope of the faculty of imagination: he argues that the range of changes in shape and size which we understand the wax to be capable of undergoing cannot be encompassed in the imagination. Why? If Descartes takes 'countless' to mean "infinite," the problem arises that it is not obvious that we can grasp infinity via any faculty.[8] It seems more likely, however, that Descartes simply means "a very great number," and a number that the faculty of imagination is not equipped to handle. The crucial point in ¶12 is simply that I "am unable to *run through* this immeasurable number of changes in my imagination" (italics added). We may also note the passage in the Sixth Meditation where Descartes argues that one of "the difference[s] between imagination and pure understanding" is that we cannot imagine a chiliagon – that is, a figure with a thousand (not an infinite number of) sides.[9] There, and arguably here, he is urging a conception of imagination which emphasizes its *limits*: just as the faculty of sense-perception is limited to sensible qualities, the faculty of imagination is confined to things I can "see ... with my mind's eye as if they were present before me" (AT 7: 72). Something like this has already been put forward in the first half of the Second Meditation: "imagination is simply contemplating the shape or image of a corporeal thing" (AT 7: 28). What is present to the mind's eye, like what is present to the physical eye, gets less and less distinct as the number of things before it gets larger.

If we accept that neither the imagination nor the senses can grasp that the wax is capable of countless mutations, and if we allow that there is only one other cognitive faculty in the running, it follows that the faculty that grasps that the wax is capable of countless mutations is the intellect.

The nature of this wax

The dominant meaning of "nature" amongst Descartes' contemporaries was "essence." Descartes often explicitly uses "nature" in this sense (e.g., *Principles* I.53, AT 8A: 25); and indeed the "Synopsis of the Meditations" appears to give us reason to believe that M2 is largely concerned with the essence of the mind and of corporeal things (AT 7: 12–13). But the "I" and "this wax" are individual things (*particularia*), and in the scholastic tradition that the Second Meditation is largely respecting, *particularia* cannot have essences. It is a scholastic axiom that only species or kinds of things have essences.[10] From this perspective, expressions like "the nature of this piece of wax" (or "the nature of this 'I'") would appear to be grammatically ill-formed. And yet Descartes does employ such expressions.[11]

I propose a definition and two principles which might help us here. The definition is this: "the nature of this particular thing" *means* "what 'pertains to' or 'belongs to' this particular thing" (and the task of clarifying what *this* means will occupy the rest of this subsection).[12] This definition can then be linked in turn to the nature or essence of the kind. The first of the two principles is (1) that anything which does not pertain to the particular cannot be part of the nature of the kind. So anything that does not pertain to this wax cannot be part of the nature of corporeal things. The arguments of M2¶¶11–12, as we will see, endeavor to show that no sensible attributes belong to the essence of corporeal things. The second principle is (2) that anything which does pertain to the particular is a mode of an essential attribute of the kind. So anything that pertains to the wax is a mode of the essence of corporeal things. M2¶12 shows, as we will see, that extensibility, flexibility and changeability pertain to the wax, and since these are all manifestly modes of extension, it follows that at least part of the essence of corporeal things is extension.[13]

"What is . . ." questions – for example, "What is this 'I'?" or "What is this wax?" – are, at least sometimes, questions about what pertains to a particular. Not always: such questions sometimes receive answers that specify the kind of thing the particular is (answers such as: "thinking thing," "corporeal thing"). Descartes expends considerable energy on the issue of what kind of thing "this 'I'" is, which he does not do in the case of "this wax." (Perhaps there is no comparable difficulty about the kind to which "this wax" belongs: it is *wax*, which in turn belongs to the more general kind *corporeal thing*.) But "What is this wax?" in M2¶¶11 and 12 is asking, not what kind of thing the wax is, but what belongs to or pertains to it. Descartes argues that no sensible qualities pertain to it, and that extension, flexibility, and changeability [*mutabile*] do pertain to it.[14] The real issue, then, is what is meant by "pertain to" or "belong to." Once we have a handle on the issue we can use the principles just outlined to elicit essences (of kinds) from a consideration of particulars.[15]

There are two obvious interpretations of ¶¶11 and 12 (involving two different conceptions of "subtraction" and hence of "pertaining to"), neither of which is wholly satisfactory. On one interpretation, "subtraction" means "change": Descartes' claim is that whatever cannot *change* while a particular corporeal thing persists pertains to it, and conversely that whatever can change does not really pertain to it; on the second interpretation, "subtraction" means "loss", so here Descartes' claim is that whatever attributes cannot *be lost* while a particular corporeal thing persists pertains to it, and conversely that whatever can be lost does not really pertain to it.

The first ("change") interpretation of the notion of "pertaining to" sees Descartes' reasoning as applied in the first instance in M2¶11 to *determinate* sensible properties. For example, when heated, the wax loses the color white, it ceases to have the texture hard, it loses the smell of honey, etc., and these properties are replaced by other determinates falling under the determinables color, texture, smell, etc. In short, the wax *changes* its color, texture, and smell, but Descartes then draws the conclusion that *determinable* sensible properties do not pertain to the wax. So interpreted, the argument is clearly fallacious; after all, determinables do not change just because their determinates do. It is moreover inconsistent with the thrust of the argument of ¶12: there Descartes concludes that the determinable property (of being extended) does pertain to this wax *even though* determinate shapes, sizes, and motions vary. If this first interpretation is correct, Descartes has no sound argument for claiming that sensible qualities (qua determinates or qua determinables) do not pertain to the wax.

On the second ("subtraction") interpretation of "pertaining to," the argument in ¶11 asserts that what happens when the wax is placed in front of the fire is not that its sensible qualities *change* – that is, not that one determinate taste, smell, color, texture, etc., is replaced by another – but that all its sensible qualities are *lost*.[16] A problem with this interpretation is that ¶12 speaks of the wax as *changing* its determinate shape and size and asserts that when it does so, it assumes a different determinate shape and size. It does not lose the *determinables* shape and size or being extended. The second interpretation does not ascribe to Descartes an obvious non sequitur, but it is similarly strained. It supposes that when the wax becomes tasteless, odorless, and colorless, it loses the determinables taste, odor, and color. That would apparently make the wax imperceptible to the senses after being placed in front of the fire, which it manifestly is not.

I think nonetheless that the second interpretation of 'pertaining to' is closer to being right. It takes Descartes not to be playing fast and loose with the distinction between determinables and determinates.[17] Moreover, a powerful Cartesian argument can be constructed for the view that there *are* corporeal things – even if this wax is not one such – to which sensible qualities (qua determinables) do not pertain, i.e., which possess no sensible qualities whatsoever. For this argument, we would need to have at our disposal a handful of Cartesian positions which go well beyond the meager resources available in M2. The first is that matter is continuously divisible. The second is that there is a mechanical element to sense-perception (*sc.* particles impacting on sense-organs), which together with the first implies that there must be a lower limit to the size of particles that can affect the sense-organs, and also that there are particles below this limit. The third is that something which *cannot* affect sense organs does not possess sensible qualities (even qua determinables). If so, there are corporeal things that fall off all the scales of color, light, taste, texture, etc., which is to say that there are corporeal things to which sensible qualities (qua determinables) do not pertain.[18] We would just be left to wonder why Descartes chose to use the example of the piece of wax in ¶11, rather than an example of an imperceptible particle.

Both of the interpretations under consideration have problems. First, they require us to force the text. Both regard being extended rather than being extensible and flexible and changeable as the determinable which pertains to the wax. Second, when Descartes tells us that the residual taste is *eliminated*, and the smell *goes away*, but the colour *changes*, the first interpretation must read all three locutions as if they refer to change, i.e., the replacement of one determinate by another determinate of the same determinable; the second interpretation must read all three as if they refer to loss of the determinable.[19] A final worry is that ¶¶11 and 12 seem to be not nearly as parallel as either of the two interpretations would suggest. ¶11 is focused on defending the claim that sensible qualities do not pertain to the wax. ¶12 is focused on the very different claim that the determinables being extensible, flexible and changeable cannot be grasped by the imagination.

Nonetheless, we can now see the answer to the question "What is this wax?" – understood as a question about its "nature," i.e., what pertains to it. The wax is an extensible and flexible and changeable thing only, because these are the determinables that cannot be "subtracted" from the wax.

"Better known"

We have seen that the key sentence in ¶15 makes a distinction between "truer and more certain" and "more distinct and evident." Descartes appears to be arguing that the former phrase applies to the respective existences of "this 'I'" and "this wax," the latter to their respective natures. But what exactly is the distinction?

Plausibly, the expression "truer and more certain" alludes to Descartes' (and others') framework of degrees of certainty. It is widely recognized that at the very least Descartes distinguished between "moral certainty" and "metaphysical certainty," though there is little consensus as to how to understand these. "Moral certainty" is sometimes treated in the literature simply as *probability*. The correctness of this identification depends in part on what conception of probability one has in mind, but note that Arnauld and Nicole explicitly distinguish *between* moral certainty and probability, where probability is what the man of good sense must fall back on if moral certainty is unavailable.[20] It seems less misleading to suggest that a morally certain proposition is one which is beyond all *reasonable* doubt.[21] What is *metaphysically certain*, by contrast, cannot *in any way* be open to doubt.[22] One issue is whether we ought to speak of a third level of certainty between moral and metaphysical certainty (perhaps *absolute* certainty). I would urge that we should, by taking note that within Descartes' adaptation of the degrees of certainty framework, there are propositions which can be called into doubt *only* by a "slight and, so to speak, metaphysical … reason for doubt," namely the hypothesis that God does not exist or is a deceiver (The Third Meditation, AT 7: 36).

If we read "truer and more certain" along these lines we would understand Descartes to be asserting that the existence of this "I" has a higher degree of certainty than the existence of this wax. This seems

eminently plausible and ought to be acceptable to anyone who has
followed Descartes in the *Meditations* so far. The existence of corporeal things is not shown until M6, and the proof rests on "knowledge
of myself and the author of my being" (AT 7: 77). The existence of
corporeal things is not metaphysically certain, since it was able to be
called into doubt by the "slight and metaphysical reason for doubt."
The existence of any *particular* corporeal thing (e.g., this wax) has a
yet lower degree of certainty: we can never confirm with more than
moral certainty that our perceptions are veridical in such cases.[23] By
contrast, the certainty of my own existence cannot be called into
doubt even on the hypothesis that God does not exist or is a deceiver.
Thus that I exist could be said to be metaphysically certain.[24]

The phrase "more distinct and evident" appears to invoke the
notions of *clarity* and *distinctness*, at least if we can read "evident"
as "clear."[25] Descartes' definitions of these two terms are well
known and notoriously difficult to apply. A perception is clear
"when it is present and accessible to the attentive mind." It is
distinct when it is, in addition, "so sharply separated from all
other perceptions that it contains within itself only what is clear"
(*Principles* I.45, AT 8A: 21–22).

Descartes' claim in the second half of ¶15 is not that he perceives
the nature of this "I" clearly and distinctly, but that he perceives it
more clearly and distinctly than the nature of this wax.[26] So distinctness is evidently a matter of *degree*; it seems that the more attributes
we know of something, the more distinctly we perceive it. When
Descartes adds (in *Second Replies*) that "no one's knowledge of anything has ever reached the point where he knows that there is absolutely nothing further in the thing beyond what he is already aware
of" (AT 7: 129), he appears to admit that no perception is ever *completely* distinct.

So on what grounds does Descartes claim that I perceive the nature
of the "I" more distinctly than the nature of the wax? The first justification given in ¶15 appears to be echoed in the *Second Replies* and
Fourth Replies discussions where Descartes simply speaks of being
"better known" or more perfectly understood. He writes,

the more attributes of a thing we perceive the better we are said to know it;
thus we know people whom we have lived with for some time better than
those whom we only know by sight, or have merely heard of . . . (AT 7: 129–30)

I have never thought that anything more is required to reveal a [particular] substance than its various attributes; thus the more attributes we know, the more perfectly we understand its nature. Now we can distinguish many different attributes in the wax: one, that it is white; two, that it is hard; three, that it can be melted; and so on. And there are correspondingly many attributes in the mind: one, that it has the power of knowing the whiteness of the wax; two, that it has the power of knowing its hardness; three, that it has the power of knowing that it can lose its hardness (i.e. melt); and so on ... The clear inference from this is that we know more attributes in the case of our mind than we do in the case of anything else. (AT 7: 360)

This last, however, far from being a clear inference, seems to be a blatant non sequitur. How can an exact one-to-one correlation between attributes of the wax and attributes of the mind establish the conclusion that the mind is *better* known than the wax? In the corresponding section of M2¶15 there is no such non sequitur, since Descartes claims that "every consideration ... which contributes to my perception of the wax ... cannot but establish *even more effectively* the nature of my own mind" (italics added). Still, this simply pushes the question back: why "even more effectively"?

We can see in a general way how knowing more attributes of something contributes to its being perceived more distinctly, especially if we bear in mind that "distinct" is contraposed to "confused." If all I know about the wax is that it is white, this does not enable me to distinguish wax from snow (i.e., I might confuse the two), whereas if I know that it is white and hard, this does enable me to make that distinction, although I would need to know yet more to enable me to distinguish it from, say, quartz, and so on. This observation, however, does not help us make sense of the apparent non sequitur or the expression "even more effectively." Nor does it tell us how knowing more attributes contributes to understanding something's *nature* (i.e., in this context, what pertains to it) – and the case is not helped by the fact that several of the attributes of the wax mentioned here are sensible qualities, which, as we know by now, are not part of its nature, i.e., do not pertain to the wax. For everyday purposes we may say that the wax is (now) white, but sensible attributes are no part of its nature.

In M2¶15 Descartes adds the somewhat less problematic consideration that "much else in the mind itself ... can serve to make my knowledge of it more distinct," i.e., not all my thoughts are reflections on corporeal things. Thus I can keep adding to the list without there being a one-to-one correspondence with attributes of corporeal things. This has some plausibility, even if we remain less than entirely clear about what appears to be his favoured argument.

METHODOLOGICAL REFLECTIONS

We should be struck by at least two things from the previous section. First, Descartes does not set out his arguments in geometrical order or *in more geometrico* (*Second Replies*, AT 7: 155–59), and indeed this would have been difficult in the extreme. Insofar as we can reconstruct the arguments, we seem to be required to reach beyond the text of M2 itself, and much that goes on in the text seems to operate subliminally.

Second, the reconstructions simply bypass ¶¶14 and 16 and most of ¶13 as well. This final section of the chapter reflects on what Descartes is doing in the interstices of the arguments sketched in the previous section. I will suggest that much of what goes on in the second half of M2 may be termed *therapeutic*: Descartes is engaged in therapy directed at his readers – especially those readers "who are able and willing to meditate seriously with me" ("Preface to the Reader," AT 7: 9). Such therapy is of necessity preceded by diagnosis. Treatment – corresponding to the two aspects of the faculty of judgment identified in the Fourth Meditation – must be directed both at the intellect, moving the reader toward a recognition that the Thought and its kin are false, and at the will, attempting to combat the obsessiveness or temptation which the Thought retains even after it has been recognized to be false.

Diagnosis

Descartes himself elsewhere identifies four main "causes of error" which may be seen as types of diagnosis.[27] He writes that "The chief cause of error arises from the preconceived opinions of childhood"; the second "is that we cannot forget our preconceived opinions"; the third "is that we become tired if we have to attend to things which are not present to the senses"; the fourth "is that we attach our concepts to words which do not precisely correspond to real things."[28] In the second half of M2, the most obvious diagnostic move occurs in ¶13, which invokes the fourth cause of error. The claim there is that ordinary language conflates, and thus leads *us* to conflate, seeing with judging, as a result of which we ascribe to the eyes what is really the work of the intellect. Are there diagnostic moves in the second half of M2 corresponding to the other three causes of error? Descartes certainly refers to "the habit of hanging on to old opinions" in ¶16, which seems to advert to the second and thereby to the first cause of error. The implication is that the Thought is one of the entrenched "preconceived opinions of childhood," an opinion of which the *Meditations* will work to "free" us ("Synopsis of the *Meditations*," AT 7: 12). The only cause of error not specifically referenced is the third, although Descartes would no doubt expect us to become tired after the non-sensory thinking of the first half of the Meditation, and a colorful piece of wax would be a short-term respite.

Treatment directed at the intellect

One might expect that the best way to persuade the reader that the Thought and other preconceived opinions of childhood are false is to present arguments *in more geometrico*. Descartes evidently thought otherwise (and, I would urge, rightly so). Simply offering demonstrations that the intellect is what is required to grasp the nature of the wax, or that sensory attributes do not pertain to the wax, or that my mind is better known than this wax, would fail to persuade someone who is firmly committed to the Thought and its kin. Such an individual "cannot forget" these, and (Descartes would say) their grasp of the relevant corrective ideas is bound to be obscure or confused. Therapy directed at the intellect must consist in drawing out unnoticed implications of the Thought and enabling the reader to begin to make the distinctions required to perceive more clearly and distinctly. Such therapy *must* begin where the reader is, intellectually, at present; it must proceed gradually, and perhaps even subliminally, at least in part.

The reader is right to think that he perceives something about corporeal things at least relatively distinctly, but he takes it that this is something he grasps with the senses. The reader probably has not thought through what he takes the scope of the various cognitive faculties to be, but he can be persuaded that the Thought commits him to saying that the wax *is* its sensible qualities, which upon reflection he does not want to say.[29] The reader would be thereby presupposing a premise which is not made explicit in M2, namely that what the senses perceive are sensible qualities; he might upon reflection become aware that this premise is presupposed, and it may strike him as obvious once it is made explicit. He can likewise be persuaded that the imagination cannot grasp the countless mutations which he understands the wax to be capable of undergoing, especially if he has accepted the conception of the imagination that is supposed at ¶7. This sets him up to accept that there is something which he can grasp which is understood neither with the senses nor with the imagination.

We might ask at this point why Descartes was so coy about introducing the term "intellect." The intellect is no more than alluded to in ¶10; it appears in ¶12 only in the guise of "the mind alone" or "the understanding or the mind," and in ¶13 as "the faculty of judgement." It is finally outed as the intellect in the final paragraph, ¶16. Surely the answer is that those in the grip of the Thought are inclined to *confuse* the intellect with the imagination. Descartes' reasoning forces the reader to reflect on the powers of the senses and the imagination, and is meant to persuade him to accept Descartes' (highly deflationary, albeit apparently obvious) conceptions of these powers. If the reader accepts these conceptions, and yet takes it that we can indeed grasp that the wax is capable of a very great number of mutations, he is acknowledging that there is a power of the human mind – and 'the intellect' is as good a name as any for that faculty – which is different both from the senses and from the imagination.

The way is then paved to an understanding of the metaphysical notions of *pertaining to, nature,* and *essence.* We asked in the previous section why Descartes chose to use the example of the piece of wax, rather than an imperceptible particle, which would have made a far more cogent case for the claim that there are corporeal things to which sensible qualities do not pertain. The question almost answers itself, however: first Descartes would have had to persuade his reader that there are imperceptible particles, which in turn would have required him to convince the reader that matter is continuously divisible *and* that there is a mechanical element to sense-perception *and* that something which cannot affect the sense-organs does not possess sensible qualities. The reader at this stage in the *Meditations* is not yet ready to accept any of this. We might even suggest that

Descartes' argumentation in the wax discussion is *deliberately* left unclear: as long as the reader accepts that the determinables being extensible, flexible and changeable do pertain to the wax, he may be able to return to the example of the wax (after completing the *Meditations*) and recognize that it doesn't really work for showing that sensible qualities are not part of the essence of corporeal things, without its defects having done any real harm.

Any reader who has followed Descartes thus far is ready to accept that this "I" has a higher degree of certainty than this wax. The "I" is, in this sense, better known. The more difficult claim to accept is that the nature of this "I" is known more distinctly than the nature of this wax, so it is toward this claim that most of ¶15 is directed. Yet what appeared to be Descartes' favored argument was not obviously cogent. I do not have a good explanation or defense of the thinking there. Perhaps he was concerned that by this time his reader would have become tired, attending to things that are not present to the senses.

We can understand why Descartes' treatment can only be effective on those readers "who are able and willing to meditate seriously with me." We can also see why "[p]rotracted and repeated study is required to eradicate the lifelong habit of confusing things related to the intellect with corporeal things, and to replace it with the opposite habit of distinguishing the two" (*Second Replies*, AT 7:131). Descartes hopes that he has helped the reader to register how and why this habit is a bad one.

Treatment directed at the will

The most obvious place at which the second half of M2 aims at treatment directed at the will is in ¶14. The strategy is to instill *shame*, and perhaps involves a correlative attempt to inculcate the right type of pride, where the treatment targets the will in particular just because shame and pride are such powerful motivators.[30] We, who surely want "to achieve knowledge above the ordinary level," ought to "feel *ashamed* at having taken ordinary ways of talking as a basis for doubt." Any doubt that my knowledge of the nature of the wax is "more perfect now" than it was when I was in the grip of the Thought "would clearly be foolish." The remainder of the paragraph, which may seem arbitrarily to bring in a contestable and undefended distinction between animals and humans, may also be seen as part of

124   KATHERINE J. MORRIS

the treatment strategy: we should surely be *ashamed* to content ourselves with a level of distinctness in our perceptions which a (mere) animal could possess. Instead we should strive for the sort of perception which "requires a human mind" and so is worthy of a human being. One might suggest that it is all part of the same strategy that Descartes labels the Thought and other such views as preconceived opinions of childhood: we grown-ups ought to be *ashamed* at having failed to put away our childish things.

The second half of the Second Meditation exemplifies the intertwining of Descartes' metaphysics, epistemology and metapsychology. It illustrates a number of central Cartesian positions, and it also illustrates the reasons for communicating them in the form of Meditations.

NOTES

1. The starting point for this chapter was the chapter on M2 in an as-yet unpublished manuscript written by myself and the late Gordon Baker; I have had to re-think much of that chapter without the benefit of Gordon's illuminating insights. References in the text to paragraph numbers (e.g., ¶ 12) are to paragraphs in M2 unless otherwise specified.

2. Note that in this chapter I am using the term 'attribute' in the way that Descartes uses it in the *Meditations* and *Replies*, to refer more broadly to a property or feature of a substance. See for example *Second Replies*, AT 7: 161. Descartes unpacks a more technical understanding of 'attribute' in *Principles* I.53–62.

3. But we might keep in mind the question: does the Thought really entail that the wax *is* its sensible qualities?

4. That is, it is perceived by the mind insofar as the mind is not considered in its union with the body. Since the faculties of sense-perception and imagination depend on that union, the phrase 'the mind alone' seems to be referring to the intellect.

5. Descartes also uses the phrase "what the wax consists in" (for example at the end of ¶ 12).

6. It is presumably obvious that the senses cannot either.

7. That Descartes subscribes to (a) is evident from elsewhere, e.g., *Principles* IV.190–95.

8. There is little doubt that in the end Descartes supposes that the wax *is* capable of an infinite number of mutations; this presupposes the axiom that modes of extension are all continuous quantities (for example the Fifth Meditation, AT 7: 63). A line is by its essence infinitely divisible and

infinitely extensible; and between any two numbers there are other numbers; and given any number there is a bigger one. So too the wax is capable of taking on an infinite number of shapes. But this is not the issue in M2.

9. AT 7: 73. Descartes says here that the figure I imagine is simply a "confused representation of some figure" which "differs in no way from the presentation I should form if I were thinking of a myriagon, or any figure with very many sides" (AT 7: 72).

10. Even if it is not always made explicit, the acceptance of this axiom is shown in scholastic discussions of essence, e.g., Suarez (1998 [1597], 44), who always refers to "the essence of man," not of this or that man.

11. For example in M2¶¶ 12 and 15.

12. CSM's occasional translations of *pertinere* as "to belong to" or "to be relevant to" (likewise *removeo* as "to take away") disguise the fact that these are technical terms.

13. The principle that every substance has just one essential attribute is then needed to rule out there being something else which belongs to the essence of corporeal things.

14. I take it to be obvious, or as meant to be obvious, that these aren't sensible qualities.

15. This process is not to be confused with the process of concept-formation called `abstraction' that is attractive to empiricists. Gassendi conflates the two things (*Fourth Objections*, AT 7: 271–72), and Descartes objects to his account (*Fourth Replies*, AT 7: 359).

16. Note that subtraction is not supposed to strip a particular corporeal thing of all its attributes, thereby yielding a property-less substance ('prime matter' in scholastic terminology, or 'a something I know not what' in Locke's ironic phraseology). This is an interpretation that Gassendi wrongly puts on M2¶11 (*Fifth Objections*, AT 7: 271). Rather Descartes makes a distinction between properties that do pertain to this wax and properties which do not.

17. That he should muddle these up seems altogether implausible in view of the prominence in scholastic thinking of the contrast between potentiality and actuality (of which the determinate/determinable distinction might be seen as a special case).

18. See also *Principles* IV.201, AT 8A: 324–25.

19. And it must also read ¶ 11's "the shape is lost" in the opposite way, as suggesting that the shape *changes*.

20. Arnauld and Nicole 1996 (1683), 264, 270.

21. Or "having sufficient certainty for application to everyday life" (*Principles* IV.204-5, AT 8A: 327–28) as, for example, the proposition that Rome is a town in Italy.

22. For example *Principles* IV.206, AT 8A: 328–29.
23. The Sixth Meditation, AT 7: 82–90; *Discourse* IV, AT 6: 37–38.
24. This is a controversial claim and would take some argument to reconcile with M3¶4 (AT 7: 35–36); I am prepared to offer such arguments, but to do so would take us too far afield in the present context.
25. And the French version provides some justification for this.
26. This passage from ¶15 confuses things, however: the perception I have of the nature of the wax "can be imperfect and confused, as it was before, or clear and distinct as it is now, depending on how carefully I concentrate on what the wax consists in." Perhaps we can read this as only claiming clarity (a necessary but not a sufficient condition for distinctness), inasmuch as it is clarity which is associated with "attention" or "concentration"; or perhaps "clear and distinct" merely means "more clear and distinct than it was before."
27. *Principles* I.70, AT 8A: 34–35. Descartes' most specific target here is the judgment that we "perceive colors in objects." This judgment bears a family resemblance to the Thought.
28. *Principles* I.71–74, AT 8A: 35–38.
29. No doubt the reader has been reared on a one-sided diet of examples of corporeal things, e.g., a stone whose sensory qualities are relatively stable. Descartes shakes him up with an example of something which no one could deny is a corporeal thing, but whose sensory qualities are markedly volatile. This is a thing that is less plausibly *defined* by its sensory qualities.
30. See also *Passions* III.204–6, AT 11: 482–83.

6 The Third Meditation: causal arguments for God's existence

INTRODUCTION

It is often thought that Descartes' epistemic project in the *Meditations* falls apart in the Third Meditation. Although some readers recoil at the method of universal doubt, which is the hallmark of the First Meditation, if one is a foundationalist about knowledge, it is at least plausible to begin from a clean slate by doubting all of one's former beliefs. Assuming one approves of Descartes' method, one also finds the main insights of the Second Meditation to be compelling. I cannot doubt that I exist, nor that I am a thinking thing. But readers report that after that concession their reserves of charity run dry. By the end of the Third Meditation no one remains on board with Descartes' project. The problem lies with his efforts to prove God's existence by invoking scholastic and Platonic principles. In the Third Meditation, he famously presents two causal (or cosmological) arguments that rely on antiquated doctrines about degrees of reality and different kinds of being, and bizarre principles of causality – none of which seem "evident by the natural light." Descartes claims to be leaving the past behind, to be an innovator using only the resources of his own mind to determine what can be discovered about the nature of reality, but what he presents in the Third Meditation leaves a startlingly different impression. Ironically, his arguments failed to convince even those readers sympathetic with scholasticism, such as Johannes Caterus, who expresses deep reservations in the *First Objections* (AT 7: 92–95). If Descartes' arguments fell flat with his contemporaries, they are received with even greater aversion today. One influential philosopher has quipped that the causal proofs appear to have come from Mars![1]

Given this reception, trying to change readers' perceptions of the causal arguments is a tall order, but that is exactly what I hope to do in this chapter. In the next section, I begin by reconstructing a simplified version of the first causal argument. The aim of this reconstruction is to show that – at its core – Descartes' proof is simple, elegant, and fairly plausible, at least as compared to other arguments of its kind. The core argument eludes most of the objections that have been leveled against the more complex, "scholastic" version, but it also raises an important interpretive question: why does Descartes present the latter if he has the resources for a simpler and less contentious demonstration? On pages 135–40, I attempt to answer this question. On pages 140–44, I take up the second causal argument in order to show that it too can be formulated in simple terms. I also explain the sense in which the arguments are "reducible to one" and how God can be the cause of himself.

THE FIRST CAUSAL ARGUMENT

The "core" argument

A simplified version of Descartes' first causal argument can be formulated as follows:

(1) I have an idea that represents an actually infinite being having all perfections.
(2) Everything that exists has a cause of its existence.
(3) The only possible cause of this idea is an actually infinite being.
(4) Therefore, an actually infinite being exists.[2]

To determine whether this core argument succeeds, let us take each of the premises in turn. Like all causal arguments, Descartes' first effort starts from some known effect and then posits God as its only possible cause. Traditional cosmological arguments, such as those found among Aquinas' Five Ways, often take as their premise the existence of the universe or something else known through the senses. But the epistemic status of Descartes' meditator is highly constrained. At the beginning of the Third Meditation, the hyperbolic doubts of the First Meditation have not been discharged and if the reader is meditating faithfully he must not affirm anything that admits of even the slightest doubt. Among other things, he is doubting the existence of physical objects and treating the reports of his senses as if they were false.[3] However, in the Second Meditation he discovered that he exists and is a thinking thing. He can be certain of these two propositions at least as long as he is attending to them. As a thinking thing, the meditator can also be certain that he has ideas, among them the idea of God. The objects of his ideas are subject to doubt, but the meditator cannot doubt that he has these ideas or that they have the content that they do. The immediate deliverances of consciousness are indubitable. Thus, Descartes' first causal argument starts from the meditator's idea of God and the second from his existence as a thinking thing, which possesses that idea.

Early in the Third Meditation Descartes attempts to classify his ideas based on their causal origin into three mutually exclusive and jointly exhaustive categories: innate, adventitious, and invented. The hope is that this taxonomy might enable him to determine whether anything exists outside him, but Descartes acknowledges very quickly that he does not yet have a means for classifying his ideas into one category or another. This effort may seem like a false start, but in fact it helps direct the meditator's attention to an important distinction that is crucial to both causal arguments, namely, the one between innate and invented ideas, the latter being ideas for which the meditator is causally responsible. The first causal argument is as much a proof that the idea of God is innate as it is a demonstration of God's existence. We infer that God exists *as* the cause of our idea of him – "the mark of the craftsman stamped on his work" (AT 7: 51). The argument also hinges on the claim that the idea of God is unique. The meditator can be the cause of his ideas of all other things, such as those of other people, animals, angels, and of course fictitious beings. This is not to say the meditator *is* the cause of all those ideas. On the contrary, Descartes ultimately affirms that the idea of oneself as a thinking thing is also innate. But since the ideas of all things other than God are of finite substances, and the meditator is a finite substance, he could be their cause. What is special about the idea of God, according to Descartes, is that *it represents an actually infinite being.*[4] His strategy is to argue that because this idea represents something actually infinite, and because it is unique in this regard, the meditator cannot be its cause. The meditator forms new ideas by drawing upon other ideas at his disposal, but since the idea of God is unique, there is no other idea upon which to draw.

Descartes' first premise is a powerful one, which it must be since he aims to prove both that God exists *and* that he has all of the perfections that Christian theologians have traditionally assigned to him. Descartes takes that to be one of the advantages of his causal argument over previous versions, which fail to deliver on the divine nature.[5] I am not going to argue that this premise is unassailable, only that one can appreciate why he thinks he is entitled to it given the nature of his project and given what the meditator has discovered so far. Contemporary readers often object to the version of the proof that he presents in the Third Meditation on the grounds that it is too scholastic. But there is nothing especially scholastic about the first premise. In fact, it deviates from at least one important tradition among medieval philosophers of denying that we can have positive knowledge of God's essence.[6] We can know God only negatively (Pseudo-Dionysius *et al.*), as the cause of creaturely attributes (Maimonides), or by analogy (Aquinas). Contrary to these philosophers, Descartes affirms that we can have a clear and distinct idea of God's essence.

Given this medieval tradition, Descartes anticipates that some readers will object to the claim that we, with our finite intellects, can *understand* an actually infinite being. To respond, he draws a distinction between knowing and grasping: I can know *that* God is infinite even though I do not grasp all of his properties nor fully understand what it means to be infinite.[7] A deeper objection would be to deny that one even has an idea of God, or at least the idea that Descartes purports to have. This is the tack taken by some of his contemporaries, such as Hobbes, though his version of the objection assumes that ideas are corporeal images – a claim that Descartes vehemently rejects.[8] A more charitable critic might grant that ideas are modifications of the mind, regarded as a thinking, non-corporeal thing, but still object that we do not have one that represents an actually infinite being. Descartes acknowledges that, if true, this criticism would be devastating:

But if no such idea is to be found in me, I shall have no argument to convince me of the existence of anything apart from myself. For despite a most careful and comprehensive survey, this is the only argument I have so far been able to find. (Third Meditation, AT 7: 42)

Both versions of the causal argument – and, for that matter, the ontological argument of the Fifth Meditation – depend on the claim that we
have an idea of God. In some contexts, especially when responding to
critics, Descartes takes it as obvious that we have such an idea and
accuses those who deny it of being lazy, stubborn, and/or weak-
minded.[9] Anyone who uses the word "God" in a sentence and understands what they are saying has an idea of such a being.[10] But in other
contexts, Descartes allows that even readers who are meditating faithfully may have trouble discovering their innate idea of God. Indeed, he
tells one of his correspondents that some readers may not discover this
idea even after reading the *Meditations* a thousand times.[11] Descartes
has a philosophical explanation for this, but we must look outside the
Meditations proper to find it.

It is sometimes said that Descartes has a dispositional theory of
innate ideas: to say that an idea is innate does not entail that it is
always consciously present. Rather, "we simply mean that we have
within ourselves the faculty of summoning up the idea" (AT 7:189).[12]
Descartes maintains that our innate ideas often need to be triggered
or "awakened," to use the Platonic language that he sometimes
encourages.[13] In other places, he suggests that our inability to perceive one of our ideas is the result of philosophical prejudice ingrained
by habit, especially the tendency to conceive of things using sensory
images.[14] He recognizes, therefore, that it is incumbent upon him to
play the role of the Socratic midwife, massaging the intellect of his
meditator in order to dispel these prejudices and induce the proper
ideas. Some commentators hold that Descartes must *argue* for the
claim that we have an idea of God, but this denies his commitment to
the doctrine of innate ideas. If the idea of God is innate, Descartes'
task is simply to help the meditator become aware of it, so that she
can discover its contents.[15]

In the Third Meditation, Descartes attempts to do this by addressing a potential objection to the first causal argument. A meditator
might suspect that he could form the idea of an actually infinite being
by negating the idea of himself as finite. If that were true, then there
would be no need to posit God as the cause of the former. But
Descartes wants the meditator to notice that the idea of God as
actually infinite is *prior to* the perception of the finite. "For how
could I understand that I doubted or desired – that is, lacked something – and that I was not wholly perfect, unless there were in me

some idea of a more perfect being which enabled me to recognize my own defects by comparison?" (AT 7: 45–46). In *Fifth Replies*, he puts the point somewhat differently: we do not form an idea of the infinite by negating the finite; on the contrary, we conceive of the finite by limiting the infinite, for "all limitation implies a negation of the infinite" (AT 7: 365). One might be tempted to read Descartes as saying that we conceive of the finite *through* the infinite, but that would put him very close to Spinoza and encourage the suggestion that there is only one substance, which he abhors. It would also make the idea of God temporally prior to, or at least contemporaneous with, the idea of oneself as finite, but in the *Meditations* the latter is discovered first. Descartes' claim is the more minimal one that the idea of oneself naturally recalls the idea of God. The idea of myself as finite, imperfect, and dependent triggers the idea of something infinite, perfect, and independent. As we shall see below, this is not Descartes' only means for awakening the meditator's idea of God, but it is the main one. Its success depends of course on whether we have the innate idea Descartes says we have.

(2) Everything that exists has a cause of its existence.

The second premise of the argument is a statement of the general causal principle, *ex nihilo, nihil fit*, which has a long pedigree in philosophy.[16] Unlike the other causal principles employed in the Third Meditation, the *ex nihilo* principle does not make any assumptions about degrees of reality or different kinds of being. For that reason, it does not state that everything has a *sufficient* cause, only that it has *some* cause. Every major early modern rationalist (and even some empiricists like Locke) accepts this general principle, as does Aristotle and his scholastic followers. So from the perspective of these traditions at least, this second premise is unobjectionable.[17] Descartes is also not violating the strictures of his own method of doubt, for the meditator has already discovered that there are some very simple and self-evident truths – such as the fact that he exists, $3 + 2 = 5$, etc. – which cannot be doubted while one is presently attending to them. Descartes takes the *ex nihilo* principle to be among these truths.

(3) The only possible cause of this idea is an actually infinite being.

For the purpose of appreciating the simplicity of the core argument, this premise is key. As noted above, Descartes asks the meditator to take stock of his ideas and to notice an important difference between the idea of God and the ideas of all finite substances, namely, he could be the cause of the latter. These other ideas can be constructed by borrowing elements from the idea he has of himself or, in the case of ideas of angels, by borrowing elements from the idea of himself and the idea of God, since the idea of an angel represents a substance more perfect than himself but less perfect than God.[18] Later in the Third Meditation, Descartes recognizes that even the clear and distinct elements in his ideas of corporeal things, such as extension, shape, position, and motion, could be derived from the idea he has of himself. These elements are not part of that idea of a thinking thing, but since they are merely modes of a finite substance and he is a finite substance, he could be their cause (AT 7: 45).

In drawing our attention to this contrast between the idea of God and the ideas of all other things, Descartes is appealing to an intuitive account of how invented ideas are formed: one takes other ideas – or their elements – and combines them in novel ways.[19] Of course, an empiricist might object that the idea of God is formed in the same way.[20] Descartes attempts to block this objection by prompting the meditator's awareness that the idea of an actually infinite being is unique. If that is right, then the meditator could not have borrowed the content of this idea from any other source, and thus the idea could only come from something outside of him! This is why Descartes reserves the term "infinite" for God, and applies the term 'indefinite' to the divisions of matter, the vastness of the extended universe, and other things that we might be inclined to call "infinite."[21] Still, even if the idea of God is singular in this way, one might envisage another way to construct it using only the resources of one's own mind.[22] I might notice that I, like the supremely perfect being depicted in my idea, am a thinking thing. My knowledge is finite and imperfect by comparison, but it seems to increase gradually. Perhaps it could be increased to infinity, at least conceptually. So what is the meditator supposedly doing? He is taking an element in his idea of himself as a finite being, such as knowledge or power, and augmenting or enlarging it. To construct an idea of God by this means, one would have to follow the same procedure for each of the perfections that is finitely instantiated in oneself – power, goodness, duration, etc. – and then compound the products of that process. But Descartes wants the meditator to discern that the first task is impossible. The idea of divine knowledge is of something *actually* infinite, that is, a *completed infinity*. But the idea produced by augmenting the idea of finite knowledge would be only of a *potential infinity*. One cannot form an idea of actual infinity by endlessly augmenting the idea of something finite, any more than one can produce an infinite number by endlessly adding finite numbers.[23] Speaking in the Third Meditation of this proposed method for constructing an idea of God, Descartes writes:

But all this is impossible. First, though it is true that there is a gradual increase in my knowledge, and that I have many potentialities which are not yet actual, this is all quite irrelevant to the idea of God, which contains absolutely nothing that is potential; indeed, this gradual increase in knowledge is itself the surest sign of imperfection. What is more, even if my knowledge always increases more and more, I recognize that it will never actually be infinite, since it will never reach the point where it is not capable of a further increase; God, on the other hand, I take to be actually infinite, so that nothing can be added to his perfection. (AT 7: 47)

It will not help to object, as some of Descartes' contemporaries do, that one might have derived the idea of God from one's family or associates, reading books, etc., for this only pushes the problem back a step. Descartes can extrapolate from his own case that no finite being could form the idea of actually infinite knowledge or omniscience, etc., by augmenting the ideas of finite attributes.[24] Earlier we noted that Descartes takes the idea of God to be conceptually prior to the idea the meditator has of himself. One might add that the idea of actual infinity is also prior to the idea of potential infinity. One sees that the product formed by endlessly augmenting the idea of finite knowledge is incomplete only because one has a prior idea of the completed infinity that is God.[25] In addition to showing why he could not be the cause of his idea of God, this exercise illustrates again that the meditator has such an idea, thus bolstering Descartes' efforts to motivate the first premise of the argument.[26]

Apart from the conclusion, which follows validly from the premises, this completes the simple version of the causal argument. To summarize briefly in a way that emphasizes its strength, the argument depends on one's having attained an idea of God as actually infinite, a very general and intuitively plausible causal principle, and a simple cognitive exercise that shows that one could not be the cause of said idea. Again, there is no appeal to bizarre principles of causality or to antiquated doctrines about degrees of reality and different types of being. To be sure, the theistic proof that Descartes presents in the Third Meditation relies on such principles and doctrines, but the point of this reconstruction has been to demonstrate that he does not need them. He has the resources for a more compelling argument that puts his scholastic predecessors to shame, both for its simplicity and because it delivers on the nature of God in a way that they cannot.

The Scholastic Version of the Argument

The simplified version of the first causal argument is unlikely to persuade most readers today, but it is clearly superior to the elaborate, scholastic version that Descartes presents in the Third Meditation. So why then does he present the latter? One general suggestion is that cosmological arguments were the stock and trade of scholasticism and Descartes saw himself as writing for an audience steeped in that tradition, and so employs principles and doctrines that strike us as wildly improbable but which he could reasonably expect would resonate with his seventeenth-century readers. This is certainly part of the story, but there is a deeper explanation.

In the previous section, I noted that Descartes maintains that philosophical prejudices – formed in childhood and ingrained by long habit – constitute one of the main obstacles to discovering one's innate idea of God as an actually infinite being.[27] As he reveals in the *Second Replies*, the philosophical prejudices in question pertain to the habit of conceiving of everything in corporeal terms, including immaterial beings such as the soul and God. If one is regarding God as a corporeal being, then one is thinking of him as finite and corruptible rather than as infinite and supremely perfect, as required by the causal arguments.[28] The controversial doctrines that Descartes marshals in order to formulate the first causal argument are designed to dispel these prejudices or, short of that, to exploit them in such a way that the meditator will nevertheless be persuaded that God exists.

Let us turn now to some of these doctrines that readers have found so puzzling. I will not attempt to formulate the more complex version of the first causal argument, which has been treated at length by others. Instead, I will focus on explaining how these doctrines of old are designed to dislodge prejudice, exploit the meditator's tendency to conceive of everything in corporeal or sensory terms, and induce his innate idea of God. Where possible, I will also indicate how, in Descartes' hands, these doctrines are more innocuous than they seem.

Perhaps the most important bit of metaphysical machinery that Descartes invokes is that being is scaled or admits of degrees. This doctrine is sometimes known as "the great chain of being" and has its roots in Plato's and Aristotle's philosophies. Medieval proponents of this doctrine countenanced a continuous scale of being from inanimate objects all the way up to God, with plants, animals, humans, and angels falling in between. These days, philosophers have little sympathy for the claim that reality is scaled. One tends to regard existence in simpler terms: either something exists or it does not. Descartes' view is closer to ours than it might seem, for his version of the scale contains only three distinct levels. From greatest to least, they are 1) God or infinite substance, 2) finite substances (i.e., created minds and bodies), and 3) modes. This shows that Descartes is not simply taking over doctrines from the scholastics but adapting them for his own purposes and, in this case, conforming them to his substance-mode ontology. He enlists the traditional hierarchy – which plays no other role in his philosophy – merely as an instrument for achieving three specific goals relating to the causal arguments. First, it highlights that the proper conception of God involves regarding him as *actually infinite*. As noted above, the natural tendency to conceive of everything in corporeal terms makes it difficult to regard him in this way. Using terms that he believes the meditator accepts, Descartes illustrates that corporeal beings occupy a much lower place in the conceptual order than God does. Second, the first causal argument hinges on the claim that the idea of an actually infinite being is unique, a point that is reflected in the structure of the scale. In fact, because his scale is discontinuous he is able to stress that God is *sui generis*.

Third, the scale of being underscores Descartes' strategy of argument. Notice that on his three-point division, degrees of reality are a function of differences in ontological independence.[29] God or infinite substance occupies the highest end of the scale (i.e., is said to have the greatest degree of reality) because he does not depend on anything for his existence. Finite substances are one step lower because they do not depend on anything except God for their existence, and modes – because they depend in turn on finite substances – constitute the lowest end of the scale. As Descartes writes, "a substance is more of a thing than a mode ... and ... if there is an infinite and *independent* substance, it is more of a thing than a finite and *dependent* substance" (*Third Replies*, AT 7:185, emphasis added). The salient contrast is between finite and infinite substance. The relevance of this contrast to Descartes' strategy is clearest in the second causal argument, where I am supposed to observe that as a finite being, I *depend* for my existence on something else and therefore could not be the cause of myself. Moreover, my ultimate cause must be something that is ontologically *independent*. Commentators sometimes complain that modes depend on finite substances in a different way than the latter depend on God, thus upsetting the symmetry of the scale.[30] Granted, but that only shows that from within Descartes' strict metaphysics the scale of being is an artificial construct; again, he is using it in the context of the causal arguments merely as a means to an end.

Another claim that readers of the Third Meditation often find perplexing is that ideas enjoy two types of being, formal and objective. These terms and the distinction itself are owed to scholasticism, as Descartes acknowledges in the French edition of the *Meditations*, where he speaks of "what the philosophers call" formal and objective reality (AT 9: 32). These notions are not as controversial as they once seemed, for commentators have come to see that "formal reality" is actual existence. "Objective reality," by contrast, is the type of being that an idea has in virtue of its representational content and so is often referred to as "representational reality." Descartes adopts this distinction in order to direct the meditator's attention toward the representational character of ideas and away from their status as modes of mind. Only then will she be able to see that the idea of God is of something actually infinite and thus requires a cause other than the meditator. Considered merely as modes, all ideas are caused by the mind itself, of which they are modes, but given their representational character, they might require external causes.[31] Given his empiricist tendencies, the meditator is likely to think that he caused his idea of God and, indeed, all ideas not deriving from the senses. The distinction between formal and objective reality thus plays a vital role in Descartes' argumentative strategy, which is to show that the meditator cannot be the cause of this one very unique idea.

Without question, the most controversial aspect of Descartes' discussion in the Third Meditation is his appeal to two causal adequacy principles that are put forth as variations on the *ex nihilo* principle. Let us refer to the first of these as the formal reality principle (FRP): everything that exists must have a cause for its existence with at least as much formal reality. Let us refer to the second as the objective reality principle (ORP): the objective reality of an idea must have a cause with at least as much formal reality as the idea has objectively. What is interesting about these principles for our purposes is the way in which Descartes tries to persuade us of their truth. In some places, he derives them from one version of the *ex nihilo* principle together with the implicit assumption that reality is scaled.[32] In other places, however, he treats them as basic or primitive truths[33] and, given the meditator's penchant for conceiving of things in sensory terms, tries to persuade us of their intuitive force by appealing to empirical examples. I shall focus on the latter.

Before discussing any of these examples, it is instructive to consider Descartes' famous comparison in the Third Meditation between ideas and images or pictures: ideas are "as it were the images of things" (*tanquam rerum imagines*) (AT 7: 37). This is important because only a few pages later he attempts to motivate the ORP by using the same analogy: "ideas are in me like <pictures, or> images which can easily fall short of the perfection of the things from which they are taken, but which cannot contain anything greater or more perfect" (AT 7: 42). Pictures of course are perceived through the senses, and it is in this general context that Descartes uses empirical analogies, such as the analogy of heat, to convince us of his two additional causal principles.

Heat cannot be produced in an object which was not previously hot, except by something of at least the same order <degree or kind> of perfection as heat ... But it is also true that the *idea* of heat ... cannot exist in me unless it is put there by some cause which contains at least as much reality as I conceive to be in the heat. (AT 7: 41)[34]

The heat example is invoked here to motivate first the FRP and then the ORP. Although Descartes uses examples of this kind to help meditators mired in the senses, doing so is not without risks. As noted on page 130, some of Descartes' contemporaries took his analogy between ideas and images too literally and concluded that ideas are corporeal. Others, including some recent commentators, have taken the analogy with heat as indicating a commitment to a causal likeness or so-called "heirloom" principle, according to which any property in the effect must be in the cause.[35] The latter claim is clearly belied by Descartes' view that even as a purely thinking thing, he could be the cause of his ideas of corporeal things such as shape and motion.[36] The two causal adequacy principles require only that the cause have the proper *degree* of formal reality, not that it be like the effect in any other respect. So why take these risks? Descartes may have thought that such misunderstandings were unavoidable and, in any case, that they were risks worth taking to help persuade a confused meditator who might otherwise be unreachable.

Before closing this section, let us examine one last attempt to motivate the ORP that often goes unnoticed, but which brings the discussion in the Third Meditation full circle. Having attained certainty about his own existence in the Second Meditation, Descartes' general aim in the Third is to determine whether anything outside of him exists. He notes at the beginning of this text, just after introducing the threefold classification of ideas, that in everyday life the most common judgments we make about external objects are formed on the basis of our sensory ideas. We judge that physical objects cause these ideas and that the latter "resemble" them. Descartes then argues that while such judgments *seem* to be taught by nature, they are in fact based on "blind impulse" and therefore should not be trusted (AT 7: 38–40). In at least two passages outside the *Meditations* proper, however, he indicates that we *can* justify such judgments based on the ORP. For example, in the *Second Replies* he writes: "[The ORP] is the sole basis for all the beliefs we have ever had about the existence of things located outside our mind. For what could ever have led us to suspect that such things exist if not the simple fact that ideas of these things reach our mind by means of the senses?" (AT 7: 135, cf. AT 7: 165). Descartes' primary aim in this passage, however, is not to justify our everyday judgments of sense, but to motivate the ORP itself. He is arguing that we *ought* to be committed to this principle given how entrenched such judgments are for us. Here again, he is appealing to ordinary sense experience to motivate his causal principles. The fact that they *can* be motivated in this way is likely one reason he employs them in the context of the *Meditations*, given the epistemic status of the meditator.

THE SECOND CAUSAL ARGUMENT

One of the controversies concerning Descartes' causal arguments is whether in fact there are two distinct arguments or whether the second is merely an extension of, or a variation on, the first. If Descartes' presentation in the Third Meditation is any indication, there certainly seem to be two distinct proofs, the first from the idea of God and the second from the existence of the meditator qua thinking thing. But in a letter to Mesland, he writes:

It does not make much difference whether my second proof ... is regarded as different from the first proof, or merely as an explanation of it ... Nevertheless, it seems to me that all these proofs based on [God's] effects are reducible to a single one ... ("To [Mesland], 2 May 1644," AT 4: 112)[37]

We can regard them as distinct arguments since there are differences between them, but they are reducible to one in that they have the same structure: they both depend on the *ex nihilo* principle and the idea of God. In keeping with the latter, Descartes consistently describes the second argument as an attempt to demonstrate God's existence "from the fact that we, who possess the idea of God, exist" (*Second Replies*, AT 7:168).[38] As we shall see below, the arguments also deploy the same strategy, namely to show that the proposed "effect" in each argument cannot be caused by the meditator.

   Given the close relation between the two proofs, why does Descartes find it necessary to introduce a second one? In the *First Replies*, he addresses this issue explicitly in the context of comparing the idea of God to the idea of a highly intricate machine (another sensory analogy). The point of the analogy is that the idea of God, as rich in perfection as it is, requires a sufficient cause as much as the idea of a highly intricate machine. But he also draws our attention to an important *dis*analogy between these two ideas: it is easier to grasp that the idea of an intricate machine requires an external cause because few of us have the necessary expertise in mechanics to produce such an idea ourselves. But "because the idea of God is implanted in the same way in the minds of all, we do not notice it coming into our minds from any external source, and so we suppose it belongs to the nature of our own intellect" (*First Replies*, AT 7: 105–106). Descartes' claim is that since the idea of God is innate, everyone possesses it and is thus more likely to take his own mind to be its source.[39] Ironically, the very fact that the idea of God is innate provides a reason for doubting that God caused it![40] Descartes responds by arguing that even if this reason for doubt proved to be justified, the mind that possesses the idea would still require a cause that was actually infinite.

Like the first causal argument, the second can be formulated without invoking any of the controversial causal principles that have come to be associated with both arguments, as follows:

(1) I exist as a thinking thing that has an idea of an actually infinite being having all perfections.
(2) Everything that exists has a cause of its existence.
(3) The only possible cause of my existence is an actually infinite being having all perfections.
(4) Therefore, an actually infinite being (i.e., God) exists.

The first premise is just a statement of the *cogito*, combined with a report on one of the meditator's ideas. The second is the general causal (*ex nihilo*) principle previously discussed. As with the first causal demonstration, the linchpin of the argument is the third premise. In this instance, Descartes employs three different sub-arguments to persuade the reader of its truth. He varies these sub-arguments to answer potential objections and to aid meditators who are having trouble grasping the truth of premise (3). The general strategy of each of them is to argue that if the meditator were self-caused then he would be God. Self-causation sounds absurd, for when one says that "x causes y" part of what one means ordinarily is that (a) x is distinct from y and (b) x is prior to y. But a thing cannot be distinct from, or prior to, itself.[41] At the end of this section we shall discuss how Descartes escapes these difficulties. He recognizes of course that there are possible causes of his existence other than himself and God. Indeed, in the Third Meditation he presents the second causal proof as an argument from elimination and enumerates several possible causes – God, oneself, one's parents, or "some other beings less perfect than God" (AT 7: 48). However, Descartes focuses on eliminating the possibility that he is self-caused for two reasons. First, once the argument is complete, he can use this point to show that unlike himself, God *is* self-caused in an important sense. Second, by eliminating the possibility that I am self-caused, I can summarily rule out that I was caused by any being less perfect than God. This too is similar to the procedure of the first causal argument, where, as we observed, Descartes argues that if I cannot cause my idea of God then nor can any other finite being.

Given space constraints and in the interests of highlighting the simplicity of Descartes' causal arguments, I shall focus on the first of Descartes' three sub-arguments for premise (3) and only sketch the second. The first might be called the "argument from omnipotence":

   (i)   If I had the power to cause my existence *ex nihilo* then I would be omnipotent.
   (ii) I am not omnipotent.
   (iii) Therefore, I do not have the power to cause my existence *ex nihilo*.
   (iv) By parity of reasoning, no other finite being could cause me either.
   (v)   Therefore, the only possible cause of my existence is an actually infinite being having all perfections, including omnipotence.[42]

The crucial premise is clearly the first, the point of which is that if I caused my own existence then I would in effect be God. As for (ii), Descartes asserts quite plausibly that he, as a finite thinking thing, is imperfect in various ways. He knows, for example, that he lacks omniscience from the fact that he doubts certain things. Similarly, he knows that he lacks omnipotence from the fact that he desires things that are beyond his grasp.[43] Premise (iv) is an instance of the argumentative strategy noted above that runs through all three sub-proofs. Any finite being, in virtue of being finite, is going to lack omnipotence. The final conclusion in step (v) appeals implicitly to one's idea of God as a being having all perfections, including omnipotence. This idea is mentioned in the first premise of the main argument. Here, one might complain that the conclusion is too strong, given the premises, for what if my creator has omnipotence but no other perfection? Descartes anticipates this type of objection in the Third Meditation and replies by stressing that among all of the attributes that we find contained in the idea of God, unity or simplicity "is one of the most important" (AT 7: 50). So a being that has one perfection has them all.

In the *First Replies*, Descartes claims that the second causal argument bypasses a difficulty that besets scholastic versions of the cosmological argument: why not suppose that the meditator, rather than being created by God, is part of a chain of finite causes that extends back infinitely? The scholastics often responded that an infinite regress is inconceivable and therefore impossible.[44] They then posited God as the "First Cause" – i.e., the uncaused cause or, in Aristotle's memorable phrase, the unmoved mover. Descartes agrees that a regress is "beyond my grasp," but he does not think it follows from this limitation of his intellect that a regress is impossible (*Second Replies*, AT 7: 106). On the contrary, some regresses actually occur: e.g., matter is divided indefinitely and the universe is indefinitely extended. So, on his view, the regress objection is fatal to traditional versions of the cosmological argument. The scholastics have no way of ruling out the possibility that the universe is the product of an infinite series of finite causes, and positing God as the First Cause begs the question. Descartes develops a second subargument to show how his version of the second causal argument bypasses this objection. Descartes argues that the meditator's duration can be divided into moments that do not depend on one another and, given this, he depends for his existence on something other than himself *at every moment*.[45] There can be no question of whether he, at this moment, might be the product of an infinite series of finite causes; God must be the immediate and total cause of his preservation.[46]

Although Descartes seems to be right about this advantage of his argument, he still must confront the question of what causes God, given the universal character of the causal principle. Part of the force of his criticism of the scholastics is that positing God as the First Cause is inconsistent with that principle. So how does Descartes avoid violating the causal principle himself? Here, rather infamously, he declares that God is *causa sui*, but the notion of self-causation is thought to be incoherent for the reasons given earlier.[47] Arnauld takes him to task for this assertion and, as a way of being helpful, both he and Caterus propose that it be understood negatively: *God has no cause*.[48] But Descartes rejects this proposal, insisting that it be understood positively and that God is the cause of himself in a sense *analogous to* an efficient cause.[49] Despite appearances, Descartes' position is a coherent one, as the following considerations will indicate. In an effort to clarify his view, Descartes tells Arnauld that strictly speaking God is only the *formal* cause of his own existence, where the term "formal" refers to the divine essence. This means that God's essence is the "cause or reason" (*causa sive ratio*) why he needs no efficient cause. Still, God is *causa sui* in a positive sense given his "inexhaustible power" or omnipotence (*Fourth Replies*, AT 7: 236). Descartes does not mean to suggest that God bootstraps himself into existence by sheer power. The point is rather that, given his omnipotence and ontological independence, God is the *reason* for his own existence.

In fact, a better way of characterizing what Descartes sees himself as doing is to say that he is employing a version of the principle of sufficient reason (PSR). As the quotation above suggests ("cause or reason"), he conceives of the causal principle as a version of the PSR. He is even more explicit in the Geometrical Exposition, appended to the *Second Replies*:

> Concerning every existing thing it is possible to ask what is the cause of its existence. This question may even be asked concerning God, not because he needs any cause in order to exist, but because the immensity of his nature is the *cause or reason* [*causa sive ratio*] why he needs no cause . . . (AT 7: 164–65, emphasis added)

Descartes' use of the PSR in this context is typically overlooked[50] because he does not employ it anywhere else and because it is thought that unlike Leibniz and Spinoza, who make regular use of the PSR, Descartes must reject it given his commitment to divine voluntarism. Since absolutely everything depends on the divine will, there are no reasons for things apart from that will.[51] But while that doctrine may constrain Descartes' use of the PSR, it does not bar him from using it in this one case, since it is God's essence (not his will) that provides the sufficient reason for his existence.

CONCLUSION

The primary aim of this paper has been to illustrate that Descartes' causal arguments for God's existence have been criticized, and even dismissed out of hand, unfairly. At their core, the arguments are simple, elegant, and relatively plausible, especially as compared to medieval versions. They are designed to mark an advance over the latter, first, by delivering on the nature of God and, second, by showing how one can vindicate the universal character of the causal principle even in the case of God. Descartes' arguments have not received the respect they deserve, I have argued, because readers have not understood his reasons for formulating them using scholastic and Platonic doctrines, nor have they appreciated the ways in which he adapts these doctrines for his own purposes. Descartes saw himself as writing for an audience steeped in these traditions and also one that was mired in the senses and so casts his arguments in a way that will exploit the reader's prejudices.[52]

NOTES

1. This remark is attributed to Ian Hacking.
2. In a previous paper (2006), Alan Nelson and I offer another way of simplifying the first causal argument. The discussion in this section owes much to Nelson and that earlier treatment.
3. Descartes explicitly distances his version of the causal argument from scholastic versions that proceed from sensory effects. See *First Replies*, AT 7: 106.
4. This does not mean that God *actually* exists, for that would beg the question. Rather, the point is that the idea represents a *completed* infinity, as opposed to a merely potential one. This contrast plays a pivotal role in the argument, as will become clear.
5. See, e.g., *Principles* I.22, AT 8A: 13.
6. Beyssade (1992) argues that Descartes' concept of God combines two divergent theological traditions without inconsistency.
7. Cf. "To [Mersenne], 27 May 1630," AT 1: 152; the Third Meditation, AT 7: 46; *First Replies* AT 7: 113–14. Williams (1978, 129–30) criticizes this distinction.
8. See *Third Set of Objections with Replies*, AT 7: 179–81.
9. See, e.g., *Second Replies*, AT 7: 135, *Third Replies*, 7: 183. Some deny they have the idea of God but do so in name only (*Third Objections*, AT 7: 139).
10. "To Mersenne, July 1641," AT 3: 392–93.
11. "To Hyperaspistes, August 1641," AT 3: 430.
12. Cf. *Comments on a Certain Broadsheet*, AT 8B: 357–58 and the passage cited in note 11.
13. See, e.g., the Fifth Meditation, AT 7: 63–64. For two contrasting interpretations of Descartes' doctrine of innate ideas, see Jolley 1990, ch. 3 and Nelson 2008.

14. See, e.g., *Second Replies*, AT 7: 135. Also see Nolan 2005.

15. Presumably, no argument could reveal the latter. Descartes recognizes of course that his efforts may fail, which is part of the point of his remark to Hyperaspistes. See note 11.

16. Strictly speaking, there are two different principles here (one positive and one negative), and Descartes invokes each at different places in his work. The negative principle states that "nothing cannot be a cause." He asserts this typically in the context of the causal arguments as a ground for the scholastic causal principles. See, e.g., the Third Meditation, AT 7: 40; *Second Replies*, AT 7: 135. A statement of the positive principle, which constitutes premise (2) of the core argument, can be found in *Second Replies* (AT 7: 164–65). Following a general suggestion by Hume, Dicker (1993, 116–17), wonders whether Descartes conflates the two principles, but I do not find evidence of that.

17. I am bracketing Hume's famous criticism, which came later. See *A Treatise of Human Nature*, I.iii.3.

18. The Third Meditation, AT 7: 43. Cf. *Second Replies*, AT 7: 139.

19. For a concise statement of this view, see *Fifth Replies*, AT 7: 362. For a perspicuous discussion of the ontology of both innate and invented ideas, see Nelson 1997.

20. Locke (*Essay Concerning Human Understanding*, II.xxiii.33–34) and Hume (*Enquiry Concerning Human Understanding*, 2.6) both claim that we form the idea of God in this way.

21. See *First Replies*, AT 7: 113 and *Principles* I.27, AT 8A: 15.

22. Incidentally, Descartes does think that if one is confused or incautious, one could "construct an imaginary idea of God," e.g., if one were to conceive of him as an "utterly perfect corporeal being." That would be an example of having confounded one's ideas of God and body. See *Second Replies*, AT 7: 138.

23. This analogy is mine, but Descartes advances a similar one in *Second Replies*, AT 7: 140.

24. See *Second Replies*, AT 7: 136.

25. This is one way of interpreting Descartes' remarks in *Fifth Replies*, AT 7: 365.

26. Incidentally, this point explains why Descartes sometimes affirms that one *could* form an idea of God's infinite understanding, for example, by indefinitely extending the idea of one's own finite understanding. See, e.g., *Third Replies*, AT 7: 188. Descartes is not conceding the empiricist's objection. Rather, the mental process of augmenting is just a heuristic tool. It produces the idea of a potential infinity, which reveals that one has a prior idea of a completed infinity, viz., the idea of God. Descartes sometimes says that the very ability to amplify creaturely perfections

shows that we have "an idea of something greater, namely God" (*Fifth Replies*, AT 7: 365).

27. See *Second Replies*, AT 7: 130–31, 135.
28. See *Second Replies*, AT 7: 138.
29. Curley (1978, 130–31) makes this same point.
30. See, e.g., Kenny 1968, 134.
31. The Third Meditation, AT 7: 40–41.
32. See the Third Meditation, AT 7: 40–41 and *Second Replies* AT 7: 135. In these places, he uses the "negative" formulation of the *ex nihilo* principle, i.e., nothing cannot be a cause. See note 17.
33. This is especially true in the *Principles*, where he presents all three causal principles as "evident by the natural light" (AT 8A: 11–12).
34. Descartes' English translators use angled brackets to indicate material added in the French edition, to distinguish it from the original Latin.
35. *Second Objections*, AT 7: 123. See, e.g., Cottingham 1986, ch. 3 for the former, and Delahunty 1980 for the latter. There are of course other reasons that commentators have attributed a causal-likeness principle to Descartes – e.g., he sometimes states his causal principles rather baldly, though I suspect that the reason he does so is because he wants to encourage the analogies from sense experience. See *Second Replies*, AT 7: 135.
36. The Third Meditation, AT 7: 45.
37. Cf. *First Replies*, AT 7: 105–6.
38. Cf. the Third Meditation, AT 7: 48, and *Principles* I.20, AT 8A: 12.
39. Cf. *Principles* I.20, AT 8A: 12.
40. I am not claiming that "innate" means "caused by God," though Descartes thinks our innate ideas *are* so caused. Incidentally, this account also explains his otherwise odd concession in the *Second Replies*: "we can find … within ourselves a sufficient basis for forming the idea of God" (AT 7: 133). He is *not* conceding that we do cause this idea, only that it is innate.
41. See Aquinas, *Summa Theologiae* Ia, 2.3.
42. See *First Replies*, AT 7: 110.
43. See, e.g., the Third Meditation, AT 7: 45–46.
44. Some scholastics also urged that the finite series itself would require a cause.
45. The Third Meditation, AT 7: 48–49.
46. See *First Replies*, AT 7: 106–7. Here, one might recall the traditional Christian doctrine of continual creation, according to which God not only creates but also *preserves* finite beings. However, to invoke that doctrine in this context would be to beg the question of God's existence. So Descartes appeals instead to considerations about the nature of the

meditator's duration. Incidentally, Descartes takes up the issue in the Third Meditation of whether the objective reality of ideas can be caused by other ideas and whether there can be an infinite regress of such causes. He affirms the former, perhaps in part to allow for the possibility that an invented idea could derive its objective reality from one or more innate ideas. But he denies the latter; the objective reality of all ideas must ultimately be caused by something with formal reality, just like pictures (AT 7: 42). This seems right, for the alternative would be to hold that there is a realm of fictional or representational entities that is causally self-contained.

47. Descartes tries to block at least one of these reasons in the *First Replies* by arguing for causal simultaneity: a cause is simultaneous with its effect (AT 7: 108). For further discussion, see Secada 2000.

48. See *First Objections*, AT 7: 95; *Fourth Objections*, AT 7: 208.

49. *First Replies*, AT 7: 109–110; *Fourth Replies*, AT 7: 240.

50. One notable exception is Davidson 2004.

51. Melamed and Lin 2010 argue that Descartes' philosophy is "deeply antithetical to the PSR" for this reason.

52. I would like to thank David Cunning, Nicholas Jolley, Alan Nelson, and Al Spangler for comments on previous drafts of this chapter.

7   The Third Meditation on objective being: representation and intentional content

My topic here is Descartes' Third Meditation – but not the causal principles and proofs that have probably been the target of more philosophical irk than anything else in Descartes. Rather, I am concerned with the language in which they are couched, where Descartes speaks of an "objective" component, feature, or mode of ideas, a bit of medieval shoptalk he uses to distinguish among ideas insofar as they represent different things. Taking ideas objectively (rather than "materially") differentiates them according to what the "Preface to the Reader" identifies as the "thing[s] represented by" operations of the intellect (AT 7: 8). The Third Meditation then refers to the degree of perfection of what the idea is *of* or *about* as its "objective reality," in contrast to the reality that is "actual or formal" [*actualis sive formalis*; AT 7: 41–2], which properly belongs to causes. In these slightly oblique ways, Descartes uses the notion of objectivity to introduce issues of mental content and its representation in ideas. But I will argue that the Third Meditation takes only a first step towards accounting for the representational content of Cartesian ideas: it asks how it is possible for our ideas to have (stable) content, and finds the condition of possibility in the content of the particular idea of God. If I am right, the content of Cartesian ideas is to be understood in a less internalist way than is typical.

I am hoping to avoid several moves that have bedeviled much commentary. One is a hermeneutical fault: failing to respect the context of Descartes' claims, particularly the "order of reasons" that structures the *Meditations* and the distinctions made among objective, formal, and material components of ideas. The other seeks to explain the mind's grasp on things (its ultimate objects) through representational relations that are (somehow) established independently of any mental act. I shall argue that this approach inverts the priorities governing Descartes' philosophy of mind, which insists that relations of representation derive from the mental activity of being directed at an object – that is, from intentionality. This priority seems a basic commitment of Descartes' thought, although other aspects of intentionality and objective reality are developed only over the course of the *Meditations*. Understanding the status of mental content, in particular, requires working out the ontology of possibility, essences, and their causes, which is not complete before Meditation Five. Within the process of working out that ontology, the Third Meditation idea of God as the positive infinite is pivotal, for it underwrites the claim that everything I think about depends on an unlimited causal power and perfection existing in God.[1] God's power and perfection also guarantee that my mind is able to reach its ultimate intentional objects, that is, *the things themselves*.

A BIT OF BACKGROUND

As Caterus points out in *First Objections*, Descartes' terminology of objective reality is bit of philosophical vernacular, borrowed from the long history of medieval and late scholastic philosophy. His talk of degrees of objective "reality" is somewhat less standard, but *Second Replies* extends the notion to "'objective perfection', 'objective intricacy', and so on" (AT 7: 161). The Third Meditation likewise slides from objective "reality" to objective "mode of being" (*modus essendi*; AT 7: 42). I will use "objective being" as the catchall term, although later I will say something about why Descartes specifically uses "objective reality" for classifying ideas in terms of their representational content. But for all their common currency, Caterus is puzzled by Descartes' demand that objective being requires a cause sufficient to its degree of reality, since he (Caterus) understands objective being as no more than an empty description (*nuda denominatio*; AT 7: 92–3), a mere label applied to the thing targeted by a mental act.

The roots of the debate between Caterus and Descartes lie in medieval and Aristotelian approaches to cognition that treat it as involving assimilation between the knower and the known.[2] Thomas Aquinas explains this assimilation through the sharing of a form, typically received into the soul (initially) through sense-perception. But since a form, e.g., of blue or of square in the intellect does not make the intellect become blue and square, such forms are there only immaterially and intentionally. They are curiously hybrid, inhering differently in different sorts of subjects, yet somehow the same, and somehow producing an intentional, or better *representational*, relation between the intellect and its targets. Some later Thomists cash out this relation by taking the act of cognition to give rise to a distinct, though dependent concept, which explains how the form inheres in the intellect. The concept thus formed is an intrinsically representational entity that provides the medium by which the intellect is directed at things instantiating the form materially. Some historians have traced Descartes' notion of objective being to this dependent concept.[3] But that seems unlikely: if anything, the Thomist account should be an ancestor of what was later dubbed the "formal concept," or the idea taken formally.

Instead, King argues that it was Duns Scotus who introduced the terminology of "objective being" to describe how content is present in the intellect. And Normore identifies his follower William of Alnwick as the first to pair formal and objective "modes" in differentiating between contents and mental acts.[4] Objective being applies to the being of what is known, its *esse cognitus*, and is introduced in the context of considering the exemplars or archetypes in God's mind; it is thus independent of existing things. Scotus suggests that the status of the *esse cognitum* as an *object* is also in some way distinct from its being known, even when the object in question depends on God's creative intellect for its being. That is because knowing is a relational state, requiring that the agent's act be related to a content. We might understand the distinction minimally as taking *esse cognitum* under different descriptions: *esse cognitum* can be understood solely as a dependent feature of the act, or as a content with properties other than those of the act by which it is conceived. As such, the content may be differentiated differently from the act. Similarly, Alnwick understands *esse cognitum* formally as just the cognition; understood objectively, it is differentiated by the intentional objects that "terminate" cognition. In this line of thought, *esse cognitus* has a "diminished" kind of being, less than that of actual things, but still requiring a cause.[5]

At the turn of the seventeenth century, philosophers such as Francisco Suárez and Eustachius a Sancto Paulo gave slightly new

twists to the common distinction (*vulgaris distinctio*) between formal and objective "concepts."[6] The formal concept is the intellectual
act, which Suárez characterizes as "a true positive thing inhering as a
quality in the mind." Both then identify the objective concept
as what the formal concept represents, which (unlike the Scotist
view) may simply be the thing itself, or could be an *ens rationis*, a
being of reason, with only objective being in the intellect. Moreover,
both describe the formal concept as a mental "word," by which, as
Suárez puts it, "the intellect conceives of some thing or common
account [*rationem*]." The objective concept, in turn, serves as "the
object and matter around which the formal concept revolves and to
which the eye of the mind directly tends." The use of the verbal
metaphor turns the intentional relation between formal and objective
concepts into a kind of *semantic* relation. But Suárez also insists that
the objective concept determines the formal concept, and so the
formal concept cannot count as a merely arbitrary vehicle for convey-
ing semantic content. I suggest that we think of the formal concept as
a *mode of presentation* of the objective concept, but with the caveat
that the object falls intrinsically under various proper descriptions.[7]
This gloss makes sense of the examples Suárez and Eustachius offer
for the objective concept, which may be singular (e.g., a human being),
or something universal and common (e.g., human nature). It may also
be a mere being of reason, but not in the sense of an idiosyncratic
mental construct. Even when we think of things that do not exist,
esse objective describes a real possibility, something that could be the
subject of a science. For this reason, Suárez associates *esse objective*
with *esse essentiae*, the being of an essence.[8] Still, Suárez (like Scotus)
thinks of such objective being as "diminished." As real possibilities,
essences are "real and apt" for existence. But that indicates only "a
kind of aptitude or better lack of repugnance to being produced by God
with such an *esse*."[9] Possible being itself neither needs a cause, nor has
causal force itself. At the same time, *how* beings of reason become
objects of thought, with the particular contents they have, calls for
explanation. In this sense, they require efficient causes, for which
Suárez thinks the intellect suffices.[10]

Descartes' reply to Caterus' objection that objective being needs no
cause seems to borrow elements from these various ways of understanding content. Descartes retorts that Caterus has misunderstood
how he uses "objective being," insisting that the "idea of the sun" "is

the sun itself existing in the intellect ... objectively ... in the way in which objects normally are in the intellect" (AT 7: 102). This sounds akin to Suárez's and Eustace's assimilation of the objective concept to the things themselves.[11] But as Scotus and Alnwick do, Descartes insists that taking ideas objectively supplies different conditions of differentiation from ideas taken formally. It is those differences in specific content for which Descartes requires causes. And as we will see, the intellect does not always suffice to explain such differences in content.

The diverse demands Descartes makes of objective being are, I suggest, the result of how he conceives of the position of created human minds, and indeed, the task for the entire *Meditations*. Unlike Scholastic empiricists, Descartes cannot simply assimilate either the objective or formal being of ideas to existing things encountered in sense-perception. For he maintains that our thinking is active and spontaneous, determining the shape of its acts autonomously and in ways that cannot be explained merely by its "inputs" (which I take to be one of the lessons of Meditation Two). Still, we are not God, or even a demiurge: we do not create the being of things, but seek to fit our ideas to the natures of things already existing. The threat raised by the second set of hyperbolic doubts in Meditation One is that our ideas do not revolve around such natures as their "object and matter." Lacking an account of how robust forms enter the mind and shape its intentional acts, Descartes needs another way to anchor our thinking to real content.

INTENTIONALITY AND REPRESENTATION IN DESCARTES

Understanding the content of ideas becomes yet more challenging since Cartesian metaphysics has no ground for representation *other than* mental acts. Extended things differ from minds in having only quantitative modes expressible in geometrical terms and transferable through efficient causation. The transfer of motions and indefinite divisibility explain the diversity of arrangements and local motions found among extended substances. But they are not enough to account for the "aboutness" of intentionality and representation. Only a mind can provide the representational relations that make something into content, by taking it as an object.

In fact, Descartes' commitment to deriving representation and content from mental intentionality may predate the full development of his metaphysics of extension. The early *World, or Treatise on Light* illustrates how an idea represents an object by analogy with how a bit of language (spoken or written) signifies its content. Descartes uses the comparison to claim that even the operation of "natural" signs (such as "laughter and tears" for joy and sadness) does not require them to resemble what they represent. Language enjoys considerable signifying success although words "signify nothing except by human convention." Now, I take it that relations of resemblance are simply the most plausible candidates for a kind of independent, non-mental relation connecting a sign and its meaning. Descartes frequently refers to such relations as crucial parts of the alternative accounts he rejects.[12] But the lesson here extends well beyond rejecting resemblance as the basis for representation: the linguistic analogy shows that signification works because "it is our mind which ... represents [the] meaning to us" (AT 11: 4).

In describing the linguistic analogy, Descartes also insists that we may remain oblivious to the character of the sign, and even of the signifying relation it bears, when focusing on what it signifies. Speaking as an absent-minded polyglot, he remarks that we may "hear an utterance whose meaning we understand perfectly well, but afterwards we cannot say in what language it was spoken" (ibid.). So, holding that relations of representation cannot extend beyond the mind's intentional "reach" on its objects does not commit him to an implausible view about the transparency of representation. It does not, for instance, require that the mind is somehow conscious of all its dependent representational relations, much less that it *decides* to establish those relations, or that they are just what we suppose them to be.

In contrast, some commentators suppose that Descartes takes brain states, or (in a different vein) sensations of bodily states, such as a feeling of dryness in the throat, to be representational.[13] But we can admit that Descartes allows special roles for phenomenal states, or even the arrangements of extension constituting brain states in representing the world: such states may "naturally" cause us to think of other things (the configuration of my environment, thirst). What I deny is simply that brain states and the like are *intrinsically* representational, independently of a mind's relating them to an object.[14]

I take it that such states are examples of the natural institutions established by God to stimulate us to form a thought of some object. Their role is primarily causal, no different in kind from the role played by words heard in a familiar language in prompting us to think of what they signify. It remains the province of minds to give words their intentional relations to meanings, and more generally to forge relations of representation in the world by their intentional activities. And I think we will find that Cartesian minds have the resources to introduce intentional representation into a world otherwise bare of it, if we allow that they can interact with at least some of what they manage to represent.

TWO STORIES ABOUT THE REPRESENTATIONALITY OF CARTESIAN IDEAS

The possibility of such interaction is what one familiar account of the representationality of Cartesian ideas seems to deny. In honor of its venerable status, I will dub this species of account the "same old story" (SOS). And an old story it is, one that can be traced to Thomas Reid's attack on the Cartesian "way of ideas" for hanging a veil of ideas between minds and the non-mental world, and thereby making external-world skepticism intractable.[15] Much as Reid did, different versions of the SOS commonly start with the distinction between mental acts and ideational objects, using the terminology of an idea taken "materially" and an idea taken "objectively" to characterize how an act of the mind represents an object, while attributing "formal" reality to the former, and "objective" to the latter.[16] The SOS can then trade on the thought that the object is simply a way of taking the idea to maintain that the object so represented is itself a mental entity, in the sense that its *esse* is *in-esse*, and requires being lodged in the mind. The idea taken objectively may then bear a representing relation to another, external thing, e.g., a bit of extension, but the primary object of an idea remains within determinate internal boundaries, so that the idea and its primary object are located fully in the (metaphorical) head. The result is a kind of "internalism" about mental ontology and an extremely "narrow" view of mental content.[17]

As you might guess, I think the SOS goes astray on objective being. For one, it assimilates the distinction between formal and objective realities to the material and objective ways of taking ideas.[18] The account also imposes high costs, while promising only uncertain benefits.[19] The SOS typically charges those costs to Descartes himself, understanding him to be so under the spell of the skeptical worries of the dreaming doubt that he treats all experience as internally indiscernible from a cocoon of mental imagery. Reid's version of the SOS assumes that the proper objects of our ideas are internally accessible and explicable, and that the task of the *Meditations* is to establish their correspondence to independent, external things. But his gloss supposes that the mind's act terminates at internal intentional objects. The SOS thereby violates just the features of Descartes' philosophy of mind I have emphasized. First, it pushes the operation of representation beyond the edges of the mind's intentionality, at least insofar as it hopes to achieve some reference to the external world. At the same time, it treats mere presence to mind as sufficient for something to qualify as an object – and thus avoids explaining the role of intentionality. The SOS also faces textual troubles with Descartes' insistence that the things we perceive through our ideas have objective being in our intellect and that objective being is a mode of being of the thing itself (*First Replies*, AT 7: 102–103).

The SOS retains some currency in accounts of the metaphysics of Cartesian ideas.[20] But several important accounts, concerned particularly with sense-perception, offer something of a "new take" (NT) on Cartesian representationality.[21] The NT does not locate the representing relation between act and object, but instead, distinguishes between presentational and causal features of ideas. Ideas present some qualities or contents to the mind insofar as something is "in" the mind. They also have causes, which in the case of sense-perceptions lie outside the mind. For the NT, ideas of sense-perception represent their causes by referring to them (under standard conditions). The presentational features of ideas, in contrast, provide information, although that information may mislead. The NT thus differs from the SOS, first, by accommodating sensory misrepresentation through its distinction between presentational representation and causal-referential representation: sensory ideas normally present information attributable to the physical things that are their salient causes, but sometimes the qualities that sensory ideas present do not properly belong to their causes. In making this split, the NT refuses to treat the presentational features of an idea as the farthest terminus

the mind can reach and thus as an indispensible way station for connecting the mind to the things the idea represents. Nevertheless, the
NT still reverses the dependence of representation on intentionality.
And perhaps because it focuses on sensory ideas, which seem to cleave
what is in the head from its external causes, the NT may likewise seem
to treat the presentational features of the idea as if they were obstacles
between the mind and the sense-perception's causal content. Indeed,
both the SOS and the NT shape the intentional relation between
representing and represented in ways that create problems for the
very idea for which Descartes develops the machinery of objective
reality and its causes in the Third Meditation: the idea of God.

CONTEXT AND ORDER IN MEDITATION III

I propose that we understand the main task of the Third Meditation as
a matter of developing an account of how we can hang on to steady
mental content after the destabilizing doubts of Meditation One. The
Meditations as a whole is structured according to an "order of
reasons,"

[which does] not attempt to say in a single place everything relevant to a given
subject [*tout ce qui appartient à une matiere*] ... [but reasons] in an orderly
way from what is easier to what is harder ... ("To Mersenne, 24 December
1640," AT 3: 266)[22]

Respecting the order of reasons demands that we attend to how the
Second Meditation gathers the rubble left by the First Meditation so
as to characterize the nature of the mind as better "recognized"
[*notior*] than that of the body.[23] After affirming that I am *cogitans*
(cogitating or thinking) and that various specific acts cannot be distinguished from my thinking (AT 7: 28–29), the meditator turns
abruptly to analyzing a perception of a piece of wax. The point of
the examination is not to advance our understanding of wax in particular, or bodies more generally, but to clarify the mental activity
involved in merely *seeming* to perceive a body. Indeed, at this point in
the *Meditations*, Descartes' narrator is in no position to assert anything about bodies as such: not even that they are possible beings, or
that they have some specific nature (e.g., being extended). Instead,
what the wax passage establishes is that it takes a *mentis inspectio* –
an "inspecting" by the mind – to perceive. This *mentis inspectio* does

not seem to be a distinct kind of mental act, for the narrator is ready to generalize its involvement to all the forms of human thinking considered so far. It is simply what allows the meditator to think of the wax as the same (in some unspecified sense) through a series of changing appearances. We can understand this activity as the mind's directing itself towards a target, above and beyond its reception of inputs (whether sensory or imaginative). It is an intentional activity.

But Meditation Two is not the final word on intentionality. It acknowledges content only in passing, and says nothing about either its ontological status or information-bearing function. When the meditator emphasizes the certainty with which I "seem to see, to hear, to be warmed," it is the acts *as* acts that warrant certainty, not their contents. The SOS assumes that the meditator is committed to affirming the certainty of her grasp on internal, mind-dependent objects. Reading the Meditation as focused on mental acts rather than content undermines that assumption. To be sure, the meditator does not deny that mental acts have contents, offering examples ranging from the wax, to the smell of honey, to coats and hats crossing a square, to the various propositions that are the targets of the modes of doubting, willing, etc. But the examples are diverse, and the meditator remains studiously neutral about how they might (or might not) illustrate features of content. In short, Meditation Two remains agnostic about content, and even about the possibility of purely intentional objects. Instead, it focuses on establishing that the mind engages in an activity of intend*ing*.

It is Meditation Three that turns directly to mental contents, by introducing the objective components of ideas through the quasi-technical notion of their objective reality. To unpack the notion, many commentators refer us to formal reality, making it the touchstone notion from which objective reality is derived: "in effect, reality *simpliciter*."[24] Yet neither Meditation Three, nor even the "geometrical" arrangement of arguments at the end of *Second Replies* follows this order: both speak *first* of objective reality, and *then* turn to formal reality.[25] This is particularly marked in *Second Replies*, in which the third definition describes the "objective reality of an idea" as the "being [*entitatem*] of the thing represented by an idea, insofar as it is in the idea." Only then does definition four declare that "the very same is said to be formally in the objects of ideas when it is in itself just the same [kind] as we perceive," and "eminently when [it] is not of the same kind, but is so great as to be able to take its place" (AT 7:161*).[26] Moreover, the definitions explicitly make formal and eminent being explanatorily dependent on objective being, and do so in at least two slightly different ways: 1. something counts as "in" an object formally when it is there in the same way as an idea represents it to be; and 2. formal (or eminent) being is a way of being belonging to the objects of our ideas when they are not considered as being (only) in the intellect. The Third Meditation likewise introduces objective reality first. It then offers yet another way of explaining the formal in terms of the objective by describing the "actual or formal" mode of being as what belongs to the causes of my ideas taken objectively (AT 7: 42). This makes sense in the context of Meditation Three, for the meditator cannot yet assume that the "being represented by an idea" could exist in itself, and so can only speak about the degree of reality that must belong to the cause of the idea taken objectively. Indeed, Meditation Three says relatively little about the notion of formal reality other than attributing it to the nature of causes, and brings in the formal reality belonging to an idea only implicitly (if at all) when considering what the meditator herself could cause. None of these various accounts makes the differences between objective and formal being a matter of how a quality inheres *in* its subject. Instead, the decisive difference is whether the object itself is considered to be in the intellect, or (also) outside it. It is thus a matter of the metaphysical location of the *subject* of inherence.[27]

That is telling, since the Third Meditation introduces objective reality – and the entire topic of the representational content of ideas – as a way of classifying thoughts before addressing their truth or falsity. Here is another point where the SOS may go astray, for it supposes that the meditator should have no uncertainty about the internal characteristics of ideas at this stage of the game: whatever lies within the head (including ideas in their intrinsic representational character) should be cognitively accessible and secure. But the meditator is less sanguine, for she emphasizes that the hyperbolic doubts of the First Meditation still operate. As such, the entire Third Meditation is subject to the worry that God may have created her nature incapable of grasping the truth, leaving her incapable "ever of being fully certain about anything" (AT 7: 36*) – including the results of the previous Meditation and the meditator's halting bids to describe the internal contents of the mind. The Third Meditation opens with tentative and indecisive attempts to taxonomize ideas. But not only does the meditator use extremely hedged language for classifying differences among "forms" (formas) of ideas (AT 7: 37–8*), she eventually abandons them all, treating the ideas so described merely as "certain ways of thinking" (cogitandi quidam modi) with no recognizable inequalities (AT 7: 40*). She then finds that she can differentiate ideas insofar as they represent one thing (rem) rather than another. So, it is diversity in their contents, not their "forms," that differentiates ideas. Even here, however, the meditator avoids specifying content in any fine-grained way, simply distinguishing ideas that represent "substances" from those representing "modes and accidents," and the idea by which I think (intelligo) the infinite God from ideas that exhibit finite substances. In doing so, the meditator keeps her ontological commitments modest by refusing to assume that the metaphysical distinctions in question apply to anything. The distinctions are simply a matter of what "as a way of speaking" (ut ita loquar) is called objective reality. All that matters is that it admits of degree.

Odd as this approach might be,[28] differentiation by degree of reality seems as generic and noncommittal a device as Descartes can find in his ontology. It applies to all modes of being, objective, formal, and eminent, indifferent to the status of the subject of inherence. Descartes' examples of different degrees of reality among modes, finite substances, and God suggest that the differences track whether something is a quality, a subject, or an infinite subject. As such, the degree is a matter of how a being inheres in its subject, and differences in degree measure relations of ontological dependence: the more independent, perfect, or complete some being is, the higher its degree of reality. Because degree of reality is a matter of ontological dependence, it makes sense that Descartes uses it as a measure of the sufficiency of a cause to its effect. For Descartes, as for his predecessors, adducing causal powers served a wide variety of explanatory purposes: one is making the ontological support for dependent beings intelligible. As such, the general causal principle of the Third Meditation could be understood simply as a version of the principle of sufficient reason.

But the corollary causal principle that follows is another matter: it demands that the objective reality of an idea must have a cause with at least the same degree of formal reality (AT 7: 41). The principle thus applies the demand for sufficiency *across* objective and formal modes of being. One might think that the object represented by an idea would *ipso facto* have a high degree of dependence (on the mind) – and thus a correspondingly low degree of reality. But that would collapse objective being into a dependent being, treating it not as mental content, but as a mental mode, property, or event. The *Meditations* is in not yet in any position to treat the objective mode of being in this way (that is, as an idea taken materially), if only because it is working from the first-person standpoint of the meditator. Instead, I suggest that the Third Meditation has not yet settled how to think of objective being, or of the contents of intentional acts in general. In this vein, we can understand the causal corollary to be less robust than it might first seem: it states that the only cause sufficient to explain an idea's content is one that has at least the degree of ontological independence represented by that content and is located in a subject the existence of which does *not* depend on the represented content. The meditator describes this second demand as a requirement that the cause have the kind of reality appropriate to causes (AT 7: 42); we might say that it is a demand that the cause of my mental content be stable, or at least as stable as the content is represented as being.

Yet even this demand by itself does not go far, because the meditator remains remarkably uncertain about how her mental content is, in fact, represented. Consider the so-called "rule of truth" that appears at the very start of the Meditation: it posits "all that to be true [*illud omne esse verum*] which I perceive as genuinely clear and distinct" (AT 7: 35*). But it is not first offered as a reliable rule, only proposed speculatively as a possible generalization of previous results. It also remains tentative and provisional about *what counts* as the content of ideas and perceptions: the content is whatever can be picked out as "all that" (*illud omne*) and counted "true" (*verum*). But the meditator fails to specify what is thus picked out. With only the results of the Second Meditation on which to rely, she should not yet assert that "all that" exists, or even commit herself to what "all that" is. Instead, as we find out in Meditation Five, the truth rule concerns whether what I perceive clearly and distinctly has a genuine, or "true and immutable" nature. Such true and immutable natures may exist nowhere outside of me [*si extra me ... nullibi*] ... but what belongs to this content is not put together by me, nor does it depend on my mind [*a me non efficta est, nec a mente mea dependet*]. (AT 7: 64*)

The idea of a true thing has content that is independent of the meditator's thinking it: it has a determinate nature, essence, or form that describes what it is to be that thing. For this reason, at least some of the properties of a true thing are susceptible of demonstration, and judgments about those properties are susceptible to formal truth. What we must bear in mind, however, is that *none of these features of the truth-rule has yet been established at the beginning of Meditation Three*. The meditator does not even know whether the contents of her ideas are stable enough that they could exist independently.

FROM APPARENT POSSIBILITY TO THE GROUND OF ALL POSSIBILITY

Because of the lingering skeptical doubts, Descartes begins Meditation Three assuming rather less about both the broad and narrow content of our ideas than did his medieval and Renaissance forerunners. Thus, we should not assume – as some commentators do – that we can cash out the contents even of clear and distinct ideas in terms of possible things.[29] Meditation Three has not yet earned the conceptual capital to suppose that the content of any idea represents real possibility. Even if all mental acts are intentionally directed, as Meditation Two suggests, the content of those acts may be no more than an unstable effigy, stitched together by the efforts of thinking. Conceivability in this sense does not entail real possibility, that is, an essence that could (but may not) be instantiated outside of the mind. All that it provides, so to speak, is an *apparent* possibility. This is so even for clear and distinct ideas. The meditator has introduced clarity and distinctness as promising qualities to qualify an idea for the truth rule (AT 7: 35). But the rule has only been proposed, not established. Indeed, it is not even clear that the meditator as yet has the wherewithal to decide which ideas are genuinely clear and distinct. Some ideas may seem to represent real things; I may even be utterly convinced of the real being of their objects when I entertain such ideas, but that is only to say that their objects *seem* to me to be possible. Making the move from such apparent possibilities to real possibilities is the work of several Meditations. But Meditation Three takes the decisive step, for it lays down the conditions for the real possibilities of objects (and things) and finds it to be the same as the condition for the mind's existence. It does so by demonstrating that in order even to think that one has the idea of the infinite God, the infinite, incomprehensible God must be a genuine possibility. In short, the causal arguments for God's existence bootstrap their way into showing that the independence of content in the idea of God is a condition for having the idea itself. In doing so, they do not apply the notion of objective reality so much as develop the understanding of content implicit in it.

Let me unpack this thought. The immediate task the Third Meditation meditator confronts upon realizing that her thinking can be differentiated by its termini, by what she seeks to think, is to determine whether she has indeed succeeded in hitting upon some real object, an objective reality sufficiently great that it represents a real possibility. The meditator cannot simply assume she has succeeded, and so at first the objective reality in the idea of God must be treated merely as an apparent possibility. But that object is presented according to a variety of detailed descriptions. The meditator specifies what "I think by the name God" (*Dei nomine intelligo*): a substance that is infinite, independent, and a host of "summa"-properties (AT 7: 45*). It is by attending to how all such things are (*omnia talia sunt*) that it seems less and less possible that she could be their source. The meditator then proceeds to develop the thought that what the idea presents to her is the positive infinite, something prior to the perception of the finite limits by which she characterizes herself. Indeed it is the perception of the infinite that allows her to acknowledge (*agnoscerem*) her own defects (AT 7: 46).

Here we can make use of the notion of a mode of presentation. The idea of God presents its object as genuinely infinite, utterly different from and prior to the mode of presentation by which the mind perceives itself. As the example of my idea of myself (qua meditator) shows, even an idea that seems clear and distinct, and thus utterly reliable, can be presented opaquely: although I cannot think of myself as not-thinking, "this I that I know [*ego ille quem novi*]" (AT 7: 27) may be much more than I know. And although I cannot simultaneously think of myself and doubt that I exist, nothing in my idea of myself guarantees that I must exist or will continue to exist; nor does it explain how I *can* exist. The metaphysical imperfection of the meditator is why the threat of uncertainty still looms at the beginning of Meditation Three. But the mode of presentation of the idea of God – that by which God appears possible – is different. Descartes demands that even the appearance of a possible object of thought demands some sort of explanation – that is, a cause. In most cases, this demand will be utterly trivial: there may be some mode of presentation in the mind, but not one that will require anything more than the mind's substance as a source. If that mode does in fact present a real object, the meditator's mind has the resources to explain that fact, and if it does not present a possible object, the meditator can appeal to her defects as the (privative) cause of the idea's mutilation. In contrast, to think of something under the mode of the positive infinite is not something for which any finite mind is ontologically sufficient. I, the meditator, cannot generate even the appearance of the positive infinite, for I am not, so to speak, big enough to contain it within me. In this case, the mode transparently presents at least the degree of reality of its object: it must be a presentation of the real possibility of the infinite. And as the object of my idea, that degree of reality determines its cause. Only the actual, infinite God is capable of producing such a real possibility, although that being may in fact greatly transcend what the idea presents. In short, to so much as have the conceptual *appearance* of the positive infinite requires that the positive infinite be a real possibility. For unlike Suárez, Descartes demands an explanation, some cause, for possibility itself. As Descartes makes clear elsewhere, God is the source of possibilities. In this case, then, God is the source of Its own possibility. By establishing the existence of such a God, Descartes secures the ground for real possibilities. By establishing that such a God is the cause of my existence (insofar as I have certain special ideas), Descartes secures the grounds for trusting that I, the meditator, am capable of grasping truth.

As this gloss shows, the mode of presentation of an idea need not be really distinct from the content it presents: God is presented *as* the positive infinite and God *is* positively infinite. But as Descartes often insists, God can (and should) also be thought of as incomprehensible. We finite minds can know God, but not embrace Its full nature: our minds "touch" what we think, without embracing it.[30]

The idea of God is, of course, *sui generis*. Nonetheless, it shows that the objective being of an idea cannot always be limited to what is "in the head."[31] More generally, Descartes seems to explain the stability of the contents of our ideas through our interaction with what the ideas represent – first and foremost, with God, but also with the "true and immutable" natures described in the Fifth Meditation. Such interaction allows those contents to constrain our thought, so that we have real contents and a stable semantics for our ideas. On this view, Descartes is far from the internalist navel-gazer that popular rumor makes him out to be. But that does not make him an externalist by default. Descartes understands the contents of our ideas, and perhaps even what gives form to our thought, through multiple levels of explanation, in which the finite mind contains within itself the mark of the incomprehensible infinite, and what exists nowhere "outside" the mind may yet be independent of it. The spatial metaphors used by contemporary philosophy of mind to describe the boundaries of the mind and the breadth of its content simply fail to do justice to the complicated web of causes and ontological dependence that Descartes weaves.[32]

NOTES

1. The "doctrine of the eternal truths" that Descartes elaborates in his correspondence holds that we must grant God the power to make and unmake eternal truths – and thus the being of *possibilia*, essences, and values – "as a king lays down laws" ("To Mersenne, 15 April 1630," AT 1: 145).

2. See Brown 2008, 197. I offer a somewhat different assessment of Descartes' debt to this tradition.

3. See, e.g., Michael Ayers (1998, 1064) who describes this concept as an "internal object of thought." But cf. Brown 2008, 198–99.

4. King 2004, 75 n. 25, and Normore 1986, 233. Although I am not providing a history of reception but only general background, we might note that Scotism was alive and well in early seventeenth-century France (Ariew 1999, 45 and 41).

5. On this last point, see Normore 1986, 233. For relevant primary texts, see Duns Scotus 1963, 258, paragraphs 31–32, and 469, paragraph 26; and Alnwick 1937, 26.

6. Suárez, 1965, 2.1.1, and ACS 1998, 33. I use "ACS" to abbreviate Ariew, Cottingham, and Sorrell 1998. Unless otherwise indicated, all relevant passages from Suárez come from D.M. 2.1.1, translated in ACS 1998,

33–4, although the translations above are mine. References to Eustachius are from *Summa philosophiae quadripartite* I. dis.1, ques.2 and 1.dis. 2, ques. 3, translated in ACS 1998, 93–4.

7. It is thus important not to think of the relation exactly as we now think of that between sense and reference. In a way, the object assimilates sense and reference, insofar as it embodies a "meaning" found in the structure of the world; even mere beings of reason may conform to the structure of the world.

8. See Ayers 1998, 1066.

9. Suárez 1965, D.M. 31.2.2.

10. D.M. 54.2.1–7, in Doyle 1995, 66–71. Thanks to Gideon Manning for bringing these passages to my attention.

11. But cf. Ayers 1998, 1068.

12. See, e.g., *Optics*, AT 6: 112–14.

13. See, e.g., Simmons 1999 for the latter.

14. Denying such intrinsic representationality carries costs for explaining the perception and behavior of non-human animals. I will bite that bullet, however.

15. See, e.g., Reid 1983, 114.

16. See Kaufman 2000; without endorsing it, Simmons (forthcoming) offers a taxonomy.

17. For this terminology, see C. Brown 2011.

18. It is tempting to do so, as Gassendi did in *Fourth Objections*, AT 7: 285. For accounts of why this is an error, see Clemenson 2007, 45–46, and Lionel Shapiro 2012, 386–87.

19. These costs are metaphysical (positing an odd mental entity), epistemological (inserting a curtain of ideas between the mind and its targets), and explanatory (doubling the relations of representation).

20. See Ayers 1998, 1068, and Brandom 2002, 354–55, although cf. 24–6.

21. The NT seems to appear first in Wilson's revision of her earlier views (1999, 69–83). Simmons (1999) presents a functionalist version of the NT (see also her forthcoming). The gloss I offer above follows Wilson's focus on ideas of sensory-perception. Other kinds of ideas have different etiologies, which would require adjusting the account suitably.

22. See also "Preface to the Reader," AT 7: 8–10.

23. The *sit notior* in the subtitle *quod ipsa sit notior quam corpus* indicates that the nature of the mind is more prominent, eminent, or marked than is the body, rather than that it is better understood discursively.

24. Wilson 1978, 105.

25. I owe this point to Annette Baier.

26. References marked with an asterisk are modified from the translations of CSM.

27. See Clemenson 2007, 20–21.
28. See also *Third Objections*, AT 7: 185.
29. For example, Margaret Wilson (1982) seems to jump the gun at p. 108.
30. See, e.g., "To [Mersenne], 27 May 1630," AT 1: 152, and *First Replies*, AT 7: 113–14.
31. Indeed, in this case, not even the mode of presentation seems confined within the head. In general, I suspect that diverse ideas may show a wide variety in the status of and relations between the modes of presentation and content, without those relations being sufficient for sorting ideas by their epistemic reliability. But cf. Lionel Shapiro 2012.
32. I'd like to thank many people for patient and constructive help: to start, Sean Greenberg and Joseph Dowd at the Scientia Workshop of the University of California-Irvine, the colloquium audience at the University of Calgary (with hat tips to Ron Wilburn, Nicole Wyatt, Mark Migotti, Ann Levey, Noa Latham, and Allen Habib), the members of the Early Modern Workshop at the California Institute of Technology, especially Gideon Manning and Patricia Easton, and John Kardosh for some acute points. I am grateful for the able research assistance of Juan Santos Castro and the support of a Standard Research Grant from the Social Sciences and Humanities Research Council of Canada. Most of all, I want to express enormous gratitude to David Cunning, whose kindness and hard work (even when sorely tested) are a model for editors everywhere.

8 The Fourth Meditation: Descartes' theodicy *avant la lettre*

The Fourth Meditation begins with a résumé of the epistemic achievements of the *Meditations* thus far. Descartes says that he has succeeded in becoming accustomed to leading the mind away from the senses to the objects of the intellect alone. The first such object is the human mind as a thinking thing, the idea of which he derives from his own existence in the *cogito*. The second such object is God, the assertion of whose existence is such that "the human intellect cannot know anything that is more evident or more certain" (AT 7: 53). It is important that the existence of God have this paramount certainty because the certainty of all else, even that of the *cogito*, depends on it.[1] For since God as a perfect being is incapable of deception, the faculty of judgment that He has given us must be reliable so long as it is used correctly. Thus, concludes Descartes, he is now in a position to achieve knowledge of the rest of the things still unknown to him. But there remains an obstacle to be overcome before he can proceed. He must provide what Leibniz later called a *theodicy*.

WILL AND JUDGMENT

There is a residual doubt left from the previous Meditation, the resolution of which is the aim of this Meditation. Descartes' doubt now concerns how it is that he is capable of error. Having shown how knowledge is possible, he must now show how error is possible, for the fact of the matter is that he has erred quite often. Indeed, that he has made errors and is thus imperfect is an important premise in the Third Meditation argument that a perfect God exists who would not deceive him by creating him with a faculty of judging that when used

168

properly goes awry. The essence of Descartes' account is that it is not God who is responsible for our errors, but us, insofar as our faculty of judgment is a function of our will. We fall into error when we do not use our will properly in the course of judging.

We judge properly when we use our will to assert only what the intellect clearly perceives to be true. But since the will has a scope greater than the intellect, it can assert what the intellect does not clearly perceive to be true, and in so judging we thereby run the risk of error. When error does occur, it thus depends on us rather than on God, because we did not use our will properly. Simply put, we willingly erred. In this, Descartes anticipates the later concept of an ethics of belief. He writes elsewhere that

every philosopher and theologian – indeed everyone who uses his reason – agrees that the more clearly we understand something before giving our assent to it, the smaller is the risk we run of going wrong; and, by contrast, those who make a judgement when they are ignorant of the grounds on which it is based are the ones who go astray. (*Second Replies*, AT 7: 147)

Descartes takes willful error to be irrational, and he also takes it to be immoral. Despite the apparent trivialization of it here, the idea that errors of willful belief are morally wrong is an important one in Descartes' theodicy. Even if by good luck one's belief turns out to be true, its very willfulness leaves one "at fault" (*culpa*).[2]

Curiously, it was only Gassendi who, among the Objectors to the *Meditations*, queried the fundamental premise of Descartes' theodicy that the will can have greater scope than the intellect. Gassendi objects that the will is not of greater extent than the intellect, which, if anything is of greater scope, since "there are many things which we understand only obscurely, so that no judgment or pursuit or avoidance occurs in respect of them" (*Fifth Objections*, AT 7:314–15). But Gassendi's critique misfires. For this suspension of judgment is precisely Descartes' recommendation in cases of obscurity:

If . . . I simply refrain from making a judgment in cases where I do not perceive the truth with sufficient clarity and distinctness, then it is clear that I am behaving correctly and avoiding error. (Fourth Meditation, AT 7: 59)

So Gassendi's rhetorical question as to whether the will can extend to anything that escapes the intellect is ambiguous. In one sense, it can do so and does – whenever we go wrong by assenting to what is not clearly and distinctly perceived to be true. But in another sense, the will does not have a greater scope than the intellect, for "when[ever] we direct our will towards something, we always have some sort of understanding of some aspect of it" (*Fifth Replies*, AT 7: 377). The sense that is relevant to Descartes' theodicy is the first.

It is in the *Meditations* that this view, that judgment is a function of the will, appears for the first time. Nowhere in Descartes' previous writings does he mention it, and nowhere in what he might have read is it to be found. Thus, while it may be true, as Gilson first proposed and many others have assumed since, that Descartes models his epistemic theodicy on previous attempts to deal with the problem of evil, it cannot be, as Gilson suggested, that he just adapted Aquinas' (or anyone else's) theodicy to his own purposes.[3] Indeed, that judgment is a function of the will may be Descartes' most novel view; yet, among his critics, none but Gassendi (and he only as an afterthought) even noticed the innovation.[4] The reason for this neglect is that Descartes introduces the view indirectly, not to say imperceptibly, and in such a way that it appears entirely unobjectionable. For he insinuates that by judgment he means an action, but this can belong only to the will, which for him is active, and not to the intellect, which is entirely passive.

This is not the first time in the *Meditations* that judgment has importantly arisen. In the Second Meditation Descartes argues that the piece of wax is known more clearly and distinctly by the mind alone than by the senses or the imagination. An animal might be capable of sensory perceptions of the wax, but when the wax is "stripped" of its outward forms to be considered in its nature, judgment is required. We say that we *see* men crossing the square below, but in fact we *judge* that men are there upon seeing their caps and coats. We also judge that wax has an underlying nature. The intellectual perception that is practiced in the Second Meditation provides us with first-hand knowledge of the nature of the human mind – as something that is capable of judgment – and a similarly non-sensory knowledge of its existence. Animals do not have intellectual perception and they do not have judgment. In the language of the Third Meditation, where Descartes argues that he has a materially true idea of God, animals are capable of no more than materially false ideas, but human beings can have materially true ideas both of the wax and of the human mind.

Despite the obvious importance of judgment, the term for it appears infrequently in the *Meditations*, and nowhere does Descartes give an explicit definition of what he means by it, not even in the Fourth Meditation, where the role of that concept is essential. The reason for the apparent neglect is that he there uses the term synonymously with another term for which he does give an explicit definition, one that is just sufficient for his epistemic purposes. When he inquires into the nature of his errors, he finds that they depend on two causes, each of which on its own is nevertheless impeccable. First is the faculty of knowing, that is, the intellect; but "all the intellect does is enable me to perceive the ideas about which I can make a judgement [*de quibus judicium ferre possum*], and in just this respect it contains no error strictly speaking" (AT 7: 56, my translation). Second is the faculty of choosing or freedom of the will (*facultate eligendi, sive … arbitrii libertate*); but this faculty too is incapable of error. Indeed, Descartes thinks, we cannot understand how it could be any more perfect than it already is. Now, there is an enormous problem of translation at this point. For when Descartes next refers to this faculty, to say that it is with respect to it that we most bear the image and likeness of God, he calls it "the will, or freedom of choice [*voluntas, vel arbitrii libertas*]." That is, if our standard translation is to be consistent, he is saying the faculty of choosing is freedom of choice, or that the will is freedom of the will, both of which look to be either syntactically awkward or just tautological.

In crucial texts over just two pages Descartes deploys, in the standard translation, the following three equivalences, which trade on electing (choosing): "judgment or choice" (*judicandum vel eligendum*, AT 7: 58); "the faculty of choice or freedom of the will" (*facultate sive … arbitrii libertate*, AT 7: 56); and "will or freedom of choice" (*voluntas, sive arbitrii libertas*, AT 7: 57). The problem lies with the term *arbitrium*, for which there is, however, a translation that both gives us the definition we need (of *judgment*), and that is unproblematically consistent. The translation is *decision*. To have a will, that is, a faculty of choosing, is to have freedom of decision.

The Latin etymons are instructive, and also easy to understand because they are close, sometimes identical, to the English derivatives. *Arbitrium* is from *ar* (*ad*) and *beto*. An *arbiter* is one who goes to something, to see or hear it, ultimately to decide or settle it. The (deponent) verb form is *arbitrari*, meaning to be, and act as that person, to make the decision. The *arbitrium* is the decision, or judgment, or the power to make it; thus it can mean: mastery, authority, power, will, or free will. Note that free will, *liberum arbitrium* does not mean that the decision is arbitrary in the sense of being capricious or indifferent. Least of all should the usual translation of this expression, *free* will, be taken to indicate that freedom is somehow a property of the will. Presumably, whatever decision is made should be made on the basis of what the arbiter sees. *Judicium* is implicated in the sense of this term.

A *judex* is one who makes or passes a *judicium*, and whose activity is described by the verb *judicare*. These terms are derived from *jus*, law or right, itself related to a Sanskrit term that means *to join*. Certainly, there are differences of nuance and context for uses of *arbitrium* and *judicium*; but Descartes uses the terms as if they were synonyms. This is not a linguistic issue, still less a quibble over translation, but a philosophical issue of classifying together mental activities as ones for which we are responsible.

Though Descartes' principal concern is with the true, and with the will's connection to the true, there is an implicit parallel treatment of the will's connection to the good throughout the Meditation. First, both the true and the good involve constraint on the will – either evidence, or the clear and distinct perception of the truth, or grace, "a divinely produced disposition of my inmost thoughts" (AT 7: 58). To fully perceive the true is to assert the true, and to perceive the good is to pursue the good.[5] Although this is not to say that perception and assertion are identical. Were they, the theodicy would collapse.[6] Second, the will's connection to the true and its connection to the good both involve freedom and thus responsibility (AT 7: 57–58). This parallel makes plausible Descartes' synonymous use of a*rbitrium* and *judicium*.

Decision is an idiomatic way to render Descartes' use of both *arbitrium* and *judicium*. I can *decide* to do something, but I cannot *judge* to do it. I can *judge* that something is true, and thus believe it; but I can also *decide* that it is true, which at least implicates that I believe it. And to *decide* to do something is to do it willingly. The word idiomatically captures both aspects of what Descartes wants to assign to the will's activity: belief and responsibility. Decision is the preferable term, but judgment is sometimes more idiomatic, and unfortunately is entrenched in the literature. It is acceptable so long as it is taken in the broader sense.

What motivates the novel, voluntarist theory that construes judgment as an action, thereby placing it under the aegis of the will? It must be a new, and severe problem, one that arises only as a result of the previous Meditations. This suggests that the doubt remaining at the beginning of the Fourth Meditation that implicates the divinity in our errors derives from the novel, hyperbolical doubt of the Third Meditation as to whether God creates us incapable of truth. What Descartes needs is an alternative explanation of how we err such that it is possible for us to err even though we are created by a truthful God. That is, the proof of a truthful God is by itself insufficient for Descartes' purposes. If this motivation is kept in mind, much of the difficulty that critics have found in the theory, certainly its incompleteness as an account of the will, can be excused. Descartes' aim is not to provide a complete account of the will, but only one that is just sufficient to explain how we are capable of going wrong while yet seeking, and indeed attaining truth. His discussion of the will is driven entirely by his epistemological project of the *Meditations* as a whole.

Descartes nonetheless does offer a fair amount by way of explicating the notion of judgment. Early in the Third Meditation, he engages what later was to be called the thesis of sighted agency, namely that no one acts blindly in the sense of acting without the determination (in some sense) of perception. Broadly speaking, the will depends on the intellect. For Descartes, volition necessarily involves thought insofar as it is a *form* of thought. Some thoughts are "like images of things," the ideas of a man, or of a chimera, for example. "Other thoughts have various additional forms: thus when I will, or am afraid, or affirm, or deny, there is always a particular thing which I take as the object [*subjectum*] of my thought, but my thought includes something more than the likeness of that thing" (Third Meditation, AT 7: 37). Among these thoughts are judgments, and other volitions.

Elsewhere Descartes speaks of *form* in connection with judgment. He does so in the *Comments on a Certain Broadsheet*, where he makes clear that the additional form (on top of perception) is affirmation or denial. By correction of his errant disciple, Regius, he says that

I saw that over and above perception, which is a prerequisite of judgement, we need affirmation and negation to determine the form of the judgement, and also that we are often free to withhold our assent, even if we perceive the matter in question. Hence I assigned the act of judging itself, which consists simply in assenting (i.e. in affirmation or denial) to the determination of the will rather than to the perception of the intellect. (AT 8B: 363)

Thus, at least as far as these texts are concerned, Descartes differs from the later, generally Cartesian Port-Royal *Logic*, which treats affirmation and denial as acts differing in themselves. For Descartes, the negation in a denial is built into a proposition that is assented to, the opposite of which activity is *suspension*, or the withholding of assent. To affirm is to assent to a positive proposition, and to deny is to assent to a negative proposition. Not to assent is to do nothing, the doubt of suspension.[7]

TRUTH AND FALSITY

In the important distinction among thoughts that Descartes draws above between ideas and judgments, the standard translation renders *subjectum* as 'object', thus suggesting that Descartes' concern is with the intentionality of thought – that he thinks that all agency is sighted precisely insofar as volition, as a form of thought is always about or is directed toward something. Now, the issue is by itself complicated, both in Descartes' texts, and in the work of those in the period who claimed to be defending his views. Notably, Arnauld took all thought, including even sensations, to be intentional in this sense, while Malebranche reserved intentionality to perception only of ideas.

The issue between Malebranche and Arnauld had not been clearly decided by Descartes. But he did draw a distinction relevant to it, that between material truth and falsity as opposed to formal truth and falsity. As is suggested by his proleptically Fregean notion of assertion, Descartes distinguishes predication, or the formation of a proposition, from the assertion of it. In this he again differs from the Port-Royal *Logic*, according to which "the verb both connects the subject and predicate, and has assertive force; hence forming a proposition is the equivalent of judging it."[8] For Descartes, there is a sense in which propositions come already formed. This is because truth is not a relation between a combination of linguistic items (a sentence) and some state of affairs, but an object itself, namely an essence: "there is no distinction between truth and the thing or substance that is true" ("To Clerselier, 23 April 1649," AT 5: 355). Thus, the Euclidean theorem that its interior angles equal a straight angle expresses both the essence of a triangle and a truth, such that the difference between that sentence (as opposed to the proposition it expresses) and a (non-sentential) name for the essence is only a matter of convention.[9] The notion of truth here adumbrates what Locke later called *metaphysical*.[10] On the other hand, "falsity [and, presumably, truth] in the strict sense, or formal falsity [and truth], can occur only in judgments" (The Third Meditation, AT 7: 43). Of formal falsity, more below.

The standard translation of *subjectum* is not exactly a *contresens*, nor even a misdirection in suggesting the issue of intentionality. But the translation of *subjectum* as 'object', instead of the more natural 'subject', nonetheless has the effect of obscuring Kenny's useful proposal that *subjectum* is used by Descartes in the scholastic sense of *materia*, or matter. This reading comports nicely with the proto-Fregean account of judgment above, a version of which Kenny uses to provide Descartes both with a justification for treating judgment as an act of the will, and a solution to a problem raised by that treatment. The problem "is that the object of the intellect is truth, that of the will goodness; that error is a matter of falsehood, and sin of badness."[11]

On Kenny's account, the *matter* of a judgment might be read as a Fregean *sense*, and an *act of will*, which Descartes calls its *form*, might be read as the indication of its reference, which for Frege is *the true*, and for Descartes, we might add, is the relevant essence. The details of Kenny's account are less than perfectly clear, but the direction of it is obviously promising. For, with the Fregean distinction in hand, "both assertions and proposals may be described in terms of affirmation and negation; both may be characterized as 'assent' or 'dissent'; both as forms of commitment. Assent to both a proposition and a proposal may be sincere or insincere, rash or cautious, right or wrong."[12] Alas, according to Kenny, the account is not the direction Descartes takes, for he is confused, as may be seen in the following "strange" argument:

Now as far as ideas are concerned, provided they are considered solely in themselves and I do not refer them to anything else, they cannot strictly speaking be false; for whether it is a goat or a chimera that I am imagining, it is just as true that I imagine the former as the latter. As for the will and the emotions, here too one need not worry about falsity; for even if the things which I may desire are wicked or even non-existent, that does not make it any less true that I desire them. Thus the only remaining thoughts where I must be on my guard against making a mistake are judgements. (The Third Meditation, AT 7: 37)

Now, Kenny thinks that judgments do not differ in these terms from ideas, that they too considered in themselves cannot be false, even if what is judged is false. The confusion is supposed to lie in Descartes' failure to account for what J. L. Austin called the *onus of match* (or perhaps what John Searle later called *direction of fit*). Obviously, affirmations should fit the world; but how volitions are supposed to be matched or to fit in the opposite direction is not made clear by Kenny. Nor is it clear just how this alleged gap in Descartes' view relates to the strange argument. But no matter; for Kenny's proto-Fregean suggestion itself helps to dispel the alleged strangeness of the argument.

The will, with its volitions, is, like the intellect, with its perceptions, impeccable. Descartes does not put it this way, but we might say that taken by themselves volitions, like perceptions, are materially *true* as modes of the mind.[13] But, unlike perceptions, volitions cannot be materially *false*. That is, volitions do not "represent non-things as things," as the intellect sometimes does, because it is not a faculty of representation at all. Only when the volition informs the perception in a judgment, which inherently contains a representation or reference, can it be false, and then, as we have seen, its falsity is *formal*, which occurs *only* in judgments.

Nor is this the only disanalogy between intellect and will. Connected with it is the difference in their operation. As essences, intellect and will are indivisible, binary notions. They occur entirely or not at all. But the intellect can vary in terms of the clarity and distinctness of its perceptions, that is, in how well it represents its object. To put it more precisely, it can more or less closely approximate the perception of truth. The will, however, does not vary in this or any other way. Indeed, if the will tracked the intellect exactly, Descartes' explanation of error, and with it his theodicy, would fail.

WILL AND FREEDOM

Descartes' view of judgment as dependent on the will is, although entirely novel, not at all unintuitive. By contrast, his view that the will and freedom are identical is unintuitive, but not at all novel. This view of the will is found in a debate whose roots extend to the previous century and the Protestant Reformation. Luther and Calvin were read by the Council of Trent, which condemned their views, as heretically denying free will and thereby moral responsibility in humans. Roughly put, these Reformers were seen as holding that divine grace is necessary and sufficient for salvation, that those and only those endowed with grace are saved, which left no role for human freedom in the salvific drama. However, exactly which contrasting view of freedom was endorsed by the Council was left unclear. Later in the century, the Jesuit Luis de Molina sought to clarify the Catholic position. To be sure, grace was necessary for salvation, but everyone had it, and so the difference that distinguished the saved from the damned was due to human freedom. The will was taken to be indifferent in the sense that its exercise of any given choice it might make could have been otherwise under the same circumstances. In short, he proposed a view that nowadays would be called libertarian.

Other thinkers in the Counter-Reformation saw Molina's view as tending toward the opposite heresy of Pelagianism, that grace is not necessary for salvation and that those who are saved effectively save themselves. These thinkers appealed instead to the views of Augustine. One of them was the Cardinal Bèrulle, who charged a member of the French Oratory that he had founded with the refutation of Molina's view. Guillaume Gibieuf duly published *De libertate* (1630), a work that drew the official approbation of, among others, Bishop Cornelius Jansenius, who ten years later published the *Augustinus*, which intensified and extended the debate to the point of becoming the single most important seventeenth-century text on the will. What Jansenius said about it is long and obscure. Moreover, his book came be regarded as heretical, and five propositions said to be in some way contained in the book were officially condemned. The defenders of Jansenius argued variously that either the propositions were not in the book, or that they were not there in the sense in which they were condemned, the result of which was further condemnations and further defenses. Even if there is unclarity about some of the propositions of *Augustinus*, there are at least a couple of views that are central to the Counter-Reformation alternative that Jansenius was proposing. One is a rejection of indifference in the libertarian sense as the essence of freedom. Jansenius took over a *reductio ad absurdum* of that view from Gibieuf: the virtuous, who are most entrenched in a habit of doing good, and the vicious, who are most entrenched in their habit of doing evil, would be the least indifferent, the least free, and the least worthy of reward or punishment.[14] A second view is that freedom consists instead in *spontaneity*, a necessity of a certain kind. The language used to draw the distinction between it and the sort of necessity that destroys freedom varied: the language of internal versus external constraint, for example, or necessity versus compulsion. But the thrust is tolerably clear: the free is what is under our control such that it occurs just in case we will it. In fact, whatever is in our power is so in virtue of our will, which is therefore essentially free. "This is the very root of all freedom," said Jansenius.[15] To have a will is to be free.

A theological question debated in the period illustrates the difference between the Molinist and Jansenist views. It had long been held that the saints in heaven who stand face to face with God are utterly fixed in their beatific vision and are thus, like Christ in this life, literally impeccable – incapable of sin. Their time of trial is over (as the time of trial is over for the damned, who are no longer capable of virtue or earning merit). On the other hand, the saints cannot be deprived of their will, which would leave them less than human. One solution to the apparent inconsistency in their state is to distinguish between the will and its freedom. This was the view of the Molinists, who conceived of the beatific vision as voluntary but not free. The saints in heaven have a will, but it is no longer indifferent. For the Augustinians, the voluntary is the free, so the saints in heaven are free; but the beatific vision remains permanent because the attraction that necessitates the will is permanent as well.

Now, Descartes generally sought to avoid theological issues,[16] but on this one it would have been hard to avoid taking a stance, at least by implication. And so, in an important letter, Descartes shows his Augustinian hand. He explains that if we saw clearly that what we are doing is evil, it would be impossible for us to sin, so long as we saw it in that fashion; that is why they say that 'whosoever sins does so in ignorance.' And we may earn merit even though, seeing very clearly what we must do, we do it infallibly, and without any indifference, as Jesus Christ did during his earthly life. ("To Mesland, 2 May 1644," AT 4:117)

The only difference between this state and the beatific vision as the Augustinians understand it is its lack of guaranteed permanence due to the fallibility of our attention to our clear perceptions. In short, Descartes pretty clearly commits himself to the Augustinian view of the connection between the will and freedom. No surprise, then, that when about to define the will, Descartes refers to "the will or freedom of choice" (AT 7: 56).

Anything other than an Augustinian stance would have been a surprise. Despite his cautious aversion from theological dispute, Descartes saw it as important that his views on sensitive issues such as freedom be compatible with theological orthodoxy. And so in the period leading up to the publication of the *Meditations*, he was at pains to have them agree with the views of Gibieuf, whom he clearly took to represent orthodoxy. Moreover, Descartes sought to have Gibieuf get the Sorbonne to approve the work, and he cannot reasonably have expected Gibieuf to do this if he subscribed to the Molinist view that Gibieuf had been tasked with refuting.

The most important reason for Descartes to have taken an Augustinian stance is that without it, his epistemological program collapses. In the Fourth Meditation he says of the *cogito* that

I could not but judge that something which I understood so clearly was true; but this was not because I was compelled so to judge by any external force, but because a great light in the intellect was followed by a great inclination [*propensio*] in the will, and thus the spontaneity and freedom of my belief was all the greater in proportion to my lack of indifference. (AT 7: 58–59)

In this well noted passage, Descartes recapitulates what he has just explained, that freedom and indifference vary inversely, presumably such that that perfect freedom of assent would be an *internal* force in response to irresistible evidence. Indeed, if belief were not always constrained by his perception in this way, doubt would still be possible, and the goal of certainty would be forever out of reach in this life.

Most, though not all, libertarian interpretations of Descartes take him to have later radically altered the view of the *Meditations*, or to have given it up altogether. The linchpin text of these interpretations is another text, at least related to his correspondence with Mesland, in which Descartes appears to contradict the great light passage: "... it is always open to us to hold back (*nobis licet nos revocare*) from pursuing a clearly known good, or from admitting a clearly perceived truth, provided we consider it a good thing to demonstrate the freedom of our will by so doing" (AT 4: 173). The very comprehensive reading by Ragland uses this text to back-read the great light passage in an effort to construe it in libertarian terms (Ragland 2006). But this translation of the text is open to questions that in conjunction with the conditional clause, and the rest of the text, suggest a reading that is not only compatible with the Augustinian reading of the great light passage, but supportive of it.[17]

With this non-libertarian view of freedom and the will, its historical context, and a recognition of Descartes' larger epistemological program, it becomes possible to provide a consistent and straightforward reading of an earlier central text of this Meditation – one that has bedeviled the literature. Descartes says that it is with respect to the will, in its essential and strict sense, that he in some way bears the image and likeness of God. He adds that

this is because the will simply consists in our ability to do or not to do something (that is, to affirm or deny, to pursue or avoid); or rather [*vel potius*], it consists simply in the fact that when the intellect puts something forward for affirmation or denial or for pursuit or avoidance, our inclinations are such that we do not feel we are determined by any external force. (AT 7: 57)

It is the *vel potius* clause that has been found problematic. For with it Descartes seems to be either correcting what he has just said, or explaining what should not have needed any explanation, or playing a rhetorical trick of bait-and-switch. With varying degrees of discomfort, interpreters have tried to shoehorn the clause in ways that are problematic to various accounts based on the rest of the text, including, for example, the suggestion that Descartes is here offering two different and incompatible views of freedom and that *vel potius* is a conjunction.[18]

The text looks very different, however, and less uncomfortable, once it is realized that the first clause was a neutral way to describe the will used by *all* sides in the debate over freedom. The *vel potius* clause can then be read as Descartes' way of cementing his agreement with the Augustinians. The reason for the neutral first clause is that in a well-heeded text, the fourth canon of the sixth session (1547), the Council of Trent had declared that grace can always be resisted, that is, that human free will (*liberum arbitrium*) can always dissent, "if it should will to do so [*si velit*]."[19] The ability to choose one way or other that is asserted in the first clause is what Descartes was bound to affirm. It was affirmed no less by Jansenius and his defenders such as Arnauld, who clearly were no libertarians. The second, *vel potius* clause of Descartes' definition lays out his own way of understanding Trent's conditional clause. We may be constrained by evidence to assert (or be constrained by grace to pursue), but because the constraint is internal to us, the assertion (or pursuit) is free. If the constraint had been different, so would the volition have been different, but no less free because of the identity of will and freedom. It is here that Descartes sets himself apart from the Molinists, for whom the soul's willing to resist would be a separate, indifferent act of willing.[20]

MOTIVATIONS: DIVINE AND HUMAN

The explanation of error as consisting in an inappropriate use of the will on our part does not quite relieve God of the responsibility for our errors. For the fact remains, acknowledged by Descartes, that God could have created him incapable of error just by giving him irresistible perceptions of the truth. Nor does it help, given that possibility, to construe error, as Descartes does, as "not something real which depends on God, but merely a defect" (AT 7: 54). This ontological gambit, previously deployed by many in dealing with the general problem of evil, perhaps would allow Descartes to explain why there should be the *possibility* of a mismatch between the intellect and the will; for it is part of our nature, standing as we do between the pure being and perfection of God on the one hand and nothingness or non-being on the other, that our intellect be finite, not possessing pure perception of everything. Only God has an infinite intellect in this sense. But it does not explain why God would allow such an avoidable mismatch to *occur at all*. It could have been that however essentially imperfect we are, we nonetheless never fall into error. So the theodical problem stands.

The answer to this problem lies in an appeal to the imperfection that generates it. God is "immense, incomprehensible and infinite"

(AT 7: 55), and we are none of these. So it is to be expected that there should be many things of whose causes (*causas*) we are ignorant. And here Descartes makes an extracurricular gesture on behalf of his anti-Aristotelian physics. "For this reason alone I consider the customary search for final causes to be totally useless in physics; there is considerable rashness [*temeritate*] in thinking myself capable of investigating the <impenetrable> purposes of God" (ibid.).[21] Final causes are proscribed not because they are unintelligible, or vacuous (the upshot of the New Science), or because God has no purposes (Spinoza's later view), but because they cannot be known, at least not by reason alone. So the question becomes, what is the equivalent here of the evident sort of explanation that can be given in physics (i.e., mechanism)? And the answer that Descartes then provides is the one above, appealing only to ideas of the intellect and will, which ideas are irresistibly evident.

Moreover, when considering whether the perfection of the world befits the perfection of its creator, says Descartes, it is the whole world that must be taken into account, and not just the limited part of it occupied by him with his imperfection. For what by itself might be imperfect might be nonetheless perfect as a part of the whole. This proto-Leibnizian observation, also with a long history before Descartes, is not an explanation of why he in particular was not provided only with irresistibly evident perceptions of the truth, but of why no such explanation can be forthcoming. Such an explanation would require knowledge beyond the ken of any finite intellect. And that is all that Descartes needs for his theodicy. It is sufficient for us to know that there exists a God whose reasons are good, and this Descartes has demonstrated.

In her classic work on the *Meditations*, Wilson raises a question which is nowhere addressed by Descartes, but which is nonetheless pertinent. It concerns motivation – not God's, but ours. Why would anyone ever misuse the will by assenting without the natural light, without the clear perception of the truth? Notwithstanding that we might "by pure chance" arrive at the truth, such an epistemological shot in the dark is always a misuse of freedom for which we are culpable (AT 7: 61). Wilson offers four reasons, immediately dismissing the first three as inadequate.[22] Still, her dismissed reasons, however inadequate as *motives* for misuse of the will, enhance the plausibility of characterizing that misuse in terms of Descartes' ethics-of-belief epistemology.

First, one might assent to what is but obscurely perceived because one *wants* it to be true. Such wishful thinking would naturally be motivated by self-interest. One wants it to be true because one's interest would be served by its being true. Except in cases where such desires might help *bring about* its truth, this motivation is nothing but delusional *selfishness*. The remedy: assent only when forced to do so; do not go epistemically off on your own.

Second, one might be led by "a sort of lust for knowledge." This way of putting it suggests the temptation of Adam and Eve, the promise of which was that they would be like unto God. The antidote to such unjustifiable *pride*, the sin of an even earlier occasion, would be the epistemological humility that figures so centrally in Descartes' theodicy.

Third, one might think of the will as "wandering among confused perceptions like a lost soul with no fixed purpose in life: embracing this or that one for no definite reason." (An image might be the aviary in the *Theaetetus*: one reaches into the cage and grabs a bird from any number of different species.) This account, which suggests the libertarian view, denies that we need a motivation beyond the will itself – which is why Wilson dismisses it: "... we can't just decide to believe or assent to something, and forthwith believe or assent to it." The sin of doing so, or acting as if we were doing so, would be an instance of what Descartes calls *temerity* (a term that often appears in Church condemnations of heretical views).

Wilson's preferred account appeals to a "natural bent" we have for assenting to the attraction of ideas that are materially false, i.e., ideas that represent non-things as things. Now this account comports nicely with Descartes' theodicy, for the paradigm of such materially false ideas is the gamut of our sensations, which are given to us for their survival value. The consumption of what is tasty contributes (at least generally, as he explains in the Sixth Meditation, consistent with the simplicity of the physical system) to the keeping of mind and body together. This biological utility justifies the errors they often occasion. (Indeed, sometimes they are required, as when action is urgent and there is no time to ascertain the absolute truth of the situation.)[23] In theological terms, the natural bent would be the result of original sin – concupiscence, as it was called. How on this account the sin of Adam is to be explained, still more the Ur-sin of Satan, is a problem – one on which the theologically intrepid Malebranche, like Milton, later had much to say. The theologically cautious Descartes was silent.

Wilson's bottom line is that Descartes' account of error "makes it no less consistent with God's goodness than sin is on the traditional [Christian] account."[24] This less than perfect success seems a fair assessment, especially in light of the Church's rejection of both Reformationist denials of freedom and the Pelagian assertions of it, without indication of a positive account that makes us both responsible for sin and yet dependent on God. Similarly, Descartes' theory makes us responsible for error but without claiming that every error in one's life can be avoided. But Descartes' theodicy need not show that on every occasion one can avoid error by not assenting, which Wilson argues is *empirically implausible*."[25] That would set too high a standard, one that Descartes nowhere asserts. At the *end* of the Meditation, he makes the following, Augustinian concession: "Admittedly, I am aware of a certain weakness in me, in that I am unable to keep my attention on one and the same item of knowledge at all times" (AT 7: 62).[26] No surprise here at such breakdown of attention, for if it were permanent, the time of trial would be over, and we would have a minor version of the beatific vision. But when it does break down there is a remedy: "By attentive and repeated meditation I am nevertheless able to remember [to withhold judgment] as often as the need arises, and thus get into the habit of avoiding error."

NOTES

1. For example, the Fifth Meditation, AT 7: 69.
2. The Fourth Meditation, AT 7: 60. For a full treatment of Descartes' project in these terms, see Davies 2001.
3. Gilson 1913, 284.
4. It was Kenny who first noticed all this, in his seminal article (1972, esp. 7–9). The novelty stands, but more needs to be said here because of the texts cited by Petrik 1992, 19–27.
5. "To Regius, 24 May 1640," AT 3: 64; *Discourse* Three, AT 6: 28.
6. See Newman, 2008, 341–42 on Curley, 1975.
7. For more, see Buroker 1996.
8. Arnauld and Nicole 1996, ed. introd. xxiv.
9. "To Mersenne, 22 July 1641," AT 3: 417–18.
10. *Essay concerning Human Understanding*, 4.5.11.

11. Kenny 1972, 10.

12. Kenny 1972, 15.

13. *Materialiter* is one of the terms Descartes uses to describe how ideas, and presumably all mental states, are taken as operations of the mind. See the preface to the *Meditations* (AT 7: 8).

14. For example, Gibieuf 1630, bk. 1, ch. 1, p. 13.

15. *Augustinus*, III, bk. 6, ch. 5; pp. 261–62.

16. For example, "To Mersenne, 30 September 1640," AT 3: 184.

17. Lennon 2013.

18. Kenny 1972, 18–19. Other commentators who have to shoehorn the text include Ragland 2006 and Wee 2006.

19. Canon 4, session 6; Denzinger 1963, 378.

20. Lennon (forthcoming).

21. See also *Principles* III.1–2.

22. Wilson 1978, 144–45.

23. See also *Principles* II.3.

24. Wilson 1978, 150.

25. Ibid., 149.

26. See also Janowski 2004, 53.

9 The Fourth Meditation: Descartes and libertarian freedom

INTRODUCTION

The Fourth Meditation has not always received its due attention in the literature. Indeed, commentators have upon occasion elected to leave out any discussion of this Meditation, moving (as if seamlessly) from commentary on the Third Meditation to commentary on the Fifth.[1] To proceed in this way is to suggest that excision of the Fourth Meditation does not result in any significant loss in understanding the *Meditations*, or Descartes' larger system.

This chapter will show how the Fourth Meditation is central to Descartes' account of the nature of the will and human freedom. To fully understand this account, we will need to situate the claims of the Meditation within the context of Descartes' wider *oeuvre*. We will also need to consider the context of earlier medieval debates on free will, as Descartes is generating his account against the background of these.

OVERVIEW OF THE FOURTH MEDITATION

By the end of the Third Meditation, Descartes takes himself to have established the existence of God – a being that "cannot be a deceiver, since it is manifest by the natural light that fraud and deception depend upon some defect" (AT 7: 52). The Fourth Meditation examines in greater detail the result that God cannot be a deceiver. The key difficulty for the result is this. Descartes finds in himself a faculty of judgment, which "like everything else, I received from God" (AT 7: 54). He then remarks:

Since God does not wish to deceive me, he surely did not give me the kind of faculty which would ever enable me to go wrong while using it correctly.

186

An analysis of his concept of (a perfect) God tells him that He created finite minds and that He would not create us in a defective manner. However, "when I turn back to myself, I know by experience that I am prone to countless errors." Note that Descartes is concerned here primarily with *epistemic errors*. The concern in the Meditation is not with "sin, i.e. the error which is committed in pursuing good and evil," or with matters pertaining to "the conduct of life," but "with the error that occurs in distinguishing truth from falsehood" ("Synopsis of the *Meditations*," AT 7: 15.)

In the Fourth Meditation, Descartes puts forward various arguments to explain how it is possible for a finite mind to make epistemic errors in a universe that was created in its entirety by a non-deceiving God. Some of the arguments explain our proneness to error by pointing out that our imperfection perhaps enhances the overall perfection of the universe. Other arguments appeal to the "immense, incomprehensible and ungraspable" nature of God (AT 7: 55), and emphasize the inability of a finite thinker to grasp the overall purposes of God in creating her as error-prone.

There is however a further argument that examines the thinker's faculties not in relation to the larger universe, but as they are in themselves. Here Descartes argues that error is the result of his improper use of the will in inappropriately affirming or denying what the intellect presents to it. Since his errors result from his *own* improper use of will, they do not have their source in God but in himself. They thus cannot be taken as evidence of God's deception. I shall call this argument the Argument from Free Will (hereafter AFW).

AFW has a larger historical context, and indeed Descartes' views on free will are framed by, and revolve around, two opposing accounts of human freedom that were heavily debated in medieval times. On one side of the debate were the Dominican intellectualists, who maintained that the will is free when it is determined to choose what the intellect apprehends to be the best course of action.[2] The final outcome of deliberation by the intellect is commonly called the "last practical judgment," and the intellectualists held that the free will is always determined in its choice by this last judgment. That is, the will is free when its choices are *determined* by the intellect. The intellectualists were thus compatibilists in respect of free will – they accepted that freedom was *compatible* with the will being determined (in specified ways). They held further that freedom *required* that the will is determined (in these ways).

On the other side, the Jesuit voluntarists supported a libertarian or incompatibilist position.[3] They held that the will is free only when it is *not* determined to choose any particular outcome. On this view, the will is free only in the case that, when all antecedent conditions prior to willing have been fully specified, it is still open to the agent to have done otherwise than she did.

With this background in place, let us return to Descartes' account of free will in AFW. This account is prima facie compatibilist. Descartes first points out that the will "consists in the ability to do or not do something," and then notes that there are different grades of freedom:

In order to be free, there is no need for me to be inclined both ways; on the contrary, the more I incline in one direction – because I clearly understand that reasons of truth and goodness point that way ... the freer is my choice ... [T]he indifference I feel when there is no reason pushing me in one direction rather than another is the lowest grade of freedom; it is not evidence of any perfection of freedom ... For if I always saw what was true and good, I would never have to deliberate about the right judgment or choice; in that case, although I should be wholly free, it would be impossible for me ever to be in a state of indifference. (AT 7: 57–58)

This passage asserts that the will is most free when it is determined in its choice by reasons provided by the intellect. Descartes elaborates that such determination occurs when the intellect has a clear and distinct perception – when a "great light in the intellect [is] followed by a great inclination in the will" (AT 7: 59). By contrast, when there is "no reason pushing me in one direction rather than another," the will is "indifferent" and has only "the lowest grade of freedom" (AT 7: 58). Descartes later remarks that the will is also in a state of indifference when "probable conjectures may pull ... in one direction" but "the mere knowledge that they are conjectures is enough to push my assent the other way" (AT 7: 59). What is common to cases of indifference is that the will is not determined to choose as it does: when all antecedent conditions prior to the act of willing are fully specified, the agent could have done otherwise.

This is in contrast to cases of clear and distinct perception, where Descartes holds that "although I should be wholly free, it would be impossible for me ever to be in a state of indifference." The latter claim can be taken as strong evidence that Descartes was a compatibilist: he specifies that when one is "wholly" free, one *cannot* be indifferent, and must be determined in one's choices.

The passages considered thus far ostensibly support that Descartes is a compatibilist. But we must be clear about the *version* of compatibilism in question. Unlike the medieval intellectualists, Descartes did not hold that the free will is *always* determined in its choices by the intellect. As seen above, he accepts that the will when indifferent is able to do otherwise – and he also accepts that in that circumstance the will is free (albeit at the lowest grade). Descartes is a compatibilist insofar as he accepts that there are *some* situations – i.e., when the intellect has a clear and distinct perception – when the will is both determined and free. That is, he accepts that there are instances where it is true both that

(a) the agent wills freely, and
(b) the agent could not have done otherwise.

Therefore he cannot maintain, as the traditional libertarian does, that the agent's ability to do otherwise is *necessary* for freedom.

AFW ostensibly supports a modified compatibilism, wherein Descartes accepts that actions can be both determined and free. In what follows, I shall mean by *compatibilism* the view that freedom can include being determined (but not that it always does). While AFW apparently presents Descartes as such a compatibilist, I now argue that Descartes was in fact a libertarian. My strategy for establishing this is to show that:

(1) Descartes' wider work provides good grounds for believing that he was a libertarian, albeit a non-traditional one, and
(2) the libertarian reading can accommodate all the claims that Descartes makes in AFW.

Whereas AFW ostensibly presents Descartes as maintaining that actions can be both determined and free, Descartes' wider *oeuvre* indicates that actions are free only if the agent can, *in some way*, not do as she did.

CARTESIAN FREE WILL AND THE ABILITY
TO DO OTHERWISE

Apart from AFW, other texts suggest that Descartes was a compatibilist. For example, in *Second Replies* he includes among a set of axioms that

the will of a thinking thing is drawn (*fertur*) voluntarily and freely (for this is the essence of the will), but nevertheless infallibly (*infallibiliter*), towards a clearly known good. (AT 7: 166)[4]

This claim is consonant with AFW, which indicates that the will is (highly) free when drawn infallibly to what the intellect clearly and distinctly perceives.

However, other texts outside of the Fourth Meditation are not easily reconciled with the compatibilist reading. In *Principles* I.37, Descartes writes:

It is a supreme perfection in man that he acts voluntarily, that is, freely; this makes him in a special way the author of his actions and deserving of praise for what he does ... [w]hen we embrace the truth, our doing so voluntarily is much more to our credit than would be the case *if we could not do otherwise*. (AT 8A: 18–19, emphasis mine)

Here Descartes equates acting voluntarily with acting freely, and he indicates that acting voluntarily requires that we could have done otherwise. This suggests that, for Descartes, freedom requires that we are *not* determined in our choices.[5]

Further evidence of the incompatibilist position is found in a letter, likely written to Mesland in February 1645 (hereafter referred to as Mesland$_1$). Descartes accepts there that the will has a "positive faculty of determining [itself] to one or other of two contraries, that is to say, to pursue or avoid, to affirm or deny." He then remarks:

Indeed, I think it has it not only with respect to those actions to which it is not pushed by any evident reasons on one side rather than on the other, but also with respect to all other actions; so that when a very evident reason moves us in one direction, although morally speaking we can hardly move in the contrary direction, absolutely speaking we can. For it is always open to us to hold back from pursuing a clearly known good, or from admitting a clearly perceived truth, provided we consider it a good thing to demonstrate the freedom of our will by so doing. (AT 4: 173)

Descartes writes that it is "always" possible to withhold pursuit of a clearly known good or assent to a clearly known truth. As he says in *Principles* I.37, the agent is *always* able to do otherwise.

Descartes' position in Mesland₁ and *Principles* runs counter to the apparently compatibilist elements of the Fourth Meditation and *Second Replies*. Can the apparent tension be resolved?

Anthony Kenny argues that the above two passages are consistent with Descartes' being a compatibilist. He points to another letter to Mesland in May 1644 (hereafter Mesland₂), where Descartes writes:

If we see very clearly that a thing is good for us, it is very difficult – and on my view, impossible, as long as one continues in the same thought – to stop the course of our desire [to pursue it]. But the nature of the soul is such that it hardly attends for more than a moment to a single thing; hence, as soon as our attention turns from the reasons which show us that the thing is good for us ... we can call up ... some other reason to make us doubt it, and so suspend our judgment, and even form a contrary judgement. (AT 4: 116)

In Mesland₁ Descartes had maintained that it is "always open to the agent to hold back from pursuing a clearly known good." Kenny notes that Mesland₂ makes clear that this can be done "only by distracting one's attention; one cannot refrain from desiring a good [that is] clearly seen to be good."[6] As an agent seldom "attends for more than a moment to a single thing," she can be distracted from assenting to a clear and distinct perception. But as long as her attention is *focused* on the clear and distinct perception, the will is determined in a particular direction, and the agent could not have done otherwise.

Traditional libertarians like the Jesuits held that, when the antecedent conditions prior to willing are fully specified, the free agent could still have done otherwise. But if Kenny is right, Descartes holds that when the antecedent conditions prior to willing are fully specified for a clear and distinct perception, the free agent could not have done otherwise. Thus, Kenny concludes, Descartes did not think the ability to do otherwise is necessary for freedom. That is, Descartes does not require of a (free) act of the will that it "should be avoidable."[7]

Kenny's position is not entirely satisfactory. *Principles* I.37 states that "when we embrace the truth, our doing so voluntarily is much more to our credit than ... if we could not do otherwise." In other words, even when we embrace the truth through our clear and distinct perceptions, we have to be able to do otherwise or else it would be less to our credit. Again, Mesland₁ states that we may hold back from pursuing a clearly known good or assenting to a clearly known truth "provided we consider it a good thing to demonstrate [our] freedom ... by so doing." Evidently, Descartes thinks we can demonstrate our freedom by holding back from pursuit of, or assent to, what is clearly known. But if freedom is demonstrated by the ability *not* to pursue or assent to what is clearly known, the ability to do otherwise is necessary for freedom. So Descartes wants to maintain that, even in the case of clear and distinct perceptions, we must be able to do otherwise in order to be free. There is a tension between Descartes' view here and his suggestion in other passages that the will is inevitably compelled to affirm clear and distinct perceptions. Can *this* tension be resolved?

I think it can. Descartes did see some kind of ability to do otherwise as necessary for freedom. He did not think the ability to do otherwise as specified by traditional libertarians – where, when all antecedent conditions have been specified, it is always possible for the agent to do otherwise – was necessary. But he still required of the free agent that she be able to do otherwise in some robust sense. To understand what this latter ability involves, we need to revisit the notion of a clear and distinct perception. In what way would the agent be able to do otherwise when confronted with such a perception?

Here note that Descartes accepts that there is always a temporal gap – no matter how brief – between the clear and distinct perception of a truth/good, and the will's affirmation or pursuit of that truth/ good. He writes in the Fourth Meditation that, when one has a clear and distinct perception, a "great light of the intellect *is followed by* [the] great inclination of the will." That is, when one clearly perceives a good, the will is "drawn" or brought towards (*fertur*) that good. However, it is in principle always possible for the agent to have a clear and distinct perception of a truth/good, and to shift attention to some other thought *before* the will affirms or pursues that truth/ good. The agent can therefore do other than affirm or pursue, even while she is having a clear and distinct perception – it is possible for her *not* to affirm that perception and *not* to pursue that good, by the expedient of shifting her attention away almost immediately from the clear and distinct perception to some other thought.

Descartes accepts, as he tells Mesland, that if one "continues" (over some time) to clearly and distinctly perceive a good, it would be "impossible" to "stop the course of our desire" towards pursuit. One does not, however, *have* to continue in the same clear and distinct thought – one can shift one's focus to some other thought, such as the thought that one expresses one's freedom by not pursuing a particular good.

Descartes also accepts that *morally* speaking, or practically speaking,[8] it is nearly impossible for us not to pursue a clearly known good or affirm a clearly known truth. He notes in Mesland₁ that one "can *hardly* move in a contrary direction" in such cases. This is presumably because the temporal gap between having a clear and distinct perception and affirmation/pursuit is miniscule, allowing little time for the agent to shift her attention and hence to withhold affirmation/pursuit. Nevertheless, this is always possible "absolutely speaking," and so in principle it is always possible for an agent to do otherwise.

The current reading makes good sense of Mesland₁ and *Principles* I.37. It also accommodates the texts which apparently suggest that the agent is unable to avoid affirmation/pursuit when she has a clear and distinct perception. For example, Descartes' claim that the will of an agent "is drawn ... freely but nevertheless inevitably towards a clearly known good" is in effect the following:

While one is focused on perceiving a clearly known good, the will is inevitably drawn towards (pursuit of) that good. The will is also free in being drawn towards that good insofar as the agent has (in principle) within herself the resources for stopping herself from pursuing that good.

Descartes thus holds that it is always possible – even when an agent is having a clear and distinct perception – for that agent to do otherwise, in the sense that she is never *determined* to will as she did. This "ability to do otherwise" of the Cartesian agent differs from the "ability to do otherwise" of the traditional libertarian. The latter takes avoiding assent/pursuit to be possible given the *same* antecedent conditions, but Descartes, in the case of clear and distinct perceptions, takes it to be possible only through *changing* the antecedent conditions. In Mesland₂, he says that

as soon as our attention turns from the reasons which show us that the thing is good for us ... we can call up ... some other reason to make us doubt it, and so suspend our judgment, and even form a contrary judgment. (AT 4: 116)

For Descartes, we can turn our attention away from a set of reasons and then "call up" other reasons in their place. To do either of these presumably involves an act of will, and Descartes thinks that there is always at least a tiny window for such an act during a clear and distinct perception. I will denominate this ability to do otherwise the robust$_D$ ability to do otherwise.

THE AGENT'S ABILITY TO DO OTHERWISE AND OTHER ASPECTS OF DESCARTES' METAPHYSICS

Descartes embraced a version of libertarianism, insofar as he held that freedom involves having either the robust$_D$ ability to do otherwise, or (at the lowest grade) the ability to do otherwise as specified by the traditional libertarian. However, there are aspects of Descartes' metaphysics that are prima facie incompatible with the view that agents have any ability to do otherwise. I now explore two of these aspects.

First, Descartes maintains that every occurrence in the universe, including every choice made by a finite will, is wholly dependent on God. He writes in a letter to Elizabeth:

When we think of the infinite power of God, we cannot help believing that all things depend on him, and hence that *our free will is not exempt from this dependence.* ("To Princess Elizabeth, 3 November 1645," AT 4: 332, emphasis mine)

For Descartes, our free choices of will are brought about by God, as is everything else in the universe. Descartes' doctrine of continuous creation reflects this view as well: God is not just the original creator of finite substances in the universe; He also sustains these substances in existence from moment to moment. As Descartes famously puts it, there is no distinction between divine preservation and divine creation, and so God re-creates thinkers in their entirety at every moment, including their every occurrent act of will.[9]

Descartes' view here militates against a human thinker's having any ability to do otherwise. If every aspect of a finite mind is completely dependent upon God for its existence and sustenance, a thinker would be unable to choose otherwise in *any* case – whether her perception is clear and distinct or not.

Second, Descartes holds that God *preordains* everything that happens in the universe. *Principles* I.40 is headlined: "It is . . . certain that everything was preordained by God" (AT 8A: 20). Descartes then writes that we recognize that our human thoughts and actions are predestined by God when we (clearly and distinctly) understand the nature of divine power:

Now that we have come to know God, we perceive in him a power so immeasurable that we regard it as impious to suppose that we could ever do anything which was not already preordained by him.

He speaks in similar terms in his correspondence with Princess Elizabeth. Echoing the doctrine of continuous creation, he writes,

The slightest thought could not enter into a person's mind without God's willing, and having willed from all eternity, that it should so enter. ("To Princess Elizabeth, 6 October 1645," AT 4: 314)

Descartes' views on the reach and scope of the divine will are in tension with his claim that the free agent has any sort of ability to do otherwise. If the agent was preordained from eternity by God to think and will as she did, she could not have done otherwise.

First I want to examine Descartes' attempt to reconcile human freedom with divine preordination, and then consider his view on the complete dependence of the human agent on God. Perhaps the best known of Descartes' attempts to reconcile human freedom with divine preordination is found in the letter to Elizabeth of January 1646, which draws an analogy between God and a king. This defense is generally thought to be unsatisfactory,[10] however, and so I focus instead on a less-noticed defense that Descartes provides. In *Third Replies*, he responds to Hobbes' criticism that he has offered no argument that the will is free:

On the question of our freedom, I made no assumptions beyond what we all experience within ourselves. Our freedom is very evident by the natural light ... There may indeed be many people who, when they consider the fact that God preordains all things, cannot grasp how this is consistent with our freedom. But if we simply consider ourselves, we will all realize in the light of our own experience that voluntariness and freedom are one and the same thing. (AT 7: 191)

Principles I.37 equated freedom with voluntariness, and maintained that voluntariness involves the ability to do otherwise. Here, Descartes acknowledges that one cannot grasp how God's preordination of all things is consistent with human freedom. But he declares that if we

examine ourselves directly, we know "in the light of our own experience" that we have voluntariness, and hence freedom. Thus, we know
from experience that we always have voluntariness and the ability to
do otherwise.

At first sight, Descartes' response to Hobbes does not look promising. He accepts both that

(a) God has preordained all things, and
(b) we know, from experience, that we are free creatures.

His point that we cannot "grasp" how human freedom is consistent
with preordination does nothing to *justify* or *explain* how divine
preordination and our experience of human freedom can be reconciled. Rather, he merely notes that divine preordination and the freedom that we experience are consistent, and says that we cannot know
how or why that is so.

The response to Hobbes might seem to be lacking, but in the
context of his larger system Descartes' response is in fact quite
plausible. We need to examine the nature of the Cartesian God in
particular. In the Fourth Meditation, one of Descartes' attempts to
reconcile divine perfection and human error involves noting that the
nature of God is "immense, incomprehensible and infinite" while
ours is "weak and limited" (AT 7: 55). We cannot fully understand
God's nature, and hence we cannot fully understand His omnipotence. Descartes will appeal to this seemingly innocuous result to
generate the conclusion that we should not expect to understand how
all of the different pieces of reality fit together, and more specifically
that we should not expect to understand how an agent's ability to do
otherwise is consistent with the complete dependence of all substances and modifications on God.

For many thinkers from the medieval through the early modern
period, God's omnipotence involved the power to do anything that is
logically possible. Aquinas and Leibniz, among others, held that the
laws of logic are metaphysically prior to any act of divine will. God's
will is therefore constrained by these laws – thus, for example, God
cannot will a round square into existence because that would violate
the principle of contradiction.

Descartes, however, espoused a radical version of divine omnipotence wherein God has the power to do even what is logically
impossible. He held that "from eternity [God] willed ... the eternal

truths and by that very fact created them" ("To [Mersenne], 27 May 1630," AT 1: 152.) The laws of logic are among these eternal truths. Thus, these laws are not metaphysically prior to acts of divine will – they came into being *because* God willed them to be so. God willed the laws of logic, and human understanding is then circumscribed by them. Accordingly, we cannot conceive a round square, for God willed as an eternal truth the principle of contradiction. We might attempt to understand what things are like beyond the laws of logic, but any such attempt is doomed to failure. Responding to Gassendi on the question of what humans grasp by the term "infinite," Descartes notes that one needs to distinguish between "an understanding that is suited to the scale of our intellect" and "a fully adequate conception of things" (AT 7: 365). Of the former, Descartes writes that "each of us knows by his own experience ... that he has this sort of understanding of the infinite." Of the latter, he says that "no one has this sort of conception of the infinite or of anything else."

Returning now to Descartes' response to Hobbes in *Third Replies*, we see why he would state that the divine order is beyond our grasp in the context of attempting to reconcile divine preordination and human freedom. This is because we can only understand what is "suited to the scale of our intellect," and we never have a fully adequate conception of things "as they really are." But although it is pointless to try to grasp what things are like independent of the laws of logic, Descartes thinks we clearly and distinctly recognize the truth of certain claims, even if it is beyond human grasp *how* they could be true. Similarly, Descartes says (in *Principles* I.25) that we have to believe what has been divinely revealed, "even though it may be beyond our grasp." (AT 8A: 14) Pointing to the mystery of the Trinity, he states that we should not "refuse to believe it, despite the fact that we do not clearly understand it." How God can be three individuals and yet one is beyond the "reach of the human mind," for it apparently contravenes the laws of logic. However, we must still accept that God is triune. For Descartes, the clarity and transparency that marks a perception as indubitably true may come from either the natural light or divine grace.[11] The perception that God is a trinity is given by divine grace. Thus, we should accept it, though we cannot conceive how it could be so.

Descartes has the same view in the case of clear and distinct perceptions: we should accept what we clearly and distinctly perceive to be the case, even if we cannot conceive how it *could* be the case. This is especially so with respect to our clear and distinct perceptions of God and God's attributes. For Descartes, human minds can perceive clearly and distinctly God's existence and attributes, although we cannot grasp them fully and adequately. In the Third Meditation, he insists that the unity, simplicity, and inseparability of the attributes of God is "one of the most important of the perfections which I understand him to have" (AT 7: 50), but then elaborates in *Second Replies* that this unity and simplicity "has no copy in us" (AT 7: 137). Our finite intellect assigns individual attributes to God "in a piecemeal fashion, corresponding to the way in which we perceive them in ourselves"; however, "none belong to God and to ourselves in the same sense."

Descartes thus accepts that our understanding may (clearly and distinctly) tell us that God has a simplicity that encompasses all His other attributes, even if we cannot conceive how God could be simple in this way. Indeed, to the human mind the claim that the various attributes are a simple unity appears contradictory: the very differentiation into various attributes requires that the attributes are different and distinct from each other, and thus not a simple unity. Thus, we are able to clearly and distinctly perceive that God has these attributes *without being able to conceive how*.

For Descartes, then, a finite mind can have a clear and distinct perception that is apparently self-contradictory. An interpretive worry, however, is that Descartes is emphatic that what is clear and distinct cannot be self-contradictory: "[s]elf-contradictoriness in our concepts arises merely from ... obscurity and confusion: there can be none in the case of [those that are] clear and distinct" (*Second Replies*, AT 7: 152). What is clear and distinct is a function of the finite standards that God has decreed to govern both the created universe and the bounds of our human minds. If a finite mind's perception of the unity of God's various attributes is self-contradictory, does this not imply that the perception is not clear and distinct (indeed is obviously false)?

We can resolve the difficulty here by comparing the two following claims:

(a) "God's attributes are unitary."
(b) "$\sim (2 + 3 = 5)$"

Descartes would accept (b) as self-contradictory. The rules of mathematics *can* be grasped adequately by a finite human understanding – indeed, they are among the laws that God willed to structure our finite understanding – and thus any claim that breaks these laws is, by definition, a claim that finite minds would consider self-contradictory. In contrast, (a) may *seem* to be self-contradictory, but in fact it is merely ungraspable by a finite human understanding. Note that an ungraspable clear and distinct claim is not thereby *confused and obscure*. For Descartes, confused and obscure claims are those which are not clear and distinct, and are such that counter-vailing reasons can be adduced to cast doubt on them. For example, a claim based on sensory perception that "The sun is very small" would be open to doubt because "astronomical reasoning indicates that it is very large" (The Third Meditation, AT 7: 39). In contrast, Descartes says that his idea of God is "utterly clear and distinct," even while he recognizes that "the nature of the infinite is not to be grasped by a finite being like myself" (AT 7: 46). For Descartes, there are claims about God and His nature that are wholly clear and dis-tinct, yet are not fully graspable by finite minds.

Returning to Descartes' response to Hobbes in *Third Replies*, we now see it has some plausibility. Recall that Descartes had to recon-cile two incompatible claims:

(a) God has preordained all things;
(b) we know from experience that we are free creatures.

Descartes' defense involves accepting (b), while pointing out that finite minds cannot grasp how (a) can be compatible with (b). As he notes, we "cannot grasp how [God's preordination] is compatible with our human freedom." This defense is cogent given the Cartesian God's radical omnipotence, which is such that finite minds can never fully grasp the nature of His power. We know from our own experience that we are able to do otherwise. Our inability to grasp how this freedom is consistent with the scope and extent of God's power is in the end an inability to fully understand God.

In *Principles* I.41, Descartes makes a second, more precise attempt at delineating this defense of free will:

41. How to reconcile the freedom of our will with divine preordination.

But we shall get out of [our difficulties here] if we remember that our mind is finite, but the power of God is infinite ... We may attain sufficient knowledge of this power to perceive clearly and distinctly that God possesses it; but we cannot get a sufficient grasp of it to see how it leaves the free actions of men undetermined. Nonetheless, we have such close awareness of the freedom . . . which is in us, that there is nothing we can grasp . . . more perfectly. And it would be absurd, simply because we do not grasp one thing, which we know by its very nature must be beyond our comprehension, to doubt something else . . . which we experience within ourselves. (AT 8A: 20)

Descartes says here that it appears to be self-contradictory that God's infinite power determines the events in the universe and also leaves human actions undetermined. However, the semblance of contradiction merely indicates that the nature of God's infinite power is beyond the "natural reach" of our minds. It is pointless to try to understand infinite power. We know "perfectly" that we have freedom, and that suffices to assure us that we have it.

Descartes' resolution of the tension between preordination and human freedom could also be applied in the case of the relation between human freedom and the complete dependence of the human agent on God. Descartes could argue that we clearly and distinctly perceive God's infinite power sufficiently to know that we are wholly dependent on God for our existence and our choices of will, and yet we are unable to grasp how God's sustaining activity leaves our free actions undetermined. Once again, this inability just indicates that divine power is beyond the natural reach of finite minds.[12] Our awareness of being undetermined should assure us that we are free.

In sum, Descartes held a version of libertarianism that involved the robust$_D$ ability to do otherwise when one is most free, and the ability to do otherwise as specified by traditional libertarians when one is least free. Despite prima facie evidence to the contrary, there is no genuine tension between these kinds of libertarian freedom and other aspects of Descartes' metaphysics. I now bring the discussion back to the account of freedom in AFW.

LIBERTARIAN FREEDOM AND THE FOURTH MEDITATION

AFW ostensibly presents Descartes as a compatibilist. I have argued, however, that the broader Cartesian corpus shows him to be a (highly nuanced) libertarian. Can this interpretation accommodate Descartes' claims about freedom in the Fourth Meditation? I now argue that it can.

Descartes' chief claims in AFW are that the will enjoys the highest freedom when it is infallibly drawn towards a clear and distinct perception, and exhibits the "lowest grade" of freedom when it is in a state of indifference. These claims are compatible with the view that when the will has the highest freedom and is being drawn towards assent/pursuit, it still has the further freedom to avoid such assent/pursuit by a deliberate switch of attention.

My reading is also consonant with another claim that might seem to support the compatibilist interpretation. It is a claim that we have already seen:

Although I should be wholly free, it would be impossible for me ever to be in a state of indifference. (AT 7: 58)

Descartes here indicates that being "wholly free" precludes being in a state of indifference. For Descartes, a state of indifference is specifically one where the will can be pushed back and forth by opposing reasons. In contrast, when one is "wholly free," one's will is pushed inexorably to affirm or pursue what one clearly and distinctly perceives. But Descartes thinks that in this latter state the agent still has a further and inalienable power, to *avoid* such assent/pursuit. It is because she has this further power not to do as she did that she is wholly free.

Note also that while Descartes never explicitly mentions the robust$_D$ ability to do otherwise in the Fourth Meditation, there *are* indications there that he takes humans to possess it. Descartes writes that he "knows by experience that [the will] is not restricted *in any way*" (AT 7: 56–57, emphasis mine). By claiming that the will is *wholly* unrestricted, Descartes would mean that the will is never fully determined to do as it did. He also claims that he knows "by experience" that this is so. This fits with his account in Mesland$_2$, where he outlines, quite evidently on the basis of personal introspection, the process by which one can avoid assent/pursuit in the case of clear and distinct perceptions (e.g., by deliberately shifting to another thought, or "calling up" other reasons to avoid assent).

Descartes further maintains in the Fourth Meditation that, while his faculties of intellect, understanding and imagination are

weak and limited . . . the will, or freedom of choice, which I experience within me [is] so great that the idea of any greater faculty is beyond my grasp; so much so that it is above all in virtue of the will that I understand myself to bear in some way the image and likeness of God. (AT 7: 57)

The claim that the faculty of will is "so great that the idea of any greater faculty is beyond my grasp" fits well with the view that freedom involves a robust$_D$ ability to do otherwise. On my reading, the will, whether at the highest or lowest grade of freedom, is always able to do otherwise. In being thus unconstrained, it is "greater" than the faculties of intellect or sense–perception. The human capacity to understand and perceive through the senses is limited, whereas the capacity to will is not.

Descartes' claim that it is in virtue of his faculty of will that he bears the "likeness of God" is indeed significant. As seen earlier, the will of the Cartesian God is wholly unconstrained in its ability to do or not do. It is not even constrained by the laws of logic, which are what they are because God willed them to be so. For our will to bear the likeness of God's will, it must somehow "image" this lack of constraint. On my reading, it does. At both levels of human freedom, the will possesses some kind of ability to do otherwise.

In sum, Descartes' claims in the Fourth Meditation are fully in line with his account of freedom as involving the robust$_D$ ability to do otherwise. But this leads to a further question: why did Descartes not make it *explicit* in that Meditation that humans possessed this ability?

To answer this question, we must look at the overall goal of the *Meditations*. The *Meditations* is a work which aims to demolish "preconceived" opinions and build knowledge upon a lasting foundation.[13] The primary concern of the *Meditations* is therefore *epistemic*. This also holds true of the Fourth Meditation. As mentioned, Descartes says in his synopsis of the *Meditations* that the Fourth Meditation is concerned "only with the error of distinguishing truth from falsehood" (AT 7: 15). Unlike his discussions of free will elsewhere, Descartes is focused here on epistemic issues.

The Fourth Meditation offers various arguments that attempt to explain how divine non-deception is compatible with human epistemic error. Descartes does this in AFW by arguing that God is not responsible for his errors, as it is he himself who misuses his will by affirming what is not clearly and distinctly perceived. AFW also serves a further purpose. As Descartes makes clear later in the

Meditation, AFW enables him to formulate a *criterion* by which to recognize that he has reached the truth. When his will is pushed inexorably in one direction by reasons – and there are no countervailing reasons to push it in another – he knows that his perception is clear and distinct, and hence true. He now has in hand a means by which he can pick out knowledge claims of whose truth he can be certain, and which can then form the foundation for a new and stable edifice of knowledge. These are claims that are utterly compelling, but that we still have the ability to refrain from affirming.

Given the epistemic goals of the *Meditations*, it is unsurprising that Descartes did not elaborate there on the robust$_D$ ability to do otherwise. But if one reads the Fourth Meditation in the context of Descartes' wider corpus, it is evident that he ultimately thought that this ability is central to human freedom.[14]

NOTES

1. See for example Dicker 1993, 146–47.
2. Murray 1996, 32.
3. Ibid., 31–32.
4. I have departed slightly from the CSM translation here.
5. Some commentators, e.g., Christofidou (2009) and Cunning (2007, 172–74; 2010, 132–33) hold that this passage should not be read as asserting that Descartes held the ability to do otherwise as necessary for freedom. They argue that the passage, considered in full, is concerned with the contrast between automata who are fully subject to physical laws, and humans who have volitions and make choices. But in the final sentence Descartes *specifically* equates voluntariness with an ability to do otherwise.
6. Kenny 1998, 150.
7. Ibid., 139.
8. *Principles* IV.204–5.
9. The Third Meditation, AT 7: 48–49.
10. See for example Kenny 1979, 78.
11. *Second Replies*, AT 7: 147–48.
12. Descartes' God, as I have presented Him, seems wholly beyond the grasp of human understanding. One worry then is that we can never truly know God or His attributes. This issue has been much discussed (see, e.g., Bennett 1994 and Curley 1984). A detailed discussion is beyond the scope of this paper. But Descartes does note in *Second Replies* that our understanding of God's attributes (omniscience, etc.) is relative to our

finite minds, circumscribed by the laws of contradiction (AT 7: 150–51). We have to be satisfied with this sort of understanding, as we have no other sort.

13. "Preface to the Reader," AT 7: 9.

14. Some material in this chapter was taken from an earlier paper (Wee 2006). I thank the editors of the *Canadian Journal of Philosophy* for permission to include this material.

10 The Fifth Meditation: Descartes' doctrine of true and immutable natures

In the Fifth Meditation, Descartes introduces his doctrine of "true and immutable natures." There he notes that

I find within me innumerable ideas of things that even though they may not exist anywhere outside me, nonetheless cannot be called nothing; and although they in some manner can be thought by me at will, nonetheless they are not made [*figuntur*] by me, but have their own true and immutable natures [*veras & immutabiles naturas*]. Thus when, for example, I imagine a triangle, even if perhaps no such figure exists outside my thought, nor has ever existed, there is still some determinate nature, or essence, or form, immutable and eternal, which is not produced [*non effictat*] by me, nor depends on my mind. (AT 7: 64)[1]

Though the emphasis here is on mathematical ideas, Descartes moves quickly in this Meditation to a consideration of the nature that corresponds to our idea of God. On the version of the "ontological argument"[2] that he presents in this text, that nature demonstrably includes existence, and so – in contrast to the nature of a triangle – requires the actual existence outside of thought of the object to which this nature corresponds.

In this chapter, I want to consider the significance of Descartes' doctrine of true and immutable natures for his system. I begin with the connection of this doctrine to Descartes' innatism. Descartes takes the fact that true and immutable natures are not produced by him and do not depend on his mind to show that his ideas of them must be innate. Some commentators have argued that this link to innatism reveals that Descartes had a consistently "conceptualist" understanding of the way in which true and immutable natures are independent of his mind. I claim, however, that the attribution of such an understanding to Descartes is problematic.

In the remarks above concerning true and immutable natures, Descartes emphasizes the importance of distinguishing such natures from those natures that he has merely constructed. In the second section of this chapter, I consider the different ways in which he attempts to distinguish these two different kinds of nature. The suggestion in the Fifth Meditation itself is that immutable natures are distinguished by the fact that they yield knowledge of necessary properties of their objects. However, in an important passage from *First Replies*, Descartes offers the different criterion that immutable natures are unanalyzable into component parts.[3] Both criteria have been subject to counterexample, but I argue that they are more plausible – and more consistent – than critics have alleged.

In the third and final section, I consider the role that true and immutable natures play in Descartes' version (or versions) of the ontological argument. His claim in the Fifth Meditation is that since God has the nature of a being with supreme perfection, and since existence is a perfection, it follows from this nature that God exists. When pressed to defend this line of argument, Descartes offers in *First Replies* what appears to be a different sort of demonstration of the existence of God that appeals to the implications of divine omnipotence. However, I claim that the discussion in *First Replies* can be understood to be a mere clarification of the original argument in the Fifth Meditation, and that this clarification serves to address some, though not all, of the important objections to that argument.

INNATISM AND CONCEPTUALISM

The subtitle of the Fifth Meditation indicates that its main topics are "the essence of material things" and "again of God, that he exists" (AT 7: 63). Descartes' consideration of the nature or essence of material things is guided by the result in the previous Meditation that one can avoid error by restricting the will in judgment to "what the intellect clearly and distinctly reveals, and no further" (AT 7: 43). In the case of the nature of material things, such a restriction yields the identification of body with "continuous quantity, as the philosophers commonly call it." This is so because what we distinctly understand of matter is "the extension of the quantity, or rather of the thing quantified, in length, breadth and depth," as well as the various sizes, shapes and motions of the parts of that quantity, and the durations of those parts (AT 7: 63).

It is important not merely that we have a distinct conception of the quantifiable features of material things, but also that the truths concerning these features are

> so open and so much in harmony with my nature, that on first discovering them it seems that I am not so much learning something new as remembering what I knew before, or that I am noticing for the first time things that were long in me, on which I never turned my mental gaze before. (AT 7: 64)

There is an obvious allusion in the first part of this passage to the Platonic theory of recollection, and the second part indicates that this theory is to be understood in terms of Descartes' account of innate ideas. Earlier, in the Third Meditation, Descartes distinguished ideas that are innate from two other kinds of ideas – those that are "adventitious," or acquired from the senses, on the one hand, and those that are "factitious," or invented by the mind, on the other (AT 7: 38 and 51). In appealing to the Platonic doctrine in the Fifth Meditation, Descartes is endorsing the view that his ideas of the quantifiable features of material things are all innate to his mind.

The Fifth Meditation view of the innateness of mathematical ideas is connected to the earlier discussion of the wax example in the Second Meditation. There Descartes argues that his knowledge of the nature of the wax can derive neither from the senses nor from the imagination: not from the senses, since he judges that the wax remains even when its sensible qualities change, and not from the imagination, since he judges that the wax can take on more shapes than he can imagine. Descartes' conclusion is that his knowledge of the nature of wax (or any other body) derives from "a pure mental inspection [*solius mentis inspectio*]" (AT 7: 30–31). That is to say, it derives from ideas that are innate to his pure intellect, and not from the adventitious ideas of the senses or the factitious ideas of the imagination.

After alluding to the Platonic theory of recollection in the Fifth Meditation, Descartes first mentions true and immutable natures. Given what he has said about the nature of material things, it is understandable that he offers as the paradigmatic example of an immutable nature that of a triangle. The juxtaposition of the discussion of this example with the claim that mathematical truths are present in the mind even before they are noticed suggests that it is a distinctive feature of the idea corresponding to the immutable nature of a triangle that it is innate. Elsewhere Descartes explicitly links the immutability of natures and the innateness of the ideas that correspond to them, writing in correspondence that examples of innate ideas include "the idea of God, mind, body, triangle, and in general all those which represent true, immutable and eternal essences" ("To Mersenne, 16 June 1641," AT 3: 383). For Descartes, then, all ideas that represent true and immutable natures are innate to the human mind.

In the Fifth Meditation, the fact that a triangle has an immutable nature, and thus that the idea of a triangle is innate, is supposed to follow from the fact that even if no triangle actually exists external to mind, still we can demonstrate certain properties of a triangle, for example that its three angles are equal to two right angles. Descartes concludes that since these properties follow from a true and immutable nature independent of any act of his will, such a nature is not merely a mental construction, but rather something that is "not produced by me, nor depends on my mind [nec a mente mea dependet]."

There is a reading of this conclusion on which it indicates that true and immutable natures have a mind-independent reality. Most notably, Kenny has urged, on the basis of the discussion in the Fifth Meditation, that "Descartes' philosophy of mathematics ... is thoroughly Platonic; indeed he is the founder of modern Platonism." In particular, Kenny takes the triangle that "does not exist anywhere outside me" to be "an eternal creature of God, with its own immutable nature and properties."[4] Kenny is perhaps unique in holding that Descartes posits something like Platonic Forms, but others have offered "quasi-Platonist" readings of Descartes, according to which he grounds truths concerning immutable natures in an aspect of reality that is independent of our mind.[5] What is common to the various Platonistic understandings of Descartes' true and immutable natures is that they take such natures to be independent of our mind in some robust ontological sense.

In contrast, Chappell and Nolan have recently defended the view that Descartes is a "conceptualist" regarding true and immutable natures insofar as he identifies them with the "objective being" present in our innate ideas.[6] In the Third Meditation, Descartes stipulates that the objective being of an object is a mode of being "by which a thing exists in the intellect by way of an idea" (AT 7: 41). The proposal that true and immutable natures are to be identified with objective being is conceptualist insofar as it requires that the natures are merely certain features of our ideas.

According to Chappell and Nolan, when Descartes says that true and immutable natures do not depend on his mind, he means that the ideas of those natures are not factitious but rather innate to the mind. Just as Chappell claims that Descartes' true and immutable natures are simply "the ideas that God makes to be innate in us" and that "are constant and never change,"[7] so Nolan holds that these natures are innate ideas that "impose their content on our thought, compelling us to think of them in certain prescribed ways." Nolan concludes: "There is nothing in this claim that commits Descartes to a transcendental realm of extra-mental objects."[8]

There is much to be said for this sort of conceptualist reading of the passage from the Fifth Meditation. Especially telling is Descartes' claim that the properties that he can demonstrate of triangles "are certainly true, since I am clearly aware of them, and therefore they are something, and not merely nothing; for it is obvious that whatever is true is something" (AT 7: 65). Earlier, in the Third Meditation, he noted that the being by which something exists objectively in the intellect, "imperfect though it may be, is certainly not nothing" (AT 7: 41). In light of this comment concerning objective being, it would be natural to take the claim in the Fifth Meditation to be that the properties of triangles are "something" in the sense that they are present objectively in the innate idea of a triangle.

However, it seems that a conceptualist reading cannot accommodate what Descartes says in the Fifth Meditation about a true and immutable nature that is particularly important to him there, namely the nature of God as a "supremely perfect being." For this nature is presented as something that is identical not to the objective being of an innate idea, but rather to the actually existing being, God. Indeed, Descartes emphasizes that our conception of the necessity of God's existence is imposed on our mind from this external source. Thus he concludes:

And from the fact that I cannot think of God except as existing, it follows that existence is inseparable from God, and thus that he really exists; not because my thought produces this [*hoc efficiat*], or imposes any necessity on anything, but on the contrary the thing itself, namely the existence of God, necessarily determines me to think this ... (AT 7: 67)

So in the case of God, at least, it is ultimately not God insofar as he exists in our thought that compels me to think of God as existing, but rather God himself as an actual and external nature. In at least one case, then, a conceptualist account of true and immutable natures is unacceptable.[9]

But perhaps God is a special case. One could argue that in cases where natures do not require existence – namely, in all other cases[10] – there seems to be no barrier to identifying those natures with the objective being of our innate ideas. There could still be an external source of the ideas insofar as God imposes them on us – or perhaps better, insofar as He imposes on us the faculty of thought from which they arise.[11] In contrast to the case of the innate idea of God, however, the ideas do not derive their content from any extra-mental natures.

Even so, it is troubling that Descartes explicitly says that the natures corresponding to our innate ideas are themselves "immutable and eternal." We can perhaps understand the immutability of the natures in terms of the inalterability of the faculty of thought that grounds our innate ideas. But even if our mind can be said to be immutable in this sense, it seems that it cannot be said to be eternal, especially if this eternity is supposed to preclude temporal duration. For Descartes takes this sort of duration to be an essential attribute of our mind.[12]

It could perhaps be objected at this point that objective being can have certain features that our mind does not. After all, Descartes makes clear in the Third Meditation that the objective being of our idea of God can be infinite even though our mind is merely finite (AT 7: 45–46). However, in this case our idea corresponds to a possible object that can have infinite reality, namely God himself. In contrast, Descartes' official position is that all created beings have a merely temporal duration.[13] According to this position, there can be no eternal created thing, and thus no objective mode of being by which such an eternal thing "exists in the intellect by way of an idea."

One possible conceptualist response is to deny that we can take at face value Descartes' claim that true and immutable natures are eternal. Thus, for instance, we have Chappell's conclusion that "the objects and truths of mathematics are not, for Descartes, strictly and literally eternal."[14] It is clear that Descartes requires that God's true and immutable nature, at least, is strictly and literally eternal, since he identifies this particular nature with God's own atemporal existence.[15] And the fact – which Chappell grants – that Descartes gave no indication that the eternity of other created natures is a mere *façon de parler* provides further reason to question a conceptualist interpretation of his thought that is prominent in the literature.[16]

CONSTRUCTED AND IMMUTABLE NATURES

As we have seen, Descartes is particularly concerned in the Fifth Meditation to distinguish true and immutable natures from mere mental constructions. His suggestion is that what sets immutable natures apart is principally the fact that they yield knowledge of inalterable properties. An immediate problem with this criterion, however, is that it does not seem to exclude natures that are clearly constructed. Wilson has offered the counterexample of an *onk*, defined as a non-terrestrial life-form. Insofar as there are necessary conditions for being a life-form, such as having the ability to assimilate nourishment and have reproductive potential, we can derive from the nature of *onk* knowledge of properties that we cannot alter. But then given the criterion introduced in the Fifth Meditation, we would have to conclude that *onk* (or any other living creature the idea of which I concoct) has a true and immutable nature.[17] As Wilson concludes in later reflections on this example, the criterion that Descartes offers in the Fifth Meditation "lets in a whole lot of ideas that certainly, in Descartes' philosophy, would not be expected to qualify as having true and immutable natures as their content."[18]

In her original discussion, Wilson also draws attention to the fact that Descartes appears to offer a different criterion for being a true and immutable nature when commenting on his Fifth Meditation discussion in *First Replies*. Descartes' critic Caterus had pressed the objection that just as the fact that existence belongs to the nature of an existent lion does not show that such a lion exists, so the fact that existence belongs to the nature of God does not show that God exists.[19] In response, Descartes emphasizes the distinction between true and immutable natures and natures that "are made [*fictitias*] and put together by the intellect," and thus can "by the same intellect be divided, not merely by abstraction, but by a clear and distinct operation." He offers the following elaboration:

When, for example, I think of a winged horse or an actually existing lion, or a triangle inscribed in a square, I readily understand that I am also able to think of a horse without wings, or a lion that does not exist, or a triangle apart from a square, and the like, and hence that they do not have true and immutable natures [nec poinde illa veras & immutabiles naturas habere]. (AT 7: 117)

Here, what distinguishes an immutable nature from merely constructed natures is not the fact that it yields knowledge of necessary properties, but rather the fact that the nature cannot be analyzed into component parts that can be distinctly conceived apart from each other. Wilson notes that in contrast to the criterion in the Fifth Meditation, this new criterion seems too restrictive. For it appears that we can analyze the nature of a triangle, for instance, into conceptually distinct parts (e.g., being a three-sided figure and being a figure with angles). But if any object that can be so analyzed does not have an immutable nature, then pace Descartes' explicit claim in the Fifth Meditation, a triangle does not have such a nature.[20]

A further troubling feature of the passage from First Replies – which Wilson does not mention in her original discussion – is that it seems to vacillate on the question of whether a particular mathematical object has a true and immutable nature.[21] In the passage above, the indication is that a triangle inscribed in a square does not have such a nature since it can be analyzed into conceptually distinct parts. However, just a few lines later we find the following:

Besides, if I should consider a triangle inscribed in a square, not to attribute to the square what pertains only to the triangle, nor to the triangle what pertains only to the square, but only to examine what arises out of the conjunction of the two, then the nature of it will be no less true and immutable than of the square or triangle alone; but indeed it can rightly be affirmed that the square is no less than double the triangle inscribed in it, and the like, which pertain to the nature of this composite figure. (AT 7: 118)

So it seems that the criterion in First Replies for being an immutable nature not only excludes a triangle, but also does not yield a clear result in the case of the triangle inscribed in a square.

I think the discussion in First Replies is less confused than these considerations seem to suggest.[22] There is, for instance, the significant distinction there between the attribution to the square (triangle) of properties that pertain only to the triangle (square) and the attribution to the composite figure of properties that arise out of their conjunction. Whereas the nature involved in the former attribution is merely constructed, the nature involved in the latter attribution is immutable. The difference is that the properties that apply to only one part of the composite figure derive from the nature of that part alone, and not from the nature of the composite. With respect to these properties, then, the nature of the composite is a mere construction and not immutable. The immutable nature of the composite pertains only to properties that can be derived from the conjunction of the parts.[23]

At this point we have an answer to Wilson's objection that the criterion of being unanalyzable into parts is too strict insofar as it excludes Descartes' own example of the triangle. The answer is that though the properties of a triangle that derive only from its component parts reveal a nature of the composite that is merely constructed, the properties of a triangle that derive from the conjunction of the parts reveal that the composite also has a nature that is immutable. And the latter properties reveal a nature that is immutable for just the reason indicated in the Fifth Meditation, namely that they reveal features of the object that we did not construct and that we cannot alter. Though the two criteria that Descartes proposes for being an immutable nature may seem at first to compete, I think we can conclude that they are in fact complementary. For the unanalyzability criterion applies to a composite in the case where the relevant property derives necessarily from the conjunction of parts, and it can apply in this case given the inalterability criterion, since the derivation does not depend on our mind.

However, we still have Wilson's objection to the Fifth Meditation criterion that even highly contrived natures, such as that of *onk*, can have features that we did not invent and cannot alter. I propose that the best way to address this sort of objection is to consider the special relation that immutable natures bear to the basic features of reality that Descartes identified with "principal attributes." On Descartes' official position, there are three such attributes, namely, extension in the case of bodily substance, thought in the case of mental substance, and supreme perfection in the case of God.[24] My proposal on Descartes' behalf is that properties can reveal that a nature is immutable only if they derive from that nature solely in virtue of the principal attribute to which that nature is referred.

In further explicating this proposal, I want to focus on the case of the principal attribute of extension, since this is most relevant to Descartes' own example of the true and immutable nature of a triangle. The fact that the inalterable property of having interior angles equal to two right angles follows from this nature is supposed to show that the nature is immutable. But the property follows from this nature in virtue of the fact that extension has the nature that it does. Hence what ultimately allows us to conclude that the nature of the triangle is immutable is the fact that it reveals necessary features that derive from the nature of extension.[25] Descartes' remarks may seem to suggest that the immutable nature of the triangle is somehow distinct from the immutable nature of extension. According to my proposal, however, these natures are essentially linked. The nature of a triangle – or indeed of any mathematical object – can be immutable only insofar as it simply reflects the immutable structure of extension. In this way, the immutability of the mathematical natures is due to the immutability of the nature of extension itself.

I think this account of the immutability of mathematical natures sheds light on an otherwise obscure parenthetical remark in *First Replies*. Descartes indicates to Caterus that he uses examples of mathematical objects such as triangles or squares rather than of lions and horses because in the case of the latter, "their natures are not fully perspicuous to us" (AT 7: 117). Though there is no explanation here of what precisely is not fully perspicuous about these natures, I suspect that Descartes has in mind that it is not clear which necessary properties derive from the natures simply in virtue of the nature of extension. The problem is that lions and horses have the natures that they do, not simply in virtue of the nature of extension, but additionally in virtue of having a certain arrangement of parts that allows for the production of certain kinds of motion.[26] Which properties follow from natures of this kind is determined by, for instance, laws governing the interactions of the parts, and not merely the mathematical structure of extension. Likewise, in the case of *onk* the conditions for being a life-form do not follow merely from the nature of extension. Thus, the fact that these conditions are necessary does not suffice to show that the nature of *onk* is immutable. In the case of material things, the only natures

that we can take to be immutable are those that directly reveal necessary features of extension itself.

Following his discussion of the (true and immutable) natures of
material things, Descartes turns to the second topic of the Fifth
Meditation, namely "again of God, that he exists [*iterum de Deo,
quod existat*]" (AT 7: 63). An initial question is why Descartes needs
to consider the existence of God again, given that he has already
provided a proof (or, more precisely, two related proofs) of his existence in the Third Meditation. It turns out that the answer to this
question depends on the special nature of the proof in the Fifth
Meditation, which since Kant has been called the "ontological argument."[27] Though there is some controversy regarding the precise
nature of the Fifth Meditation proof in particular,[28] I think we can
extract the following basic argument. We begin with the point that
God has a true and immutable nature as much as a triangle does. In
the case of God, the nature is that of a supremely perfect being. But
just as it follows from the immutable nature of a triangle that any
such a figure must have interior angles equal to two right angles, so it
follows from God's immutable nature "that it is contradictory [*repug-
net*] to think that God (that is, a supremely perfect being) lacks
existence (that is, lacks some perfection)" (AT 7: 66). Though there
is a comparison here to the case of a triangle, Descartes notes that the
case of God is distinctive insofar as there is "no other thing of which I
can think to which existence pertains to its essence, excepting only
God" (AT 7: 68).

This distinctive feature of God serves to explain why an additional
proof of God's existence is required, since the proof in the Third
Meditation does not yield the result that God alone exists by his
very nature. What the Fifth Meditation argument serves to highlight
is the fact that the existence of God is by its nature more evident than
the existence of anything else, including the *cogito*. The argument
provides, in particular, the basis for Descartes' rhetorical question:
"What is more evident *per se* than that a supreme being, or God, to
whose essence alone existence pertains, exists?" (AT 7: 69).

However, there is room to question Descartes' claim that existence pertains to the nature of God alone. Indeed, Caterus objected

that existence seems to pertain in the same way to the nature of an existing lion. But just as the fact that existence is part of the nature of an existing lion does not show that any lion actually exists, so the fact that existence is part of God's nature does not show that God actually exists (AT 7: 99–100).

Descartes offers in response the distinction in *First Replies* – considered previously – between constructed natures, which are analyzable into parts, and immutable natures, which cannot be so analyzed. In the case of the existing lion, existence derives from a part of the nature, and thus the nature itself is a mere construction, which may in fact fail to conform to reality. In the case of God, however, existence derives from the nature itself, and so one can conclude that this nature is true and immutable, and thus does in fact conform to reality (AT 7: 117–18).

In *First Replies* Descartes also offers what appears to be a different argument for the existence of God than the one we find in the Fifth Meditation. He draws attention in particular to the "immense power" of God, the possession of which ensures that he "exists by his own power." The fact that God must exist by his own power reveals that "necessary existence is contained in the idea of a supremely powerful being, not by fiction of intellect [*figmento intellectus*], but because it pertains to the nature of such a thing that it exists" (AT 7: 119). In contrast to the Fifth Meditation, there is an explicit appeal here neither to the nature of God as a supremely perfect being, nor to the fact that existence is a perfection. Instead, the argument in *First Replies* is that God's immense power requires that he exist by his own power, and thus exist necessarily.

There is the claim in the literature that the *First Replies* argument is in fact distinct from the Fifth Meditation argument.[29] Yet in *First Replies*, Descartes himself insists that what he says there "does not differ from anything I have written before, except for the mode of explication" (AT 7: 120). And indeed, I think it is possible to understand the remarks in *First Replies* as merely an explication of the Fifth Meditation argument. For that argument leaves open the question of why we should consider existence to be a perfection. The answer in *First Replies* is that it follows from the nature of a supremely perfect being that such a being exists by its own power, or *a se*, and so exists necessarily.[30] Since only the one unique supremely perfect being can be shown to exist in this way,[31] only in the case of such a being can we say that existence belongs to its nature. This fact itself serves to rule out counterexamples such as existing lions, which cannot be shown to exist *a se*.

Even if this explication of the Fifth Meditation argument allows Descartes to parry Caterus' particular objection, one might think that other objections remain. There is for instance the point, which Leibniz made famous, that Descartes' argument shows merely that *if* God's existence is possible, then God exists. What is missing is an argument for the antecedent.[32] Descartes indicates a version of this worry in the Fifth Meditation when he considers the objection that "it is indeed necessary for me to suppose that God exists, once I have made the supposition that he has all perfections, insofar as existence is one of these, but the original supposition was not necessary." Similarly, the objection continues, even though it follows from the supposition that all quadrilaterals can be inscribed in a circle that a rhombus can be so inscribed, it does not follow that the supposition is true, and thus that a rhombus can be so inscribed (AT 7: 67). Descartes insists in response that "there is a great difference between this kind of false supposition and the true ideas that are innate in me, of which the first and most important is the idea of God" (AT 7: 68), but it cannot be said that he provides a clear and convincing argument for this response.

However, there is an even more fundamental objection to Descartes' argument that grants the possibility of God's existence, but that denies that the actuality of his existence follows. This objection leads us back to the discussion in Kant that introduced the notion of an ontological argument. In that discussion, Kant begins by allowing that we have a logically consistent concept of an "absolutely necessary being." However, he questions "whether or not through this concept we are thinking of anything at all."[33] The problem here is that judgments that concern our concepts alone are "analytic," whereas judgments that concern real objects are "synthetic." It is this gap between analytic and synthetic judgments that Kant highlights in his famous remark that "being is not obviously a real predicate, i.e., a concept of something that could add to the concept of a thing."[34]

The point that being is not a real predicate challenges an assumption that is crucial for Descartes' ontological argument, and indeed for his account of true and immutable natures. The assumption is that, as Descartes puts it, "from this alone, that I can produce from my thought the idea of something, it follows that everything that I clearly and distinctly perceive to pertain to that thing really does belong to it."[35] Thus, from the fact that he has an idea that corresponds to a true and immutable nature of a triangle, Descartes concludes that everything he clearly and distinctly perceives on the basis of this idea must hold for any actual triangle. In the special case of the idea that corresponds to the true and immutable nature of a supremely perfect being, he concludes on the basis of his clear and distinct perception that such a being exists *a se* that there is a supremely perfect being that in fact exists necessarily.

But it is this very move from the clarity and distinctness of our concepts to their applicability to real objects that Kant is questioning.[36] What Kant is requiring is some justification for holding that what is true of our concepts holds also for objects. Descartes took it to be obvious from the case of mathematical ideas that there is no gap here that needs to be bridged. But though Kant allows that mathematical truths apply to reality, he holds that this can be allowed only because our knowledge of these truths has a non-conceptual basis in spatial and temporal "intuition."[37] From his perspective, then, Descartes made a critical mistake in assimilating the cases of true and immutable natures of mathematical objects to the case of the true and immutable nature of God.[38]

NOTES

1. All translations from Descartes' texts are my own.
2. For the source of this label for the argument, see the remarks at n. 27.
3. Louis Loeb has reminded me that Descartes suggests yet a third criterion when he claims that immutable natures are distinguished from constructed natures in virtue of the fact that they have unforeseen consequences (see, e.g., "To Mersenne, 16 June 1641," AT 3: 383). I believe that the discussion below of the *First Replies* criterion sheds some light on this third criterion as well.
4. Kenny 1970, 692–93.
5. For instance, cf. the attribution of a "quasi-Platonic" view to Descartes in Wilson 1978, 171, and the attribution of a "moderate Platonic" view to him in Rozemond 2008. Rozemond offers the identification of immutable natures and the eternal truths concerning them with the objective reality as God's thoughts as an improved version of my earlier identification of

these natures and truths with divine decrees; see Schmaltz 1991. I now suspect that even merely quasi- or moderate Platonism is problematic for Descartes (see n. 16).

6. Chappell 1997 and Nolan 1997a.

7. Chappell 1997, 125.

8. Nolan 1997a, 183–84.

9. For a similar objection to Nolan's conceptualist reading, see Cunning 2010, 158–60. On Cunning's view, the true and immutable nature of an object is in general identical to the actually existing object, and not just in the special case of God. However, this view seems to conflict with the suggestion in the Fifth Meditation that an object such as a triangle – or indeed, any created thing – would have a true and immutable nature even if it didn't actually exist. Cunning has to argue that in the final analysis Descartes holds that a thing and its nature are identical ("To * * *, 1645 or 1646," AT 4: 349–50), but that the Fifth Meditation meditator does not appreciate this yet and so asserts that the nature of a thing exists "even if perhaps" the thing does not.

10. As we will see in the third section, in defending his ontological argument Descartes places particular emphasis on the fact that God's nature is distinct from all other natures insofar as it alone requires existence.

11. See Descartes' claim in the Notae in programma quoddam that he never held that innate ideas "are some sort of 'forms' that are distinct from our faculty of thinking" (AT 8B: 366).

12. Principles I.62.

13. See his claim in this 1643 correspondence with Elizabeth that our notion of duration is a "general primitive notion" that applies to "everything we can conceive" (AT 3: 665). Though he is not explicit, Descartes presumably limits the scope of this claim to created things, given his claim elsewhere that God has a non-successive existence that is distinct from our temporal duration (see, e.g., his 1648 letter to Arnauld at AT 5: 193).

14. Chappell 1997, 127.

15. I take Descartes' claim that God's existence is non-successive to indicate that it is atemporal; see n. 13.

16. Though Nolan rejects Chappell's deflationary account of the eternity of immutable natures, he nonetheless thinks that the problems with this feature do not count against conceptualism since they merely indicate the incomprehensibility of God's creation of the natures. But the difficulty here is not that God created an eternal object, but rather that he created an eternal object. His ontology seems to leave no room for such an object. I am not certain that we can find in Descartes a solution to the problem of the eternal created ground of truths concerning immutable natures that is fully consistent with everything he says. However, in

Schmaltz 2002, ch. 3, I consider the original attempt of Descartes' later followers Robert Desgabets and Pierre-Sylvain Regis to offer a solution to this problem.

17. Wilson 1978, 172. Note that in her original discussion, Wilson uses the example of *onk*, defined as "the first non-terrestrial life-form discovered by man." I am substituting for this the example of *onk-x* that Wilson introduces in her later reflections on this discussion (Wilson 1999, 102).

18. Wilson 1999, 104. Edelberg offers the technical response to Wilson's objection that the necessary properties of the *onk* follow not from the nature of that object, but rather a part of it (i.e., the nature of being a life-form) (Edelberg 1990, 510). But on this point I am inclined to agree with Wilson's later claim (Wilson 1999, 102) that her example can be modified to address this response (e.g., by focusing on the necessary conditions for being a *non-terrestrial* life-form).

19. *First Objections*, AT 7: 99–100.

20. Wilson 1978, 173.

21. As noted, for instance, in Curley 1978, 151–52. In his later reflections on this discussion, Curley reports that "so far as I can see, no one has yet produced an account of true and immutable natures which would explain Descartes' use of this notion, and the project may be a hopeless one" (Curley 2005, 48).

22. Cf. Doney's claim that though he agrees with Wilson "that Descartes' notion of a true and immutable nature is less than entirely clear and distinct, it is hard to believe that it is quite as confused as she makes out" (Doney 1993, 419). Cf. another sympathetic reading of the *First Replies* discussion in Edelberg 1990, 510–13, which nonetheless differs on points of detail from the reading offered in Doney 1993, 416–20 (see n. 23).

23. This reading contrasts with the other sympathetic readings of the *First Replies* passage cited in n. 22. Whereas Edelberg takes the initial claim that the triangle inscribed in a square does not have an immutable nature to indicate merely the weak point that the evidence "does not warrant the conclusion that the idea [of a triangle inscribed in a square] has a true and immutable nature (Edelberg 1990, 512), Doney takes this claim to indicate the stronger point that the evidence provides no reason for thinking that the idea does have such a nature (Doney 1993, 418–20). On my reading the passage indicates *both* that the nature of the composite from which properties that pertain only to the parts derive is merely constructed, *and* that the nature from which properties that pertain to the conjunction of the parts derive is immutable.

24. For the case of mind and body, see Descartes' claim in *Principles* I.53 that "each substance has one principal property that constitutes its nature and essence, and to which all its other properties are referred" and that

"extension in length, breadth and depth constitutes the nature of corporeal substance; and thinking constitutes the nature of thinking substance" (AT 8A: 25). For the case of God, see the claim in the Fifth
Meditation – to be considered further in the third section – that God
has the nature of a supremely perfect being (AT 7: 65).

25. Here I am drawing on a suggestion in Edelberg 1990, 520–21. In her
comment on this article, Wilson allows that the suggestion is promising,
but objects that it is not sufficiently incorporated into Edelberg's main
account of the conditions for being a true and immutable nature (Wilson
1999, 106–7, nn.12 and 18).

26. See, for instance, Descartes' account of the human body in terms of the
dispositions of bodily organs that allow that body to produce certain
voluntary and involuntary motions (in the *Description of the Human
Body*, AT 11: 225–26).

27. In the section of Kant's *Critique of Pure Reason*, "On the Impossibility of
an Ontological Proof of God's Existence," which concludes that "the
famous ontological (Cartesian) proof of the existence of a highest being
from concepts is only so much trouble and labor lost" (A602/B630, in
Kant 1998, 569). I return toward the end of this essay to Kant's main
objection to the Cartesian proof.

28. For instance, Doney distinguishes two different arguments in this
Meditation; see Doney 1993, 420–30. There also is the view in the
literature that this text offers not so much a proof of God's existence as
an intuitive grasp of the fact that he exists by his very nature; see Nolan
and Nelson 2006, 112–21.

29. See the discussion of this point in Doney 1993, 427–29.

30. When pressed by Arnauld, Descartes admits that strictly speaking God
cannot be said to be the *efficient* cause of his own existence. However, he
also insists that the divine nature can be said to be the *formal* cause of
God's existence; see AT 7:235–45. For further discussion of Descartes'
view of God as *causa sui*, see Schmaltz 2011.

31. On the uniqueness of God, see Descartes' claim in the Fifth Meditation
that "I cannot understand that there are two or more Gods of that kind"
(AT 7: 68).

32. See this point in Leibniz's *Discourse on Metaphysics*, §23, in Leibniz
1989, 56. For a discussion of Leibniz's attempt to remedy this deficiency
in Descartes' argument, see Adams 1994, ch. 5.

33. *Critique of Pure Reason* A593/B621, in Kant 1998, 564.

34. *Critique of Pure Reason* A596//B624, Kant 1998, 567.

35. AT 7: 65. In *Second Replies*, Descartes claims that whereas the major
premise, "that which we clearly understand to pertain to the nature of
some thing, can with truth be affirmed to pertain to this nature," is a

"useless tautology," his Fifth Meditation argument relies on the different major premise, "that which we clearly understand to pertain to the nature of some thing, can with truth be affirmed of that thing" (AT 7: 149–50). He insists that this latter premise, though not the former, can be used to establish the existence of God.

36. Or, in terms of the two major premises distinguished in n. 35, Kant is objecting that concepts alone can establish only the analytic claim that whatever we clearly understand to pertain to the nature of a thing does in fact pertain to that nature, and not the synthetic claim that whatever we clearly understand to pertain to the nature of a thing does in fact pertain to that thing as a real object.

37. For a discussion of Kant's theory of mathematical knowledge, see Shabel 2006.

38. Thanks to David Cunning, Charles Larmore, and Louis Loeb for helpful comments on earlier versions of this chapter.

11 The Fifth Meditation: externality and true and immutable natures

INTRODUCTION

In this chapter I want to focus on something that I think lies at the heart of the *Meditations*, namely Descartes' notion of externality or distinctness from the subject. This notion could also be understood as objectivity. Whatever other aims he might have had in composing the *Meditations*, one was to get clear on what it is for a thing to be independent from a subject, and also how such independence is connected to external existence. It will be argued that true and immutable natures are key to both of these aims. I argue more generally that one of Descartes' substantive achievements in the *Meditations* is his re-thinking of externality or objectivity, i.e., the question about the conditions for an idea to be directed toward an object.

In the first section of the paper, I review Descartes' First Meditation result that the senses do not give us insight into the existence of things that are external to the thinking subject. The First Meditation can be seen as problematizing the notion of external existence by leaving one to wonder what the *possibility* of external existence could mean. In the Second Meditation, Descartes offers his famous wax digression to argue that external things are not perceived through the senses but through the intellect alone. This enigmatic result signals a dramatic shift from previous accounts, even if the details of intellectual perception are not filled in.

In the second section, it will be argued that true and immutable natures are required for intellectual perception of an external object. The notion of externality from the subject will be closely tied to the notion of a true and immutable nature.

In the third section, Descartes' ontological argument is considered in the light of his doctrine of true and immutable natures. Here there is an attempt to save Descartes from the famous criticisms of Kant. Unlike Kant and Russell, Descartes does not think that all existential statements can be handled predicatively.

In section four, the way of being (or ontological status) of true and immutable natures is considered. According to commentators, Descartes seems to commit himself here both to conceptualism and Platonism. I will argue that Cartesian true and immutable natures have their being in substances themselves, in a way that explains Descartes' seemingly inconsistent positions. I will also compare Descartes' doctrine of true and immutable natures with Spinoza's intriguing theory of formal essences.

EXISTENCE AND THE PROBLEM OF EXTERNALITY

In the First Meditation Descartes worries about the priority that philosophers tend to accord to the senses. In medieval Aristotelianism, the senses were regarded as the source of all knowledge. Implicit in this way of thinking is that the distinction between what is external to the mind and what is internal to it is unproblematic: the things that we touch, see, hear, feel, and taste are in the external world, and things like perceptions, feelings, thoughts, and dreams are internal to subjects.

Descartes presents the skeptical worries of the First Meditation in part to highlight that the distinction between internality and externality is not unproblematic. In dreaming, we have experiences of things that are like the things which we experience while we are awake but which we (eventually) do not take to be independent from us and which, therefore, do not have any external location. So the point would seem to be that we do not sense externality. What creates the problem of the external world is not the distance of the things that are the objects of sense-perception, but instead their closeness to the subject. The mind seems to be in a way continuous with the data provided by the senses.

It has become widely accepted that it was not so much Descartes' aim to successfully respond to the skeptic's worries about the trustworthiness of sensory perception, but instead to change the way we think about the world; and most of all Descartes wanted to lead us away from the senses.[1] This leads him to intellectualize the notion of an external thing. After having degraded sense-based information, he leaves us with the question of how the notion of an external object is to be understood and also the question of what is meant by existence. The first question is acute if the notion of externality is to be intellectualized, for it leads to the question how intellectualized external objects could exist. This latter question naturally raises the question about what it means for something to exist. It seems then that Descartes' attitude to skepticism is much the same as that of Kant. As is well-known, Kant thought that it was a scandal that philosophers had not been able to solve the problem of skepticism, and his Copernican revolution in philosophy can be seen as an attempt to build a worldview where such irritating skeptical questions lose their force. Descartes also thinks that skeptical questions need to be completely re-interpreted. In the Second Meditation, he begins to investigate the notion of existence and after that turns his attention to the notion of externality.

In the *cogito*-argument Descartes aims to show that "I exist" is true insofar as I think (AT 7: 27). The point of the argument is not only to prove that something exists, but to draw attention to existence itself. It may be a bit misleading, though, to characterize the *cogito*-argument as purporting to clarify the notion of existence in general. For Descartes, existence is a simple concept and cannot be explicated with the help of other concepts, and what the *cogito*-argument does is to show that we acquire the concept of existence by being directly acquainted with it in our active thinking.[2] But one could read the *cogito*-argument so that it identifies thinking and existence, and that, of course, would significantly decrease the number of existing things. It would then become necessary to ask whether there is some other way of existence than that given by active thinking – and one that so-called external things could enjoy.

In the latter part of the Second Meditation, Descartes considers the relation that a thinking substance has to things conceived as external. The famous discussion of wax seems to serve at least two functions: to show that mind is better known than the body, and to show that bodies qua bodies are perceived through the intellect alone. The focus here will be the second because of the close connection it has to the Fifth Meditation discussion of true and immutable natures.

Let us look at the wax example in some detail:

[T]ake, for example, this piece of wax. It has just been taken from the honey-comb; it has not yet quite lost the taste of the honey; it retains some of the scent of the flowers from which it was gathered; its colour, shape and size are plain to see; it is hard, cold and can be handled without difficulty; if you rap it with your knuckle it makes a sound. (AT 7: 30)

Descartes then places the wax close to the fire, and all of its sensible qualities change. He insists that we are still confronted with the same object, which is to say that the piece of wax remains:

But does the same wax remain? It must be admitted that it does; no one denies it, no one thinks otherwise. So what was in the wax that I understood with such distinctness? Evidently none of the features which I arrived at by means of the senses; for whatever came under taste, smell, sight, touch or hearing has now altered – yet the wax remains. (Ibid.)

The argument is simple. All of the sensible qualities of a body can change, including its shape, but still the same body remains. What makes our idea of a body an idea of *that* body is not that it has certain sensible features or other.

The upshot of the argument is that we do not perceive the wax through "vision or touch or imagination," but by an act of "purely mental scrutiny" (AT 7: 31). If we think of this as existing, we are not thinking in terms of the senses or imagination either. It is in the Fifth Meditation discussion of true and immutable natures that Descartes continues to develop the thinking here. One final step to consider before proceeding to that discussion is the a posteriori argument for the existence of God that Descartes presents in the Third Meditation, which sheds some light on how Descartes is conceiving of the existence of God.

If Descartes is right, the meditator finds in himself an idea of an infinite perfect being – that is,

a substance that is infinite, <eternal, immutable,> independent, supremely intelligent, supremely powerful, and which created both myself and every-thing else (if anything else there be) that exists. (AT 7: 45)

There are at least two ways to read the argumentation that follows. On the first, the meditator finds in himself a kind of representation or "picture" of God, and then (given certain causal principles) it is concluded that this representation had to be placed in the meditator's mind by God himself. However, this reading seems to generate a veil of intellectual perception, where the thinker is not in direct contact with the things perceived but reaches them only through an intermediate representation. The argument would then fail to secure the level of certainty of God's existence that the *cogito* secures of one's own existence.

Perhaps a more promising way to read the Third Meditation proof, and one which is better in line with the meditative aim of the *Meditations*, is as follows. When Descartes speaks of the idea of God, he is perhaps speaking of the act of thought that the meditator is performing when thinking of God. That is, the meditator finds that in thinking of God she is, as it were, being helped from the outside. This may sound strange, but I believe it is familiar from our childhood that thinking about infinity felt somehow alienating: a kind of compulsiveness and strangeness in the thought of a time never ending, an unlimited space, and a territory forbidden by the senses. I believe that Descartes would have said that it is not the finite intellect that is solely at work when it thinks of infinity: the thinking is helped by somebody or something other, and one is able to feel it. Then I would suggest that, after achieving distance from the senses in the First Meditation and feeling more at home in the realm of the non-sensory in Meditation Two, the meditator is finally able to understand in the Third Meditation that the co-operator in his attempts to think about God is God himself. It is in God's thought where the meditator finds herself while thinking of God, which for Descartes is almost a synonym for infinity.[3] If so, Descartes could formulate a principle that we might call *God-cogito*: "I think of God (=infinity), therefore God exists." Descartes does say at the end of the Fifth Meditation that if we are sufficiently reflective and detached from our senses, "I would certainly acknowledge [God] sooner and more easily than anything else" (AT 7: 69). Perhaps Descartes is also factoring in his Third Meditation view that what it is to think of a finite thing is to have an idea of infinitude and then to do the extra work of delimiting it (AT 7: 45–46). What is also important for the purposes of this chapter is that in the case of God and the "I," existence appears to be grasped similarly, and in both cases directly.

TRUE AND IMMUTABLE NATURES
AND OBJECTIVITY

In the Second Meditation Descartes does not say a lot more about external objects than that they are perceived by the intellect. This leaves us with the question of the kind of being that such objects of the intellect could enjoy. Descartes begins to consider this question in the Fifth Meditation discussion of the true and immutable natures – entities that appear to have a life of their own and are somehow opposed to the subject thinking of them. They present themselves as something other. Thus goes the famous passage from the Fifth Meditation:

But I think the most important consideration at this point is that I find within me countless ideas of things which even though they may not exist anywhere outside me still cannot be called nothing; for although in a sense they can be thought of at will, they are not my invention but have their own and true and immutable natures. When, for example, I imagine a triangle, even if perhaps no such figure exists, or has ever existed, anywhere outside my thought, there is still a determinate nature, or essence, or form of the triangle which is immutable and eternal, and not invented by me or dependent on my mind. This is clear from the fact that various properties can be demonstrated of the triangle, for example that its three angles equal two right angles, that its greatest side subtends its greatest angle, and the like; and since these properties are ones which I now clearly recognize whether I want to or not, even if I never thought of them at all when I previously imagined the triangle, it follows that they cannot have been invented by me. (AT 7: 64)[4]

In the Third Meditation Descartes learned that he was not alone in the universe – God was there too thinking with him, and now in the Fifth Meditation he uncovers some additional companions as well: true and immutable natures. We can examine these natures and demonstrate properties that are not made up – to use Kant's terminology, these properties are not analytically contained in our ideas. Such ideas are thus fruitful, and a source of information about reality. They are directed toward something other because the object of my thought necessarily has some feature that is not analytically involved in its conception: in thinking of a triangle in space and deriving the equality of its angles to two right angles, for example, I am not thinking something that is analytically true, but nor am I making things up or wandering inside my own fictions.[5]

It seems that the primary function for true and immutable natures in Descartes, as we have seen, is to give an account of objectivity. In the wax example, Descartes had argued that the things that we take to be external to us are not perceived through the senses but by the intellect or mind. The wax is really thought to be external to and independent of me, and it is thought to have a nature that is independent of its sensible qualities. In the Second Meditation Descartes refers in passing to extension as the nature of the wax, and then at the beginning of the Sixth Meditation he writes:

It remains for me to examine whether material things exist. And at least I now know they are capable of existing, in so far as they are the subject-matter of pure mathematics, since I perceive them clearly and distinctly. (AT 7: 71)

True and immutable natures thus appear to serve as the foundation of the possibility of external material things. For example, without true and immutable natures, one could doubt the objectivity of space: yes, it is true that the nature of wax is given by extension, but this does not entail anything about the wax existing as a possible independent object. Why would it be that in thinking of the wax I am thinking of something that is independent of me? The whole of space could perhaps be seen as a modification of me; I do not clearly and distinctly perceive extension as something independent of me unless I already have in hand a notion of independence or externality.

It is right at this juncture that true and immutable natures come to the aid. Figures treated in geometry give us external objectivity; the idea of a triangle has unforeseeable conclusions that are independent of me.[6] They are unlike chimeras and other objects of my own invention.

The objectivity of true and immutable natures can also be seen to provide us with an understanding of the notion of external *existence*. That an external existent is a realized true and immutable nature would first sound like a plausible way to flesh out that notion, because Descartes' argument for the possibility of external material things is based on their having a true and immutable nature as the object of mathematics. But as far as I know or understand, Descartes never quite tells what must be added to a true and immutable nature to make it an existent material thing. In addition, there is at least one true and immutable nature that is identical to the thing of which it is the nature: according to Descartes, the true and immutable nature of

God is not distinguishable from his existence and thus God exists necessarily.[7] Let us consider that nature now.

A PRIORI PROOF OF GOD'S EXISTENCE

What is so important about true and immutable natures is that properties can be derived from them that are not conceptually or analytically involved in their definitions. Descartes says that God has a true and immutable nature from which existence can be inferred and this, according to him, is enough for recognizing that God necessarily exists.[8] An argument that derives the existence of God from the concept of God has been called an *ontological argument*.[9] Descartes presents his version as follows:

But if the mere fact that I can produce from my thought the idea of something entails that everything which I clearly and distinctly perceive to belong to that thing really does belong to it, is not that a possible basis for another argument to prove the existence of God? Certainly, the idea of God, or a supremely perfect being, is one which I find within me just as surely as the idea of any shape or number. And my understanding that it belongs to his nature that he always exists is no less clear and distinct than is the case when I prove of any shape or number that some property belongs to its nature. Hence, even if it turned out that not everything on which I have mediated in these past days is true, I ought still to regard the existence of God as having at least the same level of certainty as I have hitherto attributed to the truths of mathematics. (AT 7: 65–66)

One rather typical way to present the ontological argument is to take it as involving a short inference from the meaning of the word God: God is said to be something that is perfect, i.e., has all the perfect-making characteristics, and thus the proposition that God does not exist involves a contradiction which entails that its negation is a necessary truth. It is clear of course that such a proof would be fallacious. If God is so defined, then what can be inferred is only the triviality that if God exists then he exists, or that if necessary existence is included in his definition, what can be inferred is that if God exists, then God necessarily exists. Descartes was well aware of such a misunderstanding. He writes (referring to Anselm's argument and endorsing Aquinas' critique of it):

'Once we have understood the meaning of the word "God", we understand it to mean "that than which nothing greater can be conceived." But to exist in reality as well as in the intellect is greater than to exist in the intellect alone. Therefore, once we have understood the meaning of the word "God" we understand that God exists in reality as well as in the understanding.' In this form the argument is manifestly invalid, for the only conclusion that should have been drawn is: 'Therefore, once we have understood the meaning of the word "God" we understand that what is conveyed is that God exists in reality as well as in the understanding.' Yet because a word conveys something, that thing is not therefore shown to be true. [*First Replies*, AT 7: 115]

In some passages Descartes does leave the impression that he is simply defining God into existence, and so appears to make the very error that he decries above. In the Fifth Meditation itself he says that "it is just as much a contradiction to think of God (that is, a supremely perfect being) lacking existence (that is, lacking a perfection) as it is to think of a mountain without a valley" (AT 7: 66). Even here, however, he attempts to correct the impression immediately: he considers the obvious objection and argues that his larger point is that "it is the necessity of the thing itself, namely the existence of God, which determines my thinking in this respect." When Descartes offers the ontological argument, it seems that most of his labor is to focus our attention on the idea of God and what it reveals about God's essence, and the way in which existence is supposed to follow from that essence is left almost as an exercise for the reader. Of course, the emphasis on the idea of God is understandable if Descartes thinks that by attending to it we would simultaneously see God as existent, but why should Descartes think this? I cannot give a complete answer, but I hope the following may help.

When we think of a possible non-existent thing, we are also thinking that there is something that could realize that possibility. For example, when I am thinking of what kind of bread to bake this afternoon, I have in my mind several alternatives. I also have recipes, and I know how flour, yeast, water, eggs, and other ingredients can combine to make those alternatives real. Possibilities thus seem to require material, and for something to be the thought of a possible non-existing thing, it must be grounded on this material. Possibility seems to require that there already be elements and also that there is a way for the elements to join together to make the possibility actual.

However, in the case of God the situation is different. God cannot be conceived to be non-existing in the sense that something could have failed to form into him. This is because God is by definition an independent entity. Thus, there should be some other way to think of God's non-existence. Of course, one might also ask how God's existence should be thought, if it is not thought the way the existence of other (bodily) things is conceived; and one might argue from the lack of an answer to the impossibility of such an existence. However, with his many-faced *cogito*-argument Descartes showed that the existence of the self (or "I") is conceived in a very special way. That is, the self is pure activity, and not a spiritual matter that is formed.[10] God's existence is similar of course, if God is pure activity. For the thinking substance, to exist is to think, nothing more. Descartes certainly did not want to say that finite thinking selves have an essence that entails existence, i.e., that they are necessary existents. Finite minds depend on God for their existence,[11] but God is wholly independent. He cannot be thought as a created (dependent) substance, and therefore if the only two ways of existence are existence as a realization from something already existing and existence as active thinking, then God cannot be thought to be non-existent. In addition, if Descartes is right that for God there exists a true and immutable nature that is indistinguishable from God's existence, then it is hard to see how God could be thought as non-existent. Thus, the ontological argument here looks rather strong.

The point in Descartes' a priori argument seems both simple and ingenious. One way to think of something as non-existent requires that we think of matter that is not formed in the way required for the existence of the thing. If the thing is not a matter-form combination but is still a dependent thing, like the thinking "I," then its non-existence can be conceived as a function of the behavior of the thing on which its existence depends: for example, if we think that space does not require any matter but is dependent on something else such as God, then we can think of its non-existence as being founded on the decision of God not to create it. Finally, a thing could be conceived as non-existent if it could be shown that the thing does not have a true and immutable nature, i.e., that it would be like a chimera. We cannot conceive of God as non-existent in either of the first two ways, and if we assume that God has a true immutable nature we cannot conceive of him as non-existent in the third way either. His non-existence would thus be inconceivable. His essence would not differ from his existence, which is to say that he exists.

The line of reasoning presented above may sound odd. However, I believe that the oddity is due to our stubbornly thinking of existence as the *realization* of an essence or at least as the realization of properties by things that *already are there*. This kind of thinking has been prevalent, I dare to say, from Kant to today. Think for example of Bertrand Russell's celebrated treatment of negative existentials.[12] To put it bluntly, Russell held that all existential statements say something about a given totality of things: the sentence "The king of France exists" says *that among the existent things* there is (exactly) one that has the (complex) property of being the king of France. So, fundamentally we are confronted with a kind of matter-form thinking about existence: the predicates give the form, and the existing things the matter. On this approach, a negative existential statement – say, "The king of France does not exist" – would mean that among the existent things there is nothing that satisfies the description "The present king of France," and "God does not exist" would mean that there is nothing in the world which satisfies the definition of God as the being which is "infinite, <eternal, immutable,> independent, supremely intelligent, supremely powerful, and which created both myself and everything else (if anything else there be) that exists" (The Third Meditation, AT 7: 45).

But this same approach to analyzing sentences like "I exist" is untenable. There is no description that could replace the "I," or the speaker, in such a sentence, and this is not due to any epistemological failure (i.e., a contingent failure to find a suitable description), but is built into the very notion of first-person existence. Such existence as pure activity is creative existence; it is activity which constitutes that existence and not some already existent matter that is being formed in some way.[13] When Descartes begins to seek out additional existents at the start of the Third Meditation, the only model that he has for an existent is the "I," and so it is plausible to think that that is the sort of thing for which he would be on the lookout. And such a being he finds in God, who is the source and basis of everything that is or could be, and because God is the source and basis of everything, his non-existence is completely inconceivable.

I think that Descartes' ontological argument can also be clarified with the help of some of Spinoza's remarks in the second scholium to 1p8 of the *Ethics*. There Spinoza writes:

This is how we can have true ideas of modifications which do not exist; for though they do not actually exist outside the intellect, nevertheless their essences are comprehended in another in such a way that they can be conceived through it. But the truth of substances is not outside the intellect unless it is in themselves, because they are conceived through themselves.

The point here is that to have ideas of non-existent things, there must be something that we think as existent. For example, I can think of the tree I am now looking at as non-existent because I can think of the space as not being occupied by this tree. That is, I can think the space as not being modified the way it now is. But let us now try to think about the non-existence of space. It seems that this is rather problematic. For Spinoza that could mean nothing but the annihilation of all thought, as Kant argued, and having a thought with no content is not thinking about something specific, such as space, as non-existing.[14] Here the point again is that conceiving something as not existent requires that we have to relate the thing so conceived to something that does exist. Moreover, a true thought about a non-existent should show how the thing could be generated from its ground. It is here that true and immutable natures make their entrance again. Of the ground of possibility, we should have a clear and distinct idea, and then, focusing on that fruitful ground, we can infer what is able to flow from such a ground. The moral of the story is that logical consistency is not enough for possibility; it must be grounded on something existing.

It is very well known that in *The Critique of Pure Reason* Kant criticized what he called the "famous ontological (Cartesian) proof of the existence of a highest being from concepts" (A602/B630).[15] The criticism is rather easy to repeat, but what Kant meant by it is not completely clear. He writes:

Being is obviously not a real predicate, i.e., a concept of something that could add to the concept of thing. It is merely the positing of a thing or of certain determinations in themselves. In the logical use it is merely the copula of a judgment ... Now if I take the subject (God) together with all his predicates ... and say **God is**, or there is a God, then I add no new predicate to the concept of God, but only posit the subject in itself with all its predicates, and indeed posit the object in relation to my concept. (A598–99/B626–27)

What Kant intends to say is that that the expression "the actual X" does not purport to signify a concept but an object. The expression "a hundred actual dollars" is used to refer to an object whereas "a hundred possible dollars" refers to a concept, and the latter may be

true of an actual object and be the suitable concept of it. The fundamental insight here is that if existence were a real predicate, then
there could be no complete conceptual characterization of an object
which would not involve existence.[16] The answer to "What is this?"
could not be given without mentioning existence and that Kant found
to be odd.

However, it seems that Descartes' argument does not look like
the one Kant has in mind. What was important for Kant was that
thinking or understanding never directly reaches its objects, and
thought is discursive, with a dualism between concepts and actual
things. This kind of dualism, of course, forces a rather biased attitude to the ontological argument: Kant has to think of it as a conceptual proof in which the judgment negating the existence of
God is contradictory, and this is why he devotes so much space to
arguing that existence cannot be a real predicate of a thing that
would add something to it. In brief, Kant thought that "the existent
X" signifies an object whereas X (thought here as a description)
signifies a concept. The existent X may then be an object of which
the concept X is true. Thus, existence should not be involved in the
definition of any thing, and the ontological argument as a conceptual proof loses its force.

Descartes, however, was not arguing in the way that Kant supposed. Descartes was not thinking that existence is part of the meaning of the word "God" but that, in having a thought that is directed at
the *in re* nature of God, one has to grant his existence. This is not very
different from the *cogito*-argument; there Descartes made an existential discovery by being directly acquainted with something – thinking
activity. In the Fifth Meditation ontological argument, Descartes'
point is to show not that there should be something that would
correspond to his idea of God but that existing God is what he is
thinking about directly. When we evaluate the force of Kant's critique of the ontological argument, we should bear in mind that it is
deeply rooted in his own theory of thought and understanding. It is a
matter beyond the scope of this paper whether this theory is the
correct one. Nor have I finally settled the question at the other
extreme of whether Descartes' ontological argument is successful.
What I believe I have shown is that there is no room for the sort of
master argument that Kant was seeking to show that any ontological
argument is misguided. Kant may have shown that it is impossible to

prove the existence of God from concepts alone, but that is not what Descartes was trying to do.

ONTOLOGY OF TRUE AND IMMUTABLE NATURES

Much of the recent discussion around Cartesian true and immutable natures has been concerned with the question of their way of being or ontological status.[17] Descartes does not address the question directly, and what he does say seems to be open to different interpretations. In the remainder of the paper I propose a Spinozistic interpretation.

Descartes' and Spinoza's conceptions of God as a pure activity are closely related to each other. For both, God's active essence is just the way God exists. His existence is not a realization of an essence, but is an activity that is and has always been. We might also express this by saying that at the highest level of being there is no fundamental difference between existence and essence. For Spinoza, God is the ultimate true and immutable nature and the ground of all possibility. The question about other true and ultimate natures is then the question about how they are included in God's essence. Spinoza does not speak very much about true and immutable natures, but prefers the term *formal essence*. The place where he considers these and their relation to God is *Ethics* 2p8:

> The ideas of singular things, or of modes, that do not exist must be comprehended in God's infinite idea in the same way as the formal essences of the singular things, or modes, are contained in God's attributes.

Formal essences for Spinoza are contained in the attributes of God, which for him means that they are involved in the essence of God. Because Spinoza (unlike Descartes) takes extension to be an attribute of God, the question about the ontology of geometrical essences in particular is the question about how geometrical essences are contained in God. Let us consider an example.

A geometrical essence, such as the formal essence of a triangle, is in Spinoza's view not something that is over and above the extended substance, roughly space. That is in part to say, it does not have an independent existence in a Platonic realm. Moreover, it should be added, a geometrical essence is not something that is hidden as a discrete entity in the secrets of space. What Spinoza intends by his theory of formal essences is that when we are speaking of geometrical essences we are speaking about space itself: for example, space is necessarily such that if three lines are so placed that they form a closed figure, then this figure has such and such properties. One might even put the point a bit paradoxically: for Spinoza, formal essences are not existents at all, even though anything that exists realizes a formal essence – i.e., the underlying structural features of the extension of God that are the ground of the particular modes of extension that we find actualized.

Descartes does not take an unambiguous stand on the ontology of true and immutable natures, and even seems to say mutually inconsistent things about it. It has been claimed by Kenny that true and immutable natures are Platonic entities because Descartes says that they are created.[18] At another extreme, Gewirth claims that true and immutable essences are conceptual entities, which view is supported by the *Principles of Philosophy*.[19] A problem for the first view is that Descartes is clear that true and immutable natures are eternal, but presumably he does not want to allow that any creature is eternal. A problem for the second view is that in the Fifth Meditation itself Descartes says that true and immutable natures are "not invented by me or dependent on my mind" (AT 7: 64).[20] There are ways to attempt to shore up these problems, of course, but I want to suggest an alternative proposal altogether: that Cartesian true and immutable natures like Spinoza's formal essences are structural features of substance. For Descartes (and for Spinoza), geometrical essences are not singular isolated entities, but are everywhere throughout extension.[21]

We can then also find a very natural way to understand the ontological argument of the Fifth Meditation. In the Third Meditation, Descartes has done a lot of work to show that the idea of God is not invented by the subject, and thus that the essence is not nothing but a something. However, there is no way to think the essence of God – the essence of an infinite being – as being contained in something else, and so the possibility of God cannot be treated in the same way as the possibilities of finite things. For something to be possible, there must already be some existent things on which the possibility depends, and through which the possibility can be understood. In the case of the possibility of God, the existent thing is God himself. There is no way to think of God as possible but not existing: that would mean thinking of him as being contained in or dependent on something else, which is impossible. So in the case of God, his essence is existence.²²

NOTES

1. On this, see Carriero 2009, 27–64.
2. See also *Principles* I.52, AT 8A: 25, and *Principles* I.62–63, AT 8A: 30–31.
3. On this see, De Buzon and Kambouchner 2011, 59–61.
4. It is useful to compare this with what Spinoza says in the *Short Treatise*, Part 1, Chapter 1 at footnote d/Curley 1985: 63 (this is the source of all Spinoza translations): "That other ideas exist is, indeed, possible, but not necessary. But whether they exist or not, their essence is always necessary like the idea of a triangle, or that of the soul's love without the body, etc., so that even if I thought at first that I had feigned them, afterwards I would still be forced to say that they are and would be no less the same, even if neither I nor any other man had ever thought of them. That is why they are not feigned by me, and also must have a subject outside me, which is not me, a subject without which they cannot be." I am grateful to David Cunning for reminding me of this passage.
5. For a comparison between Kant's conception of objectivity and Descartes' true and immutable natures, see Koistinen 2011.
6. Of unforeseeable consequences, see Carriero 2009, 280–317.
7. For example, the Fifth Meditation, AT 7: 66–69; and *First Replies*, AT 7: 119–20.
8. But Descartes thinks that even though it is self-evident that God necessarily exists, "it needed a close attention for [him] to perceive this" (AT 7: 69).
9. The name "ontological argument" is due to Kant.
10. Alanen defends this view in Alanen (forthcoming).
11. For example the Third Meditation, AT 7: 45, 49, and *Principles* I.51–52.
12. See Russell 1903, and Kant 1992, 119–20.
13. Hintikka (1962, 16) is helpful here: "In Descartes' argument the relation of cogito to sum is not that of a premise to a conclusion. Their relation is rather comparable with that of a process to its product. The indubitability of my own existence results from my thinking of it almost as the sound of music results from playing it or (to use Descartes's own metaphor) light in the sense of illumination (lux) results from the presence of a source of light (lumen)." However, I would like to go further and say that the relation of *cogito* to *sum* is that of identity. Active thinking is a way to exist.
14. See Kant 1992, 122–26.

15. In his chapter to this volume, Tad Schmaltz also considers Kant's criticism of the ontological argument.
16. On this, see A599/B627.
17. For example Kenny 1970, Nolan 1997a, Gewirth 1970, Chappell 1997, Schmaltz 1991, Cunning 2003. I have mainly followed here Schmaltz's discussion of this debate.
18. See Kenny 1970, 692–700.
19. Gewirth 1970, 678–79. This view is developed and then defended in Nolan 1997a and Chappell 1997.
20. See Schmaltz 1991 for a further discussion of problems with these views, and also the chapter by Schmaltz that appears earlier in this volume.
21. Of the different positions, the one that comes closest to what I have been suggesting is in Cunning 2003.
22. I am grateful to Joseph Almog, David Cunning, and Arto Repo for their most helpful comments.

12 The Sixth Meditation: Descartes and the embodied self

The following discussion considers two ways in which Descartes approaches the nature of the self. It is proposed that the *Meditations* answers two distinct questions – *What am I?* and *Who am I?* Even though the text answers each question differently, we should not regard the two answers as in conflict with one another. A deeper appreciation of Descartes' comments about the self throughout his corpus helps to reduce the apparent conflict between the self he defines as a 'thinking thing', and the self as constituted by a mind-body union. Contrary to what may seem to follow from the Second Meditation identification of self and thinking thing, a case can be made that our natural state is the lived experience of the embodied self. To remove ourselves from this state takes an extraordinary and unsustainable effort.

The exercise in which we are about to engage has important ramifications for how we think about Descartes' contribution to metaphysics and the philosophy of mind. We are all familiar with a certain caricature of the self that Descartes is alleged to have propagated, and one that contemporary philosophers of mind are apt to use when setting up their own views in opposition. Paul Churchland writes, for example, that "as Descartes saw it, the real *you* is not your material body, but rather a nonspatial thinking substance, an individual unit of mind-stuff quite distinct from your material body."[1] To accept this caricature requires ignoring a vast amount of textual material and assuming that the "you" in Churchland's statement would have been unambiguous for Descartes. Terms referring to the self are indeed ambiguous for Descartes, and unavoidably so.

WHAT AM I?

The question that dominates the Second Meditation and much subsequent scholarship on Descartes' account of personal identity is the question: "What am I?" Although the subject of the Second Meditation is not the identity of the person per se, but rather "The nature of the human mind, and how it is better known than the body" (AT 7: 23), Descartes frames the debate around an examination of whether the "I" (*ego*) can be known with certainty to refer to something which exists, and if so, what its nature is. He rejects various candidates for the referent of "I", such as a rational animal, a mechanical body, a fine-grained material element that permeates the rest of the body ("something tenuous, like a wind or fire or ether" [AT 7: 26]), or anything that requires the imagination to be conceived. About the existence and nature of each of these I may be deceived, and yet there is something I cannot doubt when I turn my attention to my thought. "What then am I?," he asks. The answer is simple and shocking: I am "a thing that thinks" (AT 7: 27).

Why should this conclusion be so shocking? It seems quite uncontentious that we are thinking things. Indeed, rationality had since antiquity been seen as the *differentia* for our species. What is shocking in Descartes' statement is the apparent *reduction* of the human being to its *differentia* and the *exclusion* of the indisputable fact of our embodiment. "I am a thing which thinks" could have seemed a fairly ordinary statement provided that it implied nothing more than a harmless kind of abstraction – *abstraction without precision*, to borrow a technical term from the medievals. For Descartes' Scholastic readers, "I am a thinking thing" would no more have excluded the truth of "I am a body" than "I am a body" would have implied the lack of a rational soul.[2] But few Scholastics would have accepted anything like Descartes' real distinction of mind and body, preferring to think of the soul as the substantial form of the body and the two as constituting one thing in nature.[3] By the Sixth Meditation, however, it is clear that *abstraction with precision* is precisely what Descartes has in mind.

From the Third, Fourth, and Fifth Meditations, we learn of God's existence and the veracity of clear and distinct ideas. In the Sixth Meditation we discover another self-evident proposition: that whatever can be clearly and distinctly understood is capable of being created by God so as to correspond exactly to our idea. If, therefore, we can clearly and distinctly understand one thing apart from another, we know that they are really distinct because we know that God could create one without the other.[4] Knowing from the Second Meditation that I exist and at the same time that "nothing else belongs to my nature or essence except that I am a thinking thing," I can infer that "my essence consists solely in the fact that I am a thinking thing" (AT 7: 78). The clear and distinct idea I have of myself as a thinking thing involves no idea related to extension, and the distinct idea I have of body, conversely, does not presuppose any idea that involves the idea of thinking substance. Together with the principles related to God's power to create separately what can be clearly and distinctly conceived separately, and that whatever can be conceived apart must be really distinct, Descartes draws the conclusion that mind and body are really distinct (ibid.). And here it is not just *my mind* which is really distinct from *my body*; it is "I" who am really distinct from my body:

[O]n the one hand I have a clear and distinct idea of myself, in so far as I am simply a thinking non-extended thing; and on the other hand I have a distinct idea of body, in so far as this is simply an extended, non-thinking, thing. And accordingly, it is certain that I am really distinct from my body, and can exist without it. (Ibid.)

The Latin text indeed asserts that it is me (*me*) and not merely my mind that is really distinct from my body (*meo corpore*). The French edition makes the identification between me and my mind even more explicit, adding: "that is, my soul, by which I am what I am."[5] At this point the case seems pretty conclusive. What am I? I am essentially and exclusively my mind.[6]

It is this stronger conclusion that was so deeply shocking to Descartes' critics. Hobbes (no Scholastic himself) attempts to block the passage of the *cogito* argument to the conclusion that I am *only* a thinking thing by pointing out the following fallacy. From the fact that I can know with certainty that I am performing some action, X (e.g., thinking), it does not follow that I am simply X (a thinking thing). To assume so would involve a conflation of a property with its subject. No conclusions follow, according to Hobbes, about the nature of the mind from the observation that it is indubitably thinking (*Third Objections and Replies*, AT 7: 172–74).

We can ignore as question-begging Hobbes' own peculiar reasons for thinking that the subject of thought must instead be corporeal[7] while granting his observation that Descartes is premature in thinking that he has an answer to the question: What am I? Although Descartes is adamant in his reply to Hobbes that the Second Meditation leaves open the question of whether the thing that thinks is corporeal or not (AT 7: 174–75), the discussion purports to be about "the nature of the human mind." In addition, the Second Meditation discussion treats the existence of bodies as neither here nor there when it comes to the functioning of the human mind, in a way that makes the work of the Sixth Meditation real distinction argument much easier.

Although the argument for the real distinction of mind and body involves not just thinking about mind and body in abstraction from one another, but, as he will later say in his response to Arnauld's objections, in *exclusion* from one another (*Fourth Replies*, AT 7: 226), much more of the Sixth Meditation is devoted to exploring their union rather than their distinctness. It is certain, Descartes announces mid-argument, that I have a body "that is very closely joined to me" (AT 7:78). The reason for this shift in focus is that Descartes does not want his view aligned with an instrumentalist understanding of the relationship between mind and body. In *Fourth Objections*, Arnauld denies that instrumentalism can be avoided, objecting that the real distinction argument

takes us back to the Platonic view ... that nothing corporeal belongs to our essence, so that man is merely a rational soul and the body merely a vehicle for the soul – a view which gives rise to the definition of man as a 'soul that makes use of a body'. (AT 7: 203)

Descartes responds:

Now someone who says that a man's arm is a substance that is really distinct from the rest of his body does not thereby deny that the arm belongs to the nature of the whole man. And saying that the arm belongs to the nature of the whole man does not give rise to the suspicion that it cannot subsist in its own right. In the same way I do not think that I proved too much in showing that the mind can exist apart from the body. Nor do I think I proved too little in saying that the mind is *substantially united* with the body, since that substantial union does not prevent our having a clear and distinct concept of the mind on its own as a complete thing. (AT 7: 228, emphasis added)

The distinction between an instrumental relationship and a true union is that in the latter, the components united are in some sense incomplete (or *in potentia*) to one another – if not with respect to their existence, then with respect to the unique composite they form. Descartes wants to argue that two substances can be complete with respect to being really distinct substances, while being incomplete with respect to some composite they form in nature:

If the reason for calling them incomplete is that they are unable to exist on their own, then I confess I find it self-contradictory that they should be called substances, that is, things which subsist on their own, and at the same time incomplete, that is, not possessing the power to subsist on their own. It is also possible to call a substance incomplete in the sense that, although it has nothing incomplete about it *qua* substance, it is incomplete insofar as it is referred to some other substance in conjunction with which it forms something which is a unity in its own right ... The mind and the body are incomplete substances when they are referred to a human being which together they make up. But if they are considered on their own they are complete. (AT 7: 222)

This "unity in its own right" is the whole human being, which, despite the real distinction of mind and body, is not something Descartes thinks can be reductively analyzed in terms of the substances of which it is composed. The idea of it cannot, for example, be derived from the ideas of mind and body considered jointly, but has to be known on its own terms, and *a posteriori*. It is not my clear and distinct ideas of mind and body developed separately in the Second Meditation that compel me to recognize that "my own nature" consists of a composite, but rather the "teachings of nature," in particular, sensations (especially, pain) and passions, through which I experience my embodiment. It is these sensory experiences that confirm that I am a union of mind and body.

The product of reflecting on my experiences of embodiment is a different sense of self from the one Descartes relies on in the real distinction argument. This shift in thinking about the self is initially confusing. On the one hand, as later passages (e.g., The Sixth Meditation, AT 7: 80) attest, "my own nature in particular" is identified with "the totality of things bestowed upon me by God," which includes my body and all the faculties that follow from the union of mind and body. Here the "I" is "my whole [self] (*me totum*), insofar as I am a composite (*compositus*) of body and mind" (AT 7: 81, my translation). On the other hand, there is no indication that Descartes has given up his earlier assertion that "my whole [self]" (*totum me*) can exist so long as the thinking thing exists whether embodied or not, for "I can clearly and distinctly understand myself as whole without these faculties [of sense and imagination]" (AT 7: 78). Prima facie, all this makes little sense. Am I one thing (my mind) or two (my mind and my body)?

We can see the confusion generated by these two ways of thinking about "my whole self" if we try to employ both in a single train of thought. Let us call the thinking thing that I am the "minimal self" and the combination of mind and body, the "maximal self." From a metaphysical perspective, the answer to the question what I am at any given moment is thus either this thinking thing (minimal self) or this thinking thing united to this particular chunk of extension (maximal self). But then what I am looks completely indeterminate. Assuming in accordance with *Principles* I.60 that any particular chunk of *res extensa* is a substance, the answer to the question "What am I?" when applied to the maximal self at any given time is that I am two substances (a mind and a part of matter in a certain God-affixed combination). Intuitively, that is a very unnatural way for me to think about myself. First, I am inclined to think that I am one thing, not two, and saying that I am one *composite* does little to reduce the sense of plurality anymore than referring to a group of soldiers as 'one army' eliminates the sense of plurality. Second, since the matter that constitutes my body is continuously replaced, what I am metaphysically is continuously changing, and yet I persist. If, in answer to the question, "What persists?," we retreat to the minimal self – i.e., the thinking thing, which, being unextended, does not suffer from replacement of parts – then the claim that the composite has a metaphysical status turns out to be spurious, as is the claim that I am not just a mind, but a body as well.

What emerges from Descartes' attempt to clarify the nature of the union, when pressed by Princess Elizabeth in correspondence, is a somewhat different emphasis on "the maximal self" as our natural state of being. He begins his response in the usual way, explaining the different ways in which substances and the union are known. There are, he writes, three "primitive" notions: of the soul alone, of body alone and of their union, and correspondingly, three ways in which each is known ("To Princess Elizabeth, 28 June 1643," AT 3: 690–95). The soul is conceived through pure intellect, the body (as extension) through the intellect aided by imagination, but the union is only known clearly through the senses and obscurely through the intellect. It is

the ordinary course of life and conversation, and abstention from meditation and from the study of things which exercise the imagination, that teaches us how to conceive the union of the soul and the body. (AT 3: 692).

Descartes claims that he can spend only a few hours a day on thoughts that occupy the imagination (e.g., geometry, mechanics), and only a few hours a year on thoughts which occupy the intellect alone (e.g., metaphysics). The rest of his time is given over to "the relaxation of the senses and the repose of the mind" (AT 3: 693). In these passages, the implication is that the self which is identified with the pure intellect is not one we can inhabit for very long; that it takes a supreme mental effort *not* to think using the senses; and that it takes a substantial though diminished effort by comparison to think using the imagination. All this seems rather strange in the context of the *Meditations*.

Perhaps more perplexing is that what I am seems to be either the whole, which includes both the mind and the body, or a part, the mind. We may wonder whether a whole is always *just* the sum of its parts or something more, but we generally tend to think that a whole is *at least* the sum of its parts. Descartes' flipping back and forth on the nature of the *me totum* seems to violate our most fundamental intuitions about the relationship between wholes and parts.

One possibility is that *me totum* is, for Descartes, ambiguous, depending on whether the question is "What am I?" or "Who am I?" If that were so, the answer to the first question might well be the minimal self – the thinking thing – since that is all that is essential to my existence, while the answer to the second question is the maximal self, since who I am includes all the properties which are true of me by virtue of my unique relationship to matter "in this human life," as Descartes sometimes says (e.g., The Sixth Meditation, AT 7: 90).

WHO AM I?

I doubt that today we hear much of a difference between the "What am I?" question and the "Who am I?" question, but during the Middle Ages a distinction between these questions served an obvious purpose. If you were to have asked the metaphysical question: "What is the Father, the Son, and the Holy Spirit?," the answer would have been God, that unitary, indivisible substance, creator of all things. But if you were to have asked the question: "Who are the Father, the Son, and the Holy Spirit?" the answer would have been not one but three – three *persons*: Father, Son and Holy Spirit. Much theoretical energy was expended trying to articulate what kind of distinction there could be between the three persons of the Trinity, and a variety of distinctions intermediate between the real and the merely verbal emerged to plug the gap. The most prominent of these by the end of the sixteenth century was the Scotists' *formal distinction*.[8] Although Descartes was averse to tackling the Trinity[9] or any other theological mystery head on, he was clearly familiar with debates among the Jesuits over the status of intermediate distinctions, including Scotus' formal distinction.[10] It is important to note that even if this distinction was regarded as a distinction of reason, it required a foundation in reality that was logically prior to thought.[11] In the tradition, the primary reason for thinking that the distinction between the three persons of the Trinity is metaphysically robust (and not merely verbal) is that what is predicable of one person of the Trinity is not necessarily predicable of the others. Whereas the Father is related to the Son by paternity, for example, neither the Son nor the Holy Spirit is related to anything by paternity. The Father is, moreover, the rightful *subject* of paternity, and it was generally assumed that where there is a property, there must be a subject or bearer of the property. The division of God into three (inseparable) persons allowed for the attribution of contradictory properties without invoking a contradiction, but the division was, for all that, thought to be "less than real."

In thinking about the relationship between persons and substances, Descartes arguably has the opposite problem. Whereas in the case of the Trinity we need multiple persons in one substance, Descartes requires that a single person be constituted by two substances. The analogy cannot be perfect, therefore, since there is a real division within Descartes' human being that doesn't correspond to any real division within God. What is similar in both cases, however, is that the pressure to supply different answers to the "What am I?" and "Who am I?" questions stems from the inability to account in both cases for all the predicates that can be applied if we are restricted to using a single, unambiguous subject term. We cannot understand God's relationship to Christ through paternity if we do not think of God as comprising two persons. In the case of Descartes' union of mind and body, there are properties that require a subject which cannot be either the mind or the body considered apart. These are the modes of sense perception and imagination, which depend not just on the existence of mind and body but on their union and inter-action. Since Descartes is committed to the view that every mode needs a subject, the question arises: *What is the subject of these irreducible modes of sensation?*

What Descartes needs is a subject for sensory predicates which is neither the mind nor the body and certainly not some third thing distinct from either of those (for what could that be?), but something that is *both* mind and body. That is the only way to capture how it is that there could be thoughts that depend upon movements in the body and *vice versa*. The subject of sensory predicates is the *union* of mind and body. Interestingly, Descartes never refers to this subject as a substance, although he does refer to it as a *substantial union* (*unio substantialis*) in line with certain orthodox opinions. His use of this expression to refer to the whole person raises interesting questions, which need not detain us right now.[12] The important point is that the special subject of these irreducible modes is not one that Descartes can draw from his official ontology of basic substances, and hence he needs to conceive of the union as *sui generis*. I suggest that the conceptual independence of "substance" and "person" would have been familiar to Descartes' scholastic readers, and could, therefore, have provided him with a model to think about the relationship between his basic substances and the whole human being.

Certainly, I need to be a thinking thing to sense redness, feel angry, imagine an ecologically friendly city, but I cannot be just a thinking thing if the modes in question "are absolutely dependent" upon movements of the animal spirits in the body (*Passions* I.41, AT 11: 359.). If Descartes' *person* is the irreducible subject of sensations, passions, and ideas of imagination, what is this subject, and what is its relationship to the substances of mind and body? Does the idea of the "whole me" require us to revise the official ontology of substances, attributes, and modes to include persons?

THE UNION OF MIND AND BODY

The moral to be drawn from the theological analogy is that talk of substances as opposed to persons and vice versa is appropriate as a function of the question that is under investigation. The "What is it?"/"Who is it?" distinction applies here as well. The answer to the "What is this (union)?" question is: two substances, mind and body. The answer to the "Who is this?" question is: a single person. Descartes' comments to Elizabeth imply that we spend most of our time in the state of being a single person, and while it is possible for us cognitively to transcend that state to engage in pure thought or thought aided only by the imagination, it can only be sustained for short periods of time and is, in a way, unnatural.

Much of the subsequent discussion following Descartes' introduction of mind–body union in the Sixth Meditation is devoted to establishing that the union is a functionally integrated, genuine unit, not a mere aggregate. The teachings of nature instruct me that my human body is not a mere instrument but something that is intimately felt as part of me.[13] In characterizing this relationship between the mind and the body, Descartes adopts the slogan from antiquity that I am not in my body as "a sailor is present in a ship" (AT 7: 81). I know this to be true by virtue of sensing directly (rather than intellectually inferring) the state of my body. From pain and pleasure, for example, I learn that "I am very closely joined and, as it were, intermingled with [my body], so that I and the body form a unit." As Descartes cautions Regius, it is important to reject the idea of the union as an accidentally conjoined aggregate:

Whenever the occasion arises, as much privately as publicly, you ought to profess that you believe a human to be a true *ens per se* and not [an *ens*] *per accidens* and the mind to be really and substantially united to the body not through a position [*situs*] or disposition, as you have in your last written text for this again is obnoxious to those who will object and, as for me, I judge it not to be true – but through a true mode of union as everyone admits commonly even if no one explains how it may be, nor therefore also will you be held to explain it. But however you can [explain it], as I do in the

Metaphysics, through this: that we may perceive a sensation of pain, and all other [sensations], not to be pure cogitations of the mind distinct from the body but confused perceptions of it as really united [to the body]. For if an angel were in a human body it would not sense as we do but it would perceive only the motions which are caused by external objects and through this it would be distinguished from a true human. ("To Regius, January 1642," AT 3: 493; my translation)

One question that has puzzled commentators is how much metaphysical import the experience of the union carries. Descartes does make clear that that the union is supposed to be explanatorily prior to the faculties that assure us that we have bodies:

As regards the soul and the body together, we have only the notion of their union, on which depends our notion of the soul's power to move the body, and the body's power to act on the soul and cause its sensations and passions. ("To Princess Elizabeth, 21 May 1643," AT 3: 665)

But is Descartes entitled to infer from his sensations and passions anything more than a phenomenological unity, an *experience* of unity? Sensations and passions are, after all, modes of thinking. Couldn't I be a sailor in a ship who has *illusory* experiences of her ship as an integral part of her nature?

Consider, by contrast, the more weighty meaning behind the rejection of the sailor-in-a-ship metaphor in a standard Scholastic text, namely, Aquinas' *Quaestiones Disputatae de Anima*, a. 1:

Plato maintained that the human soul not only subsisted of itself, but also had the complete nature of a species. For he held that the complete nature of the [human] species is found in the soul, saying that a man is not a composite of soul and body, but a soul joined to a body in such a way that it is related to the body as a pilot is to a ship, or as one clothed to his clothing. However, this position is untenable, because it is obvious that the soul is the reality which gives life to the body ... Now a form is of this nature. Therefore the human soul is the form of the body. But if the soul were, in the body as a pilot is in a ship, it would give neither the body nor its parts their specific nature. The contrary of this is seen to be true, because, when the soul leaves the body, the body's individual parts retain their original names only in an equivocal sense. For the eye of a dead man, like the eye of a portrait or that of a statue, is called an eye equivocally; and similarly for the other parts of the body. Furthermore, if the soul were in the body as a pilot in a ship, it would follow that the union of soul and body would be an accidental one. Then death, which brings about their separation, would not be a substantial corruption; which is clearly false. So it follows that the soul is a particular thing and that it can subsist of itself, not as a thing having a complete species of its own, but as completing the human species by being the form of the body. Hence it likewise follows that it is both a form and a particular thing.[14]

According to Aquinas, it is impossible for the human being to be a mere aggregate of soul and body for the simple reason that the body is nothing prior to its actualization by the soul. Matter is pure potentiality and cannot exist on its own. The soul is the substantial form of the human body and accounts for both the body's existence and its distinctive animate behavior. Thus, when the soul departs the body, its organs and parts are no longer, strictly speaking, *what* they were, namely, eyes, hands, a heart, etc. Death is a corruption of the material substance. The fact that the form (the human soul) can subsist in some compromised way after separation from the body does not, for Aquinas, diminish the fact that the human being is not a mere conglomerate of mutually distinct substances or that the matter of a human body cannot exist apart from a soul. Thinking, moreover, is essential to the soul and requires the availability of sensory images. Hence, the soul always retains "an aptitude and an inclination to be united to the body" even in the separated state.[15]

Aquinas' account of the human being seems far removed from the discussion of the union of mind and body in the Sixth Meditation. First, Descartes' human is a union of mutually independent substances. Second, the functions of the parts of the human body can all be conceived apart from the soul:

I might consider the body of a man as a kind of machine equipped with and made up of bones, nerves, muscles, veins, blood and skin in such a way that, even if there were no mind in it, it would still perform all the same movements as it now does in those cases where movement is not under the control of the will or, consequently, of the mind. (AT 7: 84)

Death, therefore, is not substantial corruption, but simply a rearrangement of matter which indisposes it for union with a soul.[16] As Descartes writes in his synopsis of the *Meditations*, created substances are by nature incorruptible, from which it follows that the death of a human being is not a substantial but only an accidental change or diminution in the body which composes it:

[B]ody, taken in a general sense, is a substance, so that it too never perishes. But the human body, in so far as it differs from other bodies, is simply made up of a certain configuration of limbs and other accidents of this sort; whereas the human mind is not made up of any accidents in this way, but is a pure substance. For even if all the accidents of the mind change, so that it has different objects of the understanding and different desires and sensations, it does not on that account become a different mind; whereas a human body loses its identity merely as a result of a change in the shape of some of its parts. (AT 7: 14)

Finally, Descartes is committed to the undeniable autonomy of the intellect from the senses (if only for a few hours a year!).

Although there is much, therefore, to distinguish Descartes' approach to the human being from the view adopted by Aquinas, there is also much to prevent his approach from collapsing into the Platonic view according to which a human being is an accidental aggregate of metaphysically independent items. This is because the union is, for Descartes, a whole which is greater than the sum of its parts – the subject of irreducible properties – and in that context the mind acquires a form of cognition (namely, sensation) that it would not otherwise have and from which it cannot easily extract itself. Descartes' concept of mind is thus arguably ambiguous, depending on whether we are talking about the mind as a substance or as belonging to a person. The first is a "complete" concept, as Descartes would say, something capable of existing on its own; the second is "incomplete in so far as it is referred to some other substance in conjunction with which it forms something which is a unity in its own right" (AT 7: 222).

A similar kind of ambiguity between complete and incomplete ideas of a primary substance is then exploited in relation to the human body.

THE HUMAN BODY

In "Synopsis of the *Meditations*," Descartes differentiates body "in the general sense" from the human body by the configuration of its parts (AT 7:14). This could suggest that a human body is a collection of material parts arranged in a certain way such that any change either in the matter or the configuration would alter its identity. But this seems wrong on three counts: first, because parts are constantly undergoing replacement in the human body without apparently affecting its identity; second, because configuration is a mode, and modes, being dependent upon substances for their being, cannot account for the identity of anything; and third, because some alteration in the arrangement of the parts of a human body can often be tolerated. My human body is a whole that includes my left thumb, but were I to lose my left thumb, my body would still exist and still be human. If we identify the human body with the whole arrangement of parts, and identify the whole with the sum of its parts in a given arrangement, it is difficult to make sense of the intuition that the human body can persist despite a non-vital part being accidentally removed from the whole.

In a letter to Mesland, Descartes seeks to clarify the status of the human body and what makes it human. The arrangement of matter is important for distinguishing a body as human, but this is not offered as a criterion. It is rather through the continual union of matter with one and the same soul that a human body remains the same through time:

First of all, I consider what exactly is the body of a man, and I find that the word 'body' is very ambiguous. When we speak of a body in general we mean a determinate part of matter, a part of the quantity of which the universe is composed. In this sense, if the smallest amount of that quantity were removed, we would judge without more ado that the body was smaller and no longer complete; and if any particle of the matter were changed, we would at once think that the body was no longer quite the same, no longer numerically the same (*idem numero*). But when we speak of the body of a man, we do not mean a determinate part of matter, or one that has a determinate size; we mean simply the whole of the matter which is united with the soul of that man. And so, even though the matter changes, and its quantity increases or decreases, we still believe that it is the same body, numerically the same body (*idem numero*) so long as it remains joined and substantially united with the same soul. ("To Mesland, 9 February 1645," AT 4: 166)

Descartes then asserts that despite the continual replacement of parts, there is a sense in which a human body is indivisible:

[I]t can even be called indivisible, because if an arm or a leg of a man is amputated, we think that it is only in the first sense of 'body' that his body is divided – we do not think that a man who has lost an arm or a leg is less a man than any other. (AT 4: 167)

I am not less a human then for losing my left thumb, but neither are the parts of my body dependent upon their union with my soul for their ontological status. The human body can be completely understood with respect to its status as a substance (body), but incompletely understood in contexts which call for reference to the union.

Aquinas' assumption is that were soul and body complete substances, they could not constitute a single, indivisible human being. This is not an assumption that Descartes shares. We could read Descartes as showing how an argument like Aquinas' rests on several equivocations: "Body," "divisibility," and "indivisibility" are all ambiguous terms. Hence, "I am a body" has equivocal meanings. First of all, "I" is ambiguous, depending on whether we are asking about the person or what the subject is essentially. If we take into consideration the "I" from the answer to "What am I?," the sentence is clearly false, for what I am essentially is a thinking thing. Suppose then that we are asking about the whole person. Taking "body" in the general sense, as a particular chunk of *res extensa*, "I am a body" is also false, for "body" in that case is considered independently of any particular relationship to a soul, is divisible into parts, and loses its identity under division. Taking "body" to refer to a human body, the sentence picks out a certain configuration of matter that can retain its identity through division provided that the remaining arrangement is sufficient to preserve its union with one and the same soul. To consider it true, "I am a body" must be taken as a case of abstraction without precision, as not implying that I am just a body. With the terms sufficiently disambiguated, "I am a body" could be as true for Descartes as it was for Aquinas, but we are far from the metaphysical picture that Aquinas assumes must be in place for the statement to be true. Provided that there is *some* sense in which "mind" and "body" cannot be completely understood in isolation from one another, Descartes thinks he can avoid the charge of Platonism. The completeness of mind and body considered in themselves need not, he thinks, interfere with the truth that resides in the proposition that I am a body as well as a thinking thing.

All this suggests that Descartes needs, in addition to the concepts of mind and body, a third category of the person or "union" as he indeed suggests in referring to this as a primitive notion. But it is important to understand that the union can be neither a mere aggregate of substances nor a substance itself. Descartes insists that his person is a unity, an *ens per se*. He uses this expression "being through itself" somewhat liberally. *Entia per se* include the kinds of things that come into being through accidental processes, including, for example, mice spontaneously generated from dirt.[17] So too, as Descartes explains to Regius, although there is some sense in which the union is accidental (since there is nothing in matter *demanding* union with the soul), the union is not "absolutely accidental" (AT 3: 461). Nor, however, could the union be a substance while it remains dependent for its existence on the existence of independent substances, mind and body. We cannot get to the point of accepting that the union is one thing, while it remains two substances, unless it is in a different category from that of substance.

CONCLUSION

Being a person in Descartes' framework is turning out to be a highly contextualized matter. Whether we think of ourselves in terms of the minimal or maximal self depends on which explanatory or conversational context we are in. To account for the emergent properties that differentiate a human being – i.e., its capacity to sense, feel, imagine – I must be understood to be a mind united to a certain configuration of matter by a "true mode of union" ("To Regius, January 1642," AT 3:493). Descartes' account of personal identity can tolerate a certain amount of vagueness of this sort because the concept of a person is defined by certain kinds of capacities, in particular, the capacity to integrate sensory and intellectual information, capacities which are realized throughout the course of a person's life in different parcels of *res extensa*. Variations within the machine are tolerable provided they do not impede this integration of sense and reason and general bodily integrity. This flexibility is the mark of an efficient design – "the best system that could be devised" (the Sixth Meditation, AT 7: 87).

It is in this framework that we can begin to disambiguate Descartes' confusing references to "my whole [self]" (*me totum*). Our original overarching worry was how I can be *wholly* identified as one thing, a mind, and as two, a mind and a body. Along the way, we have discovered a second worry: how can I be one thing (a union) while being composed of two, mind and body? I have suggested above that the only way to deal with these questions is to embrace the many ambiguities at work in Descartes' texts and see him as answering distinct kinds of questions: *What am I?* and *Who am I?* As we have seen, that the union of mind and body exists does not mean that its nature and existence are reducible to the nature and existence of mind and body understood separately. The very fact of the union's existing adds something to nature that wouldn't otherwise be.[18]

NOTES

1. Churchland 1984, 8.
2. Aquinas puts this distinction to work in *On Being and Essence*, ch. 2.
3. Scotus and Ockham represent exceptions in the medieval tradition in admitting a real distinction between matter and substantial form. Matter and form on their view must be able to exist apart, at least by an act of God, if there is to be any distinction between them at all. Matter remains *in potentia* to receiving a substantial form (but not conversely), and the two naturally combined form a per se unity. See, for example, Duns Scotus 1325, vii. 483; and for discussion, Cross 1998, ch. 3, and William of Ockham 1974, 161–62.
4. See also *Principles* I.60, AT 8A. 28–29.
5. This point is made by the editors of CSM 2: 54, n. 3. The French edition at AT 9B: 62 reads: "il est certain que ce moi, c'est-à-dire mon âme, par laquelle je suis ce que je suis, est entièrement et véritablement distincte de mon corps, et qu'elle peut être ou exister sans lui."
6. This passage also contains a generally unnoticed slide between distinguishing between my mind and body (in general) and my mind and my body (in particular). While this slide might not be problematic for the purposes of the real distinction argument since the general entails the particular, it raises questions about how successfully one can conceive of one's own, particular, human body apart from one's mind, a fact Descartes seems later to deny. See "To Mesland, 9 February 1645," AT 4: 165–67.
7. Hobbes is guilty of a different conflation – between the idea of *matter* and the idea of a *subject* of the act of thinking. He denies that I could know I am thinking except by thinking of the "I" as something material (AT 7: 173–74).
8. See, for example, Duns Scotus 1639, I, d.13, q.un., n.3.
9. See "To Mersenne, 6 May 1630," AT 1: 150. In "To Mersenne, 28 October 1640" (AT 3: 215–16) and "To Mersenne, 31 December 1640" (AT 3: 274), the Trinity is described as an article of faith that cannot be known by natural reason alone. Although the union of mind and body is not an article of faith, it too cannot be understood just by means of the intellect.
10. Adopting Suárez's terminology, Descartes posits a *distinction of (reasoned) reason (rationis ratiocinatae)* to mediate between the real and

merely verbal distinctions and to account for the distinction between inseparable attributes of a single, unified substance. See *Principles* I.62, AT 8A: 30; "To ***, 1645 or 1646," AT 4: 349–50.

11. This is true for Descartes' distinction of reasoned reason as well. See AT 4: 350.

12. The terminology of *unio substantialis* figured in a range of medieval debates concerning the issue of whether a composite substance just is its parts; the soul's subsistence; the relationship between Christ's human nature and the second person of the Trinity; and whether God suffers on the cross (the heresy of Patripassionism).

13. Despite Descartes' attack in the *Meditations* and elsewhere on the senses as a source of knowledge of the nature of matter, he recognizes the importance of the senses both for practical reason and the experimental sciences. See Brown 2006, chs. 3 and 6.

14. Aquinas 1949, 6.

15. Aquinas 1968, I, q.76.a.1.

16. See Descartes' rejection of the standard Scholastic account of death of the body in terms of the soul's departure in *Passions* I.6, AT 11: 330–31.

17. "To Regius, December 1641," AT 3: 460.

18. I am especially grateful to David Cunning for providing excellent feedback and advice, to Lilli Alanen and Calvin Normore for much fruitful discussion, and to the Australian Research Council for funding this project.

13 Sensory perception of bodies: Meditation 6.5

To judge from the first five and a half of Descartes' six Meditations, the senses have very little to recommend themselves. At the beginning of the *Meditations*, our sensory experience is regarded as susceptible to illusion, indistinguishable from dreaming, and of uncertain origin. Shortly thereafter the senses are judged to systematically mislead us about the nature of bodies, providing only "obscure" and "confused" perceptions of them through what may be "materially false" ideas. The senses, it seems, can't even acquaint us properly with a little piece of wax! The intellect, rather than the senses, is the epistemic hero of the *Meditations*, guiding us to such important metaphysical truths as the existence of God, the real distinction between mind and body, and even the true nature of body.[1] It is no wonder, then, that much of the secondary literature on Descartes' treatment of the senses is devoted to understanding their epistemic shortcomings.[2]

The second half of the sixth and final Meditation treats the senses in a more positive light. Here Descartes defends the claim that sensory perception is a form of thinking unique to embodied minds: it arises from the union or "intermingling" of mind and body (AT 7: 81). While sensory perception may be problematic for the purpose of doing metaphysics, he insists that it is critical to our survival as embodied minds. There is, it seems, a division of cognitive labor in the embodied human mind: the intellect is our best guide to metaphysics; the senses are our best guides to action. While the French tradition has long attended to Descartes' repurposing of the senses as guides to survival,[3] Anglo-American commentators have only more recently attended to this part of the story,[4] which is the focus of this chapter.

258

The chapter begins with a brief guided tour of the *Meditations* that highlights the treatment of the senses and explores their epistemic unraveling in Meditations 1 through 6.5. Along the way I distinguish Descartes, the author of the *Meditations*, from his fictional first-person meditator, and to avoid ambiguity I refer to the meditator with feminine pronouns (she, her). Descartes' aims in writing the *Meditations*, and in employing the arguments he does, are not always the same as those explicitly advanced by the meditator, and so it will be important to keep both in mind as we read the text. The second section turns to the repurposing of the senses as guides to survival in Meditation 6.5. The final three sections explore the details of Descartes' suggestion that the senses are guides to survival in three different aspects of sense perceptual experience: bodily awareness, so-called secondary-quality perception, and spatial perception.

THE SENSES IN MEDITATIONS I TO 6.5

The senses come under attack almost immediately in the *Meditations*. Why? The meditator tells us she wants to rid herself of false beliefs and establish a firm and lasting foundation for knowledge, and that the senses aren't up to the task. But why does *Descartes* choose to open the text with an attack on the senses? His stated goal is to provide the best possible argument for the existence of God and also an argument for the real distinction between mind (or soul) and body that might underwrite a further argument for the immortality of the soul. That, at any rate, is the goal (or one of the goals) that he presents to the dean and doctors of the theology faculty at the Sorbonne when he seeks their endorsement for the *Meditations* (AT 7: 1–6). It is also the goal he presents in his "Preface to the Reader" (AT 7: 9).[5] (He confesses a rather different goal to his friend, Marin Mersenne, but we'll come to that later.) Now Descartes' considered view is that God and the soul are proper objects of the intellect alone; unlike bodies, they are not sensible or even imaginable, but only intelligible.[6] He therefore finds it necessary to help his readers "withdraw from the senses" and to prepare them for the study of purely intellectual things.[7] It is to that end that he opens the *Meditations* with his familiar battery of skeptical arguments: sense-perceptual experiences are susceptible to illusion (where we might recall that square towers look round from a distance or that amputees

feel pains in non-existent limbs); sensory experiences are phenomenologically indistinguishable from dreams (so I can never know for
sure whether what I'm sensing is veridical); and their origin is uncertain (so for all we know they might systematically misrepresent
things). But withdrawal is never easy. The senses have a persistent
and compelling grip, and so by the end of the First Meditation, the
meditator resorts to a bit of self-deception in an effort to make the
doubts stick: she resolves to "deceive myself, by pretending for a time
that these former [sense-based] opinions are utterly false and imaginary" (AT 7: 22).[8]

Having momentarily freed herself of the grip of the senses, the
meditator has her first purely intellectual experiences in the Second
Meditation: she discovers that (a) she exists (AT 7: 25) and (b) she is (at
least) a thinking thing or mind (AT 7: 27). These beliefs resist all doubt,
and they appear not to rely on the senses, but only on the intellect.
What Descartes aims to establish here, as the title of the Meditation
indicates, is that the mind (accessed only through the intellect) is
known "better" than bodies (accessed chiefly through the senses) –
better in the sense that its existence and various modifications are
indubitable. But the meditator's senses rebel immediately:

But it still appears – and I cannot stop thinking this – that the corporeal
things ... which the senses investigate, are known with much more
distinctness than this puzzling 'I' which cannot be pictured in the imagination. (AT 7: 29)

The thought experiment with the piece of wax is then designed to
reinforce the conclusion that things accessed through the intellect are
known better than things accessed through the senses. It is meant to
show (a) that even bodies are known better by the intellect than by the
senses, at least so far as their *nature* is concerned (AT 7: 31–33); (b) that
whatever sensory knowledge of bodies we have always involves something above and beyond mere sensing, i.e., a judgment that belongs not
to the senses but to the "mind alone" (AT 7: 31); and (c) that whereas
any purported sensory knowledge about a body is dubitable, there is
always a corresponding fact about the mind that is known with certainty, namely that it thinks it knows something about the body (AT
7: 33). At last, by the end of the wax discussion, the senses fall into
submission. The Third Meditation opens: "I will now shut my eyes,
stop my ears, and withdraw all my senses" (AT 7: 34).

In the body of the Third Meditation, the meditator scrutinizes her old sense-based beliefs about bodies. What, if anything, in them is certain? That she has sensory ideas that represent bodies to her is something about which she is certain. After all, this is just to know something about her mind. But there are two beliefs that typically accompany these ideas: (a) that they are produced by bodies existing outside the mind and (b) that those bodies are just as they appear, i.e., they "resemble" or conform to her sensory ideas of them (AT 7: 35). Both beliefs fall prey to the skeptical doubts of the First Meditation, but the meditator worries especially about the belief that bodies resemble her sensory ideas of them. A counter-example presents itself immediately: she has two ideas of the sun: a sensory idea that represents it as small and an astronomical idea that represents it as large. The sun can't resemble *both* ideas, and the astronomical idea has more claim to accuracy than the sensory idea, so it must be that the sun does not resemble her sensory idea after all. The meditator goes on to judge that her sensory grasp of bodies is largely "confused and obscure" (AT 7: 43) and that her sensory ideas might be "materially false" insofar as they invite false judgments about bodies.

The Fourth Meditation also opens by reinforcing the withdrawal from the senses and reasserting the epistemic superiority of the intellect:

During these past few days I have accustomed myself to leading my mind away from the senses; and I have taken careful note of the fact that there is very little about corporeal things that is truly perceived, whereas much more is known about the human mind, and still more about God. (AT 7: 52–53)

The main order of business in this Meditation is to train the will to pledge its allegiance to the pure intellect, affirming its clear and distinct perceptions of mind and God and the like, and to refrain from passing judgment in the case of sensory perceptions and more generally in the case of any perceptions that are obscure and confused. By holding her sense-based beliefs at bay, the meditator predicts she will safely avoid falsehoods.

The Fifth Meditation turns to the topic of body. The meditator knows now that the senses mislead her about the nature of bodies. What, then, does her *intellect* have to tell her about them? The answer comes from geometry: she has a clear and distinct idea of body considered as something that has "extension ... in length, depth and breadth" (AT 7: 63). Indeed, she is capable of a full and certain knowledge of that corporeal nature which is the "subject-matter of pure mathematics" (AT 7: 71). Descartes is thereby ushering in the secret agenda of his *Meditations*: to introduce the geometrical conception of body that grounds his physics. He notoriously confesses this agenda in a letter to Mersenne as the *Meditations* is being readied for publication:

I may tell you, between ourselves, that these six Meditations contain all the foundations of my physics. But please do not tell people, for that might make it harder for supporters of Aristotle to approve them. I hope that readers will gradually get used to my principles, and recognize their truth, before they notice that they destroy the principles of Aristotle. ("To Mersenne, 28 January 1641," AT 3: 298)

Descartes' bare geometrical conception of body is definitely at odds with a sensory conception of body, which includes color, sound, flavor, odor, warmth, cold, and the like. We thus have a further reason for Descartes to insist on a withdrawal from the senses in the *Meditations*, and on the falsity of our belief that the corporeal world is as it sensorily appears: he intends to replace the Aristotelian sense-based conception of body with his purified intellectual conception of body. Thus when bodies are ushered back into existence in the Sixth Meditation, they are not the same bodies whose existence was doubted away in Meditation:

It follows that corporeal things exist. *They may not all exist in a way that exactly corresponds with my sensory grasp of them*, for in many cases the grasp of the senses is very obscure and confused. But at least they possess all the properties which I clearly and distinctly understand, that is, all those which, viewed in general terms, are comprised within the subject-matter of pure mathematics. (AT 7: 80, italics added)

The pure intellect proves itself to be the superior source not only of our knowledge of insensible things like God and the soul, but also of our knowledge of the nature of body. The senses are useful in establishing the existence of bodies (we'll look at the argument shortly), but as for the assumption that we can read the essence of body or the details of the corporeal world off our sensory experience, it is not just dubitable, but now firmly rejected as false.

If we stop here, we are left with the impression that the senses are little more than epistemic troublemakers from Descartes' point of view. They interfere with our attempt to attain purely intellectual knowledge of God and the soul – which are not sensible at all – and they offer up obscure and confused perceptions that hamper the progress of science by misrepresenting the true nature of bodies. But there is still half a Meditation left. The remainder of Meditation Six is devoted almost exclusively to the senses, and in particular to what Gary Hatfield has aptly called their "rehabilitation."[9] It is to their rehabilitation that we now turn.

MEDITATION 6.5: REPURPOSING THE SENSES

Let's back up to the start of the Meditation, which opens with an announcement of its express purpose to determine whether bodies exist (AT 7: 71). After an aborted attempt to demonstrate their existence on the basis of the imagination, the meditator adopts the following plan:

To begin with, I will go back over all the things which I previously took to be perceived by the senses, and reckoned to be true; and I will go over my reasons for thinking this. Next, I will set out my reasons for subsequently calling these things into doubt. *And finally I will consider what I should now believe about them.* (AT 7: 74, italics added)

The meditator signals that the epistemic credentials of the senses need to be re-evaluated in the light of recent meditational develop-ments. She produces a list of her previous sense-based beliefs (AT 7: 74–76) – a list that is a good deal longer, and the reasons in support of the beliefs a good deal richer in detail, than in earlier versions. She then recalls her initial reasons for calling these beliefs into doubt: the senses are subject to illusion; the experience on which they are based is indistinguishable from dreaming; and their origin is uncertain (AT 7: 76–77). This last reason gives the meditator pause, for she now knows that the origin of her cognitive faculties is a non-deceiving God. What follows is a short but pivotal paragraph:

But now, when I am beginning to achieve a better knowledge of myself and the author of my being, although I do not think I should heedlessly accept everything I seem to have acquired from the senses, neither do I think that everything got from them should be called into doubt. (AT 7: 77–78)

It is time to rehabilitate the senses.

The first step is to restore the sense-based belief that bodies exist. As it happens, the senses receive only a very small boost from the argument, for their role in it is surprisingly indirect. A sketch of the argument is as follows.[10] My senses are passive faculties for receiving sensory ideas, and these ideas require an active cause. The three clear options are myself, God, and actually existing bodies. However, I can rule out myself as the cause, since sensory ideas are involuntary – they cannot be conjured up, changed, or prevented at will. The cause must therefore be God or bodies, but I have a "great propensity" to believe that it is the latter. Of course, I also have a great propensity to believe that bodies have colors and sounds, and that propensity turned out to be wrong. However, I have a faculty that shows me the error in that propensity: the intellect shows me that bodies are all and only extended. By contrast, I find no faculty that suggests to me that God is causing my sensory ideas. God would be a deceiver if he produced sensory ideas in me and did not create me with any inkling that he was doing that and if he also gave me no way to tell. But God is no deceiver. My sensory ideas must therefore be caused by actually existing bodies.

So far so good. The meditator turns to examine more carefully her sensory perception of those existing bodies:

What of the other aspects of corporeal things which are either particular (for example that the sun is of such and such a size or shape), or less clearly understood, such as light or sound or pain, and so on? (AT 7: 80)

The meditator is asking what we are to say about the things that the senses purport to teach us about bodies but that have since been shown to be at best dubitable, and at worst decidedly false. We know, for example, that the sun is bigger than it looks, that bodies do not have the sorts of lights and sounds and pains that they sensorily seem to have, and that there are bodies even where we sense there are none. Knowing that God is the origin of her senses, the meditator reasons:

the very fact that God is not a deceiver, and the consequent impossibility of there being any falsity in my opinions which cannot be corrected by some other faculty supplied by God, offers me a sure hope that I can attain the truth even in these matters. (AT 7: 80)

Strictly speaking, God is not guilty of deception just because we are inclined to make false judgments on the basis of our sensory perceptions. With effort, we could withhold *every* sense-based judg-ment that we are inclined to make, and the relevant errors would be avoided. But there is something strange about a God who would give us sensory ideas and an inclination to believe that they are giving us information about bodies when they are not. It is more plausible (and a more effective neutralization of the charge of divine deception) to suppose that our sensory ideas teach us something about bodies after all. The meditator pursues this latter line of argumentation: "there is no doubt that *everything that I am taught by nature con-tains some truth*" (ibid.; italics added). Since by her "nature" she means "the totality of things bestowed on [her] by God," and since her senses are bestowed on her by God, what she is naturally taught by the senses must have some truth in it. Of course, the meditator has to sort out what things about body she is naturally taught by her senses and what things are the result of her own faulty (but correct-able) reasoning. God is only responsible for the former, so only they need to be true.

Descartes' key move in rehabilitating the senses is to repurpose them: he recasts the function of the senses, thereby showcasing the set of true beliefs to which they naturally guide us. The meditator knows by now that the function of the senses is *not*, as she previously thought, to reveal the corporeal world's true nature to us: I pervert the order of nature by using the senses "as reliable touchstones for imme-diate judgements about the essential nature of the bodies located outside us" (AT 7: 83). Instead the senses are given to me by nature in order "to inform the mind of what is beneficial or harmful for the composite of which the mind is a part" (ibid.). The function of the senses, in other words, is to facilitate self-preservation. They are not cognitive tools for doing metaphysics, but cognitive tools for survival.

It is important to note that it is not the preservation of myself as a *mind* that the senses govern, but the preservation of myself as a human being, that is, as a *mind-body union*: sensory perceptions "inform the mind of what is beneficial or harmful *for the composite of which it is a part*." The qualification is important. Disembodied Cartesian minds would have no need for the senses, and Descartes is not shy about saying that they do not have them.[11] Disembodied minds engage in pure intellection, and for that they need only innate intellectual ideas. The embodied human mind engages in an addi-tional task: it has a body to keep alive. Since a human body is

constantly impacted for better or worse by other bodies in its environment, an embodied mind has a great deal of (additional) cognitive
labor to do. The embodied mind is fitted with senses to take on the
work of protecting the body and monitoring its needs.

That the senses are designed for bodily self-preservation is under-
scored in the meditator's discussion of the "institution of nature" by
which God fits the types of motions in the human brain – more
specifically, the motions of tiny "animal spirits" coursing through
the pineal gland – to types of sensation in the human mind (AT 7: 87–
88). God's choice of pairings is not arbitrary: he has paired each type of
motion with that type of sensation which "is most especially and
most frequently conducive to the preservation of the healthy man"
(AT 7: 87). Motions in the brain that originate in a foot injury, for
example, give rise to sensations of pain occurring in the foot.
"Nothing else," the meditator remarks, "would have been so conducive to the continued well-being of the body" (AT 7: 88). That is
because the pain sensation stimulates the mind to do its best to get
rid of the cause of the pain, which it takes to be harmful to the foot
(AT 7: 88–89). God could have set things up so that we perceive what
is actually happening in the injured foot – say, inflammation of a
tendon, or tearing of a ligament, or build up of sodium urate in the
joints. But while perceiving these things might (or might not) inspire
curiosity, feeling pain seizes our attention and informs us in no
uncertain terms that whatever is happening is *bad* and *requires
attention.*

With the proper function of the senses in view, the epistemic
credentials of the senses are re-evaluated, and the meditator is clear
in her assessment: "in matters regarding the well-being of the body,
all my senses *report the truth* much more frequently than not" (AT 7:
89; italics mine). The truths we are taught by our sensory nature,
then, are truths that concern the well-being of our body.

The senses are reliable when it comes to their proper function, but
they are not infallible. Note the caution: "all my senses report the
truth *much more frequently than not.*" They remain subject, now
and then, to what the meditator describes as "true error[s] of nature"
(AT 7: 85). That is, sometimes the senses lead us to an action that is
not in fact conducive to our bodily well-being, as when a jaundice
patient sees both ripe and unripe bananas as yellow and thus fails to
distinguish them. There is no deception, on Descartes' view, in the

fact that a healthy person's visual system represents ripe bananas as yellow and unripe bananas as green, even though neither kind has the color it is represented to have. The reason there is no deception is that (a) representing the bananas as having these different colors helps us to differentiate them, which is what matters for action[12] and (b) any temptation we have to judge falsely that the bananas *really are* yellow or green in the way they are represented can be checked and corrected using our intellect, which will show us that they couldn't possibly have the colors they appear to have because colors are not proper modifications of extension. On the other hand, there *is* deception in the fact that a jaundice patient sees both ripe *and* unripe bananas as yellow, for his visual system fails to facilitate self-preserving action: he will reach for ripe and unripe bananas indiscriminately, leading to digestive problems. The patient's gustatory system will likely minimize the impact of the error once the unripe banana is in his mouth, but the error has still occurred, and in some cases the consequences can be more severe.

The meditator is not in a position to deny the existence of these "errors of nature," and she tries her best to explain them away on God's behalf. They are, she suggests, the inevitable result of fitting an indivisible mind with a divisible body. The mind interacts directly with only one part of the body, i.e., the pineal gland in the brain, and the psychophysiological laws that God set up between mind and body are laws linking sensations with pineal motions. The sort of pineal motion that is typically caused by an injured foot will thus always give rise to a pain-in-the-foot sensation. But since the body is divisible, that pineal motion can have aberrant causes – for example, an amputee's stump may trigger the pineal motion that his foot used to trigger. Consequently, the resulting pain-in-the-foot sensation will be an inappropriate guide to action. Motions in the pineal gland give rise to those sensations that are most conducive to self-preservation *given their usual distal bodily cause*, and God made the best possible system given that he was working with a divisible body.[13] And so "notwithstanding the immense goodness of God, the nature of man as a combination of mind and body is such that it is bound to mislead him from time to time" (AT 7: 88). The senses are not rehabilitated completely, but Descartes recasts their cognitive role in a way that removes some of the doubts of the First Meditation. As the meditator concludes, "I should not have any further fears about the falsity of what my senses tell me every day; on the contrary, the exaggerated doubts of the last few days should be dismissed as laughable" (AT 7: 89).

By the end of the *Meditations*, Descartes clearly envisions a division of cognitive labor in the embodied human mind. The intellect serves as our best guide to metaphysics, revealing to us the essential natures of things. The senses serve as our best guides to embodied self-preservation, revealing the corporeal world to us insofar as it is related to us and insofar as it can bring us benefit or harm. Each faculty is suited especially to its own task. Just as the senses are ill-equipped to do metaphysics, so, Descartes tells Princess Elizabeth, the intellect is ill-equipped to keep us alive: "what belongs to the union of the soul and the body is known only obscurely by the intellect alone ... but it is known very clearly by the senses" ("To Elizabeth, 28 June 1643," AT 3:691–92). As a work of metaphysics, the *Meditations* focuses on the intellect and on detachment from the senses, but it is important to put the *Meditations* itself in context. Metaphysics is something Descartes recommends we engage in "once in a lifetime" (AT 7: 17). More than that is downright dangerous:

I believe that it is very necessary to have properly understood, once in a lifetime, the principles of metaphysics, since they are what gives us the knowledge of God and of our soul. But I think also that it would be very harmful to occupy one's intellect frequently in meditating upon them, since this would impede it from devoting itself to the functions of the imagination and the senses. (AT 3: 695)

The senses (and imagination) are our guides to action and we must use them every day. As Descartes tells us in the opening line of his *Optics*, "the conduct of our life depends entirely on the senses" (AT 6: 81). The intellect may be the hero of Cartesian metaphysics, but the senses are the heroes of Cartesian human life.[14]

There remain important questions, however. Just *how* do the senses facilitate self-preservation? Precisely *what truths* about self-preservation do they teach us? And *in virtue of what* do they point us to these truths? Although Descartes offers some answers to these questions in the *Meditations*, we learn more by turning to his extensive writings on sensory perception in the *Optics*, *Treatise on Man*, *Principles*, and *Passions of the Soul*. The remainder of this chapter explores these three questions in the context of three broad categories of sensory perception: bodily awareness; so-called "secondary-quality" perception; and spatial perception. In all of these domains, we find Descartes developing a conception of sensory representation that we might call *narcissistic* representation – that is, representation of the world *as mattering to me*.[15] It is this narcissistic representation that makes them a suitable guide to action.

BODILY AWARENESS[16]

Let's start with the internal senses which collectively constitute our bodily awareness. These include bodily sensations (like pains and tickles), appetites (like hunger and thirst), and passions (like fear and love). The internal senses are on the front lines of embodied self-preservation, for it is through them, Descartes suggests, that we come to believe (truly) that we have a body, that its condition is well or unwell, and that we should take certain actions in order to maintain its well-being.

The first sense-based belief that the meditator reports having had prior to engaging in meditation is "that I had a head, hands, feet, and other limbs making up the body that I regarded as part of myself, or perhaps even as my whole self" (AT 7: 74). This is also the first belief to be restored in the Sixth Meditation, almost intact. The meditator is no longer tempted to identify her *whole* self with her body (she is first and foremost a mind), but she reinstates her belief that she *has* a body:

There is nothing that my nature teaches me more vividly than that I have a body that is harmed when I feel pain, that needs food and drink when I am hungry or thirsty, and so on. So I should not doubt that there is some truth in this. Nature also teaches me, by these sensations of pain, hunger, thirst and so on, that I am not merely present in my body as a sailor is present in a ship, but that I am very closely joined and, as it were, intermingled with it, so that I and the body form a unit. (AT 7: 80–81)[17]

Bodily sensations and appetites direct us to this truth by the peculiar way in which they are represented. Like all sensations, they are represented as existing on or in a body. But they are different from external sensations such as color, flavor, and odor in a number of important ways. First, they are represented as existing on or in one body to the exclusion of others: I feel hunger, thirst, pain, and titillation in one particular assemblage of bodily limbs and organs, but not in bagels, flowers, dogs, or even other assemblages of bodily limbs and organs (AT 7: 76). Second, they are a constant presence. I can close my eyes to cut off color sensations; I can cover my ears to block out sound sensations; I can hold my nose to omit odor sensations. But I cannot escape bodily sensations and appetites (without anesthesia or very powerful drugs). The body that they representationally inhabit is thus phenomenologically inescapable from me (ibid.). Third, these sensations are "internal" (AT 7: 77). Descartes never explains what this means, but as a first pass I suggest that it means that bodily sensations represent the body interoceptively – that is, they represent the body "from the inside" in such a way that it's difficult to distinguish the perceiver from the thing perceived. We use the language of "feeling" to describe this experience. When one *feels* a pain, the subject doing the feeling and the thing felt blur into one. The "external" senses, by contrast, are exteroceptive: through sight and touch I *observe* bodies, including my own, and in this experience there is a phenomenological differentiation between the perceiver and the body perceived. When I step on a nail, I may visually observe a nail entering a foot, but I do not *observe* pain in *a* foot; I *feel* pain in *my* foot or pain in a part of *me*.[18] Finally, internal sensations are generally pleasurable or painful to some extent. Since I naturally take an interest in pleasure and pain as things tied up with my own good, I naturally take an interest in the body that they are represented as located in. All of these features of the internal senses together help to confer a phenomenological sense of ownership on the body perceived through them. And this is obviously important for self-preservation. I can take an interest or not in seeing a foot destroyed; but I cannot help but take an interest when I feel *my* foot, or indeed *myself*, filled with pain. Bodily sensations, then, facilitate self-preservation by identifying one body in particular as *my* body or a part of *me*.

Descartes may think this representational state of affairs is an epistemic disaster insofar as it gets in the way of my appreciating the metaphysical fact that my mind can exist (as a pure intellect) without my body, but he nevertheless thinks it is representing something *true*. In this life, I do not exist apart from all bodies, but rather am united to one of them so as to form a unit.[19] What is more, the truth about mind-body union is not something that the intellect is in a position to reveal to us, since it will always represent all bodies as really distinct from my mind. It takes the senses to put us in the position to appreciate our embodied human existence.[20]

The internal senses tell us that we have bodies, and they also inform us of the wellness (or illness) of our bodies. Most of our internal sensations are pleasant or unpleasant: light strokes of the skin and a gentle squeeze of the hand are titillating and pleasant; pain, hunger, and thirst are unpleasant. The body parts that these sensations are felt to inhabit are thereby represented as doing well or badly. Feeling a titillating stroke on my skin is "naturally agreeable to the mind because it is a sign of robust health in the body with which it is closely conjoined" (*Principles* IV.191, AT 8A: 318) and "represents this to the soul as a good which belongs to it insofar as it is united with the body" (*Passions* II.94, AT 11: 399–400).[21] Feeling a pain in my foot, by contrast, tells me something is wrong (AT 7: 80) and incites me "to remove, as much as [I am] able, the cause of the pain as harmful to the foot" (AT 7: 88; my translation). What is more, I judge *other* bodies to be beneficial or harmful to me based in part on whether they produce pleasant or unpleasant bodily sensations in me (AT 7: 74). Although the internal senses may mislead us into thinking that titillation, pain, and the like are intrinsic properties of our bodies, when in fact they are merely sensations produced in the mind by motions in the brain, the internal senses lead us quickly and reliably to the truth concerning the condition of our body.

Passions like joy, sadness, fear, and love add another layer to the story. Descartes counts these among the internal senses (AT 7: 76).[22] Passions are like the rest of our sensations in that they ready our bodies for action and are caused by animal spirits that course through the pineal gland.[23] Furthermore, they add an extra affective and motivational layer to the experience we have both of our own bodies and external bodies. Their function, on Descartes' view, is to "dispose our soul to want the things that nature deems useful for us, and to persist in this volition" (*Passions* II.52, AT 11: 372). Thus when the body is in good health we feel not only titillation but also joy, and when the body is in bad health we feel not only pain but also sadness.[24] Through the passions we are attracted and repulsed by other bodies. When we see a bear charging toward us, the same pineal motions that represent the bear sensorily to us as large and stinky also induce a passion of fear so that we are motivated to flee. The passionate character of our sensory experience of the world thus facilitates our self-preservation by urging us to act appropriately in the face of bodies that are poised to benefit or harm us.[25]

The external senses (sight, audition, olfaction, gustation, and touch) represent bodies as having both spatial properties (size, shape, position, and motion) and qualitative properties (color, sound, odor, flavor, hot/cold). These qualities are typically dubbed "primary qualities" and "secondary qualities" respectively in the literature. Let's start with secondary quality perception. Insofar as the external senses represent bodies as having colors, odors, and the like, they, like the internal senses, lead us to misjudge the fundamental nature of body. But, Descartes suggests, the sensory representation of bodies as colored, smelly, and tasty is conducive to self-preservation in a number of ways. First, it enables us to discriminate the macroscopic bodies we encounter every day: "I had sensations of light, colors, smells, tastes, and sounds, the variety of which enabled me to distinguish the sky, the earth, the seas, and all other bodies, one from another" (The Sixth Meditation, AT 7: 75).[26] So long as we restrict ourselves to making discriminations among bodies, which is obviously necessary for interacting with them, our sense-based judgments are true:

From the fact that I perceive by my senses a great variety of colors, sounds, smells and tastes, as well as differences in heat, hardness, and the like, I am *correct* in inferring that the bodies which are the source of these various sensory perceptions possess differences corresponding to them, though perhaps not resembling them. (AT 7: 81; italics mine)

So far our nature does not lead us astray. It is only when we further judge that colors, sounds, etc., are intrinsic properties of the bodies that they help us to discriminate that we go wrong.

Second, through secondary-quality sensations, bodies are represented as things I should seek out or avoid (AT 7: 81, 83). How? Like bodily sensations and appetites, secondary-quality sensations tend to be pleasant or unpleasant, so that the objects they representationally inhabit are represented as pleasant or unpleasant. Secondary-quality sensations thereby serve as harbingers of the benefit or harm that external bodies can bring our way:

The fact that some of the perceptions are agreeable to me while others are disagreeable makes it completely certain that my body, or rather my whole self, insofar as I am a combination of body and mind, can be affected by the various beneficial or harmful bodies which surround it. (AT 7: 81)

Consider the examples of unpleasantly sharp or boringly bland flavor sensations. These arise from bodies that are physically too sharp or too soft to be digested into the blood stream, while pleasant flavors that "mildly tickle the tongue" arise from bodies that are suitable for digestion (*Treatise on Man*, AT 11: 146–47). The details are fanciful, to be sure, but they illustrate Descartes' view that secondary-quality perception is a way of representing the world *as mattering to us*.[27] Now add passions to the mix: I find myself attracted to things that are sensorily represented as pleasant and repulsed by things that are sensorily represented as unpleasant. Together, the senses and passions represent external bodies as beneficial and harmful to me and motivate me to engage with them accordingly.

While Descartes seems to think that all secondary-quality sensations are naturally pleasant or unpleasant and so are natural harbingers of benefit and harm that attract and repel us – including even color sensations[28] – he does not seem to think that secondary-quality sensations are intrinsically so. The valence of sensation depends a bit on the context in which it occurs: musical dissonance can be a pleasant relief from a monotonously consonant tune; salt and vinegar can be a pleasant relief in a dull meal; and "fashionable colors" like fuchsia and chartreuse can liven up a drab outfit.[29] The valence also depends on the condition of the perceiver's body: things that taste good when we are healthy often taste bad when we are ill.[30] The pleasantness/unpleasantness of a secondary-quality sensation, then, is both contextual and relational.[31] And this is appropriate, for the benefit and harm that bodies may cause us are themselves contextual and relational. The senses again represent bodies not simply as they are in their own nature, but as they are related to us.

SPATIAL PERCEPTION

The external senses also represent the spatial properties of bodies to us. Here, you might think, is the one place where the senses straightforwardly tell us the truth about bodies in a way suitable for metaphysics, for Descartes thinks that bodies *do* have spatial properties by their own nature. Vision represents the top of my coffee mug as circular, and so it is even in a Cartesain world. Matters are not quite that simple, however. The senses still represent the spatial properties of bodies narcissistically insofar as they represent them not as they are in themselves but rather as they are related to one's own body. For spatial perception is egocentric and perspectival. We do not see (or feel) bodies to occupy some absolute position on a cosmic Cartesian co-ordinate system, but to be located in a direction and at a distance relative to us. Our bodies are always situated as *here*, as it were at the origin of the co-ordinate system: my mug is off to the right at an arm's length away. Nor do I see (or feel) the shapes of things *simpliciter*, but how those shapes are oriented with respect to me: I see the top of my mug not simply as circular, but as oriented in such a way that I would have to tip it forward to see if there is any coffee left in it. It is only if I happen to view my mug from directly above that its top would look simply circular, and it is just this sort of rare occurrence that Descartes may have in mind when he says in *Principles* I.3 that the senses only "occasionally and accidentally show us what external bodies are like in themselves" (AT 8A: 41–42). The norm is instead that my senses show me objects *as they are spatially related to me* and yours show you objects *as they are spatially related to you.* Of course, the senses also show us the spatial relations objects have to each other, but even that information is often relative to the perceiver: from my point of view the blackboard is to the right of the coffee table, but from your point of view, sitting across from me, it is to the left of the coffee table. Having this egocentric and perspectival information is important to survival. If I'm scrambling up some rocks on a hike, I need to know not simply where the boulders are, and what size and shape they are, but where they are relative to me (at location here), whether they are big enough for me to step on and how they are oriented with respect to where I am now.[32]

CONCLUSION

Descartes' considered view of sensory perception is that while it gets in the way of our doing proper metaphysics, it is essential to the conduct of human life. Through what I've called its narcissistic representation of the corporeal world, it shows us things the intellect alone does not. It shows us that we are embodied minds, and that our bodies can suffer harm or enjoy robust health. It shows us the spatial relations that other bodies have to ours and the impact they may have on its well-being. And through its passionate nature, sensory perception also motivates us to engage in the actions necessary to insure our safety. It may behoove us to meditate our way into the posture of a disembodied angel once in a lifetime to discover important truths about God, the soul, and the fundamental nature of body. The *Meditations* is written to be our guide in that quest. But when our meditating is done, we must return to our embodied lives and trust the senses to be our guide.

NOTES

1. See Hatfield 1986.
2. For example, Alanen 1994, Bolton 1986, De Rosa 2004, Hoffman 1996, Nelson 1996, and Wilson 1990 and 1994.
3. See especially, Gueroult 1953.
4. See Alanen 2003, Brown 2006, Hatfield 2009, Lisa Shapiro 2012, and Simmons 1999, 2003, 2008, 2010–11.
5. For a thorough discussion of the background to these stated aims see Fowler 1999.
6. The Fourth Meditation, AT 7: 53; *Third Replies*, AT 7: 183; *Fifth Replies*, AT 7: 385.
7. "Dedicatory letter to the Sorbonne," AT 7: 4; "Preface to the Reader," AT 7: 9; *Third Replies*, AT 7: 171–72.
8. Unless otherwise noted, translations are those of CSM.
9. Hatfield 2009.
10. But see AT 7: 78–80.
11. "To More, August 1649," AT 5: 402.
12. The Sixth Meditation, AT 7: 75, 81, and *Optics*, AT 6: 132 33.
13. This is not to say that Descartes has offered a convincing argument. Just why does the mind have to interact with only one part of the divisible body? And why couldn't God have created better materials to work with? For discussion of the interplay between Descartes' metaphysics and physiology see Kolesnik-Antoine 2009 and Voss 1993.
14. Indeed metaphysics itself is ultimately subordinated by Descartes to a practical concern with the conduct of life (Shapiro 2008).
15. I borrow the term from Aikins 1996.
16. My treatment of bodily awareness here is deeply indebted to discussions with Colin Chamberlain, and to the work he has done on this topic in his dissertation.

17. The translation here is my own and corrects for the fact that the CSM translation misleadingly suggests that my belief that I have a body and my belief that it is damaged when I feel pain are two *separate* beliefs; to the contrary, it is in becoming aware of its needs through pain that the meditator learns she has a body. Thanks to Colin Chamberlain for pointing this out to me. Carriero 2009, 393 also notes this.

18. This, I take it, is what distinguishes the experience of a mind-body union from that of a pilot in his ship: I *feel* what's going on in my body, whereas the pilot can only *observe* what's going on in his ship.

19. "Synopsis of the *Meditations*," AT 7: 15; the Sixth Meditation, AT 7: 81. For different readings of the precise nature of this mind-body unit, see Chappell 1994, Cottingham 1985, Curley and Koivuniemi forthcoming, Hoffman 1986, Rozemond 1998, and Schmaltz 1992.

20. See "To Elizabeth, 15 September 1645," AT 3: 691–93.

21. See also *Treatise on Man*, AT 11: 143–45.

22. Also *Principles* IV.190, AT 8A: 316–18; and *Passions* I.26–28, AT 11: 348–50.

23. See Hatfield 2007.

24. *Passions* II.94, AT 11: 398–99.

25. See Brown 2006, Greenberg 2007, Hatfield 2007, Jorgensen 2012, and Lisa Shapiro 2012.

26. See *Optics*, AT 6: 133.

27. See Simmons 2008.

28. *Treatise on Man*, AT 11: 158.

29. "To Mersenne, October 1631," AT 1: 223; *Compendium Musicae*, AT 10: 91–92; *Treatise on Man*, AT 11: 150–51, 158.

30. AT 11: 147. In this latter case, however, it is unclear whether the object is producing a new sensation that is naturally unpleasant or the same sensation that now tastes unpleasant.

31. See Jorgensen 2012.

32. See Simmons 2003.

14 Descartes' dualism and its relation to Spinoza's metaphysics

The dualism of mind and body is at the heart of Descartes' system. It is, perhaps, his signature doctrine. It is hard to think of any subsequent philosophical system in the history of Western philosophy that does not prominently engage some version of "Cartesian" dualism. One of the earliest and most significant critics of Cartesian dualism was Spinoza. He regarded the correction of this doctrine as one of his most important achievements of his monistic system of philosophy. In what follows, however, we shall identify reasons for thinking that Spinoza's own system mirrors some of the defects he found in Descartes'. Despite Spinoza's highly negative appraisal of Descartes' dualism, he takes on more of it than is apparent on the surface. We shall also see how Descartes' dualism has available more philosophical resources than Spinoza recognized in his critique. This essay focuses first on Descartes' own treatment of dualism, especially as it is developed in the *Meditations* and associated texts, and then on some of the highlights of Spinoza's reaction to it.

DESCARTES' DUALISM

Descartes himself does not use Latin or French words for the term "dualism." The full title of the second edition of the *Meditations* includes, "... in which are demonstrated the existence of God and *the distinction between the human soul and the body*" (AT 7: 17, emphasis added). The demonstration appears in the Sixth Meditation; the distinction in question is a *real distinction*, a term which Descartes borrows from his medieval predecessors. The Sixth Meditation ends with a treatment of the human being as a union of mind and body;

Descartes' dualism thus embraces both the distinctness of mind and body and their being "closely joined," "as it were, intermingled [*quasi permixtum*]," and forming "a unit" (AT 7: 81). The notorious tension between these requires examination at both ends. We turn first to the duality of mind and body, and then to their union.

The demonstration of the real distinction has struck most of Descartes' readers as difficult and obscure. This makes it interesting that Descartes himself regarded it as entirely straightforward. The argument begins by recalling the connection between the truth and what is clearly and distinctly perceived.

First, I know that everything which I clearly and distinctly understand is capable of being created by God so as to correspond exactly with my understanding of it. Hence the fact that I can clearly and distinctly under-stand one thing apart from another is enough to make me certain that the two things are distinct, since they are capable of being separated, at least by God. (AT 7: 78)

Here more needs to be said about what it is to "understand one thing apart from another."[1] The clearest and most important case of things that *cannot* be understood apart from one another is that of a sub-stance and its modes. Modes are literally "ways" in which substances exist. In the *Meditations*, Descartes uses "mode" to refer to particular sensations, imaginations (AT 7: 34, 81), but an explicit treatment of how modes differ from the substances of which they are modes is given in the *Principles*. The difference is "... that we can clearly perceive a substance apart from the mode which we say differs from it, whereas we cannot, conversely, understand the mode apart from the substance" (AT 8A: 29). To distinctly perceive a mode is to under-stand a way in which the *substance* can exist. This can be put succinctly by saying that the perception of a mode *involves* the substance of which it is the mode, or alternatively, a mode is per-ceived *through* the substance of which it is a mode.[2] To perceive a mode *apart* from its substance requires an intellectual abstraction, as Descartes explains in a 1642 letter to Gibieuf:

This intellectual abstraction consists in my turning my thought away from one part of the contents of this richer idea the better to apply it to the other part with greater attention. Thus, when I consider a shape without thinking of the substance or the extension whose shape it is, I make a mental abstrac-tion. (AT 3: 475)

This suggests that a mode is clearly and distinctly perceived as a component of a "richer" idea that includes it and the substance. The continuation of this passage seems to confirm the suggestion: "the idea of the shape in question is *joined* in this way to the idea of the corresponding extension and substance..." (emphasis added). In light of all this, let us settle on expressing the point by saying that modes are perceived *through* the substances of which they are modes.[3] The idea of a mode is an idea of a determination of the substance – literally one of various *ways* in which a substance exists or can exist at different times.[4] This naturally implies that ideas of modes are complex ideas; they include as components both the idea of the substance that is modified and the determination that modifies it. This in turn implies that an idea of a modified substance can be analyzed into these two components, thus making each of them more distinct.

As we have seen, modes cannot be distinctly perceived apart from their substances, but two substances can be perceived apart from one another. Indeed, Descartes understands the definition of "real distinction" in terms of substances: "Two substances are said to be *really distinct* when each of them can exist apart from the other" (*Second Replies*, AT 7: 162). The most useful general characterization of substance is *Principles* I.51:

By *substance* we can understand nothing other than a thing which exists in such a way as to depend on no other thing for its existence. And there is only one substance which can be understood to depend on no other thing whatsoever, namely God. (AT 8A: 24)

So in the strictest sense only God is a substance, but Descartes allows that things that depend only on God's conserving them and are independent of all other things can be regarded as substances in a slightly relaxed sense of the term. All the demonstration of real distinction requires, therefore, are clear and distinct perceptions of mind and body as substances that are not one and the same. The Sixth Meditation's demonstration concludes:

Thus, simply by knowing that I exist and seeing at the same time that absolutely nothing else belongs to my nature or essence except that I am a thinking thing, I can infer correctly that my essence consists solely in the fact that I am a thinking thing. It is true that I may have (or, to anticipate, that I certainly have) a body that is very closely joined to me. But nevertheless, on the one hand I have a clear and distinct idea of myself, in so far as I am simply a thinking, non-extended thing; and on the other hand I have a distinct idea of body, in so far as this is simply an extended, non-thinking thing. And accordingly, it is certain that I am really distinct from my body, and can exist without it. (AT 7: 78)

As Descartes explains in various Replies to Objections (e.g., to Arnauld in *Fourth Replies*, AT 7: 317–31), this passage announces the attainment of the requisite clear and distinct perceptions. These perceptions of mind and body as substances have been developed in the preceding Meditations. What is perhaps less clear is how the meditator ascertains that these perceptions are non-identical. If the perceptions are non-identical in the right way, then their being clear and distinct guarantees that their objects are also non-identical in the right way, i.e., really distinct, so this is crucial.

Descartes' technical substance-mode ontology makes it easier to state briefly how the right kind of non-identity is established. All the modes that the meditator has taken to belong to herself – ideas, volitions, sensations – in the strict sense are perceived through thought[5] and cannot be perceived through extension. The opposite holds for modes of size, shape, and local motion. They are perceived through extension and cannot be conceived as thinking. These facts about perception are easily verified by a practiced meditator. Guided by the method of the *Meditations*, a diligent reader comes to simply intuit them – there is no additional argumentation that will force the intuitions upon an unskilled or unwilling meditator. The requisite intuitions will be obscured and unavailable for those who do not "meditate seriously" (AT 7: 9) with Descartes and also for those whose unfortunately sluggish pineal glands interfere with their attempts to clearly and distinctly perceive.[6] Later in the Sixth Meditation (and earlier in his synopsis of the *Meditations*), Descartes offers another meditative cognitive route to perceptions of mind and body as excluding each other:[7]

The first observation I make on this point is that there is a great difference between the mind and the body, inasmuch as the body is by its very nature always divisible, while the mind is utterly indivisible. For when I consider the mind, or myself in so far as I am merely a thinking thing, I am unable to distinguish any parts within myself; I understand myself to be something quite single and complete ... By contrast, there is no corporeal or extended thing that I can think of which in my thought I cannot easily divide into parts; and this very fact makes me understand that it is divisible. This one argument would be enough to show me that the mind is completely different from the body, even if I did not already know this from other considerations. (AT 7: 85–86)[8]

Although Descartes presents this as a secondary consideration, it is probably the most perspicuous way to get a handle on why he thought the separateness of the clear and distinct perceptions of mind and body was so easily intuited.

It remains to explain why Descartes expresses the real distinction in modal terms. Mind and body "can exist apart" (absque potest existere); nevertheless, "the question of what kind of power is required to bring about such a separation does not affect the judgement that the two things are distinct" (AT 7: 78). As a matter of fact, the meditator's mind and body are actually "closely joined" into a unified human being. Although mind and body do come apart when the body dies and corrupts, this requires no extraordinary exercise of God's power. Fatal disunification is a consequence of the laws of physics and the real distinction, but it is not constitutive of real distinction.[9] It seems we can conclude that mind and body are "separate" or "apart" in the sense relevant to their real distinction even when actually united. This is guaranteed once the meditator attains the appropriate clear and distinct perceptions of the truth. The mention of God's power in the demonstration is simply to assure the reader that no matter how closely mind and body are joined in the human being, they do not cease to be separate and really distinct.[10]

In Descartes' own version of dualism, an immediately pressing problem arises about mind-body union. There is a long interpretive tradition of reading Descartes as having absolutely no treatment of the union that would make sense even from a point of view internal to his system of philosophy. In recent years, however, scholars have been devoting more attention to readings that give a prominent role to Descartes' positive position on union. Although the unified human being is the centerpiece of the Sixth Meditation, that text provides no help with the obvious need for reconciling real distinction and union. The most important texts are two letters in Descartes' famous epistolary exchange with Elizabeth of Bohemia.

In response to Elizabeth's probing about the causal interaction of mind and body, Descartes admits that he did not intend to explain the metaphysics and epistemology of the union in the *Meditations*.[11] He identifies three "primitive ideas or notions" (AT 3: 691) that the mind "possesse[s] by nature" and are "ready made" (AT 3: 666–67): two are the innate ideas of the mind and of body that were extensively developed in the *Meditations*. The third, which is only obliquely hinted at in the Sixth Meditation, is an innate idea of the union of mind and body. The mind comes to be known by the perfectly clear and distinct perceptions of the intellect, i.e., through the innate idea of the mind itself. Body is best known when the innate idea of extension is augmented by distinctly imagined figures.[12] The innate idea of union comes to be accessed by attending to sensations instead of purely intellectual ideas. It thereby provides knowledge of the union.

It is easy to brush off Descartes' responses to Elizabeth as evasive, obfuscatory, or even as condescending bluster. If, however, the primary notion of union is recognized as an innate idea with the same cognitive function as the innate ideas of God, self, and extension, then an interesting enrichment of his dualism can be mapped out. As Descartes himself points out, it is not possible simultaneously to understand the real distinction between mind and body and their union.[13] It is therefore obvious that one cannot use clear and distinct perceptions of mind and body, i.e., use those primitive notions, to understand *how* mind and body are unified. Since mind and body are, as it were, opposites (e.g., indivisible and divisible), God's incomprehensible, infinite power is required to unify them. Nonetheless, the union is "known very clearly by the senses" in virtue of its primitive notion.[14] One might press the objection that this "very clear knowledge" of the union is worthless for understanding the central mind-body problem of causal interaction. On the other hand, the objection itself is perhaps based on an overhasty assessment of the resources of Descartes' theory of innate ideas. If there is indeed an innate idea of the union, then this idea is the only one appropriate to serve as a principle for the construction of explanations that concern the union.[15] Let us pursue this a little further.

Sensations arise in the human being simply in virtue of external bodies affecting it, and such affects are no mystery because humans are extended. If one insists on a further explanation of how the mind is affected with modes of sensory ideas, this can be treated as a request for mere verbal elaboration. When its sensory organs are affected (because they are extended), the human being has sensations. And when the human being has sensations, there are sensory ideas in its component mind simply because the human being is a union of a mind and a body.[16] In other words, the mind has the sensory ideas it does because it is a component of the mind-body composite. This provides a reply to the objection that the innate idea of union is explanatorily vacuous, as follows. When the human being senses something, it can be *inferred* that the associated mode of mind, its sensory idea, has been "caused" by the body to which it is united – the motions of its pineal gland to be more precise. This prepares us for the crucial point: namely that the further request for *how* this causation takes place is again an instance of the illegitimate attempt to perceive simultaneously mind and body both as separate (i.e., causally inter-acting with one another) and as unified (i.e., as having sensations). Similarly, the human being affects external bodies with motions, some of which are intended. That is not mysterious because the union has an extended component in contact with external bodies. The further question of *how* the mind alone affects its body is illegit-imate for the same reason. As we have already seen, it is not possible to conceive mental modes through body or vice versa. They are perceived as opposites and have nothing in common which, as Spinoza makes explicit, is a condition of causal relation. From Descartes' point of view, it does no harm to say, as he often does, that the mind causally affects the body and vice versa, because this is known simply in virtue of our awareness of the mind-body union as described in the Sixth Meditation.

Emphasizing the mind-body union in Descartes' philosophy as suggested in the preceding paragraphs makes its metaphysical role so large that it might seem to render "Cartesian dualism" an inaccu-rate appellation. In recent studies, there has been much discussion of the extent to which Descartes might have subscribed to a substance "trialism" of mind, body, and the human mind-body union.[17] It is possible that Descartes himself would not have been interested in the question of whether the human being is *really* a substance. He does prominently warn about the danger of merely verbal disputes;[18] and, on the particular issue of the unity of the human being, there is his well-known coaching of his (then) follower Regius on how to express positions in language that is inoffensive to the authorities.[19] A final Cartesian answer to the question of trialism would require determining the correct extension of the word "substance." The *wrong* way to begin that task would be to search for a clear and distinct generic idea of a (finite) substance. The method of the *Meditations* requires that the reader work with concrete clear and distinct perceptions instead of beginning with scholastic definitions. In *Principles* I.63, Descartes explicitly makes this point for the case of substance:

Indeed, it is much easier for us to have an understanding of extended substance or thinking substance than it is for us to understand substance on its own, leaving out the fact that it thinks or is extended. For we have some difficulty in abstracting the notion of substance from the notions of thought and extension, since the distinction between these notions and the notion of substance itself is merely a conceptual distinction. (AT 8A: 31)

Evidently, the best method for forming a useful, general concept of substance from specific cases is a two-step procedure. One begins with ideas of things that are indisputably finite substances and abstracts from their being either thinking or extended. Next, the features that remain after the abstraction are catalogued. We can then use the catalogue as a checklist for deciding whether to extend the word "substance" beyond the clear cases of mind and body to the disputed case of the human being.

Counting in no particular order, the first item delivered by this procedure is that mind and body can exist independently from other finite things, requiring only God's concurrence to remain in existence. This is patently untrue of the human being. The union of mind and body would obviously perish if either of its components were to cease existing. The second item is that substances have modes and that ideas of modes must be conceived through ideas of the substances of which they are modes. This is not as straightforward as the first item, but sensations, as opposed to sensory ideas, might be considered modes that depend on both mind and body, or better, on the union of mind and body. Descartes often writes that sensations "arise" from the union or are "referred" to it.[20] If so, the human being would have this feature of substantiality. Third, Descartes discovers innate primitive ideas of mind and body corresponding to those substances. In this respect, the union closely parallels mind and body because it corresponds to its own primitive notion. His finding another notion corresponding to the union makes it parallel to mind and body in that respect. This is further reinforced by the fact that innate ideas are placed in the mind by God and are not invented or put together by humans. Because God is not a deceiver, clear and distinct perceptions of them are true. This would include the truth that humans have a nature qua human beings as the meditator discovers in the Sixth Meditation (AT 7: 80–81).[21]

To sum up, there is one respect in which the union is clearly not substance-like, i.e., not like mind and like body. Its existence is not in the same way independent of other substances. That counts strongly against treating the abstracted idea of substance as applying to it. The main considerations in favor of regarding the union as a substance are these. There is an innate idea of union, and there is reason for saying that some modes depend on the union and are conceived through the idea of union. Asking whether the union is *really* a *genuine* substance would require a precise, unequivocal idea. But the idea of substance is an abstraction based on important features that mind and body have in common. These features do not settle the matter for the union. All of this suggests, I think, that an argument about whether the union is sufficiently similar to mind and body for it to receive the label, "substance," is an argument about the word. The real metaphysical issues are to be handled by taking union along with thought, extension, and God as explanatorily rock-bottom. This coheres with understanding Descartes' philosophy as ultimately based on a few simple, primitive intuitions – items that God has constructed us to understand as true so long as our perception is not clouded by prejudices or the exigencies of life.[22]

SPINOZA AND CARTESIAN DUALISM

Spinoza was one of the earliest and harshest critics of Descartes' dualism. As is so often the case, sharp disagreements rest on a very large base of shared commitments. Spinoza's metaphysics is, on the surface, straightforwardly a substance *monism*. From the right perspective, however, his monism is strikingly similar to Descartes' dualism. Spinoza, like Descartes, allows only one substance, God, in the strictest sense of the term. Descartes then relaxes the term to admit thinking substance and extended substance. Spinoza does not do this, but he does admit thought and extension as *attributes* of the one substance. Moreover, Spinoza and Descartes offer similar definitions of "attribute." Spinoza writes, "By attribute I understand what the intellect perceives of a substance, as constituting its essence" (E1d4).[23] Descartes uses the term "attribute" for what is distinct by reason from a substance: "Finally, a rational distinction is a distinction between a substance and some attribute of that substance without which the substance is unintelligible."[24] So, for example, thought is an attribute, the principal attribute of thinking substance, and extension is the principal attribute of an extended substance. This means that thought and extension are the essences of mind and body[25] and that "they must then be considered as nothing else but thinking substance itself and extended substance itself – that is, as mind and body."[26] Here Descartes strongly suggests that a substance and its principal attribute are one and the same thing differently conceived, in other words, distinguished only by reason.[27]

His treatment of the relationship between attribute and substance closely parallels what is found in Spinoza. For Spinoza, thought and extension are attributes of the one substance, God (E2P1, E2P2). Finite thinking things and extended things are modes of God and modes are conceived[28] through God: "By mode I understand the affections of a substance, or that which is in another through which it is conceived" (E1d5). Furthermore, the attributes of thought and extension are "really distinct" for Spinoza:

From these propositions it is evident that although two attributes may be conceived to be really distinct (i.e., one may be conceived without the aid of the other), we still cannot infer from that that they constitute two beings, or two different substances. (E1P10s)

Spinoza insists that thought and extension cannot be conceived through one another, which is an important feature of Descartes' real distinction. And while Spinoza's attributes express infinite essences of substance, he cannot agree with Descartes that these essences can exist independently from one another because it is necessary that all the essences belong to the one substance. One of the hardest problems in the interpretation of Spinoza's philosophy is how to reconcile the real distinction of thought and extension with their being unified in the one substance.

It is ironic that the part of Spinoza's indictment of Descartes' dualism based on the relationship between thought and extension should make trouble for his own monism, one ontological level up, so to speak. In Spinoza, Descartes' principal attributes of finite substances become the attributes of the one infinite substance. Descartes' finite substances are pushed down to the status of modes of the one substance. Descartes lacks a deep explanation of how finite thought and extension interact such that they exist in a union; Spinoza lacks a deep explanation of how the attributes can be really distinct, absolutely infinite essences that are unified in God and cannot exist apart from one another. It was suggested above that Descartes' positing a primitive notion of union might be regarded as explanation enough. We have direct knowledge of the reality of the union by conceiving sensations through our innate idea of union. We remain curious about the details of how God engineered the union, but those details are opaque to us. When we clearly and distinctly perceive mind and body, we understand them as really distinct. Those clear and distinct perceptions crowd out our awareness of the innate idea of union. When we move to Spinoza, there is a striking parallel with the diversity of God's essences. It has occurred to one commentator that the attributes are ontologically plural in a fully objective way while being somehow unified in an equally objective way. On this interpretation, we can know that the diversity of essences is real and objective, while the unity of God's essences is incomprehensible to us in detail.[29] The parallel in Descartes is the incomprehensibility of how God has unified finite thought and extension, the essences of minds and bodies.

An interesting question for any interpretation of Spinoza on the relationship between the attributes is whether he does make any provision for human cognition of God's unity. If so, he would be offering an analogue of Descartes' innate idea of substantial union. Since any finite object that can be conceived is a mode of God and every mode is conceived through attributes, there is considerable pressure to say that we conceive Spinoza's God only through individual attributes and not as a unity of infinitely many attributes. It is true that E1D6 reads, "By God I understand a being absolutely infinite, i.e., a substance consisting of an infinity of attributes, of which each one expresses an eternal and infinite essence." So if the definition is understandable it should clear matters up for us. But this is a definition of the word "God" rather than an axiom asserting something about God. It remains unclear whether E1D6 asserts that we can form a clear and distinct idea of God without conceiving individual attributes that are really distinct in Spinoza's sense. In other words, it remains unclear whether Spinoza held that we have the means to clearly and distinctly perceive God as a union. It was noted above that Descartes held that thought and extension are more distinctly perceived than the generic concept of finite substance abstracted from them. Insofar as there is pressure on Spinoza to agree that individual attributes are more distinctly perceived than is a union of ontologically distinct attributes, Spinoza is in at least as much difficulty as Descartes is in his notorious reply to Elizabeth (again, one ontological level up, of course).[30]

There is a different reading of Spinoza on the attributes of thought and extension that avoids the problem of the unity of the one substance.[31] It can be approached by noting that the problem of unity arises if Spinoza's real distinction among attributes is like Descartes' dualism in requiring that the attributes or essences are somehow ontologically separate from one another. But Spinoza and Descartes do not have exactly the same understanding of real distinction. Both agree that in cases of real distinction, one attribute cannot be conceived through another, but for Spinoza this fact about conception does not entail mutual independence. Spinoza's real distinction, therefore, more closely resembles Descartes' rational distinction. For Spinoza, no attribute of the one substance (God) can be excluded from it or from another attribute, because it is absolutely necessary that God have all the attributes (E1d6, E1P10s). Since there are strong reasons for taking Descartes' attributes to be numerically identical with substances, the parallel reading of Spinoza should also be considered. If God's attributes of thought and extension are identical to God, then the problem of unity disappears. On this interpretation, distinct attributes are distinct ways in which the intellect conceives substance, which is in line with E1d4.[32] The transitivity of identity is not violated by this reading. Consider an analogy with Frege's distinction between sense and reference. "Cicero" and "Tully" are names that can have different senses, but they refer to the same thing. The names are analogous to Spinoza's attributes, and Cicero the man is analogous to substance. It is also not the case that this treatment makes the attributes illusory, as is often charged. When one distinctly perceives absolutely infinite thought or absolutely infinite extension, the object of both perceptions is God and not some illusion.

Another advantage to taking the distinction between Spinoza's attributes to be a rational distinction is that it provides a solution to the famous problem of unknown attributes. The human mind can conceive God only through the Cartesian pair of thought and extension, but E1d6 defines God as "consisting of an infinity of attributes." Spinoza offers no explanation of this, in apparent violation of the principle of sufficient reason. If, however, attributes are ways in which thought perceives body and itself, there are no additional attributes to worry about. When Spinoza writes "infinity of attributes" he means "all the attributes," and the two are all of them. This does not sit well with all the texts, but neither does taking "infinite attributes" to mean "a number larger than any that can be conceived" or any other formula for unpacking the word "infinite."[33] Yet another advantage of interpreting Spinoza as having a dualism of attributes is that it keeps the two on a par. Ideas have a "formal reality" because they take an object (body), and bodies have an objective reality for which a conception (idea) is formed. If we instead suppose that the infinite intellect has separate ideas of more than two attributes, then thought becomes a superattribute taking the infinity of others as objects while extension is just one among the remaining infinity. This surprising asymmetry would follow from a central proposition of Spinoza's, namely E2P7: "The order and connection of ideas is the same as the order and connection of things." The order and connection of ideas would include ideas of the extra infinity of attributes and the things the infinite intellect (but not ours) conceives as following from them. Consequently, the order and connection of bodies would be the same as an infinitely small part of the order and connection of ideas. This would have many significant ramifications for Spinoza's system. For example, having thought as a superattribute pushes Spinoza's philosophy in the direction of a strange kind of Idealism in which the human mind has only one of the infinitely many actual mental apprehensions of "things" that are all identical with the mind and its body.[34]

We have considered Spinoza's attempt to enforce monism for infinite substance and now proceed to examine his treatment of human beings. At the cost of problems concerning the diverse attributes of substance, Spinoza buys an elegant theory of the relationship between the human mind and body. Where Descartes appeals to an extremely implausible story about the surface of the pineal gland as the interface of mind-body interaction, Spinoza states that "a mode of extension and the idea of that mode are one and the same thing, but expressed in two ways" (E2P7s). This suggestion of a general mind-body identity theory is then given a twist in E2P13: "The object of the idea constituting the human mind is the body, or a certain mode of extension which actually exists, and nothing else." The mind is not simply identical to the body, but it is "united" with it even more tightly than in Descartes' mind-body union. Spinoza does not need to localize a mind-body interface in the brain. The mind instead takes the entire body as its intentional object. When, therefore, the body is affected in the right way through its sense organs, the mind is confusedly aware of these corporeal affects in virtue of their being part of what the idea constituting the mind is an idea of. In this way Spinoza is able to take on board the modern, non-Aristotelian theory of the physiology of sense perception and at the same time allow for an ersatz-Cartesian treatment of the mind as conscious. He can even develop a sense in which the mind is aware of itself as a thinking thing. The only object of the mind is the body, but the body is a composite entity – necessarily so because of the divisibility of finite bodies. This means that every component of a human body is itself identical to an idea that is a component of the mind.[35] Every idea in the mind is, therefore, an idea of an idea. This follows by the transitivity of identity – every idea takes a body as object, but every body is identical to an idea.

Spinoza thus captures features of the Cartesian mind that he wants to preserve in a monistic framework. Mind and body are "unified" as strongly as possible, but the problem about causal interaction noted by Elizabeth and denounced by Spinoza (E5 Preface) is sidestepped. Yet there is at least one respect in which Spinoza appears to be almost wistful for a thoroughgoing dualism. His psychotherapy for treating unhealthy emotions requires that one first mentally separate the passion from accompanying ideas of a cause external to the body (E5P2D). Next, one must make the idea of the motion clear and distinct by joining it instead to "true thoughts" in the mind (E5P3s). There is a difficulty here because an emotion considered as a bodily affect is in fact transiently caused by bodies external to the human. So it would seem that the therapeutic process involves something very like what happens in Descartes' Second Meditation. The mind regards its ideas, even sensory ideas, as its own modes, separating them from the idea of corporeal causes. Of course Spinoza will insist that even though the idea is regarded as separate from an external cause it is, as a matter of fact, so caused. But Descartes will also say that even though meditation enables one to clearly and distinctly perceive a sensory idea as a mode of mind, that does not change the fact that it is caused by the action of external bodies on the body to which the mind is united. This parallel is further strengthened by the fact that Spinoza regards these *cogito*-like perceptions of affects as a source of self-knowledge "aroused or generated by adequate ideas" (E5P4 scholium). Instead of forging a new philosophical concept of mind, Spinoza comes close to attaching the Cartesian concept to a modified conception of mind-body union. How extensive this modification appears depends on one's philosophical perspective.

Spinoza seems to dig still deeper into the Cartesian picture of mind with his notorious doctrine of the human mind's eternity. E5P23 states that "the human mind cannot be absolutely destroyed with the body, but something of it remains which is eternal." This calls to mind how Descartes had originally claimed in the subtitle of the *Meditations* to demonstrate the immortality of the soul. After reading through the Objections before their publication, he decided to back off and claim that he was instead demonstrating the real distinction of mind and body. In his synopsis of the *Meditations*, however, he retains the doctrine that the mind, being a "pure substance" need not be (in fact is not) corrupted with the divisible human body (AT 7: 14). It may well be that Spinoza would not object to supplementing the sense in which something "remains" of the mind with a parallel sense in which something remains of the body that is eternal. But no such claim is to be found in the *Ethics*. Spinoza's doctrine of the eternity of the mind seems to rest heavily on our being able to form the right kind of idea of our mind. Since the mind is an idea of the body, an idea of the mind is an idea of an idea. The right kind of idea of the mind is one in which it is "considered without relation to the body's existence." Spinoza, along with most other early modern philosophers, unequivocally rejects the method of doubt employed in the *Meditations*. It seems, however, he should concede that basing one of the grand conclusions of his whole system on understanding the mind, which is one and the same mode as the body, without relation to the body's existence is not very far from what Descartes requires in the Second Meditation.[36]

We have seen some reasons for thinking that Spinoza retains more aspects of Cartesian dualism than his rhetoric lets on. Many of the problems of Cartesian dualism can, accordingly, be found in somewhat different forms in his monism. This need not alter an assessment of Spinoza's philosophy as a significant departure from his predecessor's. A major difference between Descartes' system of philosophy and Spinoza's is that the former was intended by its creator to be consistent with fundamental theological requirements as interpreted by the Church. The *Meditations* is dedicated to the "sacred faculty of Theology at Paris" (AT 7: 1). Spinoza was most decidedly naturalist insofar as he insisted that finite things are in no way ontologically cut off from the infinite. Finite things are not only conceived through God, but they are *in* God in a very literal sense. Descartes could not accept that.

CONCLUSION: FURTHER DEVELOPMENTS

Despite the momentous departure Spinoza's thoroughgoing naturalism represents, his system is permeated by problems connected with dualism. For many other early modern thinkers, Descartes' dualism leaves deep marks on their thought despite their setting out to oppose important aspects of it. Not even canonical empiricist thinkers avoid its influence. This essay concludes with a brief perspective on these developments.

An interesting transition from the rationalism of Descartes and Spinoza to early modern empiricism is found in the philosophy of Malebranche. It is well known that Malebranche's arguments against finite causation impressed Berkeley and Hume. Malebranche also subtly adjusts Descartes' dualism by denying that we have access to a clear and distinct idea of the essence of the mind. That effectively blocks Descartes' version of the real distinction argument depending as it does on that clear and distinct idea as well as the corresponding idea of the essence of body. Malebranche attempts an alternate argument for real distinction, but this would not be possible if the essence of body, at least, were not distinctly known.[37] Coming to Locke, we find that he agrees with Malebranche about the lack of clear and distinct access to the idea of mind, but he also makes the further move of disallowing the corresponding idea of body.

Locke holds that there is only an obscure idea of substance in general as a substrate supporting various qualities.[38] Our best available ideas of minds and bodies, therefore, are complexes including this general idea along with ideas of either mental or corporeal qualities.[39] A Descartes-style demonstration of the metaphysical real distinction of mind and body is quite impossible given the indistinctness of these ideas. Locke is, however, completely committed to the *epistemological* distinctness of mental and corporeal qualities. And since these are components of the ideas of mental and corporeal substances, they too are epistemically distinct:

Our Observation employ'd either about *external, sensible Objects; or about the internal Operations of our Minds, perceived and reflected on by our selves, is that, which supplies our Understandings with all the materials of thinking.* (2.1.2, p. 104)

These two "fountains of knowledge" which Locke calls sensation and reflection can also be called "internal sense" (2.1.4, p. 105) and external sense.[40] Locke seems to take the dualism of mental and corporeal qualities or properties as simply given. He proffers only this explanation,

... concerning the Operations of the Mind, *viz.* Thinking, Reasoning, Fearing, *etc.* which we concluding not to subsist of themselves, nor apprehending how they can belong to Body, or be produced by it, we are apt to think these the Actions of some other *Substance*, which we call *Spirit* ... *We have as clear a Notion of the Substance of Spirit, as we have of Body;* the one being supposed to be (without knowing what it is) the *substratum* to those simple *Ideas* we have from without; and the other supposed (with a like ignorance of what it is) to be the *Substratum* to those Operations, which we experiment in our selves within. (2.23.5, pp. 297–98)

We are "apt" to assign qualities found in inner sense to spiritual substance simply because we do not "apprehend" how they could be attributable to bodies. Locke has imbibed dualism, but shifted it from the metaphysical to the epistemological register. The result is a dualism of ideas of mental properties and corporeal properties, where the division is strictly along Cartesian lines.

One might get the impression that Berkeley's famous immaterialism is much farther removed from Cartesian dualism. Bodies are sensible objects and sensible objects, Berkeley maintains, are collections of ideas that exist only in minds. Nevertheless, Berkeley's system is in some other ways closer to Descartes' than is Locke's. Berkeley agrees with Descartes against Locke that we know the nature of ourselves as spirits.[41] And while sensible objects or "ideas" are decidedly immaterial, they are also completely different in nature from spirits. He writes, ". . . all the unthinking objects of the mind agree, in that they are entirely passive, and their existence consists only in being perceived: whereas a soul or spirit is an active being, whose existence consists not in being perceived, but in perceiving ideas and thinking."[42] This distinction between activity and passivity very closely resembles Descartes' Sixth Meditation distinction between the active and passive faculties involved in sensation. Descartes can use this to prove the existence of extension because the mind's activity does not include the production of sensory ideas. They must, therefore, be produced by either God or extended things, but not by God because that would involve divine deception (AT 7: 79).

Berkeley makes an adjustment here by insisting that sensory ideas (for him, simply "ideas") are in themselves passive, and there is no idea of extension, so they are non-deceptively produced by God.[43] The main point for us, however, is Berkeley's sharp segregation of our self-knowledge from our knowledge of "bodies," i.e., Berkeleian ideas. "It is therefore necessary, in order to prevent equivocation and confounding natures perfectly disagreeing and unlike, that we distinguish between *spirit* and *idea*."[44] These natures that are "perfectly disagreeing" or "in some way opposite" (AT 7: 13) are dual along Cartesian lines. The main difference, of course, is that while spirit is substantial, ideas fall into their own non-substantial category. Locke and Berkeley, like Spinoza, worked out deep objections to Descartes' version of dualism, but the influence of his doctrine also runs deep.

NOTES

1. The Latin translated as "apart" is *absque*. It could also be translated as "without" or "separate."
2. We will see below that this strongly foreshadows some aspects of Spinoza's system.

3. Descartes makes this point in various texts. See for example *Principles* I.53, AT 8A: 25; *Principles* I.61, AT 8A: 29–30; *Comments on a Certain Broadsheet*, AT 8B: 350; and *Fourth Replies*, AT 7: 223. Questions about what is perceived through what will be very important in the discussion below of Spinoza's engagement of Descartes' dualism.

4. *Principles* I.64, AT 8A: 31. The Latin word *modus* can be translated as "way," "manner," "bound," or "limit." The latter two are well illustrated by shapes.

5. The Second Meditation, AT 7: 28–29.

6. A good expression of this aspect of Descartes' philosophy is found in the fifth postulate of the Geometrical Exposition in *Second Replies*: "For there are certain truths which some people find self-evident, while others come to understand them only by means of a formal argument" (AT 7: 163–64). Another from the *Principles*: "I have often noticed that philosophers make the mistake of employing logical definitions in an attempt to explain what was already very simple and self-evident; the result is that they only make matters more obscure" (AT 8A: 8). Philosophical explanations must make use of self-evident truths and not try to analyze them – they are unanalyzable. For general discussions of Descartes' "intuitionism" see Cunning 2010, chs. 1 and 10, and Lennon 2008, ch. 3. Poor cognitive performance is linked with sluggish pineal glands in "To Meyssonnier, 29 January 1640," AT 3: 19–20.

7. Two ideas "exclude" one another when the first can be clearly and distinctly perceived while the second is "denied" of it. Descartes also says that ideas that exclude one another are "in some way opposite" ("Synopsis of the *Meditations*," AT 7: 13, and see also *Sixth Replies*, AT 7: 440–41 and 443–44). Nolan 1997b has a full account of Descartes' notion of exclusion and of the relevant secondary literature.

8. The divisibility of extension raises important difficulties that deeply concerned Spinoza and other post-Cartesian thinkers. For further discussion of the relevance of divisibility to real distinction and how this relates to Spinoza, see Smith and Nelson 2010.

9. "Synopsis of the *Meditations*," AT 7: 13–14.

10. This point is more explicit in the treatment of real distinction in *Principles* I.60, AT 8A: 28–29. For further discussion of the irrelevance of theories of modality or divine power to the demonstration, see Cunning 2010, ch. 7. For a fuller treatment of the connection between separation and the metaphysics of substances and modes see Rozemond 1998, ch. 2.

11. "To Princess Elizabeth, 21 May 1643," AT 3: 665. See also *Appendix to Fifth Objections and Replies*, AT 9A: 213.

12. See the Fifth Meditation, AT 7: 63–64.
13. "To Princess Elizabeth, 28 June 1643," AT 3: 693.
14. Just before this, Descartes tells Elizabeth that the union is "known only obscurely by the intellect alone." This might be taken to mean that the knowledge provided by the idea of union is of an odd sort and cannot be clearly and distinctly perceived. It could, however, mean that union is not intelligible until the intellect reflects on the nature of sensation. For an account of how Descartes could have held that the innate idea of union is clearly and distinctly perceivable, see Nelson 2013.
15. Garber (2001, 168–88) reveals in a striking way some of the hidden resources provided by the third primitive notion. Nelson (forthcoming 2014) develops the way in which Descartes ties philosophical and scientific explanation to innate ideas.
16. Descartes does stick to a standard vocabulary for sensation. Here I use "sensation" for something a human being does qua human being. I used "sensory idea" for a mode of the thinking thing that cannot be conceived through the body. See Nelson 2013 for further discussion.
17. A useful review of the main issues and many references can be found in Alanen (2003, ch. 2).
18. E.g., *Principles* I.74, AT 8A: 42.
19. "To Regius, December 1640," AT 3:460. For a thorough treatment of how the terminology did matter to some of Descartes' predecessors and contemporaries, see Rozemond (1998, ch. 5).
20. "For these sensations of hunger, thirst pain and so on are nothing but confused modes of thinking which arise from the union and, as it were, intermingling of mind and body" (The Sixth Meditation, AT 7: 81). "But we also experience within ourselves certain other things which must not be referred either to the mind alone or to the body alone. These arise ... from the close and intimate union of our mind with the body" (*Principles* I.48, AT 8A: 23). See also the Sixth Meditation, AT 7: 82–83; "To Gibieuf, 19 January 1642," AT 3: 479; and "To Regius, January 1642," AT 3: 493. For a good review of the considerations involved in deciding whether Descartes took sensations to be modes of the union, see Rozemond (1998, ch. 6).
21. For a much more positive assessment of Descartes on the power of innate ideas than is usual, see Nelson 2008.
22. Again, see the references cited above in n. 6.
23. Citations to Spinoza's *Ethics* are from Curley 1985 and are abbreviated in the standard way: E(thics) with the Part number, P(roposition),

D(emonstration), d(efinition), S(cholium). This chapter restricts itself to Spinoza's mature philosophy as it is expressed in his magnum opus.

24. The translation 'rational' for *rationis* here modifies 'conceptual' from CSM I 214. "Rational distinction" and "distinction of reason" are used interchangeably.

25. "Synopsis of the *Meditations*," AT 7: 12–13; *Principles* I.53, AT 8A: 25.

26. *Principles* I.63, AT 8A: 30–31.

27. The identity of a substance and its attributes is argued for in Nolan 1997b. See Sowaal 2011 for further advantages of this interpretation. Rozemond (1998, ch. 2) also reads Descartes this way, but only for the principal attribute. Hoffman 2002 instead holds that while attributes are ontologically distinct from their substances, they are inseparable from them.

28. Spinoza prefers "conceive" where Descartes uses "perceive" (E2d3). The reason for this is not relevant here.

29. Gueroult 1968, 237–40. For further critical discussion of this maneuver, see Lennon 2005.

30. Some commentators have extrapolated from the texts to suggest that Spinoza is committed to making use of generic concepts to conceive reality in ways that come apart from attributes. Bennett (1984, 42–47, 143–49) is an influential example of this strategy.

31. Here I am mostly summarizing the exposition in Shein 2009 which contains much more detail, additional arguments, and discussion of the literature.

32. Readings opposed to this understand the intellect referred to in 1d4 not as human intellect, but as God's. It is then inferred that conceptions that are in any way distinct in God's intellect must correspond to ontologically distinct items.

33. Bennett (1984, 75–80) convincingly argues that the textual evidence on how to count "infinite attributes" in inconclusive.

34. Bennett (1984, 62) discusses the "lopsidedness" that results from priv-ileging thought over extension in a way that Spinoza "should not have tolerated."

35. "...whatever we have said of the idea of the human body must also be said of the idea of any thing" (E2P13s).

36. This theme is developed some in Nelson (forthcoming 2013).

37. These aspects of Malebranche's relation to Cartesian dualism are richly detailed in Nolan and Whipple 2005 and 2006.

38. See 2.23.2, p. 296. References to Locke's *Essay* are by book, chapter, and section numbers followed by the page number in Locke 1975.

39. 2.23.4 and 2.23.5, p. 297–98 and 2.23.15, p. 305–06.

40. This obviously prefigures Kant's division of the forms of sensibility into the inner and outer with the former corresponding to appearances of the self and the latter to appearances of bodies.

41. *Principles* 142. Berkeley's *Principles of Human Knowledge* is cited by section number from Berkeley (1950).

42. *Principles* 139.

43. *Principles* 146.

44. *Principles* 139.

15 The *Meditations* and Descartes' considered conception of God

It is tempting to suppose that Descartes is sincere in his letter of dedication to the Sorbonne faculty of theology, not just in his request for their approval, but also in his comments that imply that the God of the *Meditations* is the God of religious tradition (AT 7: 1–3).[1] I think that at most Meditations One and Two include mention of this traditional being and that the meditator who conceives of it has an idea that is very confused. God is discussed in each of Descartes' six Meditations, and I will chart the development of that discussion. I argue that the idea that Descartes ends up reaching is by no means traditional.

I am arguing by extension that Descartes had good reason for refusing to engage his correspondents on theological matters. For example, Mersenne had asked him how a supremely good God could damn men for eternity, and Descartes replies that "that is a theological question: so if you please you will allow me to say nothing about it" ("To Mersenne, 27 May 1630," AT 1: 153). He announces in *Letter to Father Dinet* that "I have often declared that I have no desire to meddle in any theological disputes" and adds that "I deal only with matters that are known very clearly by natural reason, [but] these cannot be in conflict with anyone's theology" (AT 7: 598). Descartes holds that the clear and distinct perceptions of philosophy are true and that if a deliverance of faith appears to run counter to one of these, the deliverance needs to be re-understood.

Talk of divinity is fairly traditional early in the *Meditations*. In Meditation One, we are presented with the all-powerful God of religious tradition, whose immense power would enable him to deceive us if he so willed, although it is noted that this being is also said to be supremely good (AT 7: 21). In the Second Meditation there is a vague reference to "a God, or whatever I may call him, who puts into me the thoughts I am now having" (AT 7: 24). This presumably is much the same being as in the First Meditation, a vaguely threatening and unknown power, whose intentions for us are not entirely clear. But even if such a God exists and is deceiving the meditator, there is one thing that God cannot deceive him about, and that is his own existence as a thinker. The meditator might be deceived about almost everything else, but not about this.

Talk of God starts to look very different in the Third Meditation. Perhaps this is because God is an insensible being, according to Descartes, and the meditator has finally committed to "shut my eyes, stop my ears, and withdraw all my senses" (AT 7: 34). The only ideas to be entertained at this point in the *Meditations* – or at least to be given any credence – are clear and distinct ideas, and the clear and distinct idea of God at which the meditator arrives is an idea of the sum of reality or perfection. It is the richest idea the meditator can have:

It is utterly clear and distinct, and contains in itself more objective reality than any other idea; hence there is no idea which is in itself truer or less liable to be suspected of falsehood ... The idea is, moreover, utterly clear and distinct, for whatever I clearly and distinctly perceive as being real and true, and implying any perfection, is wholly contained in it. (AT 7: 46)

We might note for now that in the Fourth Meditation the meditator's own will is identified as something that has perfection (AT 7: 57), and it is also said that "man's greatest and most important perfection is to be found" in the work done by the intellect and will to develop the habit of avoiding error (AT 7: 62). Note also that Descartes holds that the physical universe is a continuous plenum (of real being)[2] and that "body, taken in the general sense, is a substance, so that it too never perishes."[3]

With the idea of God in hand, the meditator reasons that like everything it requires a cause for its existence, and that cause could only be the supreme being itself. Since deliberate deceit would show some imperfection, such a supreme being cannot be a deliberate deceiver. This conclusion is reached at the end of the Third Meditation, where there is a pause for wonder and adoration in the face of the divine light. The conclusion is then spelled out more explicitly at the start of the Fourth:

When I consider the fact that I have doubts, or that I am a thing that is incomplete and dependent, then there arises in me a clear and distinct idea of a being who is independent and complete, that is, an idea of God. (AT 7: 53)

Is this the same God that was discussed in the First Meditation? There God was said to be supremely good, as well as omniscient and omnipotent, and this is also said in the Fourth Meditation of God, whose omnibenevolence rules out his deceiving human creatures (but does not rule out his causing their ignorance). But there are also aspects of the God of the tradition that Descartes consistently refrains from mentioning as the idea of God becomes fully distinct. For example, the tradition saw God as three persons in one, but this is never said of Descartes' God. As Descartes had written to Mersenne, natural reason cannot demonstrate the tenets of faith.

Descartes' God starts to appear explicitly non-traditional in Meditation Four. We learn that God not only has an immense will and intellect, He also has an immense imagination and memory:

I perceive that [supremely great and infinite intellect] belongs to the nature of God. Similarly, if I examine the faculties of memory or imagination, or any others, I discover that in my case each one of these faculties is weak and limited, while in the case of God it is immeasurable. (AT 7: 57)

For Descartes memory and imagination are corporeal faculties that involve material extension.[4] Not much is made of the implication that God has imagination and memory; the focus of the Fourth Meditation is instead on will and intellect and how it is that human minds err if will and intellect are creatures of God. Descartes does say at the end of the Meditation that "I must not complain that the forming of those acts of will or judgments in which I go wrong happens with God's concurrence" (AT 7: 60). He adds that there is privation involved in false judgments and that such privation "is all that the definition of falsity and wrong consists in" (AT 7: 61). He says also that a privation is not anything, and so it is not willed by God.[5] Descartes will have to construct an account of how strictly speaking God is not the cause of our erroneous acts of will, and an account of how we are able to avoid error if God concurs in our acts of will, but those are not the focus of the Fourth Meditation either.

Imagination is considered again at the start of the Fifth Meditation, where the meditator says that he can distinctly imagine extensive magnitude, later said to be a true and immutable nature. He writes, "I distinctly imagine the extension of the quantity (or rather the thing which is quantified) in length, breadth and depth" (AT 7: 63). Presumably this extension is willed and known by God, as well as known by the finite thinker and imaginer, and presumably the immense divine imagination encompasses it as well. Then comes another proof of the existence of God, to add to the two proofs offered in the Third Meditation, where God was shown to be the cause both of the meditator's distinct idea of God, and of the meditator in possession of that idea. Now the nature of God is said to include necessary existence, just as the nature of the triangle is to have three sides, and to have the sum of its angles equal to two right angles. As Spinoza later pointed out, necessary being must be unique,[6] so only if God is Nature can each necessarily exist.[7] Now that we have a clearer and more distinct idea of extension, and know that it can be distinctly imagined, the supposition that extension cannot be an attribute of God is implicitly cast into doubt. Descartes thinks we have no image of God, and never says explicitly (like Spinoza) that God is an extended thing, but Descartes allows (and Spinoza would agree) that extension can be grasped by an act of "purely mental scrutiny" (AT 7: 31). For Descartes God cannot be corporeal in the sense of being "made up of a certain configuration of limbs and other accidents of this sort" (AT 7: 14), but the plenum of extension is something else entirely, and again "body, taken in the general sense, is a substance, so that it too never perishes."

In the Sixth Meditation it is made quite explicit that "by Nature in general I mean God, or else the ordered series of things created by God" (AT 7: 80). Nature in general is here implicitly contrasted with particular things. In the Third Meditation, creating had been shown to be the same as sustaining, so now we see that self-sustaining Nature is another name for God. Descartes similarly identifies God and Nature in Principles I.28, and so the Sixth Meditation claim is not just an aberration. He writes:

When dealing with natural things we will, then, never derive any explanations from the purposes which God or nature may have had in view when creating them. (AT 8A: 15)

This is definitely not the God of religious tradition, or not the tradition in which Descartes had been reared. It is not a God which can be imaged or imagined. We can imagine extended things, but to imagine infinite extension, as well as the more traditional attributes of God, would take an infinite mind.

God appears again in the Sixth Meditation proof of the existence of material things, and in a way that suggests that Descartes wants to secure a distinction between God and creatures. Descartes does say in *Principles* I.51 that "there is only one substance which can be understood to depend on no other thing whatsoever, namely God," and that "there is no distinctly intelligible meaning of the word 'substance' which is common to God and his creatures" (AT 8A: 24). If so, it would appear that there is only one substance and that it is God. But of course in the proof of the existence of material things Descartes argues that the cause of our sensory perceptions of bodies is either God *or* bodies, and he emphasizes the distinction between God and particular bodies elsewhere as well.[8] Descartes thus appears to be working with two understandings of "Nature" – there is Nature "in its most general aspect," or God, and Nature in the sense of the collection of finite bodies. If our sensations were not caused by a plurality of finite extended things (the second sense of "Nature") but caused directly by God (the first sense of "Nature"), then God would be a deceiver, so strong is our inclination to think that it is finite extended things that we are sensing. (Of course Berkeley would later resist this inclination.) So even if Descartes holds that God somehow encompasses or includes the extended world, it is not as the plurality of finite extended things, but presumably as the infinite extending force behind them, more like Spinoza's *natura naturans* instead of *natura naturata*.[9]

A final noteworthy mention of God in the *Meditations* is in the discussion of the mechanism by which a person suffers from dropsy, and cannot help feeling thirst, although her body does not need water (AT 7: 85–89). Here God (or Nature in the general sense) causes deception, even if it is unclear whether deception is specifically willed, since the immense goodness of this God is still affirmed, and we are told that the union of our mind and body has been set up as well as possible. Since it is a mechanistic universe that God or Nature sustains, occasional malfunctions of the human body are inevitable, and so presumably these are accepted by God even if they are not his aim.[10] And since, as was claimed in the Third Meditation, simplicity and unity are among the chief perfections of God (AT 7: 50), the divine will, intellect, imagination, and memory are not really separate powers.[11] Omnipotence is a feature of the divine will; omniscience is a feature of the divine intellect and memory and the all-encompassing divine imagination; and these and divine omnibenevolence are all identical. By the end of the *Meditations*, the meditator knows much better than earlier both his own and the divine nature, of which his own nature is to some extent a reflection. Because his mind is distinct from his body, the meditator does not appear to be made in the image of divine simplicity. One thing in the meditator that is not found in a greater form in God is sensation. Because sensation is passive, and yields confused ideas, it counts as an imperfection, so is not found in God, even if God is extended. God instead has what we might call "knowledge without observation" of what He does.

Understandably, when Spinoza restates Descartes' views in *Principles of Cartesian Philosophy*, he spends a lot of time on the attributes of God. God cannot be corporeal, Spinoza concludes in I.16, since that would imply limitation and divisibility. But he also makes clear that the extension which is denied of God is not active extending. Spinoza is then foreshadowing his own later distinction, in *Ethics*, between *natura naturans* and *natura naturata*. There God is not said to be a thinking thing either,[12] any more than he is an extended thing, and of course thinking in us does take time, so is divisible.[13] God is omniscient, and this without needing to be a thinker, just as God is immense, without needing to be spread out in space. If "God" is another name for Nature, then it has created and sustained the human race, whose members think they understand, to some degree, the Nature which sustains them. If Nature sustains knowers of Nature, then it is self-knowing. But our human knowledge is partial, and God is supposed to be omniscient, so even if God's omnipresence means his presence in us, our knowledge of Nature cannot be all there is to divine knowledge. Still, it is a marvel that Nature produces even partial finite knowers of Nature. All living things understand something about their environment, but we human beings have theories about the whole universe. Should our theory be true, then we count as sharing in the divine self-knowledge, just as Spinoza thought.

NOTES

1. For example Cottingham 2008, 300. See also Nolan and Nelson 2006, 105.
2. *Principles* II.11–18.
3. "Synopsis of the *Meditations*," AT 7: 14.
4. For example *Treatise on Man*, AT 11: 176–78; the Sixth Meditation, AT 7: 72–73.
5. He also says of falsity/wrongness that "when it is referred to God as its cause, it should not be called a privation but simply a negation" (AT 7: 61).
6. Spinoza, *Principles of Cartesian Philosophy* I.5, 134. See also I.11, 140. Page references to works of Spinoza are to the Shirley translation.
7. Spinoza argues that Nature is a necessary existent in *Short Treatise* (43), apparently from the premise that it cannot come from nothing and (as a substance) cannot be destroyed.
8. For example in *Principles* I.51–52.
9. For example *Ethics* Ip29, scholium.
10. We might ask – does the doctrine of double effect apply to God's intentions?
11. Also "To [Mersenne], 27 May 1630," AT 1: 153; "To [Mesland], 2 May 1644," AT 4: 119; *Principles* I.23, AT 8A: 14.
12. *Ethics* Ip17, scholium.
13. See also the Third Meditation, AT 7: 49.

BIBLIOGRAPHY

Adams, R. 1994. *Leibniz: Determinist, Theist, Idealist.* New York: Oxford University Press.

Aikins, K. 1996. "Of Sensory Systems and the 'Aboutness' of Mental States," *Journal of Philosophy* 93: 337–72.

Alanen, L. 1982. *Studies in Cartesian Epistemology and Philosophy of Mind.* Helsinki: Societas Philosophica Fennica.

    1994. "Sensory Ideas, Objective Reality, and Material Falsity," in Cottingham, J. (ed.), *Reason, Will, and Sensation,* 229–50. New York: Oxford University Press.

    2003. *Descartes's Concept of Mind.* Cambridge, MA: Harvard University Press.

    2008. "Omnipotence, Modality, and Conceivability," in Broughton and Carriero (eds.), 353–71.

    2013. "The role of the Will in Descartes' Account of Judgment," in Detlefsen, K. (ed.), *Descartes' Meditations: A Critical Guide,* 176–99. Cambridge University Press.

    forthcoming. "Self-awareness and cognitive agency," in Gustafsson, M. and Minar, E. (eds.), *Philosophical Topics.*

Allen, M. J. B. and Rees, V. (eds.), with Davies, M. 2002. *Marsilio Ficino: His Theology, his Philosophy, his Legacy.* Leiden: Brill.

Almog, J. 2002. *What Am I? Descartes and the Mind-Body Problem.* New York: Oxford University Press.

Alnwick, Fr. Guillelmus 1937. *Quaestiones disputatae de esse intellgibili et de quodlibet.* Athenasius Ledoux (ed.). Quaracchi: O.F.M.

Alonso de Villegas 1623. *The Lives of Saints.* St. Omer: English College Press.

Annas, J. and Barnes, J. 1985. *The Modes of Scepticism.* Cambridge University Press.

Anscombe, E. and Geach, P. (trans. and eds.) 1954. *Descartes – Philosophical Writings.* Edinburgh, London and Melbourne: Thomas Nelson and Sons Ltd.

306

Aquinas, St. Thomas 1882. *Opera omnia*. Rome: Editio leonina.
   1949. *Quaestiones disputatae de anima*. Rowan, J. P. (trans.). Title trans-
   lated as *The Soul*. London: B. Herder.
   1968. *Summa Theologiae*. London: Blackfriars and Eyre and Spottiswood.
   1983. *On Being and Essence*. Maurer, A. (trans.). Toronto: Pontifical
   Institute of Medieval Studies.
Ariew, R. 1999. *Descartes and the Last Scholastics*. Ithaca: Cornell University
   Press.
Ariew, R., Cottingham, J. and Sorell, T. (trans. and eds.) 1998. *Descartes'
   Meditations: Background Source Materials*. Cambridge University Press.
Aristotle 1951. *Physica*. Ross, W. D. (ed.). Oxford University Press.
   1957. *Metaphysica*. Jaeger, W. (ed.). Oxford University Press.
   1979. *De Anima*. Ross, W. D. (ed.). Oxford University Press.
Arnauld, A. and Nicole, P. 1996. *Logic or the Art of Thinking*. Buroker, J. V.
   (ed.). Cambridge University Press (orig. 1683).
Augustine 1992. *Confessions*. Chadwick, H. (ed. and trans.). New York:
   Oxford University Press.
Ayers, M. 1998. "Ideas and Objective Being," in Garber, D. and Ayers, M.,
   The Cambridge History of Seventeenth Century Philosophy, Vol. 2,
   1062–1107. Cambridge University Press.
   2005. "The Second Meditation and Objections to Cartesian Dualism," in
   Mercer, C. and O'Neill, E. (eds.), *Early Modern Philosophy – Mind, Matter
   and Metaphysics*, chapter three. New York: Oxford University Press.
Bacon, F. 2000. "The Essayes or Counsels, Civill and Morall," in Kiernan, M.
   (ed.), *The Oxford Francis Bacon*, Vol. 15. Oxford: Clarendon Press.
Baier, A. 1986. "The Idea of the True God in Descartes," in Rorty (ed.), 359–87.
Baker, G. and Morris K. J. 1996. *Descartes' Dualism*. London: Routledge.
Barnes, J. 2009. "Anima Christiana," in Frede, D. and Reis, B. (eds.), *Body and
   Soul in Ancient Philosophy*, 447–64. Berlin: De Gruyter.
Beck, L. J. 1965. *The Metaphysics of Descartes*. Oxford: Clarendon Press.
Beckwith, S. 1993. *Christ's Body. Identity, Culture, and Society in Late
   Medieval Writings*. New York: Routledge.
Bennett, J. A. W. 1982. *Poetry of the Passion: Studies in Twelve Centuries of
   English Verse*. Oxford: Clarendon Press
   1984. *A Study of Spinoza's Ethics*. Indianapolis: Hackett.
   1994. "Descartes's Theory of Modality," *The Philosophical Review* 103:
   639–67.
Berkeley, G. 1950. *The Works of George Berkeley*, Vol. 2. Luce, A. and
   Jessop, T. (eds.). London: Nelson.
Bernard of Clairvaux 1614. *Saint Bernard, his Meditations: or Sighes, Sobbes,
   and Teares, upon our Saviours* [sic] *Passion*. W. P., Maister of Artes (ed.).
   3rd edn. London: Thomas Creede.

Beyssade, J. M. 1992. "The Idea of God and Proofs of his Existence," in Cottingham, J. (ed.), *The Cambridge Companion to Descartes*, 174–99. Cambridge University Press.

Bible, The New Revised Standard Version, available on numerous on-line sites.

Black, R. 2001. *Humanism and Education in Medieval and Renaissance Italy: Tradition and Innovation in Latin Schools from the Twelfth to the Fifteenth Century*. Cambridge University Press.

Bolton, M. 1986. "Confused and Obscure Ideas of Sense," in Rorty (ed.), 389–404.

Brachtendorf, J. 2012. "The Reception of Augustine in Modern Philosophy," in Vessey, M. (ed.), *A Companion to Augustine*, 478–91. Oxford and Chichester: Wiley-Blackwell.

Brandom, Robert 2002. *Tales of the Mighty Dead*. Cambridge, MA: Harvard University Press.

Broughton, J. 2002. *Descartes's Method of Doubt*. Princeton University Press.

Broughton, J. and Carriero, J. 2008. *A Companion to Descartes*. Oxford: Wiley-Blackwell.

Brown, C. 2011. "Narrow Mental Content," *The Stanford Encyclopedia of Philosophy*. Zalta, E. (ed.). URL = http://plato.stanford.edu/archives/fall2011/entries/content-narrow/

Brown, D. 2006. *Descartes and the Passionate Mind*. Cambridge University Press.

 2008. "Descartes on True and False Ideas," in Broughton and Carriero (eds.), 196–215.

Buckle, S. 2007. "Descartes, Plato and the Cave," *Philosophy* 82: 301–37.

Burnyeat, M. 1982. "Idealism and Greek Philosophy: What Descartes Saw and Berkeley Missed," in Vesey, G. (ed.), *Idealism Past and Present*, 19–50. Cambridge University Press.

Buroker, J. 1996. "Arnauld on Judging and the Will," in Kremer, E. J. (ed.), *Interpreting Arnauld*, 3–12. University of Toronto Press.

Bynum, C. W. 1987. *Holy Feast and Holy Fast: The Religious Significance of Food to Medieval Women*. Berkeley: University of California Press.

Camerarius, P. 1603. *Les Meditations Historiques: Comprinses en deux volumes, qui contienent deux cents chapitres, reduits en dix livres …* Lyon: Antoine De Harsy.

Carriero, J. 2009. *Between Two Worlds – A Reading of Descartes's Meditations*. Princeton University Press.

Chappell, V. 1994. "L'homme cartésien," in Beyssade, J. M. and Marion, J. L. (eds.), *Descartes: Objecter et répondre*, 403–26. Paris: Vrin.

 1997. "Descartes's Ontology," *Topoi* 16: 111–27.

Christofidou, A. 2009. "Descartes on Freedom, Truth and Goodness," *Noûs* 43: 633–55.

Churchland, P. 1984. *Matter and Consciousness*. Cambridge, MA: MIT Press.

Clemenson, D. 2007. *Descartes' Theory of Ideas*. London: Continuum.

Copenhaver, B. P. and Schmitt, C. B. 1992. *Renaissance Philosophy*. Oxford University Press.

Cotgrave, R. 1611. *A Dictionarie of the French and English Tongues*. London: Adam Islip.

Cottingham, J. 1985. "Cartesian Trialism," *Mind* 94: 218–30.

1986. *Descartes*. Oxford: Blackwell Publishing.

2008. "The Role of God in Descartes' Philosophy," in Broughton and Carriero (eds.), 288–301.

Cross, R. 1998. *The Physics of Duns Scotus: The Scientific Context of a Theological Vision*. New York: Oxford University Press.

Cunning, D. 2003. "True and Immutable Natures and Epistemic Progress in Descartes's Meditations," *British Journal for the History of Philosophy* 11: 235–48.

2007. "Semel in Vita: Descartes' Stoic View on the Place of Philosophy in Human Life," *Faith and Philosophy* 24: 165–84.

2008. "Fifth Meditation TINs Revisited: A Reply to Criticisms of the Epistemic Interpretation," *British Journal for the History of Philosophy* 16: 215–27.

2010. *Argument and Persuasion in Descartes' Meditations*. New York: Oxford University Press.

Curley, E. 1975. "Descartes, Spinoza, and the Ethics of Belief," in E. Freeman and M. Mandelbaum (eds.), *Spinoza: Essays in Interpretation*, 159–89. La Salle, IL: Open Court.

1978. *Descartes Against the Sceptics*, Cambridge, MA: Harvard University Press.

1984. "Descartes on the Creation of the Eternal Truths," *The Philosophical Review* 43: 569–97.

(ed. and trans.) 1985. *The Collected Works of Spinoza*, Vol. 1. Princeton University Press.

1986. "Analysis in the *Meditations*: The Quest for Clear and Distinct Ideas," in Rorty (ed.), 153–76.

2005. "Back to the Ontological Argument," in Mercer, C. and O'Neill, E. (eds.), *Early Modern Philosophy: Mind, Matter, and Metaphysics*, 46–64. New York: Oxford University Press.

Curley, E. and Koivuniemi, M. forthcoming. "A Kind of Dualism," in Garber, D. and Rutherford, D. (ed.), *Oxford Studies in Early Modern Philosophy*.

Davidson, J. 2004. "Omnipotence: The Real Power behind Descartes' Proofs for God's Existence," *Modern Schoolman* 81: 275–94.

Davies, R. 2001. *Descartes: Belief, Skepticism and Virtue*. London: Routledge.

De Alcántara, P. 1624. *De meditatione et oratione, libellus aureus.* Dulcken, A. (trans.). Cologne: Petrus Henningius.

De Buzon, F. and Kambouchner, D. 2011. *Le vocabulaire de Descartes.* Paris: Ellipses.

De la Puente, L. 1636. *Meditationes de praecipuis fidei nostrae mysteriis, vitae ac passionis D. n. Iesu Christi, et B. V. Mariae, sanctorumq[ue] et Euangelicorum toto anno occurrentium: cvm orationis mentalis circa eadem praxi.* Melchior, R. P. (trans.). Cologne: Kinchius.

De Rosa, R. 2004. "Descartes on Sensory Misrepresentation: The Case of Materially False Ideas," *History of Philosophy Quarterly* 21: 261–80.

Delahunty, R. 1980. "Descartes' Cosmological Argument," *Philosophical Quarterly* 30: 34–46.

Denzinger, H. 1963. *Enchiridion Symbolorum.* 32nd edn. Barcelona: Herder.

Dicker, G. 1993. *Descartes: An Analytical and Historical Introduction.* Oxford: Oxford University Press.

Doney, W. 1993. "On Descartes' Reply to Caterus," *American Catholic Philosophical Quarterly* 67: 413–30.

Doyle, J. P. (ed. and trans.) 1995. *Francisco Suarez, On Beings of Reason, Metaphysical Disputation.* Milwaukee: Marquette University Press.

Drake, S. (ed.) 1957. *The Discoveries and Opinions of Galileo.* New York: Anchor Books.

Du Pont, D. 2012. *Writing Teresa: The Saint from Ávila at the Fin-de-siglo.* Lewisburg: Bucknell University Press.

Duns Scotus, J. 1325. *Ordinatio.* 2.3.1.5–6. Vatican City: Typis Polyglottis Vaticanis.

1639. *Ordinatio,* Vol. 2. Wadding, L. (ed.). Lyon: Crespin.

1963. Commentary on the Sentences and Lectura I, in *Opera Omnia,* Vol. 6. (Vatican City: Typis Polyglottis Vaticanis).

Edelberg, W. 1990. "The Fifth Meditation," *Philosophical Review* 99: 493–533.

Eustachius a Sancto Paolo 1609. *Summa philosophiae quadripartitae de rebus dialecticis, moralibus, physicis, et metaphysicis.* Paris.

Feyerabend, P. 1978. *Science in a Free Society.* London: New Left Books.

Ficino, M. 2002. *Platonic Theology.* Hankins, J. (ed.), Allen, M. J. B. (trans.). 6 vols. Cambridge, MA: Harvard University Press.

Foucault, M. 1972. *Histoire de la folie à l'âge classique.* Paris: Gallimard.

Fowler, C. F. 1999. *Descartes on the Human Soul: Philosophy and the Demands of Christian Doctrine.* Boston: Kluwer.

Frankfurt, H. 1977. "Descartes on the Creation of the Eternal Truths," *The Philosophical Review* 86: 36–57.

2008. *Demons, Dreamers, and Madmen. The Defense of Reason in Descartes' Meditations.* Princeton University Press (orig., 1970).

Galileo, G. 1957. "The Assayer," in Drake, S. (ed. and trans.), *Discoveries and Opinions of Galileo.* New York: Anchor.

Garber, D. 1986. "*Semel in Vita*: The Scientific Background to Descartes' *Meditations*," in Rorty (ed.), 81–116.

1992. *Descartes' Metaphysical Physics (Science and its Conceptual Foundations)*. University of Chicago Press.

2001. *Descartes Embodied*. Cambridge University Press.

Garfagnini, G. C. 1986. *Marsilio Ficino e il ritorno di Platone: Studi e documenti*. Florence: L.S. Olschki.

Gaukroger, S. 2006. *The Emergence of a Scientific Culture: Science and the Shaping of Modernity, 1210–1685*. Oxford University Press.

(ed.) 2006. *The Blackwell Guide to Descartes' Meditations*, Oxford: Blackwell.

Gerson, L. P. 2005. "What is Platonism?," *Journal of the History of Philosophy* 43: 253–76.

Gewirth, A. 1970. "The Cartesian Circle Reconsidered," *Journal of Philosophy* 67: 668–85.

Gilson, E. 1913. *La liberté chez Descartes et la théologie*. Paris: J. Vrin.

Gibieuf, G. 1630. *De libertate Dei et creaturae*. Paris: Cottereau.

Greenberg, S. 2007. "Descartes on the Passions: Function, Representation, and Motivation," *Noûs* 41: 714–34.

Gueroult, M. 1953. *Descartes selon l'ordre des raisons*. Paris: Aubier.

1968. *Spinoza: Dieu*. Paris: Aubier.

Hatfield, G. 1985. "Descartes's Meditations as Cognitive Exercises," *Philosophy and Literature* 9: 41–58.

1986. "The Senses and the Fleshless Eye," in Rorty (ed.), 45–79.

2003. *Descartes and the Meditations*. London: Routledge.

2007. "The Passions of the Soul and Descartes's Machine Psychology," *Studies in the History and Philosophy of Science* 38: 1–35.

2009. "The Sixth Meditation: Mind-Body Relation, External Objects, and Sense Perception," in Kemmerling, A. (ed.), *Meditationen über die Erste Philosophie*, 123–46. Berlin: Akademie.

Hedley, D. and Hutton, S. (eds.) 2008. *International Archives of the History of Philosophy: Platonism at the Origins of Modernity*. Dordrecht: Springer.

Hegel, G. W. F. 1971. *Vorlesungen über die Geschichte der Philosophie*. Vol. 3. Frankfurt: Suhrkamp, 1971. (English translation: *Lectures on the History of Philosophy*, Vol. 3, trans. Haldane and Simson. London: Kegan Paul, 1896.)

Hintikka, J. 1962. "Cogito ergo sum: Inference or Performance?," *Philosophical Review* 71: 3–32.

Hoffman, P. 1986. "The Unity of Descartes's Man," *Philosophical Review* 95: 339–70.

1996. "Descartes on Misrepresentation," *Journal of the History of Philosophy* 34: 357–81.

2002. "Descartes's Theory of Distinction," *Philosophy and Phenomenological Research* 64: 57–78.

Janowski, Z. 2000. *Index Augustino-Cartésien: Textes et commentaire.* Paris: Vrin.

2004. *Augustinian Cartesian Index.* South Bend: St. Augustine's Press.

Jansenius (Jansen), C. 1640. *Augustinus seu doctrina sancti Augustini de humanae naturae sanitate, aegritudine, medicina adversus Pelagianos et Massilienses.* Rouen: Berthelin.

Jolley, N. 1990. *The Light of the Soul: Theories of Ideas in Leibniz, Malebranche and Descartes.* Oxford University Press.

Jorgensen, L. 2012. "Descartes on Music: Between the Ancients and the Aestheticians," *British Journal of Aesthetics* 52: 407–24.

Kambouchner, D. 2005. *Les Méditations métaphysiques de Descartes,* 1. Paris: Presses Universitaires de France.

Kant, I. 1992. "The Only Possible Argument in Support of a Demonstration of the Existence of God," in Walford, D. and Meerbote, R. (trans. and eds.), *Kant: Theoretical Philosophy 1755–1770.* Cambridge University Press.

1998. *The Critique of Pure Reason.* Guyer, P. and Wood, A. (trans. and eds.). Cambridge University Press.

Kaufman, D. 2000. "Descartes on the Objective Reality of Materially False Ideas," *Pacific Philosophical Quarterly* 81: 385–408.

Kenny, A. 1966. "Cartesian Privacy," in Pitcher, G. (ed.), *Wittgenstein: The Philosophical Investigations,* 352–70. New York: Doubleday.

1968. *Descartes: A Study of his Philosophy.* New York: Random House.

1970. "The Cartesian Circle and the Eternal Truths," *Journal of Philosophy* 67: 685–700.

1972. "Descartes on the Will," in Butler, R. J. (ed.), *Cartesian Studies,* 1–31. Oxford: Basil Blackwell.

1979. *The God of the Philosophers.* Oxford: Clarendon Press.

1998. "Descartes on the Will," in Cottingham, J. (ed.), *Descartes,* 132–59. Oxford and New York: Oxford University Press.

King, P. 2004. "Duns Scotus on Mental Content," in Boulnois, O. (ed.), *Duns Scotus à Paris, 1302–2002,* 65–88. Turnhout: Brepols.

Koistinen, O. 2011. "Descartes in Kant's Transcendental Deduction," *Midwest Studies in Philosophy* 35: 149–63.

Kolesnik-Antoine, D. 2009. *L'homme cartésien: la "force qu'a l'âme de mouvoir le corps."* Presses universitaires de Rennes.

Kraye, J. and Stone, M. (eds.) 2000. *Humanism and Early Modern Philosophy.* London: Routledge.

Kristeller, P. 1979. *Renaissance Thought and Its Sources.* Michael Mooney (ed.). New York: Columbia University Press.

Larmore, C. 1998. "Scepticism," in Garber, D. and Ayers, M. (eds.), *The Cambridge History of Seventeenth Century Philosophy*, 1145–92. Cambridge University Press.
  2000. "La structure dialogique de la Première Méditation," in *Philosophie* 65: 55–72.
  2006. "Descartes and Skepticism," in Gaukroger (ed.), 17–29.
  2008. *The Autonomy of Morality*. Cambridge University Press.
Leibniz, G. W. 1989. *G. W. Leibniz: Philosophical Essays*. Ariew, R. and Garber, D. (ed. and trans.). Indianapolis: Hackett.
Lennon, T. M. 2005. "The Rationalist Conception of Substance," in Nelson, A. (ed.), *A Companion to Rationalism*. Oxford: Blackwell.
  2008. *The Plain Truth*. Leiden: Brill.
  2013. "Descartes's Supposed Libertarianism: Letter to Mesland or Memorandum concerning Petau?," *Journal of the History of Philosophy* 51: 223–48.
  forthcoming. "No, Descartes Is Not A Libertarian," in Garber, D. and Rutherford, D. (eds.), *Oxford Studies in Early Modern Philosophy*, Oxford University Press.
Leone, M. 2010. *Saints and Signs: A Semiotic Reading of Conversion in Early Modern Catholicism*. Berlin: De Gruyter.
Locke, J. 1975. *An Essay Concerning Human Understanding*. Nidditch, P. (ed.). Oxford University Press.
Malebranche, N. 1997. "Elucidations of the Search After Truth," in Lennon, T. M. and Olscamp, P. (eds. and trans.), *The Search After Truth*. Cambridge University Press, 533–753.
Marion, J.-L. 1996. *Questions cartésiennes II: Sur l'ego et sur Dieu*. Paris: Presses Universitaires de France.
McNamer, S. 2010. *Affective Meditation and Invention of the Medieval Compassion*. Philadelphia: University of Pennsylvania Press.
Melamed, Y. and Lin, M. 2010. "Principle of Sufficient Reason," *Stanford Encyclopedia of Philosophy*, ed. Edward Zalta. http://plato.stanford.edu/entries/sufficient-reason/
Menn, S. 1998. *Descartes and Augustine*. Cambridge University Press.
Mercer, C. 2000. "Humanist Platonism in Seventeenth-Century Germany," in Kraye and Stone (eds.), 238–58.
  2002. "Platonism and Philosophical Humanism on the Continent," in Nadler, 25–44.
  2012. "Platonism in Early Modern Natural Philosophy: The Case of Leibniz and Conway," in Horn, C. and Wilberding, J. (eds.), *Neoplatonic Natural Philosophy*, 103–26. New York: Oxford University Press.
Montaigne, M. 1999. *Les Essais*, Villey, M. (ed.). 3rd edn., 3 vols., Paris: Presses Universitaires de France. (English translation: *The Complete*

Essays of Montaigne. Frame, D. [trans.]. Stanford University Press, 1965.)

Murray, M. 1996. "Intellect, Will and Freedom: Leibniz and His Precursors," *Leibniz Society Review* 6: 25–59.

Nadler, S. (ed.) 2002. *A Companion to Early Modern Philosophy*. Malden, MA: Blackwell.

Nelson, A. 1996. "The Falsity in Sensory Ideas: Descartes and Arnauld," in Kremer, E. J. (ed.), *Interpreting Arnauld*, 12–32. University of Toronto Press.

   1997. "Descartes's Ontology of Thought," *Topoi* 16: 163–78.

   2008. "Cartesian Innateness," in Broughton and Carriero, 319–33.

   2013. "The Structure of Cartesian Sensations," *Analytic Philosophy* 54: 107–16.

   forthcoming 2013. "The Problem of True Ideas in Spinoza's Treatise," in Melamed, Y. (ed.), *The Young Spinoza*. Oxford University Press.

   forthcoming 2014. "Logic and Knowledge," in Kaufman, D. (ed.), *Routledge Companion to Seventeenth Century Philosophy*. New York: Routledge.

Nelson, A. and Cunning, D. 1999. "Cognition and Modality in Descartes," *Acta Philosophica Fennica* 64: 137–53.

Newman, L. 2008. "Descartes on the Will in Judgment," in Broughton and Carriero, 334–52.

Nolan, L. 1997a. "The Ontological Status of Cartesian Natures," *Pacific Philosophical Quarterly* 78: 169–94.

   1997b. "Reductionism and Nominalism in Descartes's Theory of Attributes," *Topoi* 16: 129–40.

   2005. "The Ontological Argument as an Exercise in Cartesian Therapy," *Canadian Journal of Philosophy* 35: 521–62.

Nolan, L. and Nelson, A. 2006. "Proofs for the Existence of God," in Gaukroger, 104–21.

Nolan, L. and Whipple, J. 2005. "Self-Knowledge in Descartes and Malebranche," *Journal of the History of Philosophy* 43: 55–81.

   2006, "The Dustbin Theory of Mind: A Cartesian Legacy?," *Oxford Studies in Early Modern Philosophy* 3: 33–55.

Normore, C. 1986. "Meaning and Objective Being: Descartes and his Sources," in Rorty, 223–41.

Olson, M. 1988. "Descartes' First Meditation: Mathematics and the Laws of Logic," *Journal of the History of Philosophy* 26: 407–38.

Petrik, J. M. 1992. *Descartes' Theory of the Will*. Durango, CO: Hollowbrook Publishing.

Popkin, R. H. 1979. *The History of Skepticism, From Erasmus to Spinoza*. Berkeley: University of California Press.

Ragland, C. P. 2006. "Is Descartes a Libertarian?," in Garber, D. and Nadler, S. (eds.), *Oxford Studies in Early Modern Philosophy*, 57–89. Oxford University Press.

Reid, T. 1983, "An Inquiry into the Human Mind on the Principles of Common Sense," in *Inquiry and Essays*, Beanblossom, R. and Lehrer, K. (eds.). Indianapolis: Hackett.

Rodis-Lewis, G. 1954. "Augustinisme et cartésianisme," in *Augustinus Magister*, Vol. 2, Congrès international augustinien, 1087–1104. Paris: Études Augustiniennes.

Rorty, A. O. 1983. "Experiments in Philosophic Genre: Descartes' Meditations," *Critical Inquiry* 9: 545–64.

(ed.) 1986. *Essays on Descartes' Meditations*. Berkeley: University of California Press.

Rorty, R. 1979. *Philosophy and the Mirror of Nature*. Princeton University Press.

Rozemond, M. 1998. *Descartes's Dualism*, Cambridge, MA: Harvard University Press.

2006. "The Nature of the Mind," in Gaukroger, 48–66.

2008. "Descartes's Ontology of the Eternal Truths," in Hoffman, P., Owens, D., and Yaffe, G. (eds.), *Contemporary Perspectives on Early Modern Philosophy: Essays in Honor of Vere Chappell*, 279–94. London: Broadview Press.

Rubidge, B. 1990. "Descartes's Meditations and Devotional Meditations," *Journal of the History of Ideas* 51: 27–49.

Russell, B. 1903. *The Principles of Mathematics*. Cambridge University Press.

Schmaltz, T. M. 1991. "Platonism and Descartes' View of Immutable Essences," *Archiv für Geschichte der Philosophie* 73: 129–70.

1992. "Descartes and Malebranche on Mind and Mind-Body Union," *Philosophical Review* 101: 281–325.

2002. *Radical Cartesianism: The French Reception of Descartes*. New York: Cambridge University Press.

2011. "Causa sui and Created Truth in Descartes," in Wipple, J. (ed.), *The Ultimate Why Question: Why Is There Anything at All Rather than Nothing Whatsoever?*, 109–124. Washington, DC: The Catholic University of America Press.

Scribani, C. 1616. *Amor Divinus*. Mainz: Johann Albinus.

Scribani, C. and Brissel J. 1616. *Caroli Scribani e Societate Iesu, Meditationes sacrae a Ioanne Brisselio, eiusdem Societatis, nunc editae*. Mainz: Johann Albinus.

Secada, J. 2000. *Cartesian Metaphysics: The Scholastic Origins of Modern Philosophy*. Cambridge University Press.

Sextus Empiricus 1933. *Outlines of Pyrrhonism*, Bury, R. G. (trans.). Cambridge MA: Harvard University Press.

Shabel, L. 2006. "Kant's Philosophy of Mathematics," in Guyer, P. (ed.), *The Cambridge Companion to Kant and Modern Philosophy*, 94–128. Cambridge University Press.

Shapiro, Lionel 2012. "Objective Being and 'Ofness' in Descartes," *Philosophy and Phenomenological Research* 82: 378–418.

Shapiro, Lisa 2008. "Descartes's Ethics," in Broughton and Carriero, 445–64.

2012. "How We Experience the World: Passionate Perception in Descartes and Spinoza," in Pickavé, M. and Shapiro, L. (eds.), *Emotion and Reason in Early Modern Philosophy*, 193–216. New York: Oxford University Press.

2013. "Cartesian Selves," in Detlefsen, K. (ed.), *Descartes' Meditations: A Critical Guide*, 226–42. Cambridge University Press.

Shein, N. 2009. "The False Dichotomy between Objective and Subjective Interpretations of Spinoza's Theory of Attributes," *British Journal for the History of Philosophy* 17: 505–32.

Shirley, S. (trans.) and Morgan, M. (ed.) 2002. *Spinoza: Complete Works*. Indianapolis: Hackett.

Simmons, A. 1999. "Are Cartesian Sensations Representational?," *Noûs* 33: 347–69.

2001. "Sensible Ends: Latent Teleology in Descartes' Account of Sensation," *Journal of the History of Philosophy* 39: 49–75.

2003. "Spatial Perception from a Cartesian Point of View," *Philosophical Topics* 31: 395–423.

2008, "Guarding the Body: A Cartesian Phenomenology of Perception," in Hoffman, P., Owens, D., and Yaffe, G. (eds.), *Contemporary Perspectives on Early Modern Philosophy: Essays in Honor of Vere Chappell*, 81–113. Buffalo, NY: Broadview Press.

2010–2011. "Re-Humanizing Descartes," *Philosophic Exchange* 41: 53–71.

2012. "Cartesian Consciousness Reconsidered," *Philosopher's Imprint* 12: 1–21.

forthcoming. "Representation," in Nolan, L. (ed.), *The Cambridge Descartes Lexicon*. Cambridge University Press.

Smith, K. and Nelson, A. 2010. "Divisibility and Cartesian Extension," *Oxford Studies in Early Modern Philosophy* 5: 1–24.

Sowaal, A. 2011. "Descartes's Reply to Gassendi," *British Journal for the History of Philosophy* 14: 419–49.

Spinoza, B. 2002a. *Ethics*, in Shirley and Morgan, 217–382.

2002b. *Short Treatise on God, Man and His Well-Being*, in Shirley and Morgan, 37–107.

2002c. *Principles of Cartesian Philosophy*, in Shirley and Morgan, 108–212.

Stock, B. 2011. "Self, Soliloquy, and Spiritual Exercises in Augustine and Some Later Authors," *Journal of Religion* 91: 5–23.

Stone, M. 2002. "Aristotelianism and Scholasticism in Early Modern Philosophy," in Nadler, 7–24.

Suárez, F. 1965. *Disputationes metaphysicae* in *Opera Omnia*, André, D. M. (ed.). Hildesheim: G. Olms.

  1995. *On Beings of Reason, Metaphysical Disputation LIV*, Doyle, J. P. (trans.). Milwaukee: Marquette University Press.

  1998 (1597). *Metaphysical Disputations*, in Ariew, R., Cottingham, J., and Sorrell, T. (eds.), *Descartes' Meditations: Background Source Materials*. Cambridge University Press (orig. 1597).

Teresa de Jesús 1626. *Septem meditationes in orationem Dominicam septem diebus hebdomadae accommodatae*, in Martinez, M. (ed. and trans.), *Opera s. matris Teresae*. Cologne: Kinkius.

Teresa of Ávila 1904. *The Life of St. Teresa of Jesus, of the Order of Our Lady of Carmelites*, Lewis, D. (ed. and trans.). 3rd edn. Grand Rapids, MI: Christian Classics Ethereal Library.

  1921. *The Interior Castle or The Mansions*, Zimmerman, B. (ed. and trans.). Grand Rapids, MI: Christian Classics Ethereal Library.

Van Cleve, J. 1994. "Descartes and the Destruction of the Eternal Truths," *Ratio* 7: 58–62.

Van Inwagen, P. 2000. "Free Will Remains a Mystery," *Philosophical Perspectives* 14: 1–19.

Voss, S. 1993. "Simplicity and the Seat of the Soul," in Voss, S. (ed.), *Essays on the Philosophy and Science of René Descartes*, 128–41. New York: Oxford University Press.

Wee, C. 2006. "Descartes and Leibniz on Human Free Will and the Ability to Do Otherwise," *Canadian Journal of Philosophy* 36: 387–414.

William of Ockham 1974. *Opera Philosophica*. Vol. 4. St. Bonaventure, NY: The Franciscan Institute.

Williams, B. 1978. *Descartes: the Project of Pure Inquiry*. Hassocks. Harvester.
  2005. *Descartes: The Project of Pure Enquiry*. London: Routledge (orig. 1978).

Williams, M. 1986. "Descartes and the Metaphysics of Doubt," in Rorty, 117–39.

Wilson, C. 2003. *Descartes: An Introduction*. Cambridge University Press.
  2008. "Soul, Body, and World: Plato's *Timaeus* and Descartes' *Meditations*," in Hedley and Hutton, 177–91.

Wilson, M. 1978. *Descartes*. London: Routledge.
  1990. "Descartes on the Representationality of Sensation," in Cover, J. and Kulstad, M. (eds.), *Central Themes in Early Modern Philosophy*, 1–22. Indianapolis: Hackett.

1994. "Sensation and 'Resemblance'," in Voss, S. (ed.), *Reason, Will and Sensation*, 162–76. Oxford University Press.

1999. *Ideas and Mechanism*. Princeton University Press.

Winterton, R. 1627. *The Meditations of John Gerhard ... Written originally in the Latine Tongue. Newly Translated into English by Ralphe Winterton ...* Cambridge: Thomas Bucke.

INDEX